THE INVENTION OF THE ORAL

THE INVENTION OF THE ORAL

Print Commerce and Fugitive Voices
in Eighteenth-Century Britain

PAULA McDOWELL

THE UNIVERSITY OF CHICAGO PRESS

CHICAGO AND LONDON

The University of Chicago Press, Chicago 60637
The University of Chicago Press, Ltd., London
© 2017 by The University of Chicago
Published 2017
Printed in the United States of America

26 25 24 23 22 21 20 19 18 17   1 2 3 4 5

ISBN-13: 978-0-226-45696-6 (cloth)
ISBN-13: 978-0-226-45701-7 (e-book)
DOI: 10.7208/chicago/9780226457017.001.0001

The University of Chicago Press gratefully acknowledges the generous support of the Abraham and Rebecca Stein Faculty Publication Fund of the Department of English at New York University toward the publication of this book.

Library of Congress Cataloging-in-Publication Data

Names: McDowell, Paula, author.
Title: The invention of the oral : print commerce and fugitive voices in
    eighteenth-century Britain / Paula McDowell.
Description: Chicago ; London : The University of Chicago Press, 2017. |
    Includes bibliographical references and index.
Identifiers: LCCN 2016033842 | ISBN 9780226456966 (cloth : alk. paper) |
    ISBN 9780226457017 (e-book)
Subjects: LCSH: Oral tradition—England. | Oral communication—England. |
    Printing—England—History—18th century. | English literature—18th century—
    History and criticism.
Classification: LCC PR905.M37 2017 | DDC 825/.509—dc23 LC record available at
    https://lccn.loc.gov/2016033842

For

GEORGE BRIDGE

and in memory of

TOM McDOWELL

1951–1999

CONTENTS

FIGURES

ACKNOWLEDGMENTS

I must first thank Alan Thomas at the University of Chicago Press, for without his vision, experience, and trust, this book would not exist. I am grateful to the anonymous readers for the press for their reports, and to Randy Petilos for making the publication process a pleasure. Rob Koehler and Lauren Roberts provided invaluable research assistance, and my excellent copyeditor, Pam Bruton, exercised a mercifully light hand.

In 1999–2000 an American Philosophical Society Research Grant and a fellowship at the National Humanities Center allowed me to begin this book, and more recently, a grant from the Abraham and Rebecca Stein Fund at NYU helped defray publication costs. In 2014 a grant from the NYU Humanities Initiative allowed me to co-teach "Papyrus to PDF: An Introduction to Book History Now" with my colleague Charlotte Priddle, librarian for printed books at the Fales Library and Special Collections, and conversations with NYU Libraries staff continue to energize my research as well as teaching.

My colleagues and students in the Department of English make NYU an ideal intellectual environment in which to work. In 2006 Clifford Siskin and his collaborators invited me to co-organize an International Working Conference at NYU, "Mediating Enlightenment Past and Present," and that occasion and the volume of essays that resulted, *This Is Enlightenment*, edited by Clifford Siskin and William Warner (Chicago: University of Chicago Press, 2010), have stimulated my thinking ever since. Like Michael McKeon at Rutgers University, John Guillory and Mary Poovey at NYU have been intellectual exemplars: I am constantly inspired by their dedication and their determination to get the story right. Mary read drafts of chapters 2 and 4 and provided helpful feedback; readers of *The Invention of the Oral* have her to thank that my Henley chapter is not even longer than it is. Wendy Lee and Maureen McLane valiantly read the entire manuscript at the final hour, and other colleagues, including Christopher Cannon, Elaine Freedgood, Lisa Gitelman, and Phil Harper, crucially never stopped asking me, "How's the book?" Jordan Hall and other members of the Eighteenth-Century British Literature Workshop make NYU an ideal place to do eighteenth-century studies.

Beyond NYU, many supporters, interlocutors, and earwitnesses have contributed to the making of this book. For their support and scholarly models, I am grateful to Paula R. Backscheider, J. Paul Hunter, and John J. Richetti. Over the last decade, I have shared portions of this book with numerous audiences at conferences and universities. Speaker series come and go, but I remain grateful to Robert Darnton and the Princeton University Center for the Study of Books and Media; the Early Modern Center at the University of California, Santa Barbara; the Bloomington Eighteenth-Century Workshop at Indiana University; the Print Culture Series at Simon Fraser University; Al Coppola and the Columbia University Seminar on Eighteenth-Century European Culture; the NYU Atlantic History Workshop; Leah Price and the Harvard University Seminar in the History of the Book; Susan S. Lanser and the Eighteenth-Century Seminar at Harvard; and, most recently, the organizers of the Stanford University Symposium "Novel Knowledge," an event honoring my teacher, mentor, and friend John Bender. Ballad scholarship underwent something of a Renaissance during the years in which I wrote this book; I particularly benefited from conversations with Patricia Fumerton, Meredith McGill, Maureen McLane, James Mulholland, Ruth Perry, and members of the Working Group on Ballads that I directed at the Rutgers Center for Cultural Analysis from 2005 to 2006. Last but not least, I am grateful to Kathleen Lynch, Owen Williams, and the Executive Committee of the Folger Institute at the Folger Shakespeare Library for inviting me to serve, along with Adam Fox, as codirector of a 2013 Faculty Seminar on what I called "The Orality/Literacy Heuristic." Along with an interdisciplinary group of participants, we examined the legacy of the "orality and literacy" rubric and its implications for research in the early modern humanities.

‹∞›

A version of chapter 3 was published in *PMLA* 121, no. 1 (January 2006): 87–106, and a version of chapter 7 appeared in *Ballads and Broadsides in Britain, 1500–1800*, edited by Patricia Fumerton and Anita Guerrini, with the assistance of Kris McAbee (Surrey, UK: Ashgate, 2010). I am thankful for permission to reprint from the Modern Language Association and Taylor & Francis, respectively.

Fig. 0.1. William Hogarth, *Beer Street* (1751). Photograph: Courtesy of the Lewis
Walpole Library, Yale University. For a surviving preliminary sketch
without the book-toting porter, see Pierpont Morgan Library
Department of Drawings and Prints, E.18.13.

In the center front of *Beer Street* (1751), William Hogarth depicts two fish-wives (fig. 0.2) reading and singing a broadside ballad. This engraving and its companion piece, *Gin Lane*, were published in support of legislation to control the sale of alcohol that resulted in the Gin Act of 1751. In *Gin Lane*, gin is depicted as a destructive liquor that brings poverty and ruin; here, in *Beer Street*, beer is portrayed as an invigorating drink that promotes industry and individual and social well-being. It is significant that one or both of these fishwives are *reading* as well as singing the ballad, for in mid-eighteenth-century Britain, as much as 50 percent of the female population could not read, and laboring women such as these street hawkers were the most *un*likely to be able to read in actual fact. It is also significant that these particular hawkers are *fishwives* (rather than, say, some other kind of street vendor such as the vegetable seller appearing to their left). As Hogarth would have been aware, in the visual and verbal texts of this period the "Billings-gate fishwife" was commonly associated with the most vulgar plebeian discourse. The term "Billingsgate" had come to refer not only to the fish market and docks beside the Thames but also to a type of foul, abusive language characterized by hyperbole and slang. Fishwives' distinctive harangues were among the best known of the "London Cries" (a verbal and visual print product as well as oral genre), and the aggressive orality of fishwives and oyster wenches was an omnipresent literary trope. (In Alexander Pope's *Dunciad* [1728–43], "shameless *Billingsgate*," the daughter of Queen Dulness, is the winner in a street brawl, having beaten "fair *Rhet'ric*" to the ground.)[1] Fish-wives were associated with the verbal intimidation of reluctant customers and with antielite sentiments. But remarkably, in Hogarth's engraving even the fishwives are sitting politely, pausing momentarily to enjoy "A New

Fig. 0.2. William Hogarth, *Beer Street* (1751), detail. Photograph: Courtesy of the Lewis Walpole Library, Yale University.

Ballad on the Herring Fishery by Mr. Lockman" (a friend of Hogarth's who wrote ballads in support of protective legislation aiding the British fisheries). These women pause only briefly from their work; one fishwife has not even bothered to put down her basket of fish.

Here and elsewhere in *Beer Street*, Hogarth applauds the potential role of print commerce in encouraging industry across the trades and in promoting harmony and manners even among the lower ranks. To the left of the fishwives, a contented butcher relaxes at a table spread with printed news. Visible titles show an issue of the *Daily Advertiser*, the earliest classifieds paper, and a printed transcript of an originally oral speech by King George II in which he "earnestly reco[m]mend[s]" to Parliament "the Advancement of Our Commerce and cultivating the Arts of Peace." To the right of the fishwives, a porter also pauses for a draught; he has been lugging an enormous basket filled with books. At first glance, these large, well-bound volumes appear to be another beneficial by-product of the print commerce promoted by wise government, protective legislation, and refreshing spirits. But upon second glance, we begin to detect details that give us pause. Among the weighty volumes depicted are "Modern Tragedys Vol: 12" and "Politicks Vol: 9999." Twelve volumes of modern tragedies is arguably too much; even more irrefutably, "9999" volumes of "Politicks" implies that the early eighteenth-century explosion of the press, always a preeminent forum for political debate, had now reached a tipping point where it was threatening to disrupt, rather than promote, industry and social order. But upon continued examination we see that this basket of books is en route not to potential readers but to "Mr. Pastem the Trunk maker in Paul's Ch. Yd." Here, Hogarth is a satirist of print commerce along the lines of Alexander Pope. Recalling the frontispiece to the *Dunciad*, which depicts an overladen ass carrying books to be recycled as waste paper, Hogarth implies that these "baggage books" will be used as paper to line trunks. Each of the book titles makes its own satiric point, demonstrating Hogarth's sustained reflection on the role of print commerce in advancing or hindering the development of science, literature, and art. (The other named books are "Hill on Royal Societies," "Lauder on Milton," and "Turnbul on Ant[ient] Painting"—all works that Hogarth loathed.) This is not wisely regulated, beneficial trade but unregulated commerce, with major, potentially negative implications for all areas of society and human knowledge. A surviving prepatory drawing of *Beer Street* shows that Hogarth added the book-toting porter only in a later stage of the image. Previously, the porter's space was occupied by a shoe-maker displaying his wares. Hogarth replaced the cobbler—a maker and mender of practical, lasting products that everyone needs—with this por-ter lugging ephemeral products to be trashed. Hogarth's simultaneous ex-ploitation of printing technology, ambivalence about print commerce, and sense of the increasing inseparability of printed texts and oral discourse was typical of authors of his era. Eighteenth-century authors' reflection on what they perceived to be an emergent "print society" and its changing relation-ship with oral discourse is also the subject of *The Invention of the Oral*.

⟨∞⟩

In eighteenth-century Britain, the dramatic proliferation of print and the specter (not reality) of mass literacy generated widespread reflection on the nature and implications of what we now call media shift. The perception of a profound change gave rise to urgent efforts to historicize different media forms and to understand their unique powers (as well as their sometimes-threatening power when working in tandem). *The Invention of the Oral* ar-gues that reflection on the spread of *print* was a key factor in shaping our modern intellectual category of "oral culture." For most English authors in 1700, the concept of oral culture did not exist, and the phrase "oral tradi-tion" would have first brought to mind a suspect Catholic theological notion.

Early eighteenth-century intellectuals rarely felt any deep admiration for societies they believed to be without a form of writing. Elite authors commonly associated the absence of writing with barbarism, and they associated what we might now call popular oral discourse with vulgarity, sedition, and religious dissent (a *lack* of culture in the sense of learning, refinement, or taste). At a time when the majority of the laboring population could not read, orality was in a sense the general condition rather than something to be especially valued. But over the course of the century, literate attitudes toward the idea of oral tradition (and what we might now call popular oral culture) underwent an epochal change. The later eighteenth century saw new ideas of oral tradition and an explosion of interest in what would later be called folk culture—a culture that was valorized for its presumed distance from the degraded present (and, I will argue, from print commerce). By the 1760s there began to emerge among educated authors and scholarly gentlemen a new elegiac mood of nostalgia for *select* oral forms and practices that seemed to be "fading into the memory of a more . . . stable and communal past."[2] At this time of spreading print and perceived rising literacy, antiquarians, poets, and others began to rethink and valorize the spoken word in new ways and to model themselves as heroic rescuers of valuable oral traditions that they depicted as on the brink of being lost.

The early eighteenth century was a time of anarchic expansion in the British book trade. As we have seen in the aforementioned examples of Hogarth and Pope, this period saw the development, if not of a concept of "print culture," then certainly of a satiric construct of print *commerce*. *The Invention of the Oral* traces the ways that eighteenth-century authors (and some visual artists) understood the historic developments happening around them having to do with printing, but its central concern is with the ways that perceptions of media shift helped to shape thinking about oral discourse, oral tradition, and what we now commonly refer to as "oral culture." In Britain, I argue, these concepts began to crystallize in their modern forms once it was ideologically useful for genteel authors to idealize a way of life that was separate from (and superior to) a world in which professional writing was now entrenched. The earliest *positive* efforts to theorize "oral tradition," and to depict popular orality as a culture (rather than a *lack* of culture), were prompted less by any protodemocratic impulse than by a profound discomfort with new cultures of reading, writing, and even speaking shaped by print.

A related concern of *The Invention of the Oral* is the relationship between emergent abstract concepts and particular local voices. Literate *models* of oral tradition, I show, were constructed in opposition not only to the perceived corruptions of an expanding print market but also to contemporary oral discourses and practices that were seen as morally or politically dangerous. The "Fugitive Voices" of my subtitle may initially evoke the evanescence of speech acts and the nostalgia often provoked by that evanescence, but it will also come to evoke "fugitive" in the sense of criminalized. "Fugitive," from the Latin *fugere*, "to flee," means something evanescent or fleeting, but it also means "one who flees or tries to escape from danger, an enemy, justice, or an owner."[3] The "fugitive voices" that I attend to include not only the idealized oral practices and forms that genteel scholars and poets mourned as disappearing but also still-pervasive, threatening oral practices such as the singing of bawdy or oppositional ballads, Dissenting preaching, fortune-telling, and slanderous or seditious speech. In eighteenth-century Britain, Anglican clergymen and Dissenters, fishwives and philosophers, rhetoricians and street hucksters competed for elbow room (and sometimes audiences) in taverns, coffeehouses, marketplaces, and streets, and it is out of their encounters—whether real or depicted in literary and visual texts—that new conceptions of the oral were forged.

The spread of print may have displaced some oral forms and traditions, as later eighteenth-century ballad scholars would lament, but it arguably energized others. The expansion of the print marketplace, I show, gave rise to new forms of oral commerce in tandem with print. From about the mid-1720s, a host of author-entrepreneurs from John "Orator" Henley, to Methodist leader John Wesley, to Irish actor-turned-elocutionist Thomas Sheridan began reevaluating the power of the spoken word, then harnessing the unique characteristics of oral discourse, *along with print*, to new commercial and ideological ends. The urban, Dissenting, and otherwise-threatening oral projects of Henley, the Methodists, and other speakers were a far cry from the feudal, masculinist culture of heroic song celebrated by ballad collectors and Ossian enthusiasts or the rural peasant traditions presented in sanitized, sentimental form by Romantic poets. Even an elocutionist like Sheridan, who offered to teach the ancient arts of oratory to new social groups, defined his own oral endeavors against the speech practices of "impolite," "vulgar," or otherwise-suspect groups. It was one thing for genteel poets, ballad collectors, and others to value sentimental or feudal oral practices; it was another thing altogether to confront and cope with loud, living, and especially urban incarnations of popular oral discourse in the immediate present. In tracing the relationship between print commerce and changing ideas of the oral, I study social, political, religious, and intellectual history in relation to one another, and I foreground a diverse cast of characters at work in order to suggest what was (and is) at stake. Like social and political theorist Don Herzog in his study of conservatism and contempt in Britain between 1789 and 1834, my goal is "to situate the abstractions, to work up a genealogical account of how some familiar views were developed."[4]

The changing media environment that I describe, then, is not one characterized by what Walter Ong called "primary orality," untainted by the written word (a coinage I will discuss further in a moment). But neither can we turn to Ong's other category, "residual orality," a term that suggests something left behind, like "residue" or detritus in a faster-moving stream.[5] Rather, what I describe in *The Invention of the Oral* is a dynamic, sometimes-volatile relationship between copresent, interdependent media forms that genteel authors increasingly *represented* as separate for ideological reasons. Eighteenth-century British writing is characterized by a heightened attempt to theorize not only the implications of print and printing but also the distinctive characteristics of oral discourse (and, especially, the potential power of print and oral discourse working in tandem). The impure oral forms and practices of urban venues—somehow tainted by their intersection with print—have not been a central part of the stories that scholars tell about early modern "oral culture." But juxtaposing *different kinds* of oral practices and forms alongside emergent nostalgic representations of lost orality can remind us of the ideological work that later eighteenth-century authors had to do to represent valuable oral traditions and practices as dying or dead. We need to be wary of literate models that associate orality or oral tradition solely with stasis or the past and that associate adaptive, urban, and/or print-inflected oral practices and discourses with contamination and decay. What we might now call "popular oral culture" has never disappeared, but it *has* changed, and by the eighteenth century, I show, it was impossible to separate either oral practices *or* ideas of the oral from print commerce.

HERALDING A PRINT SOCIETY

In recent years, theorists of "print culture" have cautioned against technological overdeterminism in assessing the consequences of printing. As Michael Warner, Roger Chartier, Adrian Johns, and others have argued, the cultural meanings and significance of print can be understood only in contextual terms.[6] (As Johns says, "the very identity of print itself has had to be made.")[7] Furthermore, I would emphasize, "print culture" does not simply appear with the introduction of printing. In Britain, there was a time lag of about three centuries between the introduction of the printing press in the fifteenth century and the crystallization of anything that we can without major qualifications label a "print society."[8] To make matters even more complex, the term "print culture" is anachronistic for the eighteenth century. No eighteenth-century author employed this term (or its post-1960s corollary, "oral culture"). As I discuss in the coda to this book, "culture" was not used as a noun signifying a "total way of life" until the nineteenth century.

In the wake of this attention to the problems inherent in the term "print culture," then, it would be foolhardy to point to any particular moment when England "became" a print society. But I do point to one especially significant moment in the history of such a *perception*. In 1695 the Licensing (or Printing) Act of 1662 lapsed for good, ending prepublication censorship as well as government restrictions on the number of printers and presses. For the first time in history, the print trade was made open to all. The decades immediately following were a time of anarchic expansion. Whereas the act of 1662 had tried to limit the total number of printers in all of England to twenty-four, within a decade of 1695 there were sixty-five to seventy printing houses in London alone.[9] Parliament repeatedly tried to renew licensing but failed to agree on specifics. Similarly, the Stationers' Company wanted (and expected) licensing to be renewed. Yet most Stationers held that the versions of the bill put forward for renewal after 1695 did not go far enough.[10] Most strikingly, these documents made no mention of the traditional privileges of the company, such as the right to control the number of printers and presses and what we would now call copyrights. The company's historic monopoly over the publishing industry was being undermined, and an older guild-based model of printing was being displaced by an openly competitive commercial model.

Contemporaries clearly had a sense that some kind of major change was taking place and that this change had major implications not only for the print trades but also for society at large. As the outspoken printer-author Elinor James urged in one of her dozens of petitions to Parliament, "Printing is not a Trade as other Trades are, but it is an Art and Mistery that ought . . . not to be made so common, as that it should be slighted and trampled under Foot."[11] For most of James's lifetime (c. 1645–1719), the English book trade was small and closely knit. (Several of James's sons, daughters, and grandchildren followed her into the family trade.) But over the course of the century, the print trade penetrated widely into the provinces. By 1800 there were hundreds of presses located throughout Britain, and the products of the press affected social life at every level.[12]

For literary authors, these shifts profoundly restructured the world of letters. But the concern of Augustan satirists such as Pope and Jonathan Swift was not simply more printers, more presses, more books (as is often assumed). These writers were not technological determinists, and they were certainly not "anti-print." Rather, these authors were astute observers of contemporary developments in the history of the press who sensed that what we would call a "technology" was being used in new ways. Printing and letters—*both* potentially valuable arts—were becoming unregulated trades whose only controls were, in effect, the market.

Literary texts are thus an especially valuable register of perceptions that a significant change was taking place. But eighteenth-century authors came to grips with the spread of print commerce in different ways. It is the distinctive self-consciousness of the authors that I discuss here, rather than any uniform set of views, that makes these poets, novelists, rhetoricians, and others powerful commentators on what we might call media shift. While some authors satirized "Grub Street," others celebrated the business of books as an important branch of British trade. In 1758 miscellaneous author James Ralph published *The Case of Authors by Profession or Trade, Stated. With Regard to Booksellers, the Stage, and the Public.* In this seventy-nine-page appeal, Ralph argued that printing one's works for pay was making a valuable contribution to national "Commerce." He effectively articulated a concept of print commerce without actually using the phrase itself. Today, Ralph is best remembered as the butt of Pope's satire in the *Dunciad*. Pope represents him as a noisy, "howl[ing]" author whose peers are screeching "Owls" (3.165–66). But in *The Case of Authors by Profession*, Ralph boldly reversed Pope's hierarchy of learned gentlemen amateurs above Grub Street hacks. In contrast to Pope, he elevated industrious "Pen-and-Ink Laborer[s]" above mere "Voluntier" or "Holiday-Writers."[13] He argued that aristocratic patronage was no longer a viable means of support, and he urged solidarity among his fellow "Laborer[s]" of the pen. "Writers by Trade" must now look to booksellers, playhouse managers, and, above all, the growing reading public to support their "Profession." Commending Hogarth for his role in promoting the Engravers' Copyright Act (1734/35), Ralph called on his fellow "Authors by Profession" to promote similar laws protecting their "Trade." Despite the Statute of Anne (1709/10), which vested copyrights in authors rather than in publishers, "Authors by Profession" lacked adequate protection of their rights.[14] In the first-ever printed call to authors to unionize, he urged his fellow "Writers by Profession" to forge a "Combination." In his rousing conclusion to *The Case of Authors by Profession*, he wrote, "of all Mankind, shall you be the last to find out the Force and Benefit of Combinations? Combine! And perhaps you would need neither Patrons nor Establishments! Combine, and you might out-combine the very Booksellers themselves!"[15]

At virtually the same time that Ralph argued for professional author-ship as a valuable branch of national "Commerce," other authors defined Britain's cultural heritage away from commercial print. In 1760 Scottish Highlander James Macpherson published *Fragments of Ancient Poetry*, claiming to have collected and translated the works of a third-century bard, Ossian, passed down chiefly by word of mouth. Macpherson's "Ossianic" publications generated enormous interest in the possibility of recovering a once-thriving native oral tradition. In 1765, clergyman and antiquarian Thomas Percy published his edited collection of ballads and songs, *Reliques of Ancient English Poetry* (3 vols.).

Percy theorized the heroic ballads in his collection as the legacy of an-cient minstrels, or "oral itinerant poet[s]."[16] Yet Percy (and, later, Macpher-son's eminent supporter, the clergyman and rhetorician Hugh Blair) rep-resented the spread of print as undermining, rather than preserving, oral traditions. In his lengthy "Essay on the Ancient Minstrels in England," ap-pended to the *Reliques*, Percy expressed his disdain for print commerce and for ballad singers who composed for print. (Ironically, both Percy's *Re-liques* and Macpherson's *Works of Ossian* went on to become phenomenal best sellers.) Whereas Ralph praised "Authors by Profession" above mere "Holiday-Writers," Percy represented his weighty (and commercially suc-cessful) volumes as the product of a gentleman's leisure hours in the coun-try, and Macpherson represented himself as motivated by patriotism rather than by his pocketbook or a desire for fame. Alert to, alarmed about, *and energized by* new institutional conditions for human uses of printing tech-nology, the diverse authors whom I discuss in *The Invention of the Oral* ar-ticulate the oral as part of their extended meditations on the new problems and possibilities of print.

THE ORALITY-LITERACY HEURISTIC

By my phrase "invention of the oral," I mean not invention ex nihilo but invention in the ancient sense of artistic or literary creativity: the sense that Jonathan Swift meant when he wrote in the "Apology" to *A Tale of a Tub* (5th ed., 1710) that "the Author was then young, his Invention at the Height, and his Reading fresh in his Head."[17] "Invention" stems from the Latin *invenire*, "to come upon, discover, find out, devise, contrive."[18] Inven-tion is the first of the five parts of classical rhetoric; in literary composition, it means "the devising of a subject, idea, or method of treatment, by exercise of the intellect or imagination."[19] This is the sense that John Dryden meant when he wrote that "the first happiness of the poet's imagination is . . .

invention, or finding of the thought."[20] "Invention" can also refer to the thing invented, whether a "device, contrivance, design, plan, [or] scheme." Just as material inventions can enable the building of objects, so invented concepts can generate further new ideas. The eighteenth-century invention of a gathering concept of the "oral" has since generated further concepts and terms such as "oral history," "oral culture," and so on.

In thinking about the invention of the category of the oral as a conceptual umbrella for an enormous variety of practices and discourses, I have benefited from the work of sociologists Geoffrey C. Bowker and Susan Leigh Star on classification and its consequences. Bowker and Star define "classification" as a "spatial, temporal, or spatio-temporal segmentation of the world" and as "a set of boxes (metaphorical or literal) into which things can be put to . . . do some kind of work." Classifications are not inevitable or natural; rather, they are constructed and "learned as part of membership in communities of practice." Bowker and Star suggest that instead of working to pinpoint what particular classifications mean or attempting to "purify . . . (un)stable systems," we should trace what particular classifications *do* and how they have been built, maintained, and used. This kind of visibility work (as I call it) means foregrounding human agents. It means "recognizing . . . the real work of politics and knowledge production. It foregrounds . . . normally invisible Lilliputian threads."[21]

In thinking about the category of the oral, I have also benefited from Peter de Bolla's work on the historical formation of concepts. De Bolla provides a taxonomy of different kinds of concepts; while some are "essentially the names for things," others "are more complex and work by providing a ladder or map which enables thought to move from one place to another." These complex concepts, which de Bolla calls "load-bearing" or "noetic," can "be thought of as small scale theories." They enable thinking across a variety of domains, and in some cases they "enable the production and discovery of new knowledge."[22] Today, "oral" is a load-bearing concept that allows us to yoke together such complex ideas as oral discourse, oral communication, oral tradition, oral culture, and orality. But in 1700, I contend, this vast yoking rubric or conceptual infrastructure did not exist. In the eighteenth century, an emergent abstract concept of the "oral" contributed to a previously unprecedented linking of diverse oral practices. As De Bolla advises, we are unlikely to learn much if we do not hold fast to a distinction between words and concepts. We don't necessarily find a particular *term* every time we detect a *concept*, or a particular *concept* every time we see a *term*.[23] I understand concepts rather as Herzog understands political theories: not as "explorations of a timeless and abstract realm of fundamental questions, but as efforts to solve problems thrown up by contingent social change." The "social world provides background conditions of intelligibility,"[24] and the meanings of terms and concepts constantly change.

The *Oxford English Dictionary* defines "oral" as "Done or performed with or by the mouth" and as "Of or relating to communication by speech."[25] These definitions may seem relatively straightforward to us, but this seeming obviousness is in fact a consequence of naturalization. Seventeenth-century English lexicographers, by way of contrast, deemed "oral" a "hard word." Before the eighteenth century, the largest English dictionary was Thomas Blount's *Glossographia: or, A dictionary interpreting all such hard words . . . as are now used in our refined English tongue* (1656). So-called "hard word" dictionaries, such as Blount's, aimed to define words that were considered rare or especially difficult (rather than to provide a complete listing of all known words). The fact that Blount included an entry for "oral" in *Glossographia* suggests that he judged it to be a hard word not already familiar to his readers. Blount defined "oral" as "(from *Os, oris*) pertaining to the mouth, visage, face, look, favor, or voyce."[26] In contrast, there is no entry in *Glossographia* for "orator," "oratory," or "oration"—suggesting that he considered these words to be relatively well known.

One hundred years later, Samuel Johnson defined oral as "ORAL, *adj.* [*oral*, Fr. *os, orris*, Latin.] Delivered by mouth; not written" (*Dictionary of the English Language*, 2 vols., 1755; see fig. 8.1). Johnson drew on earlier dictionaries such as Blount's, but his definition of "oral" marks a shift in the way that this term was understood. In defining "oral" as "not written," Johnson introduced a binary opposition between oral and written discourse. He defined oral discourse by what it is *not*. Johnson was the first English lexicographer to provide usage examples in the form of quotations from literary authors. The examples that he offered for "oral," "orally," and "oral tradition" reflect both his view of the comparative reliability of writing and oral discourse and his staunchly Protestant position on contemporary debates concerning the scriptures versus tradition as the "rule of faith." In one usage example that Johnson provides, John Locke describes "oral discourse" as fugitive and faulty. Locke compares written texts to "*Oral* discourse; whose transient faults, dying with the sound that gives them life, . . . more easily escapes observation." In another example, legal scholar and jurist Matthew Hale declares that "Oral tradition . . . were incompetent without written monuments to derive to us the original laws of a kingdom."[27] A third usage example initially seems more positive in its representation of oral discourse. Joseph Addison observes that Saint John's "*oral* testimony lasted the first century." But in the remainder of this passage, also quoted by Johnson, Addison emphasizes that the apostles were not ordinary men. God granted his messengers extraordinary longevity, so that "they might personally convey the truth of the gospel" until their "*oral* testimony" could be written down.

On the same page of the *Dictionary* where Johnson's definition of "oral" appears, definitions of "orator" and "orangewife" appear consecutively. This is a mere alphabetic (and typographic) coincidence, but for our purposes it is instructive for precisely that reason. Johnson did not possess our vast modern conceptual umbrella "orality" (a word that does not appear in these early dictionaries). Accordingly, he would not necessarily have linked "orators" and "orangewives" as two different types of powerful speakers. Johnson defines "orator" as "a man of eloquence" and "orangewife" as "a woman who sells oranges." At first glance, orators and orangewives might appear to have nothing in common. But Johnson then provides a usage example from Shakespeare that satirically depicts orangewives as powerful orators. Shakespeare warns that a man can "wear out a good wholesome forenoon in hearing a cause between an orangewife and a posset seller."[28] Like all street criers, orangewives used their oral skills and powerful lungs to advertise their goods. Similarly, eloquent orators are known for their oral arts. If Johnson had examined this page of the printed *Dictionary*, would he have noticed this commonality between orators and orangewives? We will never know. But it is only as a result of the complex historical formation of an abstract concept of the "oral," I argue, that we now lexicographically and imaginatively link such dissimilar practices as hawkers' street cries, orators' "eloquence," and lawyers' harangues. Today, the definition of "oral" in the *Oxford English Dictionary* lexicographically links such diverse (and modern) concepts and terms as "oral history," "oral poetry," "oral exams," "oral surgery," and "oral sex."[29]

In using terms such as "oral culture" or "oral communication," then, one might begin as historians Adam Fox and D. R. Woolf do in *The Spoken Word: Oral Culture in Britain, 1500–1850*, by offering their definitions.[30] Or one might take a different approach, as I do here. In this book I approach "orality," "literacy," "print culture," and so on from a historical, conceptual standpoint rather than a phenomenological one. I am not seeking early modern attitudes toward these things as if they already existed; rather, I am working to understand the historical development of these now-naturalized ideas. Like Mary Poovey in *A History of the Modern Fact*, I am interested in "the processes by which particular abstractions were produced in the first place." I agree that "to understand how . . . abstractions work now we must understand the dynamics by which they were initially generated, the semantic worlds to which they originally belonged."[31] The abstractions whose formation I consider have since taken on a force of their own in shaping research agendas. What critical anthropologist Johannes Fabian wrote of the category of the "primitive" might also be said of the "oral" and of "orality." We do not observe, or critically study, the "oral"; rather, we think, observe, and critically study *in terms of* the oral. "[Orality] . . . is a category, not an object, of Western thought."[32] My goal is not to offer a definitive meaning of "oral" but to investigate the diverse positions expressed in eighteenth-century debates and to suggest what was (and is) at stake.

A historical investigation of eighteenth-century ideas of the oral also defamiliarizes key assumptions of current media studies concerning "print culture," "oral culture," and "orality." In the eighteenth century, I argue, new ideas of the oral emerged in a complex dialectical relationship with reflection on the spread of print. Similarly, in the mid-twentieth century the concepts of "orality" and "print culture" were developed in tandem. In 1958 Walter J. Ong published *Ramus, Method, and the Decay of Dialogue,* an influential argument about the consequences of printing for Renaissance logic and rhetoric and for "orality."[33] Within the next five years, a small flood of books and articles on "orality" were published across the human sciences. The years 1962–63 alone saw the publication of such influential works as *The Gutenberg Galaxy: The Making of Typographic Man* (1962) by Marshall McLuhan; *Le pensée sauvage* (1962) by Claude Lévi-Strauss; *Preface to Plato* (1963) by Eric Havelock; and "The Consequences of Literacy" (1963) by Jack Goody and Ian Watt.[34] It is no coincidence, I suggest, that McLuhan opened *The Gutenberg Galaxy* by representing it as a companion piece to Albert B. Lord's work on "orality" and oral tradition, *The Singer of Tales* (1960). McLuhan theorized "print culture" in relation to "orality," and he employed "print culture" as one of a series of such coinages, including "typographic era," "Gutenberg era," "mechanical era," and "electric age."[35] Nor is it a coincidence that McLuhan was an English professor. Writing in the 1960s, before the appearance of the historical studies of publishing that we rely on now, McLuhan depended heavily on *literary* works (poems, plays, and novels) for his understanding of the social, cultural, and (in his view) cognitive "consequences" of print.[36] Significantly, he drew heavily on Pope's satire of the explosion of print commerce after 1695, the *Dunciad.* "It is to the *Dunciad,*" he pronounced, "that we must turn for the epic of the printed word. . . . For here is the explicit study of [the] plunging of the human mind into the sludge of an unconscious engendered by the book."[37] For McLuhan, an English professor turned media theorist, the constant references to Pope and other poets, dramatists, and novelists were not mere illustrations

of a preexisting thesis. Rather, I suggest, literary works were the medium
through which this media theorist came to identify historical continuity
and change. The eighteenth century saw the emergence of a sustained, self-
conscious discourse questioning the effects of, and relationship between,
different media forms, and this discussion took place in works like the *Dunciad* and *A Tale of a Tub*. To an extent that is seldom recognized or acknowledged today, major twentieth-century media theorists such as McLuhan and
his student Ong were unwittingly influenced by eighteenth-century literary
texts.

Shortly after McLuhan published *Gutenberg Galaxy*, Ong employed his
term "typographic culture" as part of an explicitly developed evolutionary
model of media shift with "three successive stages": "(1) oral or oral-aural,
(2) script, which reaches critical breakthroughs with the invention of the first
alphabet and then later of alphabetic moveable type, and (3) electronic."[38]
Ong's stadial model helped to shape our now-common habit of classifying
different societies according to their modes of communication.[39] In 1971 Ong
did not yet see "print culture" as a distinct phase,[40] but in 1979 Elizabeth
Eisenstein's *The Printing Press as an Agent of Change* launched the term
"print culture" into common parlance. Today, the concepts of "oral culture,"
"print culture," "electronic culture," and so on, are commonly evoked by
journalists, media theorists, literary scholars, book historians, and others.

Ong argued that "primary oral cultures (cultures with no knowledge at
all of writing)" exhibit distinctive ways of acquiring, managing, and verbal-
izing knowledge and that the introduction of writing brings with it major,
irreversible shifts. The orality-literacy heuristic, as I call it, posits orality
and literacy as parts of an equilibrium: a homeostatic balance whereby more
of one means less of the other. For Ong, once literacy is introduced, "primary
orality" disappears. Aspects of Ong's work have been debated and sometimes
rejected, but his remarkable oeuvre (more than 450 publications) may be
said to constitute a considerable part of the scaffolding on which the nexus
of fields making up "orality and literacy studies" has been built.[41] As a consequence of his works (especially his popular synthesis *Orality and Literacy*
[1982]), scholars working in a wide variety of fields addressing "orality and
literacy" are now often more familiar with Ong's usage of "orality" and his
related coinages "primary orality," "residual orality," and "secondary orality" than they are with the historical etymology of "orality."[42] Yet as I shall
show, Ong's usage of "orality" is not and has never been the only one available. The earliest recorded use of "orality" dates to the later seventeenth
century, and it means neither "primary orality" in the Ongian sense nor
simply "oral communication." This use of "orality," we shall see, appears in

a 1666 polemical work by an English Catholic priest debating oral tradition versus the scriptures as the "rule of faith."

.◌.

The predictable move in a study of the relationship between print commerce and ideas of the oral in eighteenth-century Britain would be to begin with well-known *later* eighteenth-century sympathetic representations of popular oral discourse, such as William Wordsworth's praise, in his preface (1802) to *Lyrical Ballads* (1798), for the spoken language of the common man. But part of my goal is to make sense of the dramatically *changing* literary representation of popular oral discourse over the course of the century, and accordingly, I begin with the neglected (and, in my view, more revealing) part of this story. One of the surest ways to heighten one's sensitivity to the highly ideological nature of later eighteenth-century literate representations of displaced or dying oral traditions or practices is to step back to the dramatically different representations of early eighteenth-century authors. These authors' harshly negative depictions of "vulgar" (or popular) oral discourses and practices contrast sharply with later idealizing depictions, and perhaps for this reason, these different kinds of representations have never been systematically linked or compared. But in their meditations on print commerce, I argue, the early eighteenth-century authors whom I discuss exhibit a heightened degree of self-conscious reflection on orality and its actual and potential threatening intersections with an unrestrained press. Understanding their differences from (and continuities with) later eighteenth-century authors will place the latter's real innovations *and* their continuing resistance to change in a new light.

Chapter 1 offers a wide-ranging survey of ideas of and attitudes toward oral tradition over the course of the long eighteenth century. "Tradition," from the Latin *tradere*, "to hand down," means anything passed down across generations, but in theological debates it came to signify the continuity of orthodoxy in the church. Since the Reformation, the question of tradition was a key issue of doctrinal differentiation between Protestants and Catholics. But in Restoration England, this theological issue assumed urgent political importance, as an Anglican nation experienced the reigns of two kings sympathetic to the Catholic cause (Charles II, 1660–85, and James II, 1685–88). The question of tradition was now widely debated by poets and philosophers as well as priests. Authors such as John Milton, Dryden, Locke, and David Hume explicitly debated the reliability of oral tradition in relation to writing (and sometimes print). Meanwhile, members of the Royal Society of London attempted to calculate a mathematical formula for assessing the reliability of oral testimony, and protoethnographers such as John Aubrey and Daniel Defoe scrutinized "meer tradition" while also recording traditional customs, beliefs, and tales.

Throughout the century, the dominant sense of tradition remained theological. But at the same time, the idea of tradition underwent dramatic change. New discoveries and accounts of societies without alphabetic writing generated new kinds of interest in oral tradition, and by the 1730s and 1740s, a changing political landscape in Britain increasingly allowed Britons to explore oral tradition from a protoethnographic, as well as doctrinal, standpoint. In the early 1720s Anglican reformer and clergyman Henry Bourne worked to root out "heathen" and "papist" superstitions by recording and critiquing "vulgar" (or popular) traditions and lore. But ironically, by the later eighteenth century, Bourne's *Antiquitates Vulgares; or, the Antiquities of the Common People* (1725) had helped to generate a new interest in researching and recording "popular superstitions" for their own sake. Bourne's research was rediscovered and expanded by another clergyman, John Brand, in his *Observations on Popular Antiquities* (1777). By the end of the century, a new *positive* concept of tradition as the collective wisdom of the "people" was generating a research program that led to the later founding of the Folklore Society (1878). Yet even as antiquarians, protofolklorists, poets, and others valorized certain kinds of oral tradition that they viewed as quaint and harmless, literate hostilities toward other kinds of oral tradition did not change. From Locke and Addison to Mary Wollstonecraft, Maria Edgeworth, and Hannah More, pedagogical writers castigated household servants for corrupting children with oral tales, and they associated superstitious and otherwise-"dangerous" traditions with gypsies and "Romish priests." As this long-standing Protestant bias suggests, our modern secular notion of tradition was at once a break from and an outgrowth of earlier dominant theological meanings.[43]

While chapter 1 surveys ideas of oral tradition over a 140-year period, chapters 2 and 3 examine the relationship between print commerce and ideas of the oral in two especially revealing texts. The authors of these works could hardly have been more different: Daniel Defoe (c. 1660–1731) was a Dissenting Whig tradesman who argued against press licensing and took full advantage of the opportunities of print commerce, while Jonathan Swift (1667–1745) was an Anglican Tory clergyman who was dismayed by the "license of the press." Yet both of these authors made sense of what seemed to them the new world of print commerce by linking problematic print genres and practices to dangerous and "vulgar" oral forms. In my ac-

count, these authors emerge not only as acute commentators on the potential power of an unlicensed press but also as important, neglected theorists
of *oral* discourse.

First published in 1704 but drafted around 1696–97, *A Tale of a Tub* was
written immediately after the lapse of the Licensing Act. Swift's *Tale* is traditionally read as a satire on "print culture," but in chapter 2 I read it in the
context of the development of ideas about oral discourse and oral tradition.
As a newly minted Protestant clergyman, Swift satirized Catholic theological
appeals to "oral tradition." At the same time, he associated the new "license
of the press" with a serious threat of social instability and even revolutionary
change. In a set piece on "Oratorial Machines," he draws an explicit analogy
between problematic print genres and varieties of oral discourse. For a clergyman, the most important "Oratorial Machine" was the pulpit, and for Swift,
the most dangerous preachers were Dissenters. In the terms of his oral-print
analogy, the "Pulpit" also signifies "the Writings of our *Modern Saints*": the
subversive Dissenting tracts that flooded the print marketplace after 1695.
Anticipating Pope in the *Dunciad*, Swift represents *both* Grub Street authors
and Dissenting preachers as braying asses, and he defines the unruly populace
by its organs of hearing. Whoever would manipulate mankind, the tale-teller
advises, "*must find a very good Hold at their Ears.*"[44] The unique power of
oral communication, Swift recognized, lies in its corporeality. Oral communication is rooted in the relationship between bodies, and the tools of oral
communication (tongues, ears, gesture, and so on) are readily available to all.
Eighteenth-century authors were fascinated by the physical transmission of
sounds (corporeal and otherwise), and Swift foregrounds the material bodily
stratum throughout the *Tale*. At the same time, there is a sense throughout
this work of being on the brink of a profound change. The tale-teller alludes
to (and anticipates) "great Revolutions." Now that press licensing had collapsed, Swift suggests, the new means of mass persuasion would be an increasingly organized, multimedia appeal to ears and eyes.

At the time of the Great Plague in England (1664–65), there were only
three regularly printed newspapers. But by 1722, when Defoe published *A
Journal of the Plague Year*, the public had come to depend on printed news.
Writing about events that took place sixty years earlier, Defoe was also writing across the historical period that marks the institutionalization of the
newspaper press. Looking back on the 1660s, Defoe's narrator, H.F., char-
acterizes "then" and "now" according to their modes of communication.
In the second paragraph of the *Journal*, he declares, "we had no such thing
as printed News Papers." Instead, news was "gather'd from . . . Letters . . .
and . . . handed about by Word of Mouth."[45] The *Journal* is a historical fiction,

and it is also a didactic text aimed at teaching readers how to prepare for a possible future epidemic. But it is also, I argue in chapter 3, an analysis of different modes of communication and an attempt to shape future practice. As a prolific print author, Defoe had much to gain from promoting the idea of the superior trustworthiness of print, and he embraced the prospect of a print-oriented civic order whose cornerstone would be freedom of the press and reliable news. But at the same time, as a fiction writer and political propagandist, Defoe was well aware that printed texts were not inherently trustworthy. Throughout the *Journal*, the *un*reliability of the Bills of Mortality is a central theme. Official government documents printed weekly at times of crisis, the Bills of Mortality listed the number of deaths per parish and apparent cause of death. In his concern for the credibility of print, Defoe scrutinized where the information in the bills originated. As I show, he traced this seemingly authoritative printed information back to the oral reports of the "Women-Searchers": old, poor, and illiterate women who were appointed to examine bodies and determine the cause of death. Strikingly, though, while Defoe reprinted almost verbatim the official Orders for the appointment of women searchers, he erased these women everywhere else in his text. In so doing, I argue, he worked to displace an unreliable, feminized oral "past" that in his view needed to be cut off from a more reliable, print-oriented future.

At the same time, Defoe aggressively linked popular oral discourse (cunning-women, prognosticators, mountebanks, ballad singers, and others) to contagion and superstition. Like Swift, he placed cheap print (almanacs, broadside ballads, chapbooks, and so on) on a continuum with "vulgar" oral traditions, and he associated both print and oral genres with rumors and "noise." As eighteenth-century texts amply illustrate, "noise" is a social and political category: a subjective term for unwanted sound.[46] From Ned Ward's "microcosmographies" of urban sites in the *London Spy* (1698–1700) to William Wordsworth's dramatization of his "Residence in London" in *The Prelude* (1805), eighteenth-century authors present some of their most memorable works (or set pieces within those works) as the written record of forays by themselves or their narrators though the urban soundscape: an environment that they define by aural (and oral) experiences. Defoe's depiction of disease-stricken London is striking in its emphasis on sound: shrieks, cries, moans, groans, and so on. Recent work in soundscape studies—the study of the relationship between living beings and their acoustic environments—encourages us to embed oral-aural practices in their specific spatial (and sometimes historical) contexts.[47] Eighteenth-century texts are a valuable register of our predecessors' experiences of different aural environments. As these texts powerfully show, the consumption of sound is at once physiological and psychological. Social and personal factors influence not only what we hear but what it means.

The mid- and later eighteenth century saw the explosion of debating societies, "rational entertainments" where men (and sometimes women) of a wide variety of social ranks paid a small entrance fee to hear and share views on religion, politics, and society. Chapter 4 focuses on a figure who I argue was of central importance to the emergence and institutionalization of these societies, yet one who is almost wholly neglected today. This figure is John "Orator" Henley, a notorious preacher-cum-entrepreneur who ran a public "Oratory" in London from 1726 to 1756 and was satirized by major literary authors of his time. Henley was an Anglican minister, but in 1725 he left the church to set up a new kind of religious and educational institution in the metropolis. Taking advantage of the Toleration Act of 1689, which allowed Dissenters to hold meetings for worship, he opened for business in rented rooms above a meat market in central London. For the next three decades, he supported himself by means of this unique oratorial operation and by carefully coordinated print publications.

Henley understood the Oratory to be a religious institution, but critics claimed that he had taken advantage of the Toleration Act to license a new kind of public forum: one more aptly described as a "Temple of Rebellion" than a church. The government arrested Henley at least three times, and Church of England leaders worked to have his Oratory suppressed. Why did religious and political leaders—and authors such as Pope—bother with an individual whom modern scholars have largely written off as a madman? I argue that what threatened Henley's contemporaries the most about him was not so much his increasingly heterodox ideas as the radically *public*, semi-institutionalized venue and the distinctive oral-corporeal style in which he communicated those ideas to mixed-sex audiences across the socioeconomic spectrum.

Henley was a self-conscious theorist of oral discourse. He billed himself as the "Restorer of Antient Eloquence," and he offered to teach the arts of oratory to new, marginalized social groups. Contemporaries routinely commented on his highly physical style of preaching and his studied use of gesture as well as voice. In a society where half the population could not (or did not) read, Henley was spreading his ideas orally in his own distinctive oral-corporeal style. At the same time, Henley was a prolific and innovative print author, and by linking his oral-corporeal performances to his coordinated print publications, we can begin to understand his fame (as well as the extraordinary longevity of the Oratory). Among many other kinds of evidence, I take advantage of the insights offered by two of Henley's most astute critics, Henry Fielding and Christopher Smart, who at once satirized *and imitated* his multimedia methods. Fielding satirized Henley as "Dr. Orator" in his comedy *The Author's Farce* (1730); two decades later, Smart hosted his own satiric variety show, "The Old Woman's Oratory, or, *Henley in Petticoats*." Like Henley, Smart tied his oral-corporeal performances to a periodical, *The Midwife: Or, The Old Woman's Magazine* (1750–53). Henley pioneered a new, enduring forum for the public discussion of controversial ideas, and I conclude chapter 4 by pointing to his formative (and largely unrecognized) role in the origins of modern public debating societies.

Since the Civil War period, Dissenting preachers' oral appeal to the masses was an enormous concern to Anglicans and others. But as the example of Henley suggests, in the eighteenth century, a new kind of oral entrepreneur began reassessing the power of the *spoken* word, then harnessing it, *in tandem with print*, to new commercial and ideological ends. Chapters 5 and 6 focus on the elocution movement and its relationship to varieties of oral discourse castigated as "Billingsgate rhetoric." A key figure in chapter 5 is Irish actor-turned-elocutionist Thomas Sheridan, the father of playwright and parliamentary orator Richard Brinsley Sheridan. Following Henley, but far more concerned than he was with gaining the approval of those in power, Sheridan made a new commercial opportunity out of teaching the ancient arts of public speaking. Whereas Henley's Oratory tied him to London, Sheridan traveled to major urban centers throughout the nation, offering to help men and women of the middling ranks shed the regional dialects that interfered with social advancement in the newly consolidated Great Britain. A multimedia entrepreneur like Henley, Sheridan delivered lectures on the power of oral delivery, then printed them as *A Course of Lectures on Elocution* (1762). In his oral performances, Sheridan at once celebrated and embodied those elements of spoken communication that cannot be reproduced in texts. He emphasized aspects of oral communication such as tone, cadence, and pitch, and like Henley, he celebrated gesture as the "natural language of the hands." Yet even as Sheridan taught his audiences to manipulate their body parts in public speaking (eyes, arms, hands, stance, and so on), he urged proper containment of the body. In so doing, he worked to distinguish his own "polite" oral endeavors from those of suspect social groups such as the Methodists, who were making powerful use of many of the same insights first. In contrast to these alarmingly effective orators, Sheridan lamented, "some of our greatest men have been trying to do that with the pen, which can only be performed by the tongue."[48] In an age increasingly dominated by books and reading, he argued that the propagation of texts and even of literacy was destroying the "natural" expressive force of speech. The elocutionists' arguments for the superior power of oral communication may appear to challenge widespread literate assumptions about the superiority of writing. But by rereading such arguments in the context of the critique of print commerce that I identify and analyze in this book, I show that like theorists of media shift earlier in the century, the elocutionists were theorizing *oral* discourse in large part as a means of grappling with changing political, institutional, and socioeconomic conditions for print.

In 1711 Joseph Addison proposed that if women were allowed to "plead in Courts of Judicature . . . they would carry the Eloquence of the Bar to greater heights than it has yet arrived at."[49] As a satirical example of female eloquence, he pointed to Billingsgate fishwives, who were known for their distinctive oral style. In chapter 6, I focus on the working women whom Addison referred to as the "Ladies of the *British* fishery." In the eighteenth century, "fishwives" typically referred to street criers. Fishwives' harangues were among the best known of the "London Cries"—a textual, as well as oral, genre—and the aggressive orality and animated gestures of fishwives and "oyster wenches" became a topos in literary and visual art. I begin by providing historical background on the actual fishwives of Billingsgate. I then address early modern assumptions about women's bodies—assumptions that can help us to understand, among other things, the widespread derogatory association of female genitals and fish. But my primary purpose in this chapter is to argue that in eighteenth-century literature and art, Billingsgate fishwives were considered one of the dominant figures (if not *the* dominant figure) of loud, unruly, threatening orality. Furthermore, I contend, the polite fascination with fishwives' *voices* was to a significant degree the product of literate gentlemen's reflection on the expanding world of *print*.

The term "Billingsgate" came to refer to a style of discourse that was said to be characteristic of fishwives: a style associated with colorful obscenities, verbal wit, and (more puzzlingly) the overuse of rhetorical figures and tropes. Accusations of "Billingsgate" denoted the transgression of polite style. Yet while polite rhetoricians and elocutionists defined their oratory away from what Adam Smith called "the Billingsgate language," they nonetheless acknowledged the paradox of these "rude" speakers' oratorical power. In textual representations of fishwives, we shall see, these typically illiterate plebeian women are depicted as achieving their rhetorical ends. Fishwives won their oral battles with gentlemen. In the new age of print, these representations suggest, extensive reading was undermining gentlemen's once-valued oral skills, and bookish men were increasingly cowed by the "Billingsgate rhetoric" that they condemned.

While eighteenth-century authors and visual artists associated fishwives with aggressive oral discourse, they also feared plebeian women's increased access to printed texts. As we have seen in Hogarth's depiction of a broadside-reading fishwife, a single literate member of an otherwise-illiterate group could serve as a bridge between her peers and the world of texts. Combined with these "rude" orators' supposed "natural" eloquence, this increased access to print seemed to some observers a double threat. I conclude chapter 6 by addressing the daunting methodological challenges of attempting to determine the relationship between representations of working women's voices and their actual speech. On the one hand, textual depictions of Billingsgate fishwives' voices functioned to delimit public speaking as a *male* activity. On the other hand, precisely because women's speech practices were gradually changing, Addison's satirical proposition that women might one day "plead in Courts of Judicature" no longer seems a ridiculous idea.

Throughout the century the dominant understanding of "oral tradition" remained religious. But around the 1730s, one begins to see this phrase used in a newly secular sense in protoethnographic writings[50] and in a wide range of scholarly (sometimes even popular) debates. Mid- and later eighteenth-century authors would theorize oral tradition in new ways, as I argue in chapters 7 and 8, which examine scholarly investments in ideas of the oral. Confronting a newly pluralistic literary marketplace, genteel authors increasingly looked "elsewhere" for alternative models of literary dissemination, and they found them in places and times that they represented as temporally or spatially distant from print commerce (the feudal past, the Scottish Highlands, native America, and so on).

Eighteenth-century Britain saw the emergence of an extensive print discourse about ballads. In prefaces to printed collections of ballads, in essays and commentaries in periodicals, and in many other venues, a wide variety of authors commented positively and negatively on balladry as an oral and textual practice. Chapter 7 analyzes writing about ballads from Addison's *Spectator* issues on ballads to Scottish collector William Motherwell's groundbreaking *Minstrelsy, Ancient and Modern* (2 vols., 1827), the first printed work to record ballads exclusively from oral sources. These commentators had diverse (sometimes opposing) agendas. But in writing about ballads, they all explicitly addressed the phenomenon of print commerce. In so doing, I argue, these ballad critics, commentators, and scholars, responding to the spread of print commerce in their own time, contributed to the emergence of our modern secular concept of oral tradition.

In Addison's day, the term "ballad" implicitly referred to a broadside. As we have seen in *Beer Street*, where Hogarth depicts a fishwife singing *and* reading a ballad, ballads were commonly associated with cheap print and with the "lower sort." But over the course of the century, I argue, the genteel ballad revival and the rise of ballad scholarship forged significantly new ways of conceptualizing ballads. Whereas early eighteenth-century commentators such as Addison took for granted the multimedia nature of balladry as both oral and textual, later eighteenth- and nineteenth-century scholars increasingly theorized a distinct "oral tradition" of balladry that they saw as threatened or displaced by commercial print.

Percy's *Reliques of Ancient English Poetry* intensified an already-existing interest in the collecting (and correcting) of certain *kinds* of ballads (what we would call "folk ballads" rather than bawdy ballads or topical political songs). Percy collected his relics from manuscripts and printed texts, but in "An Essay on the Ancient Minstrels in England," he represented the "Old Heroic Ballads" in his collection as the art of "oral itinerant poet[s]."[51] In Percy's conjectural history, ancient minstrels and modern balladmongers were not mutual participants in one evolving artistic tradition. Rather, the sixteenth-century institutionalization of the press in England contributed to the extinction of an earlier (and superior) cultural practice based on voice.

Today, scholars routinely reject problematic binary models of oral and textual balladry. But the most powerful way to denaturalize these binaries, I suggest, is to understand where they came from in the first place. Percy's "Essay" implicitly asks, when did ballads first become a major category of commercial print in England? In contrast, I ask, when and why did ballads first come to be valued as "oral tradition"? Eighteenth-century ballad scholars forged an increasingly sharp conceptual (not actual) separation of oral and printed ballads. By the end of the century, their heightened reflection on print commerce contributed to a new conceptualization of valuable ballad traditions as innately oral.

Chapter 8 examines the mid- and later eighteenth-century intersection of a number of scholarly, ethnographic, and literary developments that together resulted in groundbreaking new ways of thinking about societies "without the Invention of Letters." These developments include the expanding print market for travel narratives, imparting new knowledge about peoples across the globe. New information about sophisticated global populations that seemingly lacked writing began to challenge literate European assumptions that what we would call "oral societies" were lawless and barbaric. In 1688 Paul Rycaut's *Royal Commentaries of Peru*, a translation of *Commentarios Reales de los Incas* (1609) by Spanish Peruvian author Garcilaso de la Vega, taught English readers that Peruvian peoples passed down complex histories and genealogies entirely by memory. Two years later, Swift's patron Sir William Temple proposed in *An Essay Upon the Ancient and Modern Learning* (1690) that ancient priests and bards in China, Peru, and Ireland transmitted genealogies, laws, and customs "with care and exactness" by oral tradition.[52] In 1724 Jesuit missionary Joseph-François Lafitau published his influential protoethnographic work *Customs of the American Indians*, advancing the enlightened idea that "savages" without writing might nonetheless pass down by tradition a highly developed system of laws, customs, and arts.

At the same time that British readers were digesting new information about societies "without the Invention of Letters," classicists were advancing new arguments about Homeric poetry. In 1769 Robert Wood suggested in *An Essay on the Original Genius of Homer* that the "Prince of Poets" may have been illiterate. Wood's proposal was considered ridiculous by many readers, but it was taken seriously on the Continent by the German classicist F. A. Wolf, whose *Prolegomena ad Homerum* (1795) influenced nineteenth-century Homer scholars and, eventually, the twentieth-century oral-formulaic theorist Milman Parry.

The mid- and later eighteenth century also saw the flowering of research into Celtic and Gaelic oral traditions. In his *Critical Dissertation on the Poems of Ossian* (1763), Hugh Blair celebrated Ossian as a third-century "Homer of the Highlands." Macpherson's role in reconstructing the Ossianic legacy was controversial to say the least, but Blair's *Critical Dissertation* triggered extensive research into the possibility of surviving native oral traditions—in part by *assuming* their existence and calling on respected, literate gentlemen to "make enquiry in their respective parishes."[53]

Blair's *Critical Dissertation* also contributed to new stadial models of the development of human societies. Blair argued that "there are four great stages through which men successively pass in the progress of society."[54] Confronted with seemingly atemporal societies in their native Scotland—from the feudal-agricultural clans of the Highlands to the modern commercial towns of the Lowlands—a type of Scottish moral philosopher retrospectively named conjectural historians hypothesized that different peoples across the globe represented different "stages" or "ages" in an evolutionary trajectory of human societies. Each of these types of societies had its own characteristic mode of subsistence (hunter-gatherer, nomadic or pasturage, agricultural, and so on), as well as its own institutions, social arrangements, and manners. Anticipating nineteenth-century anthropologists, these moral philosophers "promoted a scheme in terms of which not only past cultures, but all living societies were irrevocably placed on a temporal slope, a stream of Time."[55]

Around the 1790s, I propose, we begin to detect the idea of communications technologies as part of this unfolding sequence. Stadial theorists began to link phases in the development of societies not only to their mode of sustenance or production but also to developments in the history of communications, including the origins of language, the invention of writing, and the introduction and spread of printing. They understood their own era as a stage or "age" that was defined by a particular set of communications practices and tools. In a vein of conjectural histories that I identify and analyze, we find a rich source for tracing the origins of modern evolutionary narratives of media shift (the idea that societies progress from "orality" to "literacy," when in fact the idea of orality is arguably invented as literacy's foil). This vein of conjectural history posited, then worked to trace the development of human communicative practices from the first cries and gestures to the spread of print. In a few of these conjectural histories, such as Dugald Stewart's *Elements of the Philosophy of the Human Mind* (1792) and other works and the marquis de Condorcet's *Sketch for a Historical Picture of the Progress of the Human Mind* (wr. 1793; pr. 1795), we see a model in which communications developments themselves trigger "stages" in human history. "The invention of printing," these authors agreed, "accelerated the progress of the human mind."[56] But not all Enlightenment authors viewed writing as a catalyst of progress. Like Jean-Jacques Rousseau, a few British authors questioned whether the invention of writing (let alone printing) had on the whole improved the human condition.

In the final section of chapter 8, I bring these developments together in a revisionary reading of Johnson's *Journey to the Western Islands of Scotland* (1775). Johnson's well-known skepticism concerning claims for the survival of ancient oral traditions in the Highlands is now typically read as an example of widespread English bias against the Scots. But Johnson's journey to and through the Highlands by boat, on horseback, and on foot was highly atypical of gentlemen of his day (both Englishmen and Lowland Scots), and his fierce resistance to contemporary claims for oral tradition is illuminating in the context of this study of changing attitudes toward and ideas of oral discourse and tradition. Johnson's relentless emphasis on the relationship between illiteracy and poverty, and his refusal of sentimental or idealizing representations of orality, offer us a new critical lens through which to rethink certain troubling aspects of later eighteenth-century genteel investments in oral tradition. The elite revaluing of certain kinds of tradition, I argue, did not necessarily have democratic consequences. Nostalgic models of the decay, displacement, or death of oral traditions served complex ideological uses and needs, but chiefly those of literate persons whose own communicative tools included writing and print. In a society where the bulk of the population performed agricultural labor, there was little elite support for the idea of government-sponsored public education. In contrast, Johnson's response to his observation of the plight of the Scottish Highlanders was consistent with his lifelong refusal to sentimentalize or justify poverty or to countenance arguments against educating the poor. His distrust of claims for oral tradition was related not only to his Protestantism but also to his sense that in modern commercial society (and what he called the new "reading nation" of Britain), the inability to read and write, while no mark against innate worth, would increasingly be a liability for Scots and Englishmen alike.

Today, the intellectual work of theorists of nostalgia such as Svetlana Boym, Nicholas Dames, Kathleen Stewart, and Susan Stewart can help us to understand the sense of loss felt by some later eighteenth-century intellectuals when it came to select oral traditions and practices of "the people." Nostalgia is a way of coping with the present as well as the past. As Kathleen Stewart suggests, "in positing a 'once was' in relation to a 'now,' [nostalgia] creates a frame for meaning."[57] The nostalgia for "lost" oral traditions and practices that I discuss in *The Invention of the Oral* was coeval with the spread of print commerce. But this nostalgia was not necessarily an attempt to *return* to the past; rather, it was a genre of reflection. Understanding the profound sense of change and loss central to the emergence of secular models of oral tradition can help us to see why even today, powerful "displacement" models of human communication (the idea that one media form displaces, rather than transforms, another), though widely acknowledged as problematic, have still not themselves been thoroughly displaced. "Great Divide" models are indeed problematic, as media theorists now routinely acknowledge, but what current theorists of media shift often miss is that these displacement models have a more than two-hundred-year history. Eighteenth-century Britain witnessed the emergence of a tremendously influential cultural narrative of orality and literacy that remodeled a reciprocal, *living* relationship as a nostalgic historical fiction of "then" and "now." To adapt Adrian Johns's statement about "print culture," the idea of "oral culture" has also had to be made. "Oral culture," as I suggest in a brief coda, is a category of the literate. For the eighteenth-century authors whom I discuss in *The Invention of the Oral*, heightened reflection on oral discourse was part of a historic coming-to-terms with the power and spread of print.

CHAPTER ONE

Oral Tradition in the History of Mediation

As for oral Traditions, what certainty can there be in them? What foundation of truth can be laid upon the breath of man?
—Joseph Hall, *The Old Religion* (1628; repr., 1686), 179

I was in a Printing House in Hell & saw the method in which knowledge is transmitted from generation to generation. . . . In the fifth chamber were Unnam'd forms, which cast the metal into the expanse. There they were receiv'd by Men who occupied the sixth chamber, and took the forms of books & were arranged in libraries.
—William Blake, *The Marriage of Heaven and Hell* (1790)[1]

In 1699 an anonymous member of the Royal Society of London published a mathematical formula for assessing the credibility of oral tradition. In "A Calculation of the Credibility of Human Testimony," printed in the *Philosophical Transactions of the Royal Society*, the author opined that "Oral Tradition . . . is subject to much Casualty," losing much of its reliability within twenty years. Meanwhile, "written Tradition, if preserv'd but by a single Succession of Copies, will not lose half of its full Certainty, until . . . Seven Thousand, if not Fourteen Thousand Years."[2] This paper has been attributed to John Craig (c. 1663–1731), an Anglican clergyman and mathematician who published at least eight papers in the *Philosophical Transactions* between 1697 and 1710. The same year that "A Calculation" appeared, Craig published *Theologiae Christianae Principia Mathematica* (Mathematical principles of Christian theology), an attempt to use mathematical reasoning to determine the reliability of human testimony. Craig calculated that several factors affect the trustworthiness of an account passed down by tradition, such as the number of original eyewitnesses, the spatial

and geographical distance from the event related, and the elapsed time since
the event took place. Addressing the question of miracles, Craig acknowledged that the miracles recorded in the Bible tested the faith of Christian believers, but he argued that the apostles were original eyewitnesses, and therefore *their* oral testimony could be believed. Alarmingly, though, Craig also
calculated that the credibility of the story of Jesus, insofar as this story had
been passed down by tradition, had expired around 800 CE. Not surprisingly,
given this verdict, some of Craig's Royal Society colleagues questioned his
wisdom in subjecting apostolic testimony to probabilistic analysis. More strikingly, though—and more significantly for us in this chapter examining the
long eighteenth-century scrutiny of the idea of tradition—other colleagues
simply questioned his math.[3]

Today, the idea of tradition is evoked in the service of diverse sociopolitical arguments. It is commonly used to evoke some kind of reassuring continuity or collective experience at times of perceived rapid change. But as
sociologist Edward Shils pointed out, "in its barest, most elementary sense,
[tradition] means simply a *traditum*; it is anything which is transmitted
or handed down from the past to the present. It makes no statement about
what is handed down."[4] The *Oxford English Dictionary* defines tradition as
"I. The action or an act of imparting or transmitting something; something
that is imparted or transmitted" and as "1. a. A belief, statement, custom,
etc., handed down by non-written means (esp. word of mouth, or practice)
from generation to generation; such beliefs, etc., considered collectively."[5]
In the Christian church, *traditio* refers to "the delivery of God's truth to
His people through the apostles" and, by extension, to "the continuity of
orthodoxy in the Church."[6]

In the eighteenth century, the question of tradition was a key issue of
doctrinal differentiation between Protestants and Catholics. Since the Reformation, theologians debated the relative authority of the scriptures as
compared with tradition as the "rule of faith." For Catholics, the tradition
of the church is of equal authority with scripture. Tradition is manifested
in the rituals, spoken words, and gestures of religious worship: it is the "Living Voice and Practice of the Church."[7] Catholic theologians argued that the
transmission and interpretation of the scriptures were subject to endless human error. Accordingly, it was safer to "shift meaning, and authority, away
from the text itself, and place both in the hands of Rome."[8] Meanwhile, Protestants promoted Luther's doctrine of *sola scriptura*. They acknowledged
that Christ's teachings were oral, and that "the Old and New Testaments . . .
had been preserved orally . . . for . . . centuries before being immortalized on
paper." But they argued that this tradition was now safely preserved in the

Bible, that the basic truths necessary to salvation were sufficiently clear, and that writing was potentially the most reliable method of preserving and communicating knowledge.[9]

As the epigraphs to this chapter suggest, the Enlightenment saw a profound interrogation of what William Blake called "the method[s] in which knowledge is transmitted from generation to generation." It saw an examination of the reliability of different modes of transmission of divine and secular wisdom and the implications thereof for knowledge, government, and faith. Enlightenment theologians voluminously debated the relative reliability of oral tradition, writing, and, sometimes, printing. Surveying the arts of transmission from Moses to modernity, they compared oral tradition with these other modes. The author of "A Calculation" compared the transmission of knowledge in "Oral Tradition" and "Written Tradition," especially "since the Invention of Printing":

> In Oral Tradition as a Single Man is subject to much Casualty, so a Company of Men cannot be so easily suppos'd to join. . . . But in Written Tradition, the Chances against the Truth or Conservation of a single Writing are far less; and several copies may also be easily suppos'd to concur; and those since the Invention of Printing exactly the same. (363)

Similarly, Anglican divine Edward Stillingfleet (1635–99) devoted sections of his more than six-hundred-page book *Origines Sacrae* (1662) to the history of writing systems, considered in relation to oral tradition. Later, another eminent Anglican clergyman, William Warburton (1698–1779), built on Stillingfleet's arguments in his own nearly thirteen-hundred-page book, *The Divine Legation of Moses Demonstrated* (2 vols., 1738–41). Both of these authors were widely read throughout the Enlightenment, and Warburton's work was celebrated by philosophers for its groundbreaking contribution to the study of "hieroglyphics"—a term then used to describe forms of picture-based writing used not only in Egypt but also in China and the New World. In debating the relative reliability of oral tradition, writing, and printing, these and other clergymen were discussing what we would now call issues of mediation. In the later seventeenth and eighteenth centuries in Britain, the most influential histories of mediation were arguably written by theologians. In turn, questions of divine intercession and the human transmission of God's Word were central to Enlightenment debates about what we would now call "media."[10]

Throughout the seventeenth century, Anglican theologians argued in texts and sermons for the centrality of the scriptures as the "rule of faith."

But in Restoration England, this debate suddenly became a matter of urgent national importance, as two kings sympathetic to the Catholic cause assumed the throne: Charles II (1660–85) and James II (1685–88). From 1660, the question of tradition was widely debated by poets and philosophers as well as priests. In *Paradise Lost* (1667), John Milton excoriated appeals to "Traditions" by corrupt clergy, whom he represented as "grievous Wolves" (bk. 12, l. 508). Like Milton, John Dryden argued for "tradition written" as the rule of faith in *Religio Laici Or a Layman's Faith* (1682). But unlike Milton, Dryden later changed his views. Shortly after the succession of James II, he converted to Catholicism, and in *The Hind and the Panther* (1687) he argued in favor of the (unwritten) tradition of the church. Meanwhile, an anonymous Protestant author who described himself as "an obscure man" published a 236-page book titled *An Enquiry Whether Oral Tradition Or The Sacred Writings, Be the Safest Conservatory and Conveyance Of Divine Truths* (1685). This author pointed out that the official Roman position as determined by the Council of Trent (1545–63) was that truth lay in *both* the scriptures and "*Oral Tradition*" as preserved by the church. But in the heated environment of political debate, he lamented, "*Oral Tradition has quite carried away the Credit*" (A4v).

In this chapter I examine the long eighteenth-century scrutiny of tradition, considering both the theological debates and the "historical processes by which non-religious uses emerged."[11] I argue that over the course of this 140-year period, the idea of oral tradition was scrutinized, debunked, and reconstituted in its modern form. Furthermore, the emergence of our modern secular notion of oral tradition was at once a break from *and* an outgrowth of earlier dominant theological meanings. Throughout the eighteenth century, the preeminent understanding of "tradition" remained theological, but a gradually shifting political and religious climate increasingly allowed authors to address the question of tradition from a protoethnographic standpoint (rather than a purely doctrinal one). From about the 1730s, one increasingly detects "oral tradition" used in strikingly new ways in a wide range of literary, historical, and philosophical writings and debates.

When philosopher and statesman Francis Bacon discussed "the organ of tradition" in *The Advancement of Learning* (1605), he was not necessarily referring to *oral* tradition. Bacon was addressing the passing down (*tradere*) of knowledge in the university curriculum. Accordingly, he classified "Speech," "Writing," and "gestures" under this rubric:

> [T]he organ of tradition, it is either Speech or Writing . . . but yet it is not of necessity that cogitations be expressed by the medium of words. For

whatsoever is capable of sufficient differences, and those perceptible by the sense, is in nature competent to express cogitations. And therefore we see in the commerce of barbarous people that understand not one another's language, and in the practice of divers that are dumb and deaf, that men's minds are expressed in gestures, though not exactly, yet to serve the turn.[12]

By "organ of tradition," Bacon meant something like our "modes of trans-mission." Today, one meaning of "organ" is "a means or medium of com-munication."[13] In the passage quoted above, Bacon initially states that "the organ of tradition . . . is either Speech or Writing," but he then adds that any "medium" capable of expressing "differences . . . perceptible by the sense" can be an "organ of tradition." Along with what he calls the "medium of words," he includes "gestures"—a means of "express[ing] cogitations" that is used with special facility by the "dumb and deaf."

For Bacon, then, "tradition" did not necessarily mean *oral* tradition. But by the mid-eighteenth century, I argue, widespread debates concerning the scriptures versus tradition as the "rule of faith" had forged so strong a link between tradition and oral transmission that by this time, "tradition" typi-cally implied oral tradition. In 1755 Samuel Johnson defined "tradition" as "1. The act or practice of delivering accounts from mouth to mouth *without written memorials*; communication from age to age; 2. Any thing delivered *orally* from age to age."[14] As is now well known, Johnson was highly skepti-cal of *contemporary* appeals to oral tradition—especially appeals made by Scottish nationalists to advance their diverse political and personal goals after the Union of England and Scotland in 1706/7. While Johnson's skepti-cism is commonly ascribed to his bias against the Scots, I would argue that much greater attention needs to be paid to the role of his Anglicanism in shaping his attitudes toward tradition. It is no accident, I would point out, that in defining "tradition," "traditional," "traditionally," "traditionary," and "traditive" in his *Dictionary of the English Language* (1755), Johnson took most of his usage examples from Protestant authors who excoriated or critiqued Catholic appeals to "Tradition." Johnson's definitions of "tra-dition," "traditional," and so on comprise a veritable Protestant catalog of anti-Catholic quotations. He provides usage examples from polemical works by Anglican divines such as Stillingfleet and from Protestant arguments by Milton and Dryden. All of these diverse authors addressed the question of tradition in a theological context. Johnson was outspoken and belligerent in many ways, but his concept of and attitudes toward tradition were entirely typical of learned Protestants of his era.

At the same time, though, while Johnson's definition of "tradition" participates in long-standing theological debates, it also exemplifies gradual change. Johnson's explication of tradition as *oral* links oral tradition to the larger category of oral discourse more generally, and his emphasis on the mechanisms of oral transmission exemplifies what I see as the heightened eighteenth-century interest in the phenomenon of oral communication. Johnson highlighted the uniquely physical nature of oral communication, for instance, when he defined tradition as "the act or practice of delivering accounts from mouth to mouth." Eighteenth-century discussions of tradition were about Protestant ideology, but they were also, increasingly, about oral communication more generally and about the changing uses and meanings of oral communication in a print society.

Johnson's usage examples reflect the critique of tradition in Protestant theology, but by 1700 the unreliability of tradition was also axiomatic in other related realms of inquiry. Philosophers such as John Locke and David Hume explicitly questioned the "Probability" of "Testimony." Whereas Locke was relatively cautious in critiquing the role of oral testimony in *religious* matters, Hume's remarks on this subject in *An Enquiry concerning Human Understanding* shocked many of his contemporaries, and in his capacity as a historian, he was even more blunt.[15] In his *History of England* (6 vols., 1754–61), Hume openly scoffed at oral tradition. Eighteenth-century historians continued to draw on oral tales, legends, and testimony as source material, but they tended to relegate these traditionary materials to the margins of histories built on the firmer foundation of material artifacts and written texts.[16] Two transitional figures whom I discuss in this chapter, John Aubrey and Daniel Defoe, extensively recorded traditional tales, legends, and beliefs. But they typically used traditionary materials for the purposes of illustration rather than as evidence, and they distanced themselves from these materials as "vulgar error." Meanwhile, in the legal realm, lawyers and jurists increasingly viewed oral testimony as a mere supplement to the written record. Oral testimony remains an important part of the trial process even today, but already by 1700, a man's oral testimony was more likely to be trusted if he could read.

But the larger transformation that I trace here is not one of the total *discrediting* of tradition as a form of transmission or mediation. Rather, it is a matter of the scrutiny and reconstitution of tradition on different grounds. Throughout the eighteenth century, religious and political concerns continued to shape literate attitudes to tradition, but after the defeat of the Jacobite uprisings in 1715–16 and 1745, clergymen-antiquarians, in particular, began to explore the question of tradition in new ways. To illustrate changing approaches to the question of tradition, I will contrast works by two different Newcastle clergymen who wrote fifty years apart. In 1725 Henry Bourne (1694–1733) published a book-length tirade against "superstitious" popular traditions, *Antiquitates Vulgares; or, the Antiquities of the Common People. Giving an Account of several of their Opinions and Ceremonies. With proper Reflections upon each of them; shewing which may be retain'd, and which ought to be laid aside.* As an Anglican divine, Bourne traced superstitious practices and beliefs to the influence of "papism," and he excoriated Catholic appeals to "tradition." Fifty years later, another Newcastle curate, John Brand (1744–1806), built on Bourne's scholarship in his own *Observations on Popular Antiquities: Including the whole of Mr. Bourne's Antiquitates Vulgares, With Addenda to every Chapter of that Work* (1777). But in contrast to Bourne, who lambasted the credulity of the illiterate "vulgar," Brand proposed that the common people, precisely because they were the most likely to be illiterate, were also the most faithful preservers of a kind of popular tradition that should now be re-evaluated and recorded by the learned. This kind of tradition was a "venerable Deposit" that was passed down by ritual, practice, and word of mouth "from Time immemorial, though erazed by public authority from the *written Word.*"[17] Brand was a clergyman, but he was also a published author, and he exemplifies authors of his day in conceptualizing oral tradition in relation not only to writing and printing in general but also to the potential degradations of the literary marketplace and the commercial press. In the late seventeenth century, John Aubrey rejected "grosse things" such as "old wives-fables," but he also anticipated these later eighteenth-century authors in lamenting what he saw as the displacement of oral traditionary materials by print.[18]

The eighteenth century also saw other intersecting developments that helped prompt a reconsideration of ideas about oral tradition. From the first century of printing, travel writings constituted a major category of the print trades, and by 1700 the dissemination of new information about sophisticated global populations seemingly "without the Invention of Letters" was generating widespread interest in what we would now call "oral societies." As I shall discuss in detail in chapters 7 and 8, the later eighteenth century saw new arguments for tradition in our modern secular sense of the passing down, over generations, of complex histories, genealogies, and works of verbal art. Conjectural historians theorized "stages" in the development of human societies characterized partly by the invention and spread of writing, *alphabetic* writing, and, most recently, printing. In the "infancy of societies," they suggested, "savage" orators passed down laws, genealogies, and customs by tradition. A handful of Homer scholars tentatively suggested that the "father of Western poetry" could not read, and in 1760 Scottish Highlander James Macpherson claimed in his *Fragments of Ancient Poetry* to have recovered the traces of a third-century "Homer of the Highlands," whose originally oral poetry might now be recovered, recorded, and preserved in print. In 1765 another Anglican clergyman-antiquarian, Thomas Percy, published *Reliques of Ancient English Poetry*, prompting a widespread genteel reconsideration of the genre of the ballad: a hybrid print and oral form in contemporary practice, but in Percy's account, the legacy of ancient oral poets esteemed by kings. Inspired by increasingly positive valuations of oral tradition, poets and novelists such as William Wordsworth and Walter Scott found inspiration for their literary creations and print publications in traditional materials such as ballads and tales. By the end of the eighteenth century, oral tradition was seen as a rich repository of vanishing values, and what Aubrey referred to as "the divine art of Printing" was increasingly represented as a destructive force.[19] Whereas Aubrey admired printing, yet circulated his writings chiefly in manuscript (if at all), William Blake printed his texts, yet satirized the press in his depiction of a "Printing House in Hell." In the new age of print commerce, Blake suggested, a once "divine" art had become a diabolical process.

In the nineteenth century, oral tradition became a research program. Traditions once castigated as superstitious "rubbish" were now venerated as "folklore"—a term coined in 1846. Yet while certain kinds of tradition were now deemed worthy of appreciation and study, other kinds of tradition continued to be lambasted by the learned. As I shall suggest in the final section of this chapter, especially fierce criticism was directed at lower-class servants and "village matrons" who were accused of damaging children's "tender Minds" with their stories of "*Goblins, Spectres,* and *Apparitions.*"[20] Locke blamed children's nurses for making grown men afraid of ghosts, and in an issue of the *Spectator* devoted to critiquing "old-wives-fables," Joseph Addison urged his female *and* male readers "*to pull the old Woman out of our Hearts.*"[21] At the turn of the nineteenth century, pioneering female educational authors such as Mary Wollstonecraft, Maria Edgeworth, and Hannah More joined their male predecessors in lambasting servants and gypsies for spreading superstitious traditions and "old wives' tales."

DEBATING "THE *ORALITY* OF THE RULE OF FAITH"

Let us turn first to the Restoration theological battleground. As Marcus Walsh has suggested, the Restoration debate about tradition was not a "set of peripheral pamphlet skirmishes, but a major war in the history of ideas, in which big guns on both sides were employed."[22] Charles II and James II favored freedom of worship for Protestant Dissenters and Roman Catholics, and while they ostensibly supported Anglican doctrine, in practice they tolerated (and promoted) arguments for tradition by English Catholics. Key works of English Catholic priest John Gother were printed by Henry Hills, the King's Printer,[23] while Anglican responses to Catholic arguments appeared under the imprint of the English church. In 1662 Edward Stillingfleet published his influential work *Origines Sacrae, Or A Rational Account of the Grounds of Christian Faith*.[24] Stillingfleet argued for the superior reliability of texts versus tradition as a means of passing down God's Word. But significantly, in advancing this argument, he devoted entire sections of *Origines Sacrae* to the history of writing technologies, considered in relation to oral transmission. The first chapter, "The Obscurity and defect of Ancient History," addresses topics such as "the want of credibility in Heathen Histories asserted and proved by the general defect for want of timely records among Heathen Nations."[25] *Origines Sacrae* was widely read throughout the Enlightenment, and sermons on related topics by Stillingfleet and others spread these debates concerning oral tradition and the origins and development of writing even to persons who could not read.

Origines Sacrae set off a flurry of printed responses. In 1665 English Catholic priest John Sergeant (1623–1707) responded in his own lengthy book, *Sure-Footing in Christianity, Or, Rational Discourses On The Rule of Faith* (244 pp.). Sergeant argued that the unreliability of textual transmission and interpretation meant that Christians must ultimately put their faith in the "Orall Tradition" of the church. (But this kind of "Orall Tradition," he emphasized, was not to be confused with "a generall and uncontroll'd Tradition.")[26] The following year, Anglican divine John Tillotson (1630–94) responded to Sergeant's arguments in his own 344-page book, *The Rule of Faith: Or, An Answer to the Treatise of Mr. J. S. Entituled, Sure-Footing, &c.* (1666). Like Stillingfleet, Tillotson argued for "written Tradition" as the most reliable repository of knowledge.

Not one to rest his quill pen, Sergeant responded almost immediately with another book, his ironically titled *A Letter of Thanks from the author of Sure-Footing to his answerer Mr. J[ohn] T[illotson]* (1666). In a passage now cited by the *Oxford English Dictionary* as the earliest recorded use of the word "orality," he praised "the *Orality* of the Rule of Faith, its Uninterruptedness, and perpetuall Assistance of God's spirit, and . . . imprinting it by the way of living Sense in *men's hearts*."[27] For Sergeant, "orality" was no mere synonym for "speech" (as the term is sometimes loosely used today).

The orality of tradition included "visible Actions" as well as spoken words: *"by Orall or Practicall Tradition wee mean a delivery down from hand to hand (by Words and a constant course of frequent and visible Actions conformable to those Words) of the Sence and Faith of Forefathers."*[28] Like Johnson, who defined tradition as "the delivery of accounts from mouth to mouth," Sergeant foregrounded the physicality of oral communication when he described *"Orall or Practicall Tradition"* as *"delivery . . . from hand to hand."*

Sergeant never implied that *"the Orality of* the Rule of Faith" meant the total absence of writing or printing. On the contrary, he held that "visible Actions," spoken words, and the scriptures work together to ensure the continuity of the faith. Sergeant praised the Catholic emphasis on tradition as a "way of coming to Faith by the open use of our Senses."[29] He emphasized that in Catholic worship, spoken words are accompanied by rituals that can be observed and assessed by anyone. This audible and visible legacy is "understandable by the rudest vulgar" yet also "able to satisfie the acutest Discoursers."[30] Sergeant's emphasis on the repeated witnessing of "visible Actions" and "the open use of our Senses" echoes the nascent discourse of empiricism. Meanwhile, his assertion that even the "rudest vulgar" could serve as guardians of tradition was also ahead of its time. Whereas most Catholic writers on the rule of faith were "positively hostile towards the phenomenon of popular transmission," Sergeant "presents an unusually positive picture of the ordinary Christian, who is seen as . . . a repository and guarantee of [tradition]."[31] As we shall see, his belief that common people might serve as guardians of tradition, rather than its destroyers, anticipated the views of a small number of late eighteenth-century ballad scholars and others who argued that the "vulgar" or "common people" were in fact the most "faithful" custodians of a valuable, *popular* oral tradition that was being undermined by the spread of print. Like the arguments of these later authors, Sergeant's remarks on tradition were prompted in part by his reflections on the spread of print. With a telling turn of phrase, he wrote that "the *Orality* of the Rule of Faith . . . imprint[ed] it by the way of living Sense in *men's hearts*."[32]

Two decades after this polemical battle of the 1660s, Sergeant, Stillingfleet, and Tillotson were still debating the question of tradition. On 27 November 1687, about a year before James II fled to France, Stillingfleet preached a highly politicized sermon at London Guildhall denouncing the fallibility of "meer Tradition" and praising the "Invention" and spread of "Letters." In this oral sermon and its later print counterpart, *Scripture and Tradition compared* (1688), Stillingfleet vigorously engaged, as he had done for the previous twenty years, with the arguments of one "J.S."[33]

Along with political exigencies, another factor shaping Restoration eighteenth-century debates concerning oral tradition was the development of modern biblical scholarship. Throughout the seventeenth century, the scriptures were subjected to new forms of textual criticism (historical, antiquarian, philological, and literary), and new findings greatly influenced polemical debates. The monumental project of compiling the King James Bible (1604–11) had "revealed the . . . human side" of the scriptures. The Bible might be the "Word" of God, but it was also "a *document* whose qualities need to be investigated and understood."[34] In 1678 and 1689 respectively, French Catholic priest Richard Simon published *Histoire critique du Vieux Testament* and *Histoire critique du text du Nouveau Testament*. A skeptical textual scholar "who is now seen as pioneering modern-day biblical criticism,"[35] Simon subjected the scriptures to new standards of documentary historicity. He examined original historical documents, checked secondary references, and so on. Attempting to protect Christianity from skepticism, he summoned all of his extraordinary intellectual resources, only to conclude that biblical texts were highly unreliable. For this reason, he argued, Christians must rely on the continuous oral tradition of the church.

Like Simon's critical histories, the textual scholarship of the Huguenot refugee Pierre Bayle (1647–1706) raised as many questions as it answered about the Bible. In 1697 Bayle published *Dictionnaire historique et critique*, a biographical dictionary that examines religious beliefs. Like Simon's works, Bayle's *Dictionnaire* was written to defend the faith, but it ultimately exposed the Bible as unstable, ambiguous, and contradictory. Confronted with the textual challenges of the scriptures, Bayle echoed Simon in concluding that the basis of Christianity necessarily lay in faith and in the unwritten tradition of the church. In advancing their arguments for or against the scriptures as the ultimate rule of faith, all these authors were attempting to undergird Christianity. But in subjecting the Bible and tradition to new standards of documentary evidence, the new textual scholarship and historiography "unwittingly turned the basic question of Christian truth into a historical one." As Joseph Levine has suggested, in the long run the new historiography "turned out to be the deadliest enemy of traditional Christianity, as the Bible dissolved into a plurality of texts." Eighteenth-century historians and philosophers adopted these devout authors' skeptical textual methods, and they used this new biblical scholarship for different (sometimes radical) ends. In developing his skeptical outlook in religious matters, historian Edward Gibbon (1737–94) honed his critical and textual skills by reading "the extraordinary series of works that had been written to defend orthodox Christianity from its . . . enemies."[36]

From the 1660s, too, the question of "the *Orality* of the Rule of Faith" was also debated in print by laypersons. Shortly after Sergeant published his earliest arguments in favor of "Orall Tradition," John Milton published his epic poem *Paradise Lost* (1667). In the following lines, Milton represents priests (such as Sergeant) as "grievous Wolves" preying on their spiritual flocks:

> Wolves shall succeed for teachers, grievous Wolves,
> Who all the sacred mysteries of Heav'n
> To their own vile advantages shall turn,
> Of lucre and ambition, and the truth
> With superstitions and traditions taint,
> Left only in those written Records pure,
> Though not but by the Spirit understood.[37]

In this passage, "traditions" are not equal to truth; rather, they "taint" truth and mislead the devout. Only the "written Records pure" of the scriptures, Milton argued, could assist the faithful in distinguishing "truth" from "superstitions."

Like Milton, John Dryden energetically participated in debates concerning "the Orality of the Rule of Faith." But unlike Milton, who remained a Protestant Dissenter after the succession of James II in 1685, Dryden converted from Protestantism to Catholicism, and he argued with equal force on both "sides" of the question of tradition. Both before and after his conversion, Dryden thoughtfully engaged with the arguments of Richard Simon, whom he admired as a "Matchless Author." In 1682 Dryden's friend Henry Dickinson published a translation of Simon's *Histoire critique du Vieux Testament*, and later that year, Dryden published *Religio Laici Or a Layman's Faith*. He implicitly worked to counter Simon's arguments about tradition when he asked this rhetorical question about "written words" versus "oral Sounds":

> If *written words* from time are not secur'd,
> How can we think have *oral Sounds* endur'd?
> Which *thus* transmitted, if *one* Mouth has fail'd,
> *Immortal Lyes* on *Ages* are intail'd:[38]

As a Protestant, Dryden acknowledged that both oral tradition and written tradition were fallible, yet he argued that *"Tradition written . . .* more
commends / *Authority,* than what from *Voice* descends." Yet even at this
stage in his spiritual development, we can detect Dryden's growing discomfort with certain aspects of Protestantism. The publication of vernacular
Bibles after the Reformation, he suggested, potentially made every man his
own interpreter of the scriptures, and he saw this as a problem. Dryden
routinely linked the *"Mouths"* of the "vulgar" or "Rabble" with "loud" and
dangerous oral discourse. But in the following lines, he also links the *textual misreadings* of "Crouds unlearn'd" to political and social disorder and
dangerous noise:

> The Book thus put in every vulgar hand,
> Which each presum'd he best cou'd understand,
> The *Common Rule* was made the *common Prey;*
> And at the mercy of the *Rabble* lay.
> The tender Page with horney Fists was gaul'd;
> *And he was gifted most who loudest baul'd.*[39]

Three years later, after he converted to Catholicism, Dryden argued in support of "Tradition" rather than the scriptures (the "Book") as the rule of
faith. In his 2,600-line allegorical poem *The Hind and the Panther* (1687),
he represented the Catholic Church as "a milk-white hind, immortal and
unchanged," and in sharp contrast to Milton in the lines from *Paradise Lost*
quoted above, he argued that the Roman Church "by Tradition's force up-
held the Truth."[40]

A now-forgotten voice in these debates is Milton's and Dryden's contemporary, the anonymous author of the aforementioned *An Enquiry
Whether Oral Tradition Or The Sacred Writings, Be the Safest Conservatory and Conveyance Of Divine Truths* (1685). This author seems to have
been something of a popularizer; he attempted to lay out his argument as
fairly and clearly as possible and to educate a broad audience about key issues and debates. A self-described "obscure man," he represented himself as
a latecomer to a "Competition" that had long preoccupied "Reverend and
Learned Persons": *"the Author is sensible, that the Competition between*
Oral Tradition *and* Scripture *has been already so* excellently *manag'd by*
Reverend and Learned Persons, *that this present Undertaking by an obscure man may be judg'd* Supernumary, *or worse."* At the same time, he expressed his hope that *"even his* Gleanings *after others plentiful* / Harvest . . .

may yet be not altogether unacceptable, *or* useless." His self-description and occasionally witty style suggest that he may have been a layperson. In one jocular moment, he mentions Ovid: a pagan author not typically cited by divines. In assessing oral tradition, he compared oral narratives to the fantastically transformed creatures depicted by Ovid. An oral story that has "travelled through many Mouths," he suggested, eventually becomes something new: " 'tis usual for Stories . . . after they have travelled through many Mouths, to be so much altered from what they were at the first, that they look like one of *Ovid's* Metamorphoses."[41]

The *tone* of the *Enquiry* also differs from most Protestant polemics of its day. In contrast to Milton's outburst above, for instance, the author adopted a respectful position in relation to the Catholic Church. His diplomacy may have been due in part to the date of his text's publication: the *Enquiry* was printed in 1685, the year that James II succeeded to the throne. The author attempted to lay out doctrinal differences fairly, and he acknowledged that there was diversity of opinion on the issue of tradition even within the Catholic Church. He proposed that recent Catholic polemicists' emphasis on oral tradition to the point of near exclusion of Holy Writ was not characteristic of mainstream Catholicism. The official Roman position was that truth was to be found equally in "Scripture *and* Tradition." But *"of later years,* Oral Tradition *has quite carried away* the Credit; *and has been by some Zealous Asserters cry'd up for the* infallible Conveyance, *and* only Rule of Faith." The author pointed not only to Anglican authors such as Stillingfleet but also to Catholic cardinal Robert Bellarmine (1542–1621) as examples of learned theologians who held that *"Tradition* is not the *onely Rule* of Faith."[42] He also worked to clarify the meaning of *non scripta.* As Bellarmine had emphasized in *De verbo Dei non Scripto* (The word of God unwritten), *non scripta* does not mean that a doctrine has *never* been written down but rather that it was not *originally* written down: *"a Doctrine is called unwritten; not because it is no where written, [but] because it was not written by the first Author."*[43]

The author of the *Enquiry* argued that contemporary polemicists wrongly opposed oral and written tradition: "the Adversaries, I have to deal with, talk of *Oral Tradition,* as a *Plenipotent* thing, which is a support to *itself,* and needs not the prop of a Pen."[44] At the same time, though, the fundamental structure of the *Enquiry* exhibits (and, in so doing, helps to construct) the oral versus written binary that I see as crystallizing in this period. The author explicitly represents "Oral Tradition" and "Written . . . Tradition" as the two different "side[s]" of a crucial "Competition": one on which human salvation depends. He divides his text into two parts, the first part on oral tradition and the second on written tradition, and throughout the book, the running page headers foreground "Oral Tradition" and "Written Tradition" as the work's dominant concerns. The author's division of his text is not a neutral gesture; rather, it is an act of classification—and of opposition. This comparative analysis of oral tradition and writing, prompted in part by recognition of the spread of print, was (I shall argue throughout this book) increasingly characteristic of British authors, and it had implications far beyond theological debates.

The author of the *Enquiry* emphasized that "both Written, and *Oral Tradition* are . . . guilty of *no small failures.*" Texts, like their authors, are subject to destruction ("violence from Enemies") and decay, and textual transmission is subject to the "carelessness" of printers and scribes:

> *Writings* have their fates, as well as their *Authors.* They are not exempt from either a *total perishing* by the oscitancy and *carelessness* of the Owners, or by *violence* from Enemies. Or at least they are liable to *corruption;* and that either *willful,* and out of design . . . or through the *ignorance,* or *negligence* of Transcribers.

But some texts, he suggested, do "escape . . . injury," and "Divine Truths" had been handled with special care. Alluding to the work of textual scholars such as Simon, he outlined for his readers some of the new critical "Methods" used to correct errors of transmission and to distinguish "*Spurious* from . . . *Genuine* Works":

> Learned Men have *Methods* (as Trial by Chronology, and the Customs and Modes of each Age; insight into the Style and Genius of an Author; Collation of Copies, with others) by which to distinguish *the Spurious* from the *Genuine* Works; and to right the Genuine by requisite *Emendations.*

Having assessed both "side[s]" of the oral/written binary that his own text helps to create, the author declared that "of the two, *Oral Tradition* is subject to the more *shortness* and *uncertainty.*" Ultimately, though, he suggested that the final "Director" in these debates must be "Reason." Men must use their individual judgment, in consultation with the "Scriptures Guidance," to assess the credibility of testimony: "we are not . . . bound to *resign our Faith universally* to the *Tradition* of the Church."[45]

The author briefly addressed the Jewish idea of the Oral Torah. He observed that "the *Jews* have amongst them an *Oral Tradition*, expository of the *Law Written*, and given (as is said by them) by God to *Moses* . . . and . . . transmitted down from one Generation to another." In the Jewish tradition, God gave Moses the Written Torah and an additional set of laws that was passed down orally from teacher to student. Eventually, after centuries of oral transmission, these laws were compiled in the Mishnah (the book of laws), accompanied by the Gemara, or rabbinical commentary. As Stephen Prickett explains, "for the *Hebrew* world tradition . . . was midrash, an ongoing debate and commentary on what was being conveyed. The law is incomplete without the associated tradition of reflection and discussion by which it was . . . absorbed."[46] But while the author of the *Enquiry* recognized the importance of the Oral Torah within the Jewish faith, he ultimately rejected this *"Oral Tradition"* as a mere invention: "Learned Men judge this fardle of *Traditions* to be a very . . . *Figment*."[47] Like Jonathan Swift—as we shall see in chapter 2—he held that the Oral Torah was a hoax ("Figment").

ORAL TRADITION AND THE PROBABILITY
OF TESTIMONY

The skeptical methods developed by seventeenth-century biblical scholars and theologians were put to different uses by Enlightenment philosophers and historians. In 1690 John Locke interrogated the "Probability" of "Testimony" as the grounds for belief in *An Essay Concerning Human Understanding*. In book 4, "Of Knowledge and Opinion," he examined the "degrees and ground of Probability, and Assent or Faith" (4.15.655). Anticipating the Royal Society discussion of oral tradition I have outlined above, Locke observed that in calculating "the Credibility of Human Testimony," multiple factors must be taken into consideration. He advised that "any Testimony, the farther off it is from the original Truth, the less force and proof it has. . . . [T]*he Hear-say of an Hear-say, is yet less considerable. So that in traditional Truths, each remove weakens the force of the proof*" (4.16.663–64, emphasis in original). Assessing the credibility of the originally oral apostolic testimony later recorded in the scriptures, Locke made a now-famous exception in the case of miracles. He acknowledged that "Propositions" of miracles "challenge the highest Degree of our Assent, upon bare Testimony." For this reason, he observed, these "Propositions" are "called by a peculiar Name, Revelation, and our Assent to it, Faith" (4.16.667). But the apostles were credible eyewitnesses, and for this reason, "the strangeness of the Fact lessens not the Assent to a fair Testimony given of it" (4.16.667). In assessing the "traditional Truths" now recorded in the Bible, he concluded, "Faith" must step in where empirical proof is lacking and reason flounders.

Whereas Locke was relatively cautious in addressing in print the question of tradition in religious matters, onetime Anglican minister John Henley used Anglican arguments against "meer Tradition" to question the hegemony of the established church. After he left the Anglican Church and registered as a Dissenter, Henley challenged Anglican leaders to produce documentary proof of their special line of descent directly from the apostles. Knowing full well that they could not do so, he argued that their inability to produce a special "Apostolical Warrant" meant that in theory, at least, *any* Christian had an "equal . . . Right" to preach the gospel:

> To tell us that there is a Succession of Men from the Apostles, is much the same as to tell us, that there is a Succession of Men from *Adam*, from *David*, or *Solomon*. But how can we know what Powers, or Privileges any of these particular Men have from the Apostles, unless they exhibit their Warrants, or authentick and known Copies of Warrants from St. *Paul*, from St. *Peter* and the Rest? Till then every Man has an equal, and none a particular Right to execute these Constitutions, or any Laws of Christ.[48]

According to Henley, Anglican arguments for the authority of writing over mere tradition also authorized Dissenters' right to preach. No one could document a right to preach descending directly from the apostles. The right to preach was therefore a *legal* right, granted by political bodies, and in England after the Toleration Act of 1689, that right belonged to anyone who met specified legal conditions (as Henley did).

In the 1740s and 1750s David Hume similarly cited Anglican arguments against "Oral Tradition" to advance his own subversive arguments. In *An Enquiry concerning Human Understanding*, he addressed the role that oral testimony plays in matters of religious belief. In section 10, "Of Miracles," he argued that "no human testimony . . . even by a sufficient number of men, of . . . unquestioned good sense, education, and learning . . . can have such force as to prove a miracle, and make it a just foundation for any system of religion." The miracle of revelation, if scrutinized according to modern standards of documentary historicity, would seem mere *"Hear-say"* (in Locke's term). Core Christian beliefs must therefore not be subjected to empirical "trials" that they can never withstand: "our most holy religion is founded on Faith, not reason; and it is a sure method of exposing it to put it to such a trial as it is, by no means, fitted to endure."[49] Complicating further the theological debates concerning "Tradition" that I have outlined above, he pointed out that both the Catholic and Protestant Churches relied on apostolic testimony that was originally oral: "the authority, either of scripture or of tradition, is founded merely in the testimony of the apostles." On the one hand, the testimony of the apostles could be trusted, for they had "evidence of the senses": the apostles "were eye-witnesses to those miracles of our Saviour, by which he proved his divine mission." On the other hand, as Anglican theologians themselves had argued (Hume cited Stillingfleet on this point), the reliability of testimony diminishes greatly over time and space. For this reason, Hume concluded (shocking many of his contemporaries), "our evidence . . . for the truth of the Christian religion is less than the evidence for the truth of our senses; because, even in the first authours of our religion, it was no greater, and it is evident it must diminish in passing from them to their disciples." In practical matters of daily life, he admitted, we cannot function without depending on the "the testimony of men, and the reports of eye-witnesses and spectators." But "a wise man" weighs the circumstances of the testimony or report and "proportions his belief to the evidence. . . . and when at last he fixes his judgment, the evidence exceeds not what we properly call probability."[50]

In writing "Of Miracles," Hume may have drawn on Craig's *Theologiae Christianae* (1699).[51] Whether or not he did so, it is striking that seven years after Hume's *Enquiry* was printed, Craig's work was suddenly republished. More than fifty years after its first appearance, an enterprising publisher decided that Craig's once-alarming text would now sell in numbers sufficiently large to warrant a new edition. In his capacity as a historian, too, Hume openly scoffed at the idea of using "oral tradition" as a historical source. In his widely read *History of England* (1754–61), he asserted that "the history of past events is immediately lost or disfigured, when intrusted to memory and oral tradition." In his view, oral transmission "disfigured" all it touched.[52]

The Protestant interrogation of tradition also shaped other contemporary discourses. In the legal realm, too, the written word gradually "came into its own as the basis of law and of legal training," and "local custom and judicial precedent were increasingly fixed in printed texts."[53] These shifts happened gradually; throughout the eighteenth century, the testimony of credible men was "accepted as valid evidence in cases of property and land disputes, and in cases involving tenants' rights."[54] As Bishop Gilbert Burnet observed in 1680, "all courts of justice proceed upon the evidence given by witnesses; for the use of writings is but a thing more lately brought into the world."[55] But the legal profession's relationship to oral sources had changed, and the career of leading jurist Sir Matthew Hale epitomizes these developments. Hale was a voluminous author who worked to rationalize and codify English law. In his *History and Analysis of the Common Law* (1713), now commonly cited as the first published history of English law, he worked to clarify the idea of the *lex non scripta* (pl. *leges non scriptae*):

> The Laws of *England* may . . . be divided into Two Kinds, *viz. Lex Scripta*, the written *Law, and Lex non Scripta*, the unwritten Law: For although . . . all the Laws of this Kingdom have some Monuments or Memorials thereof in Writing, yet all of them have not their Original in Writing; for some of those Laws have obtain'd their Force by immemorial Usage or Custom, and such Laws are properly called *Leges non Scriptae*, or unwritten Laws or Customs.[56]

The *lex non scripta* was conventionally dated to "before time of memory," or before legal history.[57] But belief in the idea of the "unwritten Law"—like belief in the continuous oral tradition of the church—should not be confused with a general belief in oral tradition. Unlike statute (or written) law, English common law is passed down in practices, precedents, and judgments. Furthermore, as Hale emphasized, the legal idea of the *leges non scriptae* does not mean that these "unwritten Law[s]" have *never* been written down, only that they were not *originally* written down: "all the Laws of this Kingdom have some Monuments or Memorials thereof in Writing, yet all of them have not their Original in Writing." Interestingly, Hale's language here echoes the passage that I cited earlier from Cardinal Robert Bellarmine, where Bellarmine worked to explain the idea of tradition in Catholic theology.

Related to the idea of the *lex non scripta* is the ideology of the "Ancient Constitution." As J. G. A. Pocock has shown, seventeenth-century proponents of the Ancient Constitution appealed to the authority of an ancient, unwritten tradition of laws and customs to further their own political goals. The ideas of the *lex non scripta* and the Ancient Constitution are examples of tradition understood as immemorial usage—a long-established procedural method, having almost the force of a law. But once again, although these ideas may have helped some eighteenth-century authors to entertain the possibility of reliable oral traditions of other kinds, neither of these beliefs should be mistaken for a *general* belief in oral tradition. As Nicholas Hudson has suggested, "neither the 'Ancient Constitution' nor 'natural law' constitute versions of oral tradition: they were advanced by

seventeenth-century scholars solely as forms of knowledge that supported
or supplemented the written codes of a literate society."[58] Furthermore, it
is important to understand that in appealing to tradition, proponents of the
ideology of the Ancient Constitution were attempting to *limit* the power
of the monarch. As Pocock has suggested, "nothing could be more mislead-
ing than to picture the vehement assertion of the antiquity of English laws
and liberties as an inert acceptance of 'traditional society.' "[59] In some ways,
as we shall see later in this book, these seventeenth-century elite appeals
to tradition anticipate later eighteenth-century gentlemen's invocations of
popular tradition to promote their own ideological and commercial goals.[60]

As Hume's skepticism concerning oral tradition suggests, eighteenth-
century historians largely "disparage[d] common report and hearsay as untrustworthy sources for understanding events in the past."[61] The great
sixteenth- and seventeenth-century antiquarians, such as John Leland
(c. 1503–52), John Stow (c. 1524/25–1605), and William Camden (1551–1623),
all drew extensively on oral sources. As Richard M. Dorson points out, "the
concept of antiquities . . . was not restricted to written and material records
of the past; it also covered oral traditions."[62] In compiling his monumental
topographical and historical survey of Britain and Ireland, *Britannia* (Latin,
1586; English, 1610), Camden consulted manuscript and printed texts, but
he also made a series of tours throughout Britain, interviewing its inhabitants and mining them for their knowledge of local history and tradition.
In 1695 *Britannia* was republished in an expanded edition by Edmund Gibson, and in the eighteenth century this edition became the vade mecum of
antiquarians.

But although early modern antiquaries made extensive use of oral sources,
they also discriminated among those sources, and they typically "attempt[ed]
to verify their statements with reference to a document." Where " 'hard'
evidence" such as texts or artifacts could be found, they were "preferred . . .
to the 'soft' evidence of folk tale, unwritten and undatable local custom,
and ancestral tradition." Antiquaries increasingly distinguished between
tradition and what we might call oral history, and they preferred the latter.
Tradition was undatable, whereas oral history was *"in hominum memoria"*: that is, "in the memory of men living."[63] Above all, antiquarians distinguished among oral sources according to the socioeconomic background
and reputed character of the informant. In his compendium *Pseudodoxia
Epidemica or Enquiries into Very Many Received Tenents and Commonly
Presumed Truths* (1646; rev. ed., 1672), Sir Thomas Browne extensively recorded information that he had gathered from oral sources, yet he also distanced himself from "Vulgar Errors" (as the familiar title of his work, *Vulgar*

Errors, suggests). Literate gentlemen's distrust of oral testimony and tradition was "a combination of epistemological skepticism and socially based distaste."[64]

In their private writings, though, gentlemen continued to record and use oral sources. In his manuscript writings posthumously published as *Table-talk*, jurist and legal scholar John Selden (1584–1654) recorded traditionary sources such as proverbs and ballads, and he argued that these materials, while untrustworthy in many ways, might nonetheless be a useful means of gathering information about popular views: "More solid things do not show the complexion of times so well, as ballads and libels."[65]

In illustrating the changing status of oral traditional sources, two especially illuminating figures are antiquary and protofolklorist John Aubrey (1626–97) and his print-oriented partial contemporary Daniel Defoe (c. 1660–1731). Today, Aubrey is best remembered for his two manuscript miscellanies, *Remaines of Gentilisme and Judaisme* (n.d., printed 1881) and *Brief Lives* (1669–96; printed 1898), neither of which was printed before the nineteenth century. (Not coincidentally, these works were printed shortly after the founding of the Folklore Society in 1878.) *Remaines* is based on Aubrey's commonplace book, in which he recorded traditional customs, practices, and beliefs, and *Brief Lives* is a gossipy collection of biographical notices, consisting chiefly of anecdotes gathered from oral conversations as well as texts. Like Selden, who recorded traditional sources without necessarily believing them, Aubrey recorded traditional materials in order to glean from them what he could. He argued that "Old customs" and "fables," while deficient as a certain kind of historical source, might nonetheless have a different kind of value that made them worth recording: "Old customes, and old wives-fables are grosse things: but yet ought [not] to be quite rejected: there may some truth and usefulnesse be elicited out of them: besides 'tis a pleasure to consider the Errours that enveloped former ages: as also the present."[66] Aubrey was fascinated with stories of ghosts and other apparitions, but he distanced himself from such materials by describing them as "old wives-fables." At the same time, though, we detect in Aubrey's works the emergence of a new perspective that will become more important later in our story: the idea that the spread of "Printing" was displacing (rather than preserving) oral tradition and that this was regrettable. As we have seen, Aubrey described printing as a "divine art"—in sharp contrast to William Blake, who represented modern commercial printing as a mindless, mechanized process rather than an art or craft. But although Aubrey idealized the "art" of printing, he also represented the spread of printing as a development that had some sad consequences for oral tradition: "Before Printing,

Old-wives' Tales were ingeniose; and since Printing came in fashion, till a little before the Civil-warres, the ordinary sort of People were not taught to reade." In a passage now commonly quoted with nostalgia by modern scholars, he at once celebrated printing and mourned what he saw as its negative consequences: "the divine art of Printing and Gunpowder have frighted away Robin-good-fellow and the Fayries."[67] Ironically, given Aubrey's depiction of the displacement of oral tradition by the "fashion" of printing, the printing of his manuscript miscellanies in the 1880s by the newly formed Folklore Society did much to *preserve* oral traditions that might otherwise have been lost. As we shall see in a moment, too (and in more detail later in this book), Aubrey anticipated late eighteenth- and nineteenth-century scholars in his suggestion that traditionary materials, while suspect in many ways, might nonetheless be appreciated for the unique insights that they offered into a now-vanishing (and in many ways valuable) "past."

Like Aubrey, Defoe drew on oral sources as early modern antiquaries had done, but he *used* them in different ways. Defoe's approach in compiling *A Tour thro' the Whole Island of Great Britain* (3 vols., 1724–27) epitomizes the changing relationship between history, tradition, and what we would now call "folklore." In preparing for his tours throughout Britain, Defoe read extensively in antiquarian and topographical writings. He was especially indebted to Gibson's edition of Camden's *Britannia* and to the expanded edition of Stow's *Survey of London* (1598) recently published by John Strype (5th ed., 1720).[68] Defoe's methods of travel exemplify the precepts of James Howell's *Instructions for Forreine Travell* (1642), an influential guidebook that was still widely read throughout the eighteenth century. According to Howell, worthwhile travel requires extensive intellectual labor, both before, during, and after one's journey. A prospective traveler should converse with experienced travelers and consult relevant histories, guidebooks, and maps. He should then "collate" what he learns from these two types of "conversation": oral conversation and also, via books, "conversation with the dead." Finally, a traveler should compare his preparatory learning with what he learns on his journey through "Optique observations." As Howell advised, "*Books* . . . and conversation with the *Dead*" are "good Teachers, and edifie infinitely; yet the study of living men, and a collation of his [the traveler's] own *Optique* observations and judgment with theirs, work much more strongly, and where they meet (I meane the living and the dead) they perfect."[69]

In *The Great Law of Subordination Consider'd* (1724), published the same time as *A Tour*, Defoe outlined a method for productive traveling. The fictional narrator of this text, a Frenchman, recalls how upon first traveling to England he read extensively. But he also took with him on his journey a companion whose oral conversation made him seem like a "walking Library, or moveable Map":

> I took with me an ancient Gentleman of my Acquaintance, who I found was thorowly acquainted with almost every Part of *England*, and who was to me as a walking Library, or a moveable Map of the Countries and Towns through which we pass'd; and we never fail'd to enquire of the most proper Persons in every Place where we came, what was to be seen? what Rarities of Nature, Antiquities, ancient Buildings were in respective Parts?[70]

This "ancient Gentleman" is not lugging folios in his backpack; rather, it is his *memory* that makes him seem "a walking Library." Throughout their journey, Defoe's narrator and his friend also conduct oral interviews with local inhabitants, choosing "the most proper Persons in every Place."

Similarly, in *A Tour* the narrator's observations are aural as well as "Optique." The narrator records not only what he sees but also what he hears. He is fascinated by tradition, yet he consistently repudiates oral tales and legends. His "rigorous recording *and* scrutiny of oral tradition is designed to endorse his own status as a 'modern' "; he represents himself as "an objective, scientifically minded observer unimpressed by what cannot be proven."[71] On the coast of Cornwall, the narrator "*hear*[s]" that "little or nothing . . . is to be seen" at Tintagel Castle. He rejects "the story of King Arthur being born and killed there" as "*a piece of tradition, only on* [sic] *oral history, and not any authority to be produced for it.*"[72] Whereas Aubrey was a manuscript author who expressed nostalgia for oral traditions that he believed to be disappearing, Defoe was a print-oriented author who embraced modernity even as he recorded oral traditions. In recording "old customs" and beliefs even as he embraced print's role in consolidating the new "Great Britain" after the Union of 1706/7, Defoe simultaneously collected, preserved, and helped to usher in new Enlightenment attitudes toward oral tradition.

As we have just seen, Defoe's narrator in *The Great Law of Subordination* relies on the experience and memory of "an ancient Gentleman." Not coincidentally the narrator's traveling companion is "ancient," "Gentle," and, above all, a man. Social rank and reputation were key factors in endowing oral testimony with authority, but the sex of the informant was perhaps the most important factor in determining whether or not oral testimony was believed. The testimony of an "ancient Gentleman" might be deemed reliable, but as the phrase "old wives' tale" suggests, old *women's* words were inherently suspicious. As Laura Gowing writes: "older women had a distinctly different standing in the community from old men: if men, with age, acquired a certain power and status that enabled some to mediate in social disputes, older women were just as likely to be defined as a source of trouble, and for female witnesses, the phrase 'old poor woman' was a marker of discredit."[73] An "old wives' tale" is by definition "an unlikely story; a widely held or traditional belief now thought to be incorrect or erroneous."[74] References to old wives' tales date back to the ancient world. In Plato's *Republic*, for instance, Socrates advises that children's nurses must not be allowed to corrupt the minds of their charges with *aniles fabulae*, or foolish tales.[75] Early Christian authors similarly warned against old wives' tales. In his First Letter to Timothy (4:7), the apostle Paul advises Christians to "refuse profane and old wives' fables, and exercise thyself rather unto godliness." Somewhat paradoxically, by the eighteenth century, "old wives' tale" was a classification not only for profane beliefs that hampered religious teachings but also for "superstitious" religious beliefs that hampered Enlightenment rational thought.[76]

Throughout his works, Defoe commonly associated old women and tradition. Traveling through Northumberland, the narrator of *A Tour* comes upon the Cheviot Hills near the Anglo-Scottish border, and he immediately recalls the ballad of Chevy Chase. He inquires of the locals whether they had "heard" of the fourteenth-century battle that is the subject of this ballad, and he learns that all the old women were familiar with it:

> We had Cheviot Hills so plain in view, that we could not but enquire of the good old women every where, whether they had heard of the fight at Chevy Chace. They not only told us they had heard of it, but had all the account of it at their fingers' end.[77]

In parts of *A Tour*, every rock, hill, or other feature of the landscape seems to trigger a tale from a garrulous local. As D. R. Woolf has suggested, "oral tradition was very closely tied to objects and visible features, either natural or man-made."[78] In the passage above, the old women's mouths spin oral tales as their fingers spin their yarn (hence the proverbial phrase for tale-telling, "spin a yarn"). Defoe also mentions stories "handed down from one Generation of old Women to another" in two works on the occult that he published simultaneously with *A Tour*. In *The Political History of the Devil* (1726), he describes the passing of traditionary materials "from one Generation of old

Women to another" (i.e., from "old Mothers and Nurses" to young women, who eventually grow old themselves):

> It is true our old Mothers and Nurses have told us other Things, but they only told us what their Mothers and Nurses told them, and so the Tale has been handed down from one Generation of old Women to another; but we have no Vouchers for the Fact other than Oral Tradition, the Credit of which, I confess, goes but a very little Way with me.[79]

Like the old women he depicts, Defoe relished listening to "oral histor[ies]," "Tales," and "Fables." But he also relished the process of empirical investigation and assessment, and he attempted to evaluate "Oral Tradition" from an empirical standpoint. A good empirical investigator, he believed, needed to assess documentary evidence ("Vouchers") to determine "Fact."

In *A System of Magick; or, A History of the Black Art* (1727), Defoe similarly links old women and oral tradition. But whereas in the passage quoted above he dismisses traditions that cannot be supported with documentary evidence, in a revealing moment in *A System of Magick* he insists that a particular "Oral Tradition" is based on fact. He says that the legendary soothsayer Mother Shipton was a "real and known Person," "not a Witch or a Prophetess, but a *Warlock* or Wizard." Furthermore, he claims that Mother Shipton accurately predicted Cardinal Wolsey's fate:

> We have abundance of merry Tales scatter'd abroad in the Oral Tradition of antient times, and among those antient things called *Old Women*, concerning Wizards: how the Kings and Princes used to consult with them, before they undertook any great Enterprize. . . . They relate the same of old Mother *Shipton* in *England*, who, (tho' so many Fables are made of her) was a real and known Person, and was not a Witch or a Prophetess, but a *Warlock* or Wizard, and 'tis certain she did foretell to Cardinal *Woolsey* [*sic*] his falling into Disgrace at Court, his Loss of the King's Favour, and his Death; all which accordingly happen'd.[80]

As this passage suggests, Defoe did not reject traditional tales outright; rather, he recorded them, then assessed their claims. To be thoughtlessly dismissive of "Oral Tradition" was hubristic. It was also potentially wasteful, for valuable insights might be lost. In *Political History of the Devil*, Defoe recounts a traditional tale of men selling their souls to the devil. But significantly, while he rejects this *particular* tale as groundless, he does not reject the *possibility* of supernatural bargains being struck. In general, he says, the "Credit" of "Oral Tradition" "goes but a very little Way" with him, but in this case he quibbles that this particular devilish bargain would have been against the law. Selling one's soul was entering into an unlawful contract, for men have no right to sell what belongs to God. Tellingly, too, after assigning little "Credit" to "Oral Tradition," he immediately notes that print is not necessarily any more reliable than oral tales. He scoffs at *both* printed texts and oral discourse when he observes that "at Salisbury the Devil, as it is said, and publickly printed, carried away two Fellows that had given themselves up to him."[81]

Like most Protestant authors of his day, Defoe linked superstitious tales and customs to the influence of papism. This association was in fact so common that Alexander Pope, himself a Catholic, satirized its conventionality in his mock-heroic poem *The Rape of the Lock* (1712). In canto 1, Pope's protagonist Belinda dreams of a "glitt'ring Youth" who whispers in her ear. This seductive orator urges the young woman to recall "all the Nurse and . . . Priest have taught": that is, the oral tradition that was passed down to her in the nursery. The lessons that Belinda learned from her nurse and priest included tales of "airy Elves by Moonlight shadows seen" and other "Truths" not "Credit[ed]" by the "Learned" (ll. 20–40). Pope's satire here is gentle; indeed, the supernatural cast of sprites, gnomes, and fairies in *Rape of the Lock* suggests that Pope himself relished fairy tales. In contrast to Pope, Defoe excoriated the superstitious tales of "old Women and Romish Priests." Traveling through Cumbria, the narrator of Defoe's *Tour* rejects the legend of Saint Bega, an Irish princess who became a saint, as the superstitious remnant of papism. He scoffs, "as for the Lady, . . . the Story is become fabulous, *viz.* about her procuring, by her Prayers, a deep Snow on *Midsummer* Day, . . . these, and the like Tales, I leave where I found them, (*viz.*) among the Rubbish of the old Women and the *Romish* Priests."[82]

Defoe's Protestant critique of tradition links him to Newcastle curate and antiquarian Henry Bourne, who published his compendium of popular superstitions, *Antiquitates Vulgares* (1725), at the same time that Defoe was writing *A Political History of the Devil*. In the seventeenth and early eighteenth centuries, the terms "vulgar," "popular," and "common" were "floating epithet[s]" rather than "precise term[s] of reference. . . . [T]hey were often hurled as insults by the learned."[83] In the wake of Browne's compendium, *Pseudodoxia Epidemica*, commonly known as *Vulgar Errors* (rev. ed., 1672), books collecting (and critiquing) "popular Errors" became an influential genre. The full title of Bourne's work was *Antiquitates Vulgares; or, the Antiquities of the Common People. Giving an Account of several of their Opinions and Ceremonies. With proper Reflections upon each of them;*

shewing which may be retain'd, and which ought to be laid aside. As this title suggests, Bourne did not set out to recover "vulgar" or popular traditions for their own sake. Rather, he aimed to demonstrate the papist or heathen origins of customs preserved by tradition and to argue which of these "ignorant" and "sinful" customs must "be laid aside."[84] Bourne was rampantly anti-Catholic; his investigation of tradition was for the purpose of eradicating popular "errors." Ironically, though, in researching and recording popular tradition and lore in order to root out "sinful" practices and beliefs, Bourne helped to preserve traditionary materials in print. In the long run, his "reforming zeal was a powerful stimulus to quasi-anthropological investigation."[85]

Throughout the eighteenth century, religious views continued to shape attitudes toward traditional materials and sources. But after the final defeat of the Jacobites in 1745, Protestant clergymen and antiquarians were freer to approach these materials in new ways. Oral traditions that had long been considered politically or doctrinally dangerous were now open to reconceptualization. *Antiquitates Vulgares* was locally printed in Newcastle, and it did not attract much attention in Bourne's lifetime. But in the 1770s, it was rediscovered by another Newcastle clergyman and antiquarian, John Brand, who expanded and transformed it in his own widely read *Observations on Popular Antiquities* (1777; rev. ed., 2 vols., 1813). Brand built his *Observations* on the scaffolding of Bourne's research, but in Brand's book, "the antiquary . . . eclipsed the curate. . . . [T]he superstitious fancies of the populace" are less "a target of reform" than "a proper subject for antiquarian study."[86] Whereas Bourne excoriated "popular superstitions" as the legacy of papism, Brand approached these and other traditional "Notions and vulgar Ceremonies" with a conviction that they were worth recording and preserving in print—not least because they now seemed increasingly alien and archaic.[87]

Like Bourne, Brand attributed many "popular Notions and vulgar Ceremonies of our Nation" to "the Times when Popery was our established Religion." After the Reformation, Catholicism was made illegal in England. But while the "written Word" could be erased by censorship, Brand proposed, "oral Tradition" could escape surveillance:

> The People [were] by no means inclined to annihilate the seemingly innocent Ceremonies of their former superstitious Faith.
>
>   These, consecrated to the Fancies of Men, by a Usage from Time immemorial, though erased by public authority from the *written Word*, were committed as a venerable Deposit to the keeping of *oral Tradition.*[88]

In contrast to the anonymous author of "A Calculation of the Credibility of Human Testimony," who thought that written tradition would long outlast oral tradition, Brand suggested that in certain circumstances, oral tradition could long outlast the written word. In the first sentence of *Observations*, Brand boldly asserts that "Tradition has in no Instance so clearly evinced her Faithfulness, as in the transmitting of vulgar Rites and popular Opinions."[89] "Faithfulness" is a weighty word for a clergyman; whereas Brand's Protestant predecessors represented Catholic appeals to tradition as a *threat* to the "Faith," Brand proposed that oral tradition—even popular oral tradition—embodied the *continuity* of the faith. "Vulgar Rites and popular Opinions" are passed down orally by "the vulgar," who are illiterate and resistant to change. In Brand's account, the "vulgar" are no longer the *polluters* of tradition but rather its most "Faithful" transmitters and preservers. In the context of long eighteenth-century debates about tradition, this statement signals a momentous shift.

Brand's revision of *Antiquitates Vulgares* helped spur a vogue for collections and glossaries of proverbial or "vulgar" speech. In the late eighteenth century, the "vulgar" came to be seen as a source of proverbial wisdom: a link to *valuable* aspects of the nation's past. In 1785 Francis Grose (c. 1731–91), an antiquary who founded and edited *The Antiquarian Repertory: a Miscellany, intended to preserve and illustrate several valuable Remains of Old Times* (vol. 1, 1775), published *A Classical Dictionary of the Vulgar Tongue*. A commercially successful collection of vernacular vocabulary and slang, this was followed by *A Provincial Glossary, with a Collection of Local Proverbs, and Popular Superstitions* (1787). Grose argued that proverbial speech was a valuable form of tradition that preserved ancient customs and worldviews, and he helped to direct an important branch of antiquarian scholarship toward the study of what we might now call "old popular speech."

Yet while polite authors increasingly collected proverbial wisdom and "popular" traditions, it is important to recognize that many (if not most) of the sources touted by these authors as taken from tradition were in fact gleaned from literary texts. In 1774 the collapse of perpetual copyright enabled wide-scale reprinting of "classic" works of literature, and antiquarians liberally quoted from the works of now-canonical English poets such as Geoffrey Chaucer, William Shakespeare, John Milton, and Thomas Gray. Meanwhile, literary authors such as William Wordsworth drew on (and imitated) traditionary materials such as ballads and tales. In his *Lyrical Ballads* (1798), Wordsworth depicted rustic country speakers who passed down their proverbial wisdom by tradition, and he famously sought to imitate "the real language of men." But Wordsworth also read and imitated the ballads in Percy's *Reliques of Ancient English Poetry* (1765). Percy represented the "Old Heroic Ballads" in his collection as the legacy of feudal bards, but he collected his "relics" exclusively from textual sources, and he extensively rewrote them to suit fashionable literary tastes.

Although Percy theorized the ballads in his collection as the legacy of oral itinerant poets, he did not especially value ballads as "oral." But as we shall see in chapter 7, later eighteenth- and nineteenth-century ballad collectors increasingly conceptualized (and valorized) the hybrid oral, manuscript, and print genre of ballads as "oral tradition." In the 1760s, too, Macpherson published the poems of Ossian, whose works purportedly had been passed down for centuries by tradition, and clergyman Hugh Blair, one of Macpherson's supporters, represented the Scottish Highlands as the site of a still-living, yet quickly disappearing oral tradition. Across the English Channel, another Protestant clergyman, Johann Gottfried von Herder (1744–1803), enthusiastically responded to Macpherson's Ossianic poetry in his own *Correspondence about Ossian and the Songs of Ancient Peoples* (1773).[90] But whereas Blair represented Ossianic poetry as the legacy of esteemed feudal bards, Herder made a different kind of contribution to the theorizing of tradition: he offered a new conception of the *volk* (folk) that transformed the "vulgar" into "a pastoral people attuned to nature and glowing with a natural morality."[91] Stephen Prickett argues that Herder was one of "very few non-Catholic writers in the eighteenth century . . . to use the word ['tradition'] freely and favourably in his writing." Herder's "passionate belief in . . . tradition was not so much a belief in the tradition of the Church . . . as a belief in the strength of national cultures as organic beings. . . . [T]radition was the memory and inherited wisdom of a culture."[92] Yet while Herder coined the word *Volksleid* (folksong) in his *Correspondence about Ossian*, it is important to note that his use of this term did not include *all* the songs of the people. Herder sharply distinguished between the *Volk* (folk) and the *Popel* (rabble). He cautioned, " 'People' does not mean the rabble in the streets, which never sings or creates but rather screams and mutilates true folk song" (Volk heisst nicht der Pobel auf den Gassen, der singt und dichtet niemals, sondern schreit und verstummelt).[93]

In the nineteenth century, oral tradition became its own research program—one that was greatly assisted by the spread of print. After Brand's death, his papers were entrusted to Sir Henry Ellis, the secretary of the Society of Antiquaries and the Keeper of Manuscripts at the British Museum. In 1813 Ellis published a significantly expanded edition of Brand's *Observations*.[94] This mammoth tome is a monument to the art of printing, as much as to oral tradition: the two sumptuous quarto volumes total about seven hundred pages of densely printed type. In Ellis's edition, Brand's footnotes sprout further footnotes. Visually, Ellis's edition of the *Observations* recalls Pope's parody of modern scholarship, *The Dunciad Variorum* (1729). In the nineteenth century, *Observations* became vastly influential: it has been described as "the cornerstone of British folklore science."[95] Ironically, it was this monumental *Dunciad-Variorum*-like *printed* text, edited by a professional librarian, that produced "popular oral tradition" as a viable object of learned study. In 1846 antiquary William John Thoms coined the term "folklore," and in 1878 a group of private gentlemen founded the Folk-Lore Society.[96] Instead of using new scholarly methods to critique "tradition" as superstitious, these gentlemen now devoted themselves to recording in print "oral" tradition as an object worthy of study and preservation.

"TO PULL THE OLD WOMAN OUT OF OUR HEARTS": ENLIGHTENMENT AUTHORS AND "OLD WIVES' TALES"

By the later eighteenth century, *some* kinds of oral tradition were considered worthy of polite appreciation. At the same time, though, long-standing hostilities to other kinds of tradition did not change. Enlightenment pedagogues traced superstitious tale-telling to old women "spinning yarns" on winter evenings and to nurses frightening children into good behavior. From John Locke to Mary Wollstonecraft, authors raged against the ghost stories and fairy tales that they claimed were spread chiefly by nurses, gypsies, and maids. Locke's *Some Thoughts Concerning Education* (1693) was one of the most influential Enlightenment works on education. Originally written to advise a friend on the education of his son, Locke's treatise was adapted by pedagogues who repeated almost verbatim his warning about the dangers of nurses and maids:

> I would not have Children troubled whilst young with Notions of Spirits; . . . I think it inconvenient, that their yet tender Minds should receive early Impressions of *Goblins*, *Spectres*, and *Apparitions*, wherewith their Maids, and those about them, are apt to frighten them into a compliance with their Orders, which often proves a great inconvenience to them all their Lives after, by subjecting their Minds to Frights, fearful Apprehensions, Weakness, and Superstition.

Locke suggested that servants' "Bug-bear" tales of "*Sprites* and *Goblins*" and "*Raw-Head* and *Bloody Bones*" could leave permanent "Impressions" on the blank slate of children's minds. Household servants might seem relatively powerless to us, but Locke suggested that their oral tale-telling gave them tremendous power. Like indelible ink stamped on blank sheets of paper by a printing press, the "Impressions" that these storytellers made on children's "tender Minds" "sink deep, and fasten themselves so as not easily, if ever, to be got out again."[97]

Beyond the nursery, too, women of the lower ranks were associated with tradition. As early as the twelfth issue of the *Spectator* (1711), Addison devoted an entire paper to the dangers of "old wives' tales." He headed this paper with a Latin motto from Persius, ". . . *Veteres avias tibi de pulmone revello*," and he then uncharacteristically paused to translate it into English. Men, as well as women, could spread old wives' tales; accordingly, Mr. Spectator advises readers of both sexes to "*pull the old Woman out of our Hearts* (as *Persius* expresses it in the Motto of my Paper)." He describes an evening that he spent eavesdropping on the traditional tale-telling of his "Land-lady's Daughters" and "young Girls of the Neighbourhood." Significantly, while listening to the girls' "Stories of Spirits and Apparitions," he read—or pretended to read—a book:

> I remember last Winter there were several young Girls of the Neighbourhood sitting about the Fire with my Land-lady's Daughters and telling Stories of Spirits and Apparitions. . . . I seated my self by the Candle that stood on a Table at one End of the Room; and pretending to read a Book that I took out of my Pocket, heard several dreadful Stories of Ghosts as pale as Ashes that had stood at the Feet of a Bed, or walked over a Church-yard by Moon-light . . . with many other old Womens Fables of the like Nature.

Opposing "old Womens Fables" to "the Dictates of Reason and Religion," Mr. Spectator advised his readers "*to pull the old Woman out of our Hearts* . . . and extinguish those impertinent Notions which we imbibed at a Time that we were not able to judge of their Absurdity."[98] Like Defoe in the examples considered earlier, Addison did not reject the *idea* of "Spirits." Rather, he held that it was unreasonable (and irreligious) to terrify oneself with "Stories of spirits," because God "holds the Reins of the whole Creation in his Hand." In sharp contrast to the "Pleasures of the Imagination" that he describes in other issues of the *Spectator*, Mr. Spectator refers here to the oral traditions propagated by "old women" and "young Girls" as "Horrours of Imagination."

A century after Locke blamed maids and nurses for making grown men

afraid of ghosts, Wollstonecraft followed his example in her translated book
of stories, *Elements of Morality, for the Use of Children* (1790).[99] Wollstonecraft recounts a story of a boy incapacitated by his fear of spirits. These
irrational beliefs, she suggests, were instilled in him by a tale-telling "old
maid." A few years later, in her pedagogical work *Practical Education*
(2 vols., 1798), Maria Edgeworth echoed Locke, Addison, and Wollstonecraft. Like them, she warned that the tender minds of children should not
be filled with ideas of "apparitions, and winding sheets, and sable shrowds."
In a chapter addressing "Taste and Imagination," Edgeworth drew on Addison's discussion of "the Pleasures of the Imagination." At the same time,
she critiqued the type of traditional tales that he classified as "Horrours
of Imagination." Quoting poet Mark Akenside, whose sentimental verse
includes a depiction of a "village matron" telling "tales" around a "blazing
hearth," Edgeworth warned that Akenside's seemingly charming depiction
of "the pleasures of the imagination" in fact illustrated what Addison called
"Horrours of Imagination" (in this case, dangerous oral tales):

> In the following poetic description of the beldame telling dreadful stories
> to her infant audience, we hear only of the pleasures of the imagination,
> we do not recollect how dearly these pleasures must be purchased by
> their votaries:

>   *   *   *   *   *   finally by night
> The village matron, round the blazing hearth,
> Suspends the infant audience with her tales,
> Breathing astonishment! of witching rhymes,
> And evil spirits. . . .
> . . . .
> At every solemn pause the crowd recoil,
> Gazing each other speechless, and congeal'd
> With shiv'ring sighs; till, eager for th'event,
> Around the beldame all erect they hang,
> Each trembling heart with grateful terrors quell'd *.

Edgeworth concludes this chapter of *Practical Education* with a recom-
mendation that opposes the rational, "prudent" middle-class mother to the
tale-telling "village matron" and lower-class female servant: "No prudent
mother will ever imitate this eloquent village matron, or will she permit
any beldame in the nursery to conjure up these sublime shapes, and to quell
the hearts of her children with these grateful terrors." In another episode,

Edgeworth's representation of laboring-class women as conduits of tradition is even more disturbing. In a passage that recalls Mr. Spectator's depiction of his eavesdropping on the tale-telling of "young Girls of the Neighbour-hood," Edgeworth depicts another eavesdropping gentleman who is simi-larly disdainful of "tattling, ridiculous wom[e]n." But unlike Mr. Spectator— a "silent man" who uses print to express his views—Edgeworth's gentleman orally (and aggressively) intervenes to "counteract" the "dangerous influ-ence" of tradition. Edgeworth writes, "We were once present when a group of speechless children sat listening to the story of Blue-beard. . . . A gentle-man who saw the charm beginning to operate, resolved to counteract its dangerous influence." The gentleman interrupts the story, then teaches the children how to interpret it. Instead of the traditional interpretation of Bluebeard's captive wife as his victim, Edgeworth's male authority figure represents Bluebeard's wife as a "tattling, ridiculous woman" who is *herself* the problem. This woman, Edgeworth advised, "lost all sympathy the mo-ment she was represented as a curious, tattling, timid, ridiculous woman."[100]

As the example of Akenside's "village matron" suggests, though, by the end of the eighteenth century, some polite authors were beginning to depict motherly rural women as conduits and preservers of valuable oral traditions. A few ballad collectors, such as Walter Scott and William Motherwell, praised women singers as the preservers of ballad traditions. (Scott espe-cially respected the literate middle-class ballad singer Anna Gordon Brown.) At the same time, though, the continued condemnation of lower-class fe-male tale-tellers reminds us that we need to be wary of generalizations about "women and orality." For a final example of continuing genteel hos-tility to lower-class women as conduits of tradition, let us consider the case of the pioneering educationalist and philanthropist Hannah More. To counteract the influence of oral tale-telling and "low" print genres such as chapbooks, More made her own highly innovative use of print. More wrote and published the series Cheap Repository of Moral and Religious Tracts (1795–98), aimed at humble readers and auditors, and with the assistance of subscribers, she priced these tracts at one penny each (and also distributed them for free). She directed her crusade against popular oral tradition not only at polite readers but also at illiterate and marginally literate laboring-class men and women themselves. In *Tawney Rachel, Or, The Fortune Teller* (1796), More tells the story of "Tawney Rachel," the wife of "poaching Giles," who attempts to cheat credulous servants out of their wages. (Ra-chel's "tawney" complexion suggests that she is a gypsy.) Rachel especially targets ignorant women and innocent children. In More's tract, this fortune-telling gypsy is a purveyor of cheap print as well as oral trickery: "Mr. Wilson, the clergyman, found her one day dealing out some very wicked ballads to some children."[101] Eventually, Rachel is found guilty of theft and sentenced to transportation. The ethnic female "other" is exiled beyond the seas, and British children (and gullible laborers) learn not to credit *this* kind of tradition.

In addressing questions of tradition, Mark Salber Phillips observes that "scholarly analyses of the history . . . of the concept of tradition remain remarkably few." Phillips suggests that "theological understandings of tradition have been relatively well discussed, if only among historians of religion and generally within the boundaries of particular religious traditions," yet "surprisingly little has been said about the historical processes by which non-religious usages emerged."[102] Phillips especially notes the lack of exchange between scholars of religious thought and "secular-minded theorists" of tradition. He points out, for instance, the total absence of any mention of religious understandings of tradition in Raymond Williams's entry for "tradition" in *Keywords: A Vocabulary of Culture and Society*.[103] (This absence is especially striking given that Williams's stated goal is to examine major historical changes in the "keywords" that he identifies.) In tracing the secularization of ideas of tradition over the course of the long eighteenth century, one of my goals has been to bridge the gulf that Phillips identifies between scholars of religious thought and "secular-minded theorists" of tradition. In chapter 2, I shall consider yet another Protestant clergyman who critiqued the Catholic appeal to "oral tradition." But significantly, while Jonathan Swift linked Catholic appeals to oral tradition to learned tyranny from above, he also linked new forms of Protestant Dissenting oral discourse to popular unrest from below. Whether critiquing Catholic (and Jewish) ideas of oral tradition, "enthusiastic" Protestant preachers, *or* the explosion of print after the lapse of the Licensing Act in 1695, Swift foregrounded "Ears" and "Tongue[s]" as powerful "organs" of sedition and dissent, and he represented commercial print as on a *continuum* with dangerous and vulgar oral practices. Swift's harshly negative satiric representations, both of popular oral practices *and* of the theological notion of oral tradition, echo the critiques of other Protestant clergymen of his time. In so doing, they contrast sharply with the increasingly sympathetic representations of the later eighteenth century.

CHAPTER TWO

Oral Tradition as *A Tale of a Tub*: Jonathan Swift's Oratorial Machines

"A GENERAL HISTORY OF EARS"

Why would anyone want to write *"A general History of* Ears"? The question arises upon encountering Jonathan Swift's satire *A Tale of a Tub* (1704). Accompanying the title page is a list of "Treatises writ by the same Author, most of them mentioned in the following Discourses; which will be speedily published" (fig. 2.1).[1] This list establishes the "Author" (Swift's narrator) as a Grub Street hack who has worn his "Quill . . . to the Pith" (44) experimenting with a dizzying array of genres: *"A Character," "A Panegyrical Essay," "Lectures," "A Description," "A Voyage," "A Critical Essay,"* and so on. His works include *"A Dissertation upon the principal Productions of* Grub-street," *"An Analytical Discourse upon Zeal," "A modest Defence of the Proceedings of the* Rabble *in all Ages,"* and most strikingly for us in this book on the relationship between print commerce and the invention of the oral, *"A general History of* Ears." In the main body of the *Tale,* the narrator compares print advertisements such as this one to the oral harangues of fairground showmen. The prefatory materials of modern texts (*"Prefaces, Epistles, Advertisements, Introductions, Prolegomena's, Apparatus's, To-the-Reader's"*) have saved him "many a Threepence, for my Curiosity was fully satisfied, and I never offered to go in, tho' often invited by the urging and attending Orator, with his last *moving* and *standing* Piece of Rhetorick; *Sir, Upon my Word, we are just going to begin"* (85).

A striking characteristic of the *Tale's* own abundant *"Prolegomena's"* is Swift's repeated dating of his composition. *A Tale of a Tub* was published in 1704, but Swift states that *"the greatest Part of that Book"* (5) was drafted in 1696–97.[2] In "The Bookseller to the Reader," the "Bookseller" states, *"it is now Six Years since these Papers came first to my Hand, which seems to*

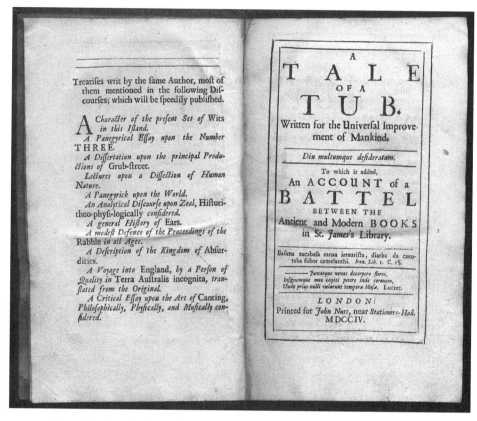

Fig. 2.1. Jonathan Swift, *A Tale of a Tub* (1704). Title page and facing page with list of "Treatises writ by the same Author." Photograph: Rare Books and Special Collections, Princeton University Library.

have been about a Twelvemonth after they were writ: For, the Author tells us . . . that he hath calculated it for the Year 1697" (19).[3] The "Epistle Dedicatory, to . . . Prince Posterity" is dated "Decemb. 1697" (24), and the "Preface" mentions "this present Month of *August*, 1697" (27).[4] In an address "To the Reader" prefacing *Battel of the Books*, the Bookseller observes: "the following Discourse . . . seems to have been written about . . . 1697" (141). Thirteen years later, when Swift added an "Apology" to the fifth edition of the *Tale* (1710), he reiterated the date of the *Tale*'s composition: "*the greatest Part of that Book was finished above thirteen Years since, 1696. which is eight Years before it was published*" (5).[5]

On the one hand, Swift's pointed dating of the composition of *A Tale of a Tub* is part of his satire on the occasionality of Grub Street writings.[6]

Swift's narrator (hereafter the tale-teller) has an odd quirk of noting the exact time and place that he is writing: "this Minute" (23), "in Bed, in a Garret" (27). Ironically, his tale has sprung not from a newsworthy event but from a "Dearth of . . . News." It is "the poor Production of that Refuse of Time which has lain heavy upon my Hands, during a long Prorogation of Parliament, a great Dearth of Forein News, and a tedious Fit of rainy Weather" (20). On the other hand, Swift's dating of the *Tale*'s composition reminds us that his text was "occasional" in important ways. In the "Apology," Swift offers an origins story that sets his satire on *"Corruptions in Religion and Learning"* (5) in its original political, religious, and media contexts. Noting the seamen's custom of throwing out a tub (or barrel) to distract a whale from a ship, he claims that he published the work to distract "the Wits of the present Age" from picking "Holes in the weak sides of Religion and Government" "during the intervals of a long Peace" (25). Swift was writing within living memory of the Civil War period and the Interregnum, and the trauma of the regicide and Cromwell's "Commonwealth" and "Protectorate" is a central concern of the second half of the *Tale*. But *A Tale of a Tub* also contains numerous references to its *own* unstable political moment (i.e., the moment of its composition). The phrase "intervals of a long Peace" suggests that peace is at best a temporary state of affairs.[7] Later, the tale-teller refers to "Times so turbulent and unquiet as these" (135). More ominously, he hints at possible "Revolutions" to come: "what I am going to say is literally true this Minute I am writing: What Revolutions may happen before it shall be ready for your Perusal, I can by no means warrant" (23).

Swift's "Preface" also foregrounds the *Tale*'s media contexts. *A Tale of a Tub* is not merely about *general* anxieties pertaining to "Grub Street" and the expanding literary marketplace; rather, I suggest, it exemplifies particular anxieties expressed in this pivotal decade in the history of the British press. In 1695 the lapse of the Licensing Act ended prepublication censorship and government restrictions on the number of printers throughout Britain. The same decade that saw the genesis and publication of *A Tale of a Tub* (roughly 1696–1704) also saw an exponential increase in the number of printers and presses. Whereas before 1695 the government had tried to limit the number of printers in all of England to twenty-four, by 1704 there were between sixty-five and seventy printing houses in London alone. By 1696 Swift was alert to the implications of new institutional and political conditions for printing. Between 1689 and 1699 he served as Sir William Temple's secretary, and in overseeing the publication of his patron's works, he acquired considerable knowledge of the workings of the book trade.[8] *A Tale of a Tub* is a valuable register of Swift's perception that some kind of major change in communications and social control was taking place: one tantamount to the beginning of a new "Age." The tale-teller rejoices to be living in "so blessed an Age for the mutual Felicity of *Booksellers* and *Authors*" (117), and he exults in the new "Liberty and Encouragement of the Press" (136). But now that press licensing had collapsed, Swift suggests, the "Danger" to the church and state is "hourly increasing, by new Levies of Wits all appointed (as there is Reason to fear) with Pen, Ink, and Paper which may at an hours Warning be drawn out into Pamphlets, and other Offensive Weapons, ready for immediate Execution" (25). Pamphlets and other "Weapons" such as political newspapers and essay journals were a specialty of Grub Street. The tale-teller notes the "factious" political writings to which "so noble a Number of Authors are indebted for their Fame" (40). Swift himself was a prolific author of political occasional materials; indeed, as Edward W. Said remarked, "nearly everything he wrote was occasional."[9] But as the tale-teller's reference to "great Revolutions" suggests, Swift associated the unlicensed press with the threat of social upheaval and even revolutionary change. Pat Rogers observes that an "undertone of social unrest" pervades the *Tale*: Swift, Pope, and other satirists of Grub Street were "born in the century of revolution. Within their lifetime they experienced every kind of disturbance which a nation can undergo. There was international conflict. . . . [and] internal dissent. . . . But it is not only the major flashpoints which make an age or a society insecure. As well as the big constitutional upheavals, there was a steady undertow of popular disturbance."[10] In Swift's view, the lapse of licensing was an invitation to dangerous "license" (especially *popular* license), now made easier by new institutional and political conditions for printing. Not coincidentally, the tale-teller plans to publish a "*Defence of the Proceedings of the* Rabble *in all Ages.*" Indeed, in adding an "Apology" for the *Tale* in 1710, Swift looked back on his drafting of the *Tale* in the aftermath of the lapse of the Licensing Act, and he pronounced this verdict on himself as a younger author: "*he was then a young Gentleman much in the World, and wrote to the Tast of those who were like himself; therefore in order to allure them, he gave a Liberty to his Pen, which might not suit with maturer Years, or graver Characters*" (5).

Writing within living memory of 1649 and 1688—the killing of one king and the exile of another—the narrator of the *Tale* alludes to (and anticipates) "Revolutions." But more puzzlingly, in celebrating the new "Liberty . . . of the Press," he declares that "no Revolutions have been so great, or so frequent, as those of human *Ears*" (129). *A Tale of a Tub* is traditionally read as a satire on Grub Street and "print culture," but following Swift's hint concerning "Ears," my chapter will read it in the context of the simultaneous development of ideas about oral communication and oral tradition and the emergent science of acoustics. In his extensive meditations on print commerce, I argue, Swift also exhibits a heightened degree of self-conscious reflection on orality (and aurality) and its actual and potential threatening intersections with a newly unrestrained press. The title of the *Tale* itself foregrounds oral genres. "A tale of a tub" is a proverbial phrase signifying idle talk, the word "tale" evokes oral storytelling, and a "tub preacher" was a derisive term for a Dissenting preacher. Not coincidentally, Swift's allegory of the three brothers, Peter, Martin, and Jack, begins with the traditional opening of oral storytellers, "Once upon a Time" (47).

Swift made sense of what seemed to him the new world of unrestrained print commerce by linking it to familiar local practices of "vulgar" or popular orality. He exhibits an intense suspicion of popular oral forms and their increasingly organized intersection with the newly available tool of print. In the opening sentence of the *Tale* proper ("Sect. I. *The Introduction*"), the narrator represents the author's challenge in the crowded literary marketplace as one of being "heard" in an unruly crowd. In an extended set piece on "Oratorial Machines," he draws an explicit "Analogy" between genres of oral discourse and varieties of print commerce. He describes "three . . . Machines, for the Use of those Orators who desire to talk much without Interruption." Lest his genius be lost on modern readers, he then explains that "this Physico-logical Scheme of Oratorial . . . Machines" is an "Analogy to the . . . Commonwealth of Writers" (39). One machine, the "*Ladder*" (i.e., the gallows), represents "Factio[us]" political writings and the popular print genre of "Last Dying Speeches" of condemned persons about to be hanged at Tyburn. Another machine, the "*Stage-Itinerant*," signifies print entertainments such as chapbooks and fairy tales. But the most important machine, "in Place as well as Dignity, is the *Pulpit*" (37). Swift was ordained as a priest in 1695, and throughout the *Tale*, he foregrounds the pulpit as the most distinguished "Machine" by which modern "Orators" exalt themselves above the crowds. His satire focuses chiefly on the Dissenting pulpit, which symbolizes "the Writings of our *Modern Saints*" (39): that is, the subversive Dissenting tracts, published since the Civil War period, that continued to flood the print market throughout the eighteenth century.

Swift *was* concerned with the making of constitutive choices about the press, but as a freshly ordained clergyman, he also knew that at a time of widespread illiteracy, ears and tongues remained the chief organs of mass manipulation. The tale-teller advises, "*it is with* Men, *as with* Asses; *whoever would keep them fast, must find a very good Hold at their Ears*" (129). Throughout the late seventeenth and eighteenth centuries in Britain, the question of effective oral "delivery" was the subject of an almost culture-wide debate, and Dissenting preachers' oral appeal to the masses was an enormous concern.[11] Anglican authors express alarm that "pulpit oratory" in the Church of England was not competing successfully for the souls of the populace, who were being seduced by "enthusiast" preachers more cunning in the use of intonation and gesture in public speaking. One of the defining dilemmas of Swift's career was how to get a *"good Hold at the . . . Ears"* of the populace in a shifting media climate. Not coincidentally, in his satire on print commerce he also rigorously analyzes styles of preaching. He satirizes both Grub Street authors and Dissenting preachers as asses with loud braying voices and enormous ears. Protestant Dissenter Jack has "a Tongue so Musculous and Subtil" (126) and has mastered the art of braying like an ass. Swift also foregrounds the potential power of oral discourse. Alarmingly, Jack's oral adeptness has earned him "Multitudes" of "Disciples" and "Devotees" (101–2).

The unique power and danger of oral communication, Swift suggests, lies in its corporeality (and so universality). The tools of oral communication are rooted in the human body (tongues, ears, breath). Throughout the *Tale*, but especially in the set piece on Oratorial Machines and the discussions of the "Learned *AEolists*, [who] maintain the Original Cause of all Things to be *Wind*" (99), Swift foregrounds the corporeal and otherwise material aspects of oral communication. As we shall see, he engages with ancient philosophical debates on the materiality of sound and hearing. He especially grapples with Lucretius's arguments in his first century BCE poem attempting to convert readers to the materialist philosophy of Epicurus, *De rerum natura*. But he does so, I suggest, not so much to satirize Lucretius as to participate in seventeenth-century debates concerning sound, speech, and hearing. Swift engages with Francis Bacon and the emergent science of acoustics; with Robert Boyle's recent experiments with air (the dominant "medium" of sound and speech); and with extensive commentary on these scientific debates and experiments by his fellow clergymen, including William Wotton (the *Tale*'s most notorious critic) and Narcissus Marsh, bishop of Ferns and Leighlin and the provost of Trinity College, Dublin (where Swift earned his BA).

Swift was concerned with the mediation of knowledge and values across spaces, places, and generations. Interwoven with the *Tale*'s satire on print commerce and its "Oratorial" counterparts is an allegory satirizing the controversial theological notion of *"Oral Tradition"* (54n). Swift's satire on oral tradition participates in the war in the history of ideas that I have outlined in the previous chapter: the debate between Protestants and Catholics concerning the relative reliability and authority of scripture versus "tradition" (the received wisdom and practices of the established church). This debate took on increased visibility and urgency in the 1680s, when James, Duke of York, a Catholic, stood next in line for the English throne. The question of the "orality of the rule of faith" was a rare issue on which Swift and his critic William Wotton were in agreement. Swift represented the spread of legitimate written documents (such as vernacular Bibles) as the best available response to Brother Peter's corrupt appeals to oral tradition to authorize "papist" innovations in the church. In his commentary on these sections of the *Tale* (eventually inserted by Swift into later editions), Wotton joined with Swift in scorning papal appeals to *"Oral Tradition"* (54n).[12] Swift associated Protestant Dissenting orality with popular unrest and gender subversion from below, but he also linked Catholic appeals to *"Oral Tradition"* to despicable learned tyranny from above.

Swift foregrounds "Ears" and "Tongue[s]" as powerful organs of sedition and dissent (and, potentially, of valuable social control), and he places commercial print on a continuum with vulgar and dangerous oral practices. His harshly negative satiric representations, both of popular oral practices and of the notion of "oral tradition," contrast sharply with later eighteenth-century sympathetic representations. At the same time, though, there is a strong sense in *A Tale of a Tub* of being on the brink of a new "Age." Now that press licensing had collapsed, Swift's text suggests, the new strategy would be a sophisticated appeal to both ears and eyes. Accordingly, the tale-teller draws his "tale" to a close by reminding us one last time of his forthcoming *print* publications (131).

PRINT COMMERCE AND THE ORATORIAL MACHINE

In a scene set in a crowded London square, Swift depicts a heated oral exchange between a *"fat unweildy Fellow"* and a *"Weaver"* to satirize not only the exploding literary marketplace but also the practice of condemning one's fellow *"Scriblers"*: "the Multitude of Writers whereof the whole Multitude of Writers most reasonably complains" (28). He "tell[s] the Reader a short Tale":

> A Mountebank in Leicester-Fields, *had drawn a huge Assembly about him. Among the rest, a fat unweildy Fellow, half stifled in the Press, would be every fit crying out, Lord! what a filthy Crowd is here? . . . At last, a* Weaver *that stood next him could hold no longer: A Plague*

confound you (said he) *for an over-grown Sloven; and who (in the Devil's Name), I wonder, helps to make up the Crowd half so much as your self? . . . Is not the Place as free for us as for you? Bring your own Guts to a reasonable Compass (and be d——n'd) and then I'll engage we shall have room enough for us all.* (28–29)

This depiction of a London crowd alive with characters and voices is actually a parable about print commerce. In the increasingly crowded literary marketplace after 1695, Swift suggests, authors and booksellers contending for readers resemble the Weaver and the *"fat unweildy Fellow, half stifled in the Press."* Swift makes numerous puns on the multiple meanings of "press" as technology (noun), crowd (noun), and physical action (verb). In the opening sentence of the *Tale* proper ("Sect. I. *The Introduction*"), he likens the modern author to an orator struggling to be "heard in a Crowd": "Whoever hath an Ambition to be heard in a Crowd, *must press*, and squeeze, and thrust, and climb with indefatigable Pains, till he has exalted himself to a certain Degree of Altitude above them" (34, my emphasis). In the new age of print commerce, he suggests, anyone who wishes to be "heard" must now "press" (i.e., print).

In the set piece that follows, the tale-teller goes on to explain the "Machines" or technologies that modern orators (i.e., authors) use to be "heard" above the crowd. He states: "the Wisdom of our Ancestors . . . has, to encourage all aspiring Adventurers, thought fit to erect three wooden Machines, for the Use of those Orators who desire to talk much without Interruption. These are, the *Pulpit*, the *Ladder*, and the *Stage-Itinerant*" (34).[13] As I have suggested, for Swift "the first of these Oratorial Machines in Place as well as Dignity, is the *Pulpit*." "[F]rom its near Resemblance to a Pillory," this machine "will ever have a mighty Influence on human Ears" (37). Swift's satire focuses on the Dissenting pulpit, but in these politically tumultuous decades both the Dissenting pulpit and its Anglican counterpart were associated upon occasion with dangerous rabble-rousing noise. In 1690 John Locke described the politicized pulpit of his day as the "Drum Ecclesiastick."[14] Twenty years later—the year that Swift wrote his "Apology"—High Church Tory Henry Sacheverell preached his riot-causing sermon entitled "The Perils of False Brethren, Both in Church and State."[15]

The aspect of Swift's satire on Oratorial Machines that most concerns us here, however, is the way that he represents cheap print on a continuum with popular oral practices. After the tale-teller explains the different venues and varieties of oral discourse that each Oratorial Machine represents, he proposes that these *oral* genres and practices symbolize genres of *print*:

"this Physico-logical Scheme of Oratorial Receptacles or Machines, contains a great Mystery, being a Type, a Sign, an Emblem, a Shadow, a Symbol,
bearing Analogy to the spacious Commonwealth of Writers, and to those
Methods by which they must exalt themselves to a certain Eminency above
the inferiour World" (39). The phrase "Commonwealth of Writers" hints at
Swift's concern with the threatening relationship between print commerce
and religiopolitical dissent. The seventeenth century saw a flood of Dissenting pamphlets and tracts during the Civil War period and Interregnum and
again after the lapse of the Licensing Act in 1695. "By the *Pulpit*," the tale-
teller explains, "are adumbrated the Writings of our *Modern Saints* in *Great
Britain*" (39). For Swift, the most threatening Oratorial Machine was the Dissenting pulpit—and by extension of his analogy, the print publications with
which Dissenting preaching worked in tandem.

Another Oratorial Machine is the *"Ladder"* (or gallows). At this venue,
too, oral communication and print publication work closely together. At
Tyburn, the "ascending Orators do not only oblige their Audience in the
agreeable Delivery, but the whole World in their *early* Publication of these
Speeches; which I look upon as the choicest Treasury of our *British* Eloquence"
(38).[16] The publication of so-called "Last Dying Speeches" of condemned persons was a lucrative sideline for the Ordinary (chaplain) of Newgate Prison,
for these printed "Accounts" of ostensibly oral "speeches" sometimes sold
in the thousands of copies. At the same time, Swift's phrase "our *British* Eloquence" evokes impassioned contemporary debates concerning effective oral
"delivery" and the "decline of pulpit oratory" in the Anglican Church. The
"Ladder" is linked not only to "Last Dying Speeches" but also to "Factio[us]"
political writings such as the aforementioned "Pamphlets, and other Offensive Weapons":

> The *Ladder* is an adequate Symbol of *Faction* and of *Poetry*, to both
> of which so noble a Number of Authors are indebted for their Fame.
> *Of *Faction*, because * * * * * * * * * * * * * * * *
> *Hiatus in MS.* * * * * * * * * * * (40)

A Tale of a Tub is notoriously characterized by a number of *"Chasms"* (13)
at strategic points in the text: long series of asterisks indicating "Defect[s]
in the Manuscript" (40n) with marginal notes such as *"Hic multa desider-
antur"* (110) and *"Hiatus in MS"* (40). A footnote on this particular occasion notes that these "Defect[s] in the Manuscript" are "frequent with our
Author, either when he thinks he cannot say any thing worth Reading, or
when he has no mind to enter on the Subject, or when it is a Matter of little

Moment, or perhaps to amuse his Reader . . . *or lastly, with some Satyrical Intention"* (40n). A few pages later, the tale-teller notes his tireless production of pamphlets for opposing political parties. His "Quill [is] worn to the Pith in the Service of the State, in *Pro's* and *Cons* upon *Popish Plots*, and *Meal-Tubs*, and *Exclusion Bills*, and *Passive Obedience* . . . . Fourscore and eleven Pamphlets have I writ under three Reigns, and for the Service of six and thirty Factions" (44).

The "last Engine of Orators, is the *Stage-Itinerant*" (38). A footnote in the text here comments: "*the* Mountebank's Stage" (38n).[17] More broadly, the category of the Stage-Itinerant includes popular entertainments that take place outdoors, such as the fairground shows that Swift satirizes later in the *Tale* (85) or the theatrical performances that William Hogarth depicts in his engraving *Southwark Fair*. The Stage-Itinerant, like the Ladder and (sometimes) the Dissenting pulpit, is "erected with much Sagacity, +*sub Jove pluvio, in triviis & quadriviis"* (38). (A note in Swift's text adds, *"In the open Air, and in Streets where the greatest Resort is"* [unnumbered note, bottom of 38].)

In fact, Swift suggests, the Stage-Itinerant "is the great Seminary of the two former [Oratorial Machines]," "there being a strict and perpetual Intercourse between all three" (38). Dissenting preachers are linked to mountebanks and gallows orators by their threatening practice of delivering their orations *"in the open Air, and in the Streets where the greatest Resort is"* (38n). Members of Dissenting groups such as the Quakers (and, later, the Methodists) were distinctive in their practice of delivering their oral "testimonies" to sometimes vast crowds in fields, streets, and marketplaces—that is, *"open Air"* sites. In the view of many contemporaries, this kind of oratory was not only highly "vulgar" but also highly dangerous, because it could be heard by the greatest number of ears. In Swift's set piece on "Oratorial Machines," the Stage-Itinerant is the "great Seminary" of gallows orators and Dissenting preachers because both criminals and Dissenters learn their techniques of oral delivery from mountebanks. Finally, for now, in the tale-teller's complex oral-as-print "Analogy," the Stage-Itinerant also symbolizes popular print entertainments, "such as, *Six-peny-worth of Wit*, Westminster *Drolleries, Delightful Tales, Compleat Jesters*, and the like; by which the Writers of and for *GRUB-STREET*, have in these latter Ages so nobly triumph'd over Time" (40). Grub Street authors specialize not only in "Factio[us]" political writings and Dissenting tracts but also, more harmlessly, in fairy tale and chapbook subjects such as *"Tom Thumb,"* "Dr. *Faustus,"* "the History of *Reynard* the *Fox,"* and "Whittington *and his Cat"* (42–43).

Swift is well known to have delighted in exposing mankind's overconfidence in the power and permanence of writing. Truisms such as *vox audita perit, littera scripta manet* (voices heard perish; letters written endure) are examples of the sort of hubris that he liked to deflate. In Swift's satire, material texts visibly decay. Indeed, he suggests, in the new age of print commerce, *most* printed texts are now ephemeral (*"half stifled in the Press"*). But as I will go on to argue now, Swift scholars have for the most part failed to notice that he equally engages with truisms and assumptions about oral communication. On the one hand, Swift satirizes the ephemerality of Grub Street writings. On the other hand, he foregrounds everything that is material, corporeal, and even (in some ancient and modern theories) permanent about sound and speech.[18] Simultaneously engaging with print commerce and with ancient philosophical debates and modern scientific discourses about sound, speech, and air, he plays with age-old tropes of both speech and writing.

In his discussion of Oratorial Machines, the tale-teller questions why it is that "for obtaining Attention in Publick, there is of necessity required a *superiour Position of Place*" (38). Offering a theory of the materiality of sound and voice, he theorizes that

> Air being a heavy Body, and therefore (according to the system of **Epicurus*) continually descending, must needs be more so, when loaden and press'd down by Words, which are also Bodies of much Weight and Gravity, as it is manifest from those deep *Impressions* they make and leave upon us; and therefore must be delivered from a due Altitude, or else they will neither carry a good Aim, nor fall down with a sufficient Force. (38)

He quotes Lucretius's *De rerum natura*: "*Corpoream quoque enim vocem constare fatendum est, | Et sonitum, quoniam possunt impellare Sensus.* Lucr. *Lib.* 4" (38). To drive home his point still further, he then quotes the same lines in English, drawing on Thomas Creech's acclaimed recent edition, which reads: "**'Tis certain then, that* Voice *that thus can wound | Is all* Material; Body *every* Sound" (38n).[19]

Epicurean philosophy held that everything consists of particulate matter: atoms that swerve, collide, combine, or otherwise dance throughout the air. Book 4 of *De rerum natura* is devoted to a theory of the senses. After a detailed explanation of vision, Lucretius gives an account of hearing and speech: both the workings of sounds in general (*sonitus/sonus*) and of voice (*vox*), a subcategory of sound (4.524–614). According to Lucretius, when we speak we force out voice-constituting atoms from deep down in our bodies. These atoms move through our windpipes and then our mouths. If we speak too long or too loudly, this particulate matter scrapes our throats and makes us hoarse. Like Swift, but for different reasons, Lucretius appears to have been keen to drive home his argument concerning the materiality of sound and voice. He reiterates this point closely, three times in some ninety lines. In addition to his first statement quoted above (in Melville's translation, "For we must confess that voice and sound also / Have bodies . . ."), he also states: "There is no doubt therefore that words and voices / Consist of bodily elements, since they can hurt" and "Therefore the voice must be made of bodily stuff, / Since much speaking diminishes the body."[20]

But Lucretius was one of Swift's favorite authors, and I would argue that in Swift's engagement with *De rerum natura* in this section, he is not so much satirizing Lucretius as using Epicurean materialism to address modern debates in natural philosophy pertaining to sound and speech. This passage on air as "a heavy Body" is a veritable encyclopedia of satiric references to seventeenth-century debates about and experiments with sound, speech, and air (the "medium" of sound). As I have suggested, Swift is responding not only to the experiments of natural philosophers such as Robert Boyle but also to commentary on these experiments by members of the wider public, including his fellow clergymen, Wotton and Marsh. The most important progenitor of Restoration experiments and debates was Francis Bacon, who described his theories of oral communication and acoustics in *Sylva Sylvarum: or a Naturall Historie in Ten Centuries* (1623; pub. 1627). Anticipating Swift's emphasis on the physical ear, Bacon represented hearing as the most immediately corporeal of the senses: "the sense of hearing striketh the spirits more immediately than the other senses, and more incorporeally than the smelling. For the sight, taste, and feeling, have their organs not of so present and immediate access to the spirits, as the hearing hath."[21] Like Swift, too, Bacon was especially interested in the acoustics of the pulpit and the technologies by which preachers and other orators seek to enhance their power. He questioned whether "sounds do move better downwards than upwards. Pulpits are placed high above the people. And when the ancient generals spake to their armies, they had ever a mount of turf cast up, whereupon they stood."[22]

Swift scholars have long recognized his engagement with seventeenth-century natural philosophy, and they have noted that one of his favorite satiric targets was Robert Boyle. Boyle died in 1691, by then one of Swift's most famous fellow Irishmen, and his death prompted widespread assessment of his works. To my knowledge, though, no previous scholar has proposed that one prompt for Swift's "*A general History of* Ears" was Boyle's recently published *The General History of the Air* (1692) (fig. 2.2). One glance at the contents of Boyle's *History of Air*, which lists topics such

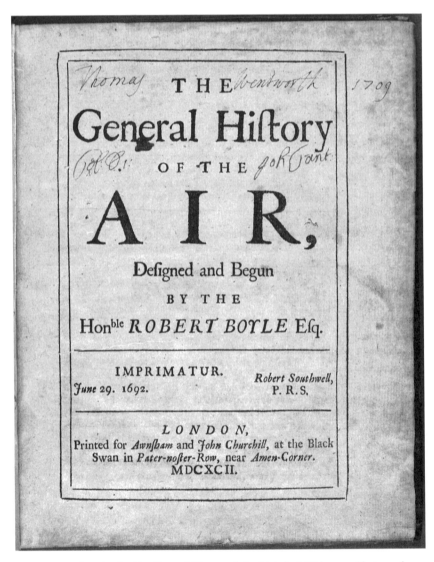

Fig. 2.2. Robert Boyle, *The General History of the Air* (1692). Title page. Photograph: By permission of the Huntington Library, San Marino, California (RB 323253).

as "Of the *Motion* of the Air, and of Winds" (chap. 15), "Of the Air as the Medium of *Sounds*, and of Sounds and Noises in the Air, and particularly Thunder; and of the Air's Operation on the Sounds of Bodies" (chap. 16), and "Of the *Weight* of the Air" (chap. 17), would have provided Swift with sufficient inspiration for his representation of words as *"weighty* Matter" or his satire of the "Learned *AEolists*," who "maintain the Original Cause of all Things to be *Wind*" (99).[23] Another publication that I believe provided Swift with satiric fodder was Boyle's *A Continuation of New Experiments Physico-Mechanical, Touching the Spring and Weight of the Air, and their Effects* (1669). In this work, the Royal Society philosopher provides detailed descriptions of his air-related experiments, sometimes illustrating these experiments with elaborate engraved plates. One of these plates shows a gentleman standing on the roof of a four-story building and operating a suction pump to determine to what height water can be raised by attraction (fig. 2.3). In the section of *Continuation of New Experiments* describing the experiment depicted in this illustration, Boyle makes several references to the weight of the air. His statement that "the Air was . . . very heavy" anticipates Swift's assertion that "Air" is "a heavy Body."[24]

Swift also satirizes broader public interest in natural philosophy, especially among his fellow clergymen (who, he implies, should be doing something else). His reference to "Air" as "a heavy Body" also echoes Wotton's *Reflections Upon Ancient and Modern Learning* (1694), where Wotton enthuses about "'The *Baroscope*, or *Torricellian Experiment'*" that "convinced the World, that the Air is an actually [sic] heavy Body; and gravitates upon every Thing here below."[25] With the misplaced enthusiasm of the tale-teller, Wotton also boasts that Boyle's "Doctrine *of the Weight and Spring of the Air* . . . has universally gained Assent from Philosophers of all Nations" (181).

The narrator of the *Tale* describes "weight[y]" *spoken* words as making "deep *Impressions*" (38) on the hearer—rather as a printing press does on paper. As further evidence for his theory of spoken "Words" as "Bodies of . . . Weight and Gravity," he notes that "in the several Assemblies of . . . Orators, Nature . . . hath instructed the Hearers, to stand with their Mouths open, and erected parallel to the Horizon, so as they may be intersected by a perpendicular Line from the Zenith to the Center of the Earth" (38–39). This image satirizes jaw-dropped auditors generally, but it also has a specific satiric target. In 1683, when Swift was in the second year of earning his BA at Trinity College (a "Hearer" in the "Assemblies of . . . Orators"), Narcissus Marsh delivered a lecture on the "Science . . . of Acousticks" to the Dublin Society. In 1684 this lecture was printed in the *Philosophical Transactions of the Royal Society* as "An introductory Essay to the doctrine of Sounds, containing some proposals for the improvement of Acousticks."[26] Swift's description of "Mouths . . . parallel to the Horizon" may have been prompted by remarks by both Boyle and Marsh. In his essay on acoustics, Marsh describes a crude visual diagram that appears at the end of his "Essay" as depicting a "*Phonical* Sphear" with a "*Semiplane*, as Parallel

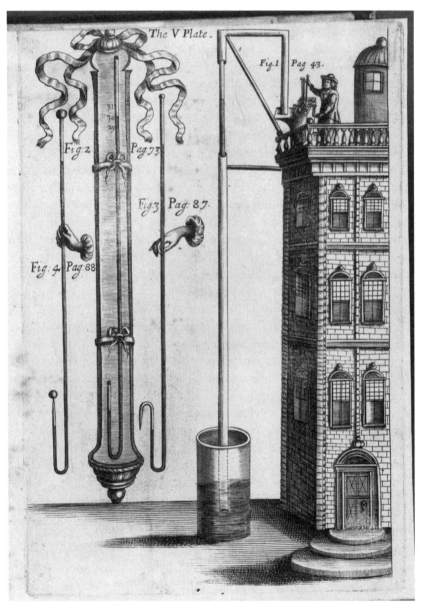

Fig. 2.3. Robert Boyle, *A Continuation of New Experiments Physico-Mechanical, Touching the Spring and Weight of the Air, and their Effects* (1669), pt. 1, pl. V, depicting portable baroscopes, a barometer, and an air-related experiment with a suction pump. Photograph: By permission of the Huntington Library, San Marino, California (RB 291380 vol. 1).

to the *Horizon*. For if it be Perpendicular thereunto, I suppose the upper extremity will be no longer *Circular*, but *Hyperbolical*, and the lower part of it suited to a greater Circle of the Earth . . . [and so on]."[27] Marsh's cryptic description echoes Boyle's much clearer description of his suction pump experiment in *Continuation of New Experiments*, where he states that the upper part of the pump is "parallel to the Horizon."[28]

Swift's tale-teller tests this theory of *"weighty* Matter" by considering one more significant arena of oratorical and acoustic achievement: the "Modern Theatre." He observes, "there is something yet more refined in the Contrivance and Structure of our Modern Theatres. For, First; the Pit is sunk below the Stage . . . [so] that whatever *weighty* Matter shall be delivered thence . . . may fall plum into the Jaws of certain *Criticks* . . . which stand ready open to devour them." While *"weighty* Matter" sinks downward to the pit, "Bombast and Buffoonry, by Nature lofty and light," float upward to *"the Twelve-Peny Gallery,"* where "a suitable Colony . . . greedily intercept[s] them" with their mouths (39). In Swift's satire, texts are ephemeral and immaterial, while *spoken* words are *"weighty,"* material substances that hearers "intercept" with their ears, mouths, and "Jaws."[29]

On the one hand, Swift foregrounds the materiality of orality and aurality. He discusses the measurable (and manipulatable) qualities of air and sound, the acoustics of different venues ("Modern Theatres," the *"Pulpit,"* the *"open Air, and in the Streets"*), and the body parts of speakers and hearers (mouths and ears). On the other hand, Swift satirizes the ephemerality—even immateriality—of written and printed texts. In "The Epistle Dedicatory, To His Royal Highness Prince Posterity," the tale-teller laments that Time's "Malice is such to the Writings of our Age, that of several Thousands produced yearly from this renowned City, before the next Revolution of the Sun, there is not one to be heard of: Unhappy Infants, many of them barbarously destroyed, before they have so much as learnt their *Mother-Tongue* to beg for Pity" (21–22). Significantly, the metaphor here is one of *hearing* rather than reading. With the exponentially increased number of works now being published, Swift suggests, printing one's works no longer means that one will be remembered (or even heard). In addition, Grub Street texts are not only temporally but also geographically "occasional." Like modern oral wit, these texts rarely transcend their immediate neighborhood: "Such a Jest there is, that will not pass out of *Covent-Garden*; and such a one, that is no where intelligible but at *Hide-Park* Corner" (27).

In adding the "Apology" to the fifth edition of the *Tale* (1710), Swift returned to his theme of ephemeral versus lasting works. He proposed that the writings of critics of earlier editions of the *Tale* are already sunk into waste Paper and Oblivion; after the usual Fate of common Answerers to Books, which are allowed to have any Merit: They are indeed like Annuals that grow about a young Tree, and seem to vye with it for a Summer, but fall and die with the Leaves in Autumn, and are never heard of any more. ("Apology," 8)

For Swift, the category of "ephemera" included the works of his critics and any author whom he didn't like.[30] But Swift admitted that not only worthless publications but also valuable "Learn[ed]" works eventually decay. He defined "Critick[s]" as "the Restorers of Antient Learning from the Worms, and Graves, and Dust of Manuscripts" (61). Nonetheless, with the hubris of the tale-teller (though much better cause) he exulted that *A Tale of a Tub* *"seems calculated to live at least as long as our Language, and our Tast* [sic] *admit no great Alterations"* ("Apology," 5).

ORAL TRADITION AS A TALE OF A TUB

Swift's desire that *A Tale of a Tub* would escape the "usual Fate" of "Writings of our Age" links his engagement with print commerce to his concern with the transmission of the Christian scriptures. The common issue linking these wildly diverse publications—Grub Street publications, Swift's satire, and the scriptures—is the much-debated question of the transmission and endurance of written and oral discourse over time. As I have discussed in chapter 1, the question of the reliability of textual transmission and interpretation versus that of oral tradition as preserved by the church had been a key issue of debate between Protestant and Catholic theologians and polemicists since the Reformation. In his religious allegory of the "three brothers," Swift satirizes Catholic arguments for oral tradition. Not accidentally, given his Protestant conviction of the potential superiority of written transmission over generations, he pointedly begins this section with the phrase of oral story-tellers, "Once upon a Time" (47).

The tale-teller recounts the story of a man whose wife had three sons "all at a Birth," whom they named Peter, Martin, and Jack. As Wotton's note explains, "By these three sons . . . *Popery,* the *Church* of *England,* and our Protestant *Dissenters,* are designed" (47n). On his deathbed, the father calls his sons together and hands them his written will. The will is pointedly a document: "here it is" (47). The will provides each of the sons with a new coat (implicitly, the doctrine or faith of Christianity) that will last *"fresh and sound as long as you live"* (47). It also contains *"full Instructions in every particular concerning the Wearing and Management of* [the]

Coats" (47). (Swift allows that some change is inherent in tradition, for the father explains that the coats will *"grow in the same proportion with your Bodies . . . so as to be always fit"* [47].) For seven years the sons follow the will's instructions exactly, until one day they realize that their coats are out of style. They search the text for passages authorizing the addition of *"Shoulder-knots"* (epaulets), but they find no textual authority to support fashionable updates: *"*they went immediately to consult their Father's Will, read it over and over, but not a Word of the *Shoulder-knot*. What should they do?*"* (54). The brothers are temporarily at a loss until Peter, the most *"Book-learned"* of the three, finds a way to evade the will's instructions: *"'Tis true, said he, there is nothing here in this Will,* *totidem verbis, making mention of* Shoulder-knots, *but I dare conjecture, we may find them in-*clusive, *or* totidem syllabis. This Distinction was immediately approved by all*"* (54). Wotton's footnote to this passage scoffs:

> *When the Papists cannot find any thing which they want in Scripture, they go to *Oral Tradition:* Thus *Peter* is introduced satisfy'd with the Tedious way of looking for all the Letters of any Word, which he has occasion for in the Will, when neither the constituent Syllables, nor much less the whole Word, were there in *Terminis.* W. Wotton. (54n)

The brothers search the will for syllables supporting *"Shoulder-knots,"* but they cannot find those either. Accordingly, the same "Learned Brother" who "found the former Evasion" (54–55) suggests that in lieu of syllables they may look for component letters (*a, b, c,* and so on): *"Brothers, there is yet Hopes; for tho' we cannot find them* totidem verbis, *nor* totidem syllabis, *I dare engage we shall make them out* tertio modo, *or* totidem literis*"* (54). Not surprisingly, given this degree of interpretive corruption, the brothers eventually find exactly what they want in the text: *"Shoulder-Knots* were made clearly out, to be *Jure-Paterno"* (55).

But the brothers are still not satisfied; they now decide that they must have gold lace. Once again, Peter struggles to find a way to evade the father's instructions. He proposes that in addition to the "Scriptory" (or written) will, their father also left them a "Nuncupatory" (or oral) will:

> *Brothers,* said he, * *You are to be informed, that, of Wills,* duo sunt genera, +*Nuncupatory and scriptory: that in the Scriptory Will here before us, there is no Precept or Mention about Gold Lace,* conceditur: But, si idem affirmetur de nuncupatorio, negatur, *For Brothers, if you remem-*

ber, we heard a Fellow say when we were Boys, that he heard my Fa-
ther's Man say, that he heard my Father say, that he would advise his
Sons to get Gold Lace *on their Coats, as soon as ever they could procure*
Money to buy it. By G——that is very true, cries the other; *I remember*
it perfectly well, said the third. And so without more ado they got the
largest *Gold Lace* in the Parish. (55–56)

Another note in the text, this time presumably by Swift himself, echoes
Wotton's scorn for Catholic theological notions of oral tradition: "+ By this
is meant *Tradition,* allowed to have equal Authority with the Scripture, or
rather greater" (55n).

Anticipating Samuel Johnson's famous challenge to James Macpherson
later in the eighteenth century—that the latter ought to be able to produce
manuscript "evidence" for his claims concerning Ossianic oral tradition—
both Swift and Wotton held that the papacy should be able to produce textual evidence for its arguments and innovations. Swift reproduces an unusually large number of Wotton's comments in this section of the *Tale.* When
Peter justifies another fashionable update by alluding to "Tradition," Wotton's note says: "*The* Popes *in their Decretals and Bulls, have given their*
Sanction to very many gainful Doctrines which are now received in the
Church of Rome *that are not mention'd in Scripture, and are unknown to*
the Primitive Church . . . W. Wotton" (58n). When Peter is rumored to have
"obtained [a] Favour from a certain Lord, to receive him into his House,"
Wotton comments: "*This was* Constantine the Great, *from whom the* Popes
pretend a Donation of St. Peter's *Patrimony, which they have been never*
able to produce" (58n). Peter routinely appeals to oral tradition to promote
his desires, and his brothers are unable to prove him wrong, because he keeps
the will locked up in the "strongbox" of Greek and Latin. Eventually, Martin and Jack get so frustrated with their brother's constant appeals to oral
tradition that they secretly make a "*Copia vera*" of the will (78). Alluding
to the Protestant translation of the scriptures into the vernacular, Swift
represents the spread of legitimate written documents as the best available
response to Peter's appeals to the orality of the rule of faith.

Swift satirizes not only the Catholic idea of oral tradition but also the
Jewish notion of the Oral Torah. In the aforementioned satire of print entertainments such as chapbooks and fairy tales in the section on Oratorial Machines, he proposes that the tale of "Whittington *and his Cat,* is the Work
of that mysterious *Rabbi, Jehuda Hannasi,* containing a Defence of the *Ge-*
mara of the *Jerusalem Misna,* and its just preference to that of *Babylon*"

(43). In Jewish tradition, God gave to Moses both the Written Torah and an additional set of laws that was passed down orally from teacher to student. Eventually, after centuries of oral transmission, Rabbi Judah ha-Nasi compiled these laws in what became known as the Mishnah (the book of laws), accompanied by the Gemara, or rabbinical commentary.[31] In his seemingly light-handed satire of popular print entertainments, then, Swift manages simultaneously to satirize both modern textual criticism (which overinterprets even fairy tales) *and* the idea of oral tradition as expressed in the doctrine of the Oral Torah.

As Swift's handling of the chapbook tale of "Whittington *and his Cat*" suggests, then, Swift was to some degree an equal-opportunity satirist. In *A Tale of a Tub*, he satirizes not only the Catholic idea of oral tradition and the Jewish notion of the Oral Torah but also what he saw as the Protestant overconfidence in the superior reliability of texts. As Peter's corrupt textual criticism shows, writing is not necessarily a more reliable form of communication than oral tradition, because fallen human beings willfully misinterpret texts (and, as we have seen, material texts decay). When Protestant Dissenter Jack obtains a copy of the will, he too grows infatuated with textual interpretation. Although the will consists of "plain, easy Directions," Jack finds in it complex meanings to justify his own desires:

> Jack had provided a fair Copy of his Father's *Will* . . . and . . . became the fondest Creature of it imaginable. For, atho' . . . it consisted wholly in certain plain, easy Directions . . . yet he began to entertain a Fancy, that the Matter was *deeper* and *darker* and therefore must needs have a great deal more of Mystery at the bottom. (123)

Whereas Peter cites *"Oral Tradition"* to justify anything he wants, Jack turns the *written* will to many uses not anticipated by his father: "He had a Way of working it into any Shape he pleased; so that it served him for a Night-cap when he went to Bed, and for an Umbrello [*sic*] in rainy Weather" (124). Later, in responding to his critics in his "Apology" for the *Tale*, Swift returned to the issue of textual (mis)interpretation. Ironically, in arguing for his complete *"Innocen[ce]"* of *"ill Meanings"* charged to him by his critics, Swift underlined the complex textual subterfuge of which he was capable:

> *There are three or four other Passages which prejudiced or ignorant Readers have drawn by great Force to hint at ill Meanings; as if they glanced at some Tenets in Religion; in answer to all which, the Author*

solemnly protests he is entirely Innocent, and never had it once in his
Thoughts that any thing he said would in the least be capable of such
Interpretations. ("Apology," 7)

The near impossibility of determining with any certainty what Swift "really" means in this passage foregrounds for us the interpretive challenges of
complex texts. But Anglicans held that despite the polysemy of language,
the fundamental truths of the scriptures were available to any sufficiently
humble reader. As a Protestant clergyman, as well as a publishing author,
Swift avoided any expression of a despairing skepticism about the *possibil-*
ity of reliable interpretation, whether of his own text or any other.

Oral tradition, Swift reminds us throughout the *Tale*, can never be
sufficiently reliable, because human memory is fallible. Immediately after
satirizing the theological idea of oral tradition in section 2, Swift begins
section 3 with the tale-teller's lament that "the unhappy shortness of my
Memory led me into an Error" (60). Later, the tale-teller observes that

> the severe Reader may justly tax me as a Writer of short Memory, a
> Deficiency to which a true *Modern* cannot but of Necessity be a little
> subject: Because, *Memory* being an Employment of the Mind upon things
> past, is a Faculty, for which the Learned, in our Illustrious Age, have no
> manner of Occasion, who deal entirely with *Invention*, and strike all
> Things out of themselves. (88; see also 133)

"*Modern Authors*" have short memories because they do not value "things
past." It is ironic, then, that their "great Design" is "everlasting Remem-
brance, and never-dying Fame" (81). Oral tradition and Grub Street writings are both unreliable sources—and significantly, the tale-teller depends
upon each of them. He states, "I shall . . . be extreamly careful and exact in
recounting such material Passages . . . as I have been able to collect, either
from undoubted Tradition or indefatigable Reading" (123).

"A VERY GOOD HOLD AT THEIR EARS"

Swift suggests that the Catholic Church makes more than one kind of corrupt appeal to the oral: not only the learned theological appeal to oral tradition to justify papal authority but also, through rituals and processions, a
tyrannic version of the fairground huckster's appeal to the ears (and eyes) of

the populace: "*Lord Peter* was also held the original author of *Puppets* and *Raree-Shows*" (70). Lord Peter is associated with tyrannic orality of several kinds, notably "*Oaths and Curses*" (13) and "argu[ing] to the Death": "he had an abominable Faculty of telling huge palpable *Lies*, upon all Occasions; and cursing the whole Company to Hell. . . . at every Word; *By G——, Gentlemen, I tell you nothing but the Truth; And the D——l broil them eternally that will not believe me*" (77). In Swift's satire, even Peter's papal "bulls" are not written documents issued by the pope but live animals associated with impolite orality. These beasts are so fond of lucre that "they would *Roar*, and *Spit*, and *Belch*, and *Piss*, and *Fart*, and *Snivel* out *Fire* . . . till you flung them a Bit of *Gold*" (72). Peter's other innovations in the church include the practice of "Auricular Confession" (69n), requiring all believers to whisper their secrets to an ass. Swift notes that "a third Invention, was the Erecting of a *Whispering-Office*, for the Publick Good and Ease . . . of all such as are in Danger of bursting with too much *Wind*. An *Asse*'s Head was placed so conveniently, that the Party affected might easily with his Mouth accost either of the Animal's Ears" (69). After depicting the Reformation in section 4, Swift focuses on Protestant Dissenter Jack, who is also, not coincidentally, associated with asses. But Jack is known for not only his "large Ears" but also his "Tongue so Musculous and Subtil" and his accomplished "*Braying*" (126). Whereas the critique of Peter focuses on his corrupt appeals to "Tradition" to justify his innovations, Swift's critique of Jack, as I will go on to demonstrate now, focuses on the alarming oral appeals of Dissenting preachers.

Jack's zeal has "given Rise to the most Illustrious and Epidemick Sect of *AEolists*" (94). A footnote here explains: "+*All Pretenders to Inspiration whatsoever*" (99n). The AEolists "affirm the Gift of BELCHING, to be the noblest Act of a Rational Creature" (100). In section 8, Swift depicts the AEolist preacher's inappropriately physical style of delivery as a loss of bodily control. After the preacher receives "new Supplies of Inspiration" via his anus, he

> swell[s] immediately to the Shape and Size of his *Vessel*. In this Posture he disembogues whole Tempests upon his Auditory, as the Spirit from beneath gives him Utterance; which issuing *ex adytis*, and *penetralibus*, is not performed without much Pain and Gripings. And the *Wind* in breaking forth, *deals with his Face, as it does with that of the Sea; first *blackning*, then *wrinkling*, and at last, *bursting it into a Foam*. (102)

A footnote in the text notes: "*this is an exact Description of the Changes made in the Face by Enthusiastick Preachers*" (102n). Private revelation, or

"Inspiration," causes an "Earthquake": not only in the preacher's face but also, it is implied, in the body politic at large: "after certain Gripings, the *Wind* and Vapours issuing forth; having first by their Turbulence and Convulsions within, caused an Earthquake in Man's little World; distorted the Mouth, bloated the Cheeks" (101).

Swift compares the AEolists' "Delivery of their Mysteries" to the practice of "antient Oracles, whose Inspirations were owing to certain subterraneous *Effluviums* of *Wind*" (102). Alluding to the oracle of Apollo at Delphi, who answered through the Pythia (a priestess in a state of possession), he notes that the delivery of ancient oracles was "frequently managed and directed by *Female* Officers, whose Organs were understood to be better disposed for the Admission of those Oracular *Gusts*, as entring and passing up thro' a Receptacle of greater Capacity" (102). These ancient oracles, he proposes, have modern counterparts: "this Custom of **Female* Priests is kept up still in certain refined Colleges of our *Modern AEolists*, who are agreed to receive their Inspiration, derived thro' the Receptacle aforesaid, like their Ancestors, the *Sibyls*" (102). A footnote here comments: "**Quakers who suffer their Women to preach and pray*" (102n). In the late seventeenth and early eighteenth centuries, the striking visibility of female leadership in Dissenting groups (including but not limited to the Quakers) generated widespread fears of illicit sexuality and gender role upheaval.[32] Swift shared these concerns, but his critique of enthusiasm is distinctive in its double focus not only on illicit sexuality but also on threatening orality. Following Rabelais, who linked ears and genitals, he suggests that the large ears of Puritan preachers such as Jack signify a comparable "Protuberancy of Parts in the [*Inferior*] Region of the Body" (130). He also proposes that this correlation between ears and genitals helps to explain the attraction of Dissenting movements for the "devouter Sisters" (130–31).

The conventional critical explanation for Jack's protuberant ears is that "the short hair, and wiglessness, of the Puritans made their ears prominent" (459n67). But as I have argued here, the prevalence of ears, tongues, and mouths throughout the *Tale* suggests a much larger pattern of satiric association and argument at work. In the second half of the *Tale*, a "great Part" of "the Remainder of this Discourse" (89) thematizes ears, tongues, and air. The Civil War period and Interregnum, the tale-teller suggests, simultaneously saw the growth of sedition and the "Growth of *Ears*": "[W]hile this *Island* of ours, was under the *Dominion of Grace*, many Endeavours were made to improve the Growth of *Ears* once more among us" (130). After the Restoration, "a **cruel King . . . arose, who raised a bloody Persecution against all *Ears*, above a certain Standard" (131). A footnote comments: "*This was King *Charles* the Second, who at his Restauration, turned out all the Dissenting Teachers that would not conform" (131n). Swift evokes the powerfully symbolic corporeal punishment of mutilating *ears* as a penalty for seditious *print* publications (a punishment inflicted upon some seventeenth-century Dissenters). But he also goes on to advance an argument about the *continuing* threat of "Seditious Preachers who blow up the Seeds of Rebellion" (100n). Swift's reference to "Colleges of *Modern AEolists*" emphasizes that Protestant Dissent was a *growing* phenomenon—especially now that William and Mary had passed the Toleration Act of 1689 ("An Act for Exempting their Majestyes Protestant Subjects dissenting from the Church of England from the Penalties of certaine Lawes").[33] Despite "so many Loppings and Mutilations" after the Restoration, Swift suggests, the Dissenting threat was continuing to spread: "if the only slitting of one *Ear* in a Stag, hath been found sufficient to propagate the Defect thro' a whole Forest; Why should we wonder at the greatest Consequences, from so many Loppings and Mutilations, to which the *Ears* of our Fathers and our own, have been of late so much exposed" (130).

Like Cromwell, Jack initially grows powerful not through violence but through *oral* effectiveness: "in all Revolutions of Government, he would make his Court for the Office of *Hangman* General; and in the Exercise of that Dignity, wherein he was very dextrous, would make use of no other *Vizard* than a long *Prayer*" (126). In Scriblerian satire, both Dissenting preachers and Grub Street authors are represented as asses with loud braying voices and enormous ears. Dissenter Jack

> had a Tongue so Musculous and Subtil, that he could twist it up into his Nose, and deliver a strange Kind of Speech from thence. He was also the first in these Kingdoms, who began to improve the *Spanish* Accomplishment of *Braying*; and having large Ears, perpetually exposed and arrect, he carried his Art to . . . a Perfection.[34] (126–27)

So pervasive is the braying ass in *A Tale of a Tub*, *Mechanical Operation of the Spirit*, and *Battel of the Books* that at one point the narrator pauses to confess, "I . . . bear a very singular Respect to this Animal, by whom I take human Nature to be most admirably held forth in all its Qualities as well as Operations: And therefore, whatever in my small Reading, occurs, concerning this our Fellow-Creature, I do never fail to set it down, by way of Common-place" (171). In *Battel of the Books*, Swift features a "malignant Deity, call'd Criticism," whose "Head, and Ears, and Voice, resembled those of an Ass"; one of her children is *"Noise"* (154). But in *A Tale of a Tub*, Jack's braying, while deafening, is a peculiar kind of noise that triggers not wakefulness but drowsiness and sleep (a renunciation of agency on the part of the hearers that is morally and politically dangerous). Jack was "the first that ever found out the Secret of contriving a +*Soporiferous* Medicine to be convey'd in at the *Ears* . . . a Compound of *Sulphur* and *Balm of Gilead*, with a little *Pilgrim's Salve"* (127).[35]

Ironically, for someone with a knack for braying, Jack has an aversion to instrumental music. To shield his ears, he becomes a habitué of London's noisiest sites, preferring to drown out music in churches with the disputes of lawyers, shrieks of schoolchildren, and harangues of fishwives: "He . . . would run Dog-mad, at the Noise of *Musick*. . . . But he would cure himself again, by taking two or three Turns in *Westminster-Hall*, or *Billingsgate*, or in a *Boarding-School*, or the *Royal-Exchange*, or a *State Coffee-House"* (127). Augustan satirists commonly took advantage of their readers' familiarity with the noise levels and kinds of oral discourse that were characteristic of various London sites. Elsewhere in the *Tale*, in a passage comparing textual satire to oral preaching, Swift links different sermon subjects to different London parishes. He then proposes that no one is greatly offended by either sermons or satire, for hearers and readers alike assume that the preacher's or author's criticism is aimed at someone else:

> It is but to venture your Lungs, and you may preach in *Covent-Garden* against Foppery and Fornication. . . . Against Pride, and Dissimulation, and Bribery, at *White Hall*. . . . And in a *City* Pulpit be as fierce as you please, against Avarice, Hypocrisie and Extortion. Tis but a *Ball* bandied to and fro, and every Man carries a *Racket* about Him to strike it from himself. (32)

In Swift's writings, Westminster and Whitehall make frequent appearances as well-known sites associated with meaningless verbosity and deafening noise. As the seat of government, Westminster was full of squabbling lawyers; it was also a fashionable meeting place, full of merchant stalls. In a passage in the "Digression concerning Madness" (sec. 9) where the tale-teller associates different oratorical venues with different kinds of patients in Bedlam, he suggests that any Bedlamite who is "eternally talking, sputtering, gaping, bawling, in a Sound without Period or Article. . . . be furnished immediately with a green Bag and Papers, and *three Pence* in his Pocket, and away with him to *Westminster-Hall"* (113–15).

Most importantly, Swift's critique of Protestant Dissent in *A Tale of a Tub*

pays detailed attention to the nature of Dissenting preachers' oral "delivery."
He depicts AEolist preachers "droning," "drivelling," "whining," and "canting" not only to bemused strangers but also to "Followers" (123) and "Devotees" (101). Jack's preaching is at once anarchically impulsive *and* shrewdly
manipulative. His "oracular Belches" stem from base bodily impulses, but
he also carefully manipulates aspects of delivery such as tone, cadence, and
pitch. The tale-teller observes that Jack's ruling passion is *"Zeal,"* then comments that this "is, perhaps, the most significant Word that hath been ever
yet produced in any Language; As, I think, I have fully proved in my excellent
Analytical Discourse upon that Subject; wherein I have deduced a *Histori-
theo-physi-logical* Account of *Zeal"* (89–92). Both the tale-teller's "Critical
Essay upon the Art of *Canting, Philosophically, Physically, and Musically
considered"* (4, 181) and *"Histori-theo-physi-logical* Account" foreground
the physiological aspects of preaching. *"Cant"* and *"Zeal,"* Swift proposes,
are at once rooted in the body and manifested in an alarmingly physical kind
of delivery that acts upon the "Senses" rather than the intellects of hearers:
"Cant and Vision are to the Ear and the Eye, the same that Tickling is to the
Touch. Those Entertainments and Pleasures we most value in Life, are such
as *Dupe* and play the Wag with the Senses" (110).[36] In turn, Swift character-
izes the Dissenting worshiper, or *"Fanatick Auditory"* (172), by his or her un-
critical style of hearing. The tale-teller notes that AEolist preachers' *"Belches*
were received for Sacred, the Sourer the better, and swallowed with infinite
Consolation by their meager Devotees" (101). The preacher's "Eloquence"
(124, 126, 180, and passim) evokes an unconscious sympathetic response in
the bodies of his audience, involving panting, swaying, sighing, and singing:
"the sacred *AEolist* delivers his oracular *Belches* to his panting Disciples; Of
whom, some are greedily gaping after the sanctified Breath; others are all the
while hymning out the Praises of the *Winds"* (102).

As in the *Tale,* so in *Mechanical Operation of the Spirit* Swift suggests
that the power of Dissenting preaching lies in the "mechanical" or physiological act of communication rather than in any particularly meaningful
content. Dissenting preaching, like Grub Street authorship, "is nothing but
a *Trade"* (178). The general subject of *Mechanical Operation* is the vanity
and danger of private revelation (or inspiration). But there is nothing uncal-
culated or natural, Swift suggests, about these orators' "skillful" "Disposition of Words":

[I]n the Language of the Spirit, *Cant* and *Droning* supply the Place of
Sense and *Reason* . . . . [T]he Art of *Canting* consists in skillfully adapt-

ing the Voice, to whatever Words the Spirit delivers, that may strike the
Ears of the Audience, with its most significant Cadence. The Force, or
Energy of this Eloquence, is not to be found, as among antient Orators,
in the Disposition of Words to a Sentence, or the turning of long Periods; but . . . is taken up wholly in dwelling, and dilating upon Syllables
and Letters. Thus it is frequent for a single *Vowel* to draw Sighs from a
Multitude. (180)

Swift represents Dissenting preachers as ridiculous, but he was not without
genuine concern that their seeming "Eloquence" might have "Force."

Swift describes the Dissenting preacher as "a little paultry Mortal, droning, and dreaming, and drivelling to a Multitude" (178). Terms like "Paultry"
and "meager" are intended to be insulting (a jab at the low social rank of
Jack and his Dissenting followers), but they nonetheless illustrate Swift's
recognition of the particular appeal of Dissenting sects to marginalized individuals and social groups.[37] Jack is a populist preacher who preaches without
discrimination to men and women of all social ranks in any venue (including the *"open Air"*). When Peter curses him to broil eternally, Jack responds
to Peter's aggressive oral style with his own colloquial dialect—another aspect of his character that links him to common people: *"What; said he; A
Rogue that lock'd up his Drink, turned away our Wives, cheated us of our
Fortunes; paumd his damned Crusts upon us for Mutton; and at last kickt
us out of Doors; must we be in His Fashions with a Pox?"* (92). Peter and
Jack are examples of Swift's extraordinary talent for capturing oral dialects,
or what Irvin Ehrenpreis called his "ear for talk."[38] Swift's earliest biographer, John Boyle, 5th Earl of Orrery, also noted Swift's talent at mimicry,
but he was dismayed rather than impressed by the clergyman's penchant for
imitating "vulgar," or popular, voices. Orrery wrote, "the vulgar dialect was
not only a fund of humour for him, but I verily believe was acceptable to his
nature."[39]

Swift's satire allows that Dissenting preachers' oral delivery has a "Force,
or Energy" (180) that gives them real power, however unwarranted. Powerful delivery, Swift feared, could lend authority to words that in reality were
nothing more than "Sound." As we have seen in his satire of wrangling
lawyers at Westminster, Swift also represented other kinds of contemporary oral discourse as characterized by a disconnection between sound and
content. In the passage quoted above, where the tale-teller assigns different
inhabitants of Bedlam to different oratorial venues in the outside world,
he also remarks of another patient, who "has forgot the common *Meaning*

of Words, but [is] an admirable Retainer of the Sound": "What a compleat System of *Court-Skill* is here described" (115).

From the fifth edition on, *A Tale of a Tub* included illustrations. One of these illustrations depicts a preacher who is elevated to a position of "Eminency above the inferior World" (39) (fig. 2.4). Outside the room, visible through a large window, a condemned man at the gallows delivers his "last dying speech," while two figures (possibly a mountebank and his merry-andrew, or "zany") perform on an outdoor stage. The original sketch for this illustration of the three "Oratorial Machines" of pulpit, gallows, and stage-itinerant differs strikingly from the published version, and it is not difficult to surmise why the original design was never reproduced.[40] In the original sketch, now surviving only in a relatively modern reproduction, there are multiple pointed references to the material bodily stratum (fig. 2.5). The preacher is notably stout and gaseous: he thumps his belly and spews out a cloud of "inspiration," or air. Meanwhile, visible out the window, cherub-like figures in the clouds are also exhaling air, causing strong winds that disturb man and nature. The preacher's "Fanatick Auditor[ies]" are similarly lively and animated; they are exclaiming with wonder, holding their guts and spewing, and otherwise making noise. (One of them may even be passing wind, as his neighbor is leaning away from him.) The preacher has managed to keep his audience seated and (for the most part) awake. In the *published* plate, by way of contrast, the preacher mechanically drones and gestures to audience members who variously listen with different degrees of attention, snooze, or turn away. In both stages of this illustration, the preachers are depicted addressing a "Multitude."[41] Regardless of the content of their sermons (or the lack of it), these preachers' enthusiastic *delivery* enables them to attract (and sometimes hold) a crowd.

In the opening sentence of section 1, we recall, the tale-teller began by advising the reader that "Whoever hath an Ambition to be heard in a Crowd, *must press*" (i.e., print) (34, my emphasis). Similarly in the last section of the *Tale* proper, the tale-teller advises the reader:

> From this brief Survey of the falling State of *Ears*, in the last Age, and the small Care had to advance their antient Growth in the present, it is manifest, how little Reason we can have to rely upon a Hold so short, so weak, and so slippery; and that, whoever desires to catch Mankind fast, must have Recourse to some other Methods. (131)

Throughout *A Tale of a Tub*, Swift links the "Mouths" of Dissenting preachers to "Seditio[n]" and "Rebellion" (100n) and advances an argument about

Pag. 35.

Fig. 2.4. Jonathan Swift, *A Tale of a Tub*, 5th ed. (1710): "The *Pulpit*, the *Ladder*, and the *Stage-Itinerant*." Photograph: Rare Books and Special Collections, Princeton University Library.

Fig. 2.5. Jonathan Swift, *A Tale of a Tub*, 5th ed. (1710). Fountaine's original design for the tub preacher. Photograph: © Victoria and Albert Museum, London. Forster Collection (F.47.E.).

the link between "Ears" and "Revolutions." At the same time, though, in choosing to print the *Tale*, he himself embraced new opportunities and methods for mass communication. Now that press licensing had collapsed, he suggests, the most effective "Method" for reaching the public would be a sophisticated appeal not only to the ears but also (via print) to the eyes. Not so surprisingly, then, the narrator of the *Tale* takes advantage of this closing moment to remind his readers one last time of his forthcoming print publications—particularly his "*general History of Ears;* which I design very speedily to bestow upon the Publick" (131).

CHAPTER THREE

The Contagion of the Oral in *A Journal of the Plague Year*

"NO . . . PRINTED NEWS PAPERS IN THOSE DAYS"

Daniel Defoe's historical fiction *A Journal of the Plague Year* (1722) opens with an oral rumor. H.F., the London saddler who is the fictional author of the *Journal*, recalls how he first overheard the news that the plague had arrived in Holland:

> It was about the Beginning of *September* 1664, that I, among the Rest of my Neighbours, heard in Ordinary Discourse, that the Plague was return'd again in *Holland* . . . . whether *they say*, it was brought, some said from *Italy*, others from the *Levant* . . . ; others said it was brought from *Candia*; others from *Cypress*. It matter'd not, from whence it came; but all agreed, it was come into *Holland* again.
>
> We had no such thing as printed News Papers in those Days, to spread Rumours and Reports of Things; and to improve them by the Invention of Men, as I have liv'd to see practis'd since. But such things as these were gather'd from the Letters of Merchants, and others, who corresponded abroad, and from them was handed about by Word of Mouth only; so that things did not spread instantly over the whole Nation, as they do now.[1]

As H.F.'s recollection suggests, the chief medium of news in 1664–65 was oral communication. What was known was a matter of rumor and discussion ("they say," "some said," "others said," "all agreed"). Foregrounding the fifty-seven-year time gap between the events that H.F. relates and the imagined posthumous publication of his "Memorandums" in 1722, Defoe represents this temporal distance in terms of contemporary shifts in modes of communication—especially the relative availability of printed news.

Looking back on events that are now only distant memories, H.F. reconstructs the earlier period as one of lack ("no . . . printed News Papers"), then draws a line between "those Days" and "now" ("as I have liv'd to see practis'd since"). Over this period, Defoe suggests, England has become more modern. Specifically, the reading public has become less vulnerably dependent on oral reports ("Word of Mouth") and increasingly able to consult fact-oriented (if never wholly factual) "printed News." He thus sets up two structural movements central to this work: moving diachronically across time, we also move synchronically across different communicative modes that in reality are coexisting and interdependent but are here represented as parts of a linear, progressive development.

In the same paragraph, Defoe continues the movement of rumor and report across voice, manuscript, and print—this time modeling government efforts to track the plague:

> [T]his Rumour died off again, and People began to forget it . . . till the . . .
> Beginning of *December* 1664, when two Men . . . died of the Plague in
> *Long Acre* . . . . The Family they were in, endeavour'd to conceal it . . .
> but as it had gotten some Vent in the Discourse of the Neighbourhood,
> the Secretaries of State gat Knowledge of it. And concerning themselves
> to inquire about it, in order to be certain of the Truth, two Physicians
> and a Surgeon were order'd to go to the House, and make Inspection.
> This they did; and finding evident Tokens of the Sickness upon both
> the Bodies that were dead, they gave their Opinions publickly, that they
> died of the Plague: Whereupon it was given in to the Parish Clerk, and
> he also return'd them to the Hall; and it was printed in the weekly Bill
> of Mortality in the usual manner, thus,
>
> Plague 2. Parishes infected 1. (5–6)

When a rumor of the plague's arrival reaches the secretaries of state, they appoint "two Physicians and a Surgeon" to visit the house suspected to harbor the infection. These gentlemen inspect "the Bodies that were dead," then orally deliver their "Opinions" concerning cause of death to the parish clerk, who writes them down. The clerk's transcription of the physicians' judgments is then printed in the official Bill of Mortality. Published weekly by the government at times of crisis and posted in public places, the bills consisted of single sheets printed on one side with the number of deaths per parish and the estimated number of deaths caused by plague and on the other side with the total number of deaths broken down according to apparent cause (figs. 3.1 and 3.2). Significantly, as the collected information

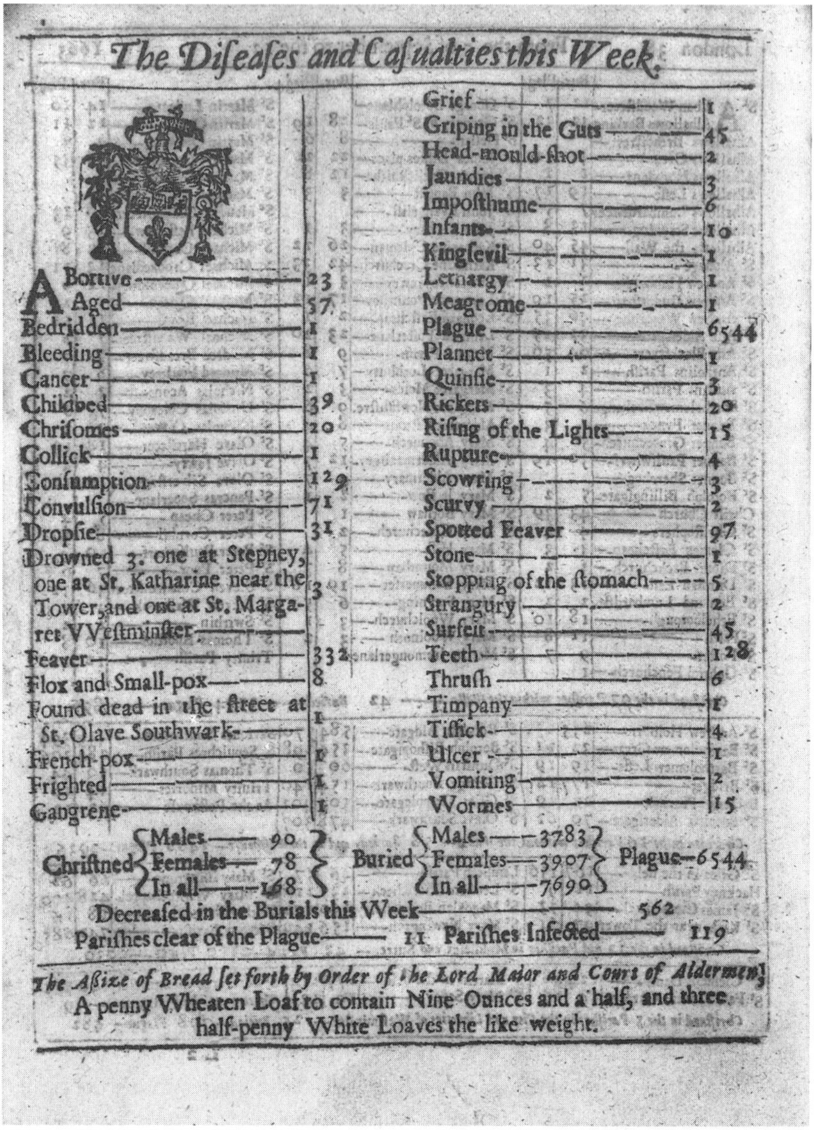

The Diseases and Casualties this Week.

		Grief	1
		Griping in the Guts	45
		Head-mould-shot	2
		Jaundies	3
		Imposthume	6
		Infants	10
		Kingsevil	1
Abortive	23	Lethargy	1
Aged	57	Meagrome	1
Bedridden	1	Plague	6544
Bleeding	1	Planner	1
Cancer	1	Quinsie	3
Childbed	39	Rickets	20
Chrisomes	20	Rising of the Lights	15
Collick	1	Rupture	4
Consumption	129	Scowring	3
Convulsion	71	Scurvy	2
Dropsie	31	Spotted Feaver	97
Drowned 3. one at Stepney, one at St. Katharine near the Tower, and one at St. Marga-ret VVestminster	3	Stone	1
		Stopping of the stomach	5
		Strangury	2
Feaver	332	Surfeit	45
Flox and Small-pox	8	Teeth	128
Found dead in the street at St. Olave Southwark	1	Thrush	6
		Timpany	1
French-pox	1	Tissick	4
Frighted	1	Ulcer	1
Gangrene	1	Vomiting	2
		Wormes	15

	Males — 90		Males — 3783		
Christned	Females — 78	Buried	Females — 3907	Plague — 6544
	In all — 168		In all — 7690	

Decreased in the Burials this Week ———— 562
Parishes clear of the Plague ———— 11   Parishes Infected ———— 119

The Assize of Bread set forth by Order of the Lord Maior and Court of Aldermen.
A penny VVheaten Loaf to contain Nine Ounces and a half, and three half-penny White Loaves the like weight.

Figs. 3.1 and 3.2. Bill of Mortality for the week of 12–19 September 1665, showing an estimated 6,544 deaths from the plague. Reproduced by permission of the Pepys Library, Magdalene College, Cambridge (PL 1595 [1], sig. L3), verso and recto.

| London 39 | From the 12 of September to the 19. | 1665 |

Parish	Bur.	Plag.	Parish	Bur.	Plag.	Parish	Bur.	Plag.
St Alban Woodstreet	23	19	St George Botolphlane	5	3	St Martin Ludgate	21	11
Alhallows Barking	41	32	St Gregory by St Pauls	32	23	St Martin Orgars	9	7
Alhallows Breadstreet	4	3	St Hellen	8	8	St Martin Outwitch	8	3
Alhallows Great	59	53	St James Dukes place	29	26	St Martin Vintrey	64	61
Alhallows Honylane	1		St James Garlickhithe	13	11	St Matthew Fridaystreet	1	1
Alhallows Lesse	29	26	St John Baptist	7	6	St Maudlin Milkstreet	3	3
Alhallows Lumbardstreet	8	7	St John Evangelist			St Maudlin Oldfishstreet	16	11
Alhallows Staining	16	10	St John Zachary	3	2	St Michael Bassishaw	17	12
Alhallows the Wall	41	30	St Katharine Coleman	44	36	St Michael Cornhil	14	11
St Alphage	25	13	St Katharine Creechurch	35	31	St Michael Crookedlane	10	10
St Andrew Hubbard	6	5	St Lawrence Jewry	8	6	St Michael Queenhithe	11	6
St Andrew Undershaft	25	22	St Lawrence Pountney	22	17	St Michael Quern	4	3
St Andrew Wardrobe	63	54	St Leonard Eastcheap	5	4	St Michael Royal	20	17
St Ann Aldersgate	33	28	St Leonard Fosterlane	34	32	St Michael Woodstreet	6	2
St Ann Blackfryers	79	65	St Magnus Parish	7	6	St Mildred Breadstreet	6	3
St Antholins Parish	6	5	St Margaret Lothbury	8	8	St Mildred Poultrey	4	2
St Austins Parish	2	2	St Margaret Moses	5	5	St Nicholas Acons	8	7
St Bartholomew Exchange	3	3	St Margaret Newfishstreet	17	13	St Nicholas Coleabby	14	13
St Bennet Fynck	1		St Margaret Pattons	5	3	St Nicholas Olaves	12	9
St Bennet Gracechurch	5	4	St Mary Abchurch	13	9	St Olave Hartstreet	20	18
St Bennet Paulswharf	35	15	St Mary Aldermanbury	20	16	St Olave Jewry	7	5
St Bennet Sherehog			St Mary Aldermary	11	10	St Olave Silverstreet	23	17
St Botolph Billingsgate			St Mary le Bow	4	2	St Pancras Soperlane	2	2
Christs Church	55	48	St Mary Bothaw	9	8	St Peter Cheap	4	3
St Christophers	6	5	St Mary Colechurch	2	2	St Peter Cornhil	10	6
St Clement Eastcheap	3	3	St Mary Hill	12	8	St Peter Paulswharf	12	12
St Dionis Backchurch	10	3	St Mary Mounthaw	9	9	St Peter Poor	6	6
St Dunstan East	20	10	St Mary Sommerset	36	34	St Steven Colemanstreet	47	40
St Edmund Lumbardstr.	4	4	St Mary Stayning	2	1	St Steven Walbrook	5	5
St Ethelborough	16	6	St Mary Woolchurch	2	2	St Swithin	11	9
St Faiths	7	6	St Mary Woolnoth	9	6	St Thomas Apostle	19	17
St Foster	10	9	St Martin Iremongerlane	1	1	Trinity Parish	13	13
St Gabriel Fenchurch	6	3						

Christned in the 97 Parishes within the Walls — 40 Buried — 1493 Plague — 1189

Parish	Bur.	Plag.	Parish	Bur.	Plag.	Parish	Bur.	Plag.
St Andrew Holborn	271	247	St Botolph Aldgate	623	589	Saviours Southwark	427	403
St Bartholomew Great	21	17	St Botolph Bishopsgate	294	256	S. Sepulchres Parish	301	214
St Bartholomew Lesse	14	12	St Dunstan West	88	79	St Thomas Southwark	57	52
St Bridget	236	180	St George Southwark	195	176	Trinity Minories	12	10
Bridewel Precinct	32	31	St Giles Cripplegate	456	373	At the Pesthouse	6	6
St Botolph Aldersgate	68	62	St Olave Southwark	530	363			

Christned in the 16 Parishes without the Walls — 65 Buried, and at the Pesthouse — 3631 Plague — 3070

Parish	Bur.	Plag.	Parish	Bur.	Plag.	Parish	Bur.	Plag.
St Giles in the fields	140	125	Lambeth Parish	48	43	St Mary Islington	68	66
Hackney Parish	22	18	St Leonard Shoreditch	183	173	St Mary Whitechappel	532	502
St James Clerkenwel	77	67	St Magdalen Bermondsey	207	180	Rotherith Parish	17	13
St Kath. near the Tower	93	66	St Mary Newington	155	152	Stepney Parish	716	686

Christned in the 12 out Parishes in Middlesex and Surry — 42 Buried — 2258 Plague — 2091

Parish	Bur.	Plag.	Parish	Bur.	Plag.	Parish	Bur.	Plag.
St Clement Danes	168	140	St Martin in the fields	286	228	St Margaret Westminster	411	399
St Paul Covent Garden	30	29	St Mary Savoy	20	19	Whereof at the Pesthouse		7

Christned in the 5 Parishes in the City and Liberties of Westminster — 29 Buried — 915 Plague — 815

L. 3

moves across modes of communication—from oral "Rumour" and "Opinion" to manuscript transcription and printed text—its status subtly shifts. The orally delivered judgments of the physicians are medical "Opinions," suggesting authoritative judgments but nonetheless resting on grounds insufficient for conclusive demonstration. Once these opinions are printed in the bills, however, they appear to acquire the status of truth. H.F. marks this transformation with a flourish, setting apart from his narrative the now-official statistics concerning plague deaths for this week of September: "Plague 2. Parishes infected 1."

Yet H.F.'s depiction here of the procedure for searching the dead so as to track the movement of the plague is most remarkable for how atypical it is of his usual representation of this process in the *Journal*. In this instance, the procedure is depicted as relatively reliable: an authoritative team of medical men, overseen by the secretaries of state, conducts an empirical observation "in order to be certain of the Truth." The presence of plague is indicated by "evident Tokens . . . upon both the Bodies," and the judgment concerning cause of death is transferred in an orderly, uncorrupted manner into the bills. Elsewhere, however, H.F. repeatedly emphasizes the impossibility of interpreting signs of plague with certainty, and he excoriates the unreliability of the Bills of Mortality. He estimates that "there died, at least, 100000 of the Plague . . . who were not put down" (83). Furthermore, even in this relatively idealized opening depiction, the secretaries of state first learn of the plague's arrival through neighborhood gossip: a "Rumour" that had "gotten . . . Vent." Nor is print any more reliable than common talk. As we have just seen, the Bills of Mortality risk "spread[ing] Rumours" precisely because orally delivered opinions immediately underlie printed texts. No form of communication, whether print, manuscript, or oral, is exempt from the "Invention of Men"—undermining any clear distinction or hierarchy among them such as H.F. tries to make at the beginning of the *Journal*. This movement from oral report to only-purportedly authoritative print is evident throughout the *Journal*—most obviously, as H.F. struggles to assess the "Stories" of the plague that he "met with, *that is* heard of, and which are very certain to be true, or very near the Truth; that is to say, true in the General" (47).

In *The Nature of the Book: Print and Knowledge in the Making*, Adrian Johns has worked to historicize assumptions about "print culture," suggesting that "what we often regard as essential elements and necessary concomitants of print are in fact rather more contingent than generally acknowledged. Veracity in particular is . . . extrinsic to the press itself, and has had to be grafted onto it." In early modern England, the commercial and cultural success of printing could come only after the technology and its products had acquired an "air of intrinsic reliability."[2] Printers, booksellers, and market-oriented authors such as Defoe had the most to gain by encouraging the idea of the superior trustworthiness of print. As his generation's most prolific printed author, Defoe contributed significantly to an emergent model of a hierarchy of forms of communication with print at its apex. In his *Essay upon Literature* (1726), he declared, "The *Printing Art* has out-run the Pen, and may pass for the greatest Improvement of its Kind in the World."[3] Yet he also knew that print had no inherent link to credibility. Human agents could use it to spread false reports as well as true. As he suggested in *The Storm* (1704), print's only inherent characteristic was the way that it "convey[ed] its Contents," whether true or false, long after the human agents who employed it were dead:

> [A] Book Printed is a Record, remaining in every Man's Possession, always ready to renew its Acquaintance with his Memory, and always ready to be produc'd as an Authority or Voucher to any Reports he makes out of it, and conveys its Contents for Ages to come, to the Eternity of mortal Time, when the Author is forgotten in his Grave.[4]

Reliability was especially crucial because of print's vast reach across time and space: "Preaching of Sermons is Speaking to a few of Mankind: Printing of Books is Talking to the whole World."[5]

Readers of the *Journal* have long puzzled over H.F.'s opening remark concerning the absence of "printed News Papers" in 1664–65. Why would H.F., a saddler, make such a statement in so prominent a place? Watson Nicholson argues that H.F.'s assertion is "so gratuitous as to cause suspicion." As a journalist, Defoe "must have been aware" that there were newspaper prototypes (though not daily newspapers) in 1664–65.[6] Frank Bastian counters that Defoe "cannot have known" of these prototypes, for if he "wished his account to be, or even only to appear, accurate, he would scarcely have invited criticism by a statement he knew to be false."[7] Yet while critics have debated Defoe's knowledge of newspaper history, none has addressed the question of how H.F.'s statement actually functions in the *Journal*. I propose that whether or not Defoe knew of the printed news genres of 1664–65, this opening statement works to set up a key structuring binary of the text: the opposition of a backward past associated with orality to a new, print-oriented modernity associated with the collection and reproduction of accurate statistics and true report. Writing in 1722 about events supposed to have taken place in 1664–65, Defoe was in fact writing across the historical period that marks the institutionalization of a recognizably modern newspaper press. In 1663–66 there were only three regularly printed sources of news: two eight-page newsbooks, the *Intelligencer* and the *Newes*, published weekly by Roger L'Estrange, and, beginning in 1666, the government organ the *Oxford* (later *London*) *Gazette*. By 1702, however, the first daily newspaper had appeared, and by 1712 "about twenty single-leaf papers were regularly published in the capital each week."[8] By 1722 the reading public had come to depend on printed news. Defoe's statement may be a comment on the relative absence of newspapers in 1664–65, but I read it as indicative of his contribution to emergent developmental narratives of media shift still with us today: particularly, the model whereby an orality that is in fact coexistent with and inseparable from print is ideologically relegated to the past.[9] The identities of both print and orality have had to be made.

Yet Defoe was as much a theorist of print as a propagandist for it. Throughout his many fictional, journalistic, and informational writings on plague, his most consuming concern is arguably the lack of credibility of the printed Bills of Mortality. In the *Journal*, H.F. laments the inaccuracy of the bills at least thirteen times.[10] When Defoe published the *Journal* in March 1722, outbreaks of the plague had been occurring on the Continent. In February he published *Due Preparations for the Plague*, a didactic text aimed at teaching readers to prepare for a future epidemic. Likewise, the *Journal* should be read as an effort to shape future practice. At times of plague, H.F. stresses, the reliability of the bills is a matter of the utmost importance, for panicked citizens will inevitably use these texts as a guide to action, even when they know that the texts cannot be read at face value as truth. H.F. notes that in 1665, "as soon as the first great Decrease in the Bills appear'd," the people abandoned caution, causing escalation of the plague: "the Bills encreas'd again Four Hundred the very first Week" (176–77).

In his concern with the accuracy of the Bills of Mortality, Defoe was addressing the lack of credibility of print. But what he was most pointedly concerned with was where the statistics came from: how they were collected and the observations, interpretations, and oral reports on which they were based. Readers of the *Journal* cannot fail to note H.F.'s concern with the bills, yet, surprisingly, no scholar has commented on the (near) erasure in this text of the officials responsible for the gathering of this information. Despite the relatively idealized scenario in H.F.'s opening paragraphs, prominent physicians did not in fact routinely make rounds of infected houses during plague time, purposely bringing themselves into contact with the deadly disease. Instead, this was the job of the "Women-Searchers," ground-level agents officially hired by the government since at least 1579 to examine bodies and determine cause of death. Depicted in contemporary illustrations and discussed in texts available to Defoe, the women searchers "played a central role in the regulation of public health in England for over 250 years" (figs. 3.3 and 3.4).[11] Defoe is well known to have used printed historical sources in composing the *Journal*. Most notoriously, he reprints in

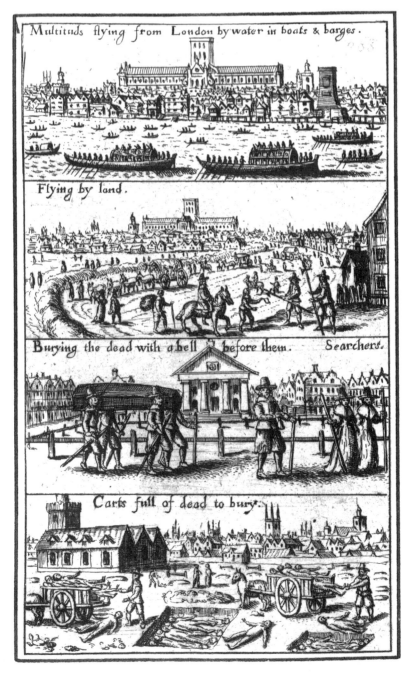

Fig. 3.3. Plague broadsheet (c. 1665) depicting women searchers in the third frame. Reproduced by permission of the Pepys Library, Magdalene College, Cambridge (PL 2973/447).

Fig. 3.4. Two frames of a nine-frame plague broadsheet (c. 1665) depicting women searchers at work. Reprinted from Walter George Bell, *The Great Plague in London in 1665*
(London: Lane, 1924), facing 105.

full and nearly verbatim the official "ORDERS Conceived and Published by
the Lord MAYOR and Aldermen of the City of London, concerning the Infection of the Plague 1665" (36–43). The Orders are instructions for tracking
and containing the plague—including a detailed directive for the appointment of "Women-Searchers in every Parish" (37). Yet, while Defoe reprints
the official Orders for the appointment of the women searchers, no critic
has remarked that these women do not appear anywhere else in Defoe's historical fiction of the plague. While all the other workers listed in the Orders
("Examiners," "Watchmen," "Nurse-Keepers," and so on) become familiar
figures in Defoe's account, the category of plague personnel most prominent

in the Orders—the women searchers—is mysteriously missing everywhere else in his text.

I propose that Defoe's erasure of the women searchers in the *Journal* paradoxically has to do with his efforts to forge a bond not previously existing between print and "enhanced fidelity, reliability, and truth."[12] Defoe knew that "printed news was only a rung above rumour on the ladder of credibility,"[13] and he was deeply invested in drawing a theoretical line between oral rumors and printed news. His erasure of the female, oral origins of the bills is part of a larger agenda in his writings to model print as separate from certain kinds of oral discourse—especially the type of suspect orality that he associated with superstitious old women. In *Due Preparations for the Plague*, he explicitly links the problem of the searchers to the larger issue of trusting print. But in the *Journal*, published only a few weeks later, he quietly erases the searchers, as part of an effort to rewrite the chaotic past of a not-yet-modern civic bureaucracy in the new, idealized image of a civic order based on the gathering and dissemination of printed news. In early modern England, the government's reliance on the oral reports of typically illiterate poor women was a striking reversal of the usual hierarchy of readers over nonreaders. Under normal circumstances, illiterate persons depended on the literate for access to printed news, but at times of plague, literate authorities grew dependent on illiterate women's readings of "tokens" on infected bodies. The searchers' orally delivered verdicts formed the basis for the Bills of Mortality (and, by extension, for the political and civil mandates based on those texts). Defoe worked to dissociate his culture from what he viewed as a destabilizing and backward reliance on orality, and I will investigate here his fictionalized containment of the contagion of the oral in the increasingly print-oriented society in which he wrote. Print—especially printed collected information, such as news—would be a major structural element in a newly far-reaching bureaucratic civic and national order, and Defoe himself would be a part of these developments, whether as journalist, informational author, reporting spy, or even writer of true histories. The *Journal* models an unreliable oral past that is—or rather should be—cut off from the print-oriented future.

Yet although Defoe works to strengthen the credibility of print by separating it from the contagion of the oral, suspect orality seeps out everywhere in the *Journal*. At least three times, H.F. exults in the plague's apparent silencing of the retailers of "vulgar" oral street culture: "all the Predictors, Astrologers, Fortune-tellers . . . and such People, were gone and vanish'd" (141–42). I shall explore this text's repeated erasure of the kind of oral street culture that H.F. shows to have been distressingly influential in this time of need, and I shall suggest how this repeated erasure of superstitious orality is related to the erasures of "Women-Searchers" and "printed News Papers" in 1664–65. While Defoe himself most likely drew on some oral sources for his knowledge of the plague,[14] his saddler character struggles to distance himself from the types of orality that he links to rumors, contagion, superstition, and a backward past. Yet H.F.'s attempted construction of a binary divide between then and now, suspect oral discourse and credible print, is wishful thinking. The idea of a more reliable print culture displacing an older oral one is an influential construct that Defoe helped to create—and at times of crisis, the *Journal* shows, the oral underpinnings of modern print culture reveal themselves in surprising ways.

"RIDICULOUS LEGENDS, CALL'D BILLS OF MORTALITY"

In a scene in *Due Preparations*, Defoe depicts two brothers debating the extent to which the Bills of Mortality can be trusted. When the "1st Brother" points out an apparent decrease in the number of plague deaths, the "2nd Brother" expresses surprise that his sibling "should lay any stress upon what [the bills] say." He notes that the seemingly impersonal data presented in the bills have fallible human origins—"the searchers and parish officers," who can be bribed: "people get their dead put in of other distempers, that their houses may not be marked or ordered to be shut up; they bribe the searchers and parish officers."[15] This exchange develops into a discussion of the serious stakes of trusting print. The first brother states, "I take things always for true when authority publishes them," but the second brother is more cautious: "I am for being imposed on by nobody, especially in a case that so nearly touches my life, as this does."[16] While the first brother holds that texts printed by "authority" must be true, the second brother prides himself on being an astute critical reader alert to the origins of printed texts. In set pieces like this one, Defoe frankly addresses the current fragility of public trust in print, and he suggests that if the nation is about to experience another plague, the government must shore up the foundations of the Bills of Mortality—or this fragile, not yet fully established trust in print will collapse.

In the *Journal*, inaccurate printed information makes an already-terrible situation worse. Whenever the citizens of London see a decrease in the number of reported plague deaths, they react foolishly, calling out to neighbors whom they had been trying to avoid: "they . . . ask'd . . . if they had heard the good News, that the Plague was abated" (190). The citizens respond to the bills with excited "talk," but their overhasty oral discourse causes further spreading of the contagion. The government responds to this "thoughtless Humour of the People" by publishing more would-be authoritative texts, giving out "printed Directions, spreading them all over the City." But these printed texts are ineffectual, for the erroneous bills have already done their damage. The people were "so surpriz'd with the Satisfaction of seeing a vast Decrease in the weekly Bills, that they were impenetrable" (177).

The seeming transparency of the bills suggests a neat chain of collected evidence, but contemporary discussions of the procedures for collecting this government-authorized information reveal a more complex dynamic. Most strikingly, these accounts make clear the central role of "antient Matrons" in this process. The statistician John Graunt, in his *Natural and Political Observations . . . Upon the Bills of Mortality* (1662) and *Reflections on the Weekly Bills of Mortality* (1665), provides the most detailed contemporary accounts. (These texts were immediately available to Defoe in *A Collection of Very Valuable and Scarce Pieces Relating to the Last Plague* [1721], printed by his own printer, James Roberts, only a few months before Roberts printed the *Journal. A Collection* was also the likely source from which Defoe obtained a copy of the 1665 Orders he then reprinted in the *Journal*.) Graunt estimated that the number of reported plague deaths was at least 25 percent too low, and he warned that "the knowledg[e] even of the numbers, which die of the Plague, is not sufficiently deduced from the meer Report of the Searchers, which onely the Bills afford." He recounts the procedures for the compilation of the bills:

> When any one dies, then, either by tolling, or ringing of a Bell, or by bespeaking of a Grave of the *Sexton*, the same is known to the *Searchers*, corresponding with the said *Sexton*.
>
> The *Searchers* hereupon (who are antient Matrons, sworn to their Office) repair to the place, where the dead Corps lies, and by view of the same, and by other enquiries, they examine by what *Disease*, or *Casualty* the Corps died. Hereupon they make their Report to the *Parish-Clerk*, and he, every *Tuesday* night, carries in an Accompt of all the *Burials*, and *Christnings*, hapning that Week, to the *Clerk* of the *Hall*. On *Wednesday* the general Accompt is made up, and Printed, and on *Thursdays* published, and dispersed.[17]

The women searchers physically examined the bodies where they lay and, "by view of the same," reached their interpretive verdicts concerning cause of death. They then orally delivered their report to the parish clerk, who wrote it down, and once a week the clerk delivered his tally to the hall of the Company of Parish Clerks. The records from the various parishes were then collated, and the "general Accompt" was "Printed, . . . published, and dispersed." This movement across different forms of communication, from oral report to written tally to printed bill, recalls the movement of rumors we saw in the opening paragraphs of the *Journal*. In this instance, however, the status of the information changes from oral, female, and inevitably subjective to printed, male, and seemingly authoritative. The final product, the printed bills, wholly obscures the searchers' verdicts and the interpretive work on which they were based.[18] (As H.F. himself admits, the symptoms of bubonic plague were easily confused with those of other diseases, and sometimes there were no signs at all: "it is impossible to know the infected People from the sound" [151].)

The government relied on women searchers well into the nineteenth century, until the position became defunct as a consequence of the Registration Act of 1836. As Walter George Bell observes, "I imagine that few people realize . . . how long was the dependence upon . . . 'searchers of the dead' for vital statistics. The old-women searchers, with their right of intrusion into the house of bereavement, exercised their office down to . . . 1836."[19] As the 1665 order for the appointment of women searchers makes clear, the official searchers were always women, for modesty norms prevented men from searching female bodies (but not the reverse). The searchers were also typically poor, frequently parish pensioners who were expected to perform these services in return for support. The Orders of 1592 state that any woman "fayling to doe that service, shall not have any Pension owt of the hospitall [or Parish]."[20] The searchers were also closely associated with illiteracy; as late as 1799, a concerned clergyman complained that "persons are appointed who cannot *write*" and that the searchers did not report directly to parish clerks but rather "trust to memory till they get home; then, child or neighbour writes what they suppose it to be."[21] These women were prohibited from seeking any other employment, and as contemporary illustrations show, they were required to carry long rods to indicate their regular contact with disease. Yet despite their pariah status, the searchers' job duties effectively put them in charge of quarantine. On the basis of their verdicts, entire households could be shut up for a month. These verdicts were also the source of the statistics printed in the bills: "They gave the information to which every statement in the Bills of Mortality is traced back."[22]

How exactly does Defoe handle the women searchers in his historical fiction? As I have mentioned, he reprints the plague Orders of 1665, which take up "a little over one-thirtieth of the entire book."[23] Issued in various forms since at least 1577, the Orders included instructions for the appointment of a set of officials from the citizenry. Here is the directive for the appointment of women searchers as it appears in Defoe's text:

> THAT there be a special care to appoint Women-Searchers in every Parish, such as are of honest Reputation, and of the best Sort as can be got in this kind: And these to be sworn to make due Search, and true Report to the utmost of their Knowledge, whether the Persons whose Bodies they are appointed to Search, do die of the Infection, or of what other Diseases, as near as they can. And that the Physicians who shall be appointed for Cure and Prevention of the Infection, do call before them the said Searchers, who are, or shall be appointed for the several Parishes under their respective Care; to the end they may consider, whether they are fitly qualified for that Employment; and charge them from time to time as they shall see Cause, if they appear defective in their Duties.
>
> That no Searcher during this time of Visitation, be permitted to use any publick Work or Employment, or keep any Shop or Stall, or be employed as a Landress, or in any other common Employment whatsoever. (37)

As I have also noted, this is the only time in the *Journal* when Defoe names the women searchers or suggests that there was a position held by "Searchers" as distinct from "Examiners"[24] or that searching was a job performed by women. H.F. is vague in specifying the procedures for determining cause of death; he typically refers to this process in the passive voice (the houses were searched) or refers to those searching as an indeterminate "they." His terminology blurs matters further. Historically, the word "searcher" was interchangeable with "visitor," but he merges "visitor" and "examiner" and elides the searchers. At the same time, he substantially enhances the role and numbers of the (male) examiners. (He briefly serves as an examiner himself.) He claims that "there were two Examiners to every District or Precinct" and that his parish had "no less than eighteen Examiners" (135, 128). (Like so many aspects of Defoe's historical fiction, these numbers have no basis in reality; rather, they are idealistic, intended to serve as a template for future practice.) H.F. is also vague about his duties as an examiner, yet he is clear about what examiners did not do. He insists that "the Examiners can not be supposed . . . to go into . . . Houses to visit and search" (135). At one ludicrous moment, he proposes that the best way to determine the cause of death was to stand outside houses suspected to harbor the plague and ask the neighbors: "we were no way capable of coming at the

Knowledge of the true state of any Family, but by enquiring at the Door, or of the Neighbours; as for going into every House to search, that was a part, no Authority wou'd offer to impose on the Inhabitants" (133). Yet Defoe is correct that examiners—as opposed to searchers—investigated general circumstances, not actual bodies. The Orders directs that examiners "enquire and learn from time to time what *Houses* in every Parish be Visited, and what Persons be Sick . . . as near as they can inform themselves" (36, my emphasis). Still, historians of the plague have concluded that examiners were in reality few in number. As H.F. notes, "I got myself discharg'd of the dangerous Office . . . as soon as I cou'd" (135).

On 18 November 1721, *Applebee's Original Weekly Journal* published a letter by one "Tom Beadle," who rails against "those ridiculous Legends, call'd Bills of Mortality." (This issue has been attributed to Defoe.)[25] One reason that Mr. Beadle links the bills with erroneous oral discourse may be that their "Foundations" were in fact oral. The printed bills are held to be no more reliable than "ridiculous Legends" precisely because they stem from the oral reports of old women. Mr. Beadle places the blame for the bills' unreliability squarely on the searchers and the negligent (male) parish clerks to whom they report. In one sentence, he uses the phrase "old Women" twice, once to refer to the searchers and once to the male clerks who transcribe—or invent—the searchers' verdicts: "the Searchers are a sort of old Women, Ignorant, Negligent; that many times the Clarks, who are not above half a Degree better old Women than the Searchers, often supply the Searchers Office, and put the Dead down of what comes next in their Heads." (We encounter the same gendering of unreliable male individuals as old women in the *Journal*, when Defoe refers to men who participate in suspect oral traditions as "*old Women* too" [21].) Like the second brother in *Due Preparations*, Mr. Beadle is convinced that the "greatest Fraud" of the bills is "from the ignorance of the Searchers, and the slight Inquiries they make after the Fact." Furthermore, until this problem is itself "Search'd into," neither the bills nor any "Calculations" based on them will be credible: "till this is Detected, and Search'd into, I expect nothing can be depended on from our Bills of Mortality." Printed texts published by the authority of the government need to be established on a firmer "Foundation" than oral reports. The searchers' verdicts—here understood as old women's unreliable oral testimony—are an embarrassingly weak link in the authority of the would-be modern government that prints the bills as truth.

Yet the truth claims of the women searchers were always already under suspicion. The 1665 Orders requires that only women of "honest Reputation" be appointed and that these women be "sworn to make due Search, and true Report." Why this suspicion of new appointees, even though these pensioners presumably had no previous records of false reporting? The answer, I propose, lies at least partly in long-standing cultural assumptions about old women and oral discourse. As I suggested in chapter 1, in early modern England, old women's words were inherently under suspicion. In juridical and other environments the testimony of old men might still be trusted, but "for female witnesses, the phrase 'old poor woman' was a marker of discredit."[26] Gender stereotypes are also evident in the etymology of "gossip": historically, a gossip was a companion invited to be present at a birth, but the term came to denote "[a] person, mostly a woman, of light and trifling character, esp. one who delights in idle talk; a newsmonger, a tattler."[27] Defoe's erasure of the women searchers has much to do with these traditional stereotypes of women's speech, and it is also related to his representation of cunning-women and female prognosticators elsewhere in this text. Like the female interpreters of dreams and clouds whom H.F. runs into on the streets, the women searchers interpreted signs on the body that could be read without literacy. But the searchers' oral reports were later printed, and thus their always-already-suspect interpretations had long-term consequences for the credibility of print: the Bills of Mortality that would "convey . . . [their] Contents for Ages to come."

"ADDICTED TO . . . OLD WIVES TALES"

While Defoe (nearly) erases the women searchers and their oral verdicts in the *Journal*, other varieties of orality and aurality seem to seep out everywhere else in this text. The book is characterized by a pervasive concern with sound, especially paralinguistic vocalizations such as "dying Groans," "dismal Shrieks," and "lamentable Cries" (33, 50, 65):

> The Voice of Mourning was truly heard in the Streets; the shriecks [*sic*] of Women and Children at the Windows, and Doors of their Houses, where their dearest Relations were, perhaps dying, or just dead, were so frequent to be heard, as we passed the Streets, that it was enough to pierce the stoutest Heart in the World, to hear them. (18)

H.F. wants more than anything else to make us hear the plague:

> I wish I could repeat the very Sound of those Groans, and of those Exclamations that I heard from some poor dying Creatures, when in the Hight [*sic*] of their Agonies and Distress; and that I could make him that read

this hear; as I imagine I now hear them, for the Sound seems still to Ring in my Ears. (86)

Even visual horrors register themselves aurally. As a church sexton says to H.F. of the burial pits, "['T]will be a Sermon to you . . . the best that ever you heard in your Life. 'Tis a speaking Sight" (54).

Paul K. Alkon suggests that Defoe's appeal to "the reader's aural imagination" in the *Journal* is "calculated to diminish his readers' sense of distance between themselves and 1665,"[28] but I would point out that while Defoe does temporarily allow us to get caught up in H.F.'s narrative, he also constantly reminds us that we are reading a written account penned long after the fact. Defoe could have depicted H.F. orally relating a story "as it happens," but instead he emphasizes that H.F.'s story is mediated by time, memory, and, above all, writing. As H.F. says, "I remember, and while I am writing this Story, I think I hear the very Sound of it" (50). He draws on oral stories, but he also tries to construct a hierarchical relation between mere oral tales and authoritative written truth. A saddler by trade, he nonetheless surrounds himself with books: "Such intervals as I had, I employed in reading Books, and in writing down my Memorandums of what occurred to me every Day" (65). His journal is filled with references to the materiality of writing: "I have set this particular down so fully, because . . ." (11). He purportedly draws on memories, yet he also foregrounds the inadequacy of memory: "As to the poor Man whether he liv'd or dy'd I don't remember" (129).

H.F. especially distances his account from oral rumors. He could fill his journal with such tales, he says, but he will not. Adam Fox argues for the cultural centrality of the "grapevine, or the spreading of news or information by word of mouth." This phenomenon, while "of the utmost importance in the dissemination of intelligence and report," still has not "received the historical attention which it deserves."[29] In the *Journal*, Defoe thematizes the workings of the grapevine and shows its centrality—danger—as a social force. At times of crisis, the scope for unfounded stories is immense, and H.F. explores in detail how rumors originate, function, and spread. He theorizes three key characteristics of rumors: they obscure their origins, feed on circumstantial details, and grow with each telling. He especially considers "Innumerable Stories . . . of the cruel Behaviours and Practises of Nurses, who tended the Sick" (55). These stories were "always placed . . . at the farther End of the Town, opposite, or most remote from where you were to hear it" (71), and "the Particulars were always the same, especially that of laying a wet double Clout on a dying Man's Face" (72). He ultimately decides that "there was more of Tale than of Truth in those Things" (72).

Oral rumors are themselves a kind of plague, for they make a bad situation worse. The deaths of two citizens near the meat market give rise to "a Rumor that the Meat was all infected . . . and spoil'd the Market for two or three Days." Rumors do their damage whether or not they are true, for "no Body can account for the Possession of Fear when it takes hold of the Mind" (188). They are not only plague-like but themselves transmitters of the plague, for, like most of his contemporaries, Defoe believed that plague effluvia were spread by breath. In his *Diary*, Samuel Pepys describes the experience of walking through the streets during the plague, desperately trying to avoid having to speak to others: "And Lord, to see how I did endeavour all I could to talk with as few as I could."[30] Defoe explicitly compared the movement of the contagion to the movement of spoken words: "The effluvia of infected bodies may, and must be indeed, conveyed from one to another by air; so words are conveyed from the mouth of the speaker to the ear of the hearer."[31] In the *Journal*, different meanings of conversing overlap: physical intimacy or proximity generates familiar talk. H.F. repeatedly links uncontained oral discourse and death, theorizing that the "ordinary Way of Infection" is "unwary conversing with those who were sick" (153). While some Londoners leave the city, others do not leave soon enough, "till by openly conversing with the other People their Neighbours, they had the Distemper upon them" (118). Writing enables distance, whereas oral communication means risking contact with the disease: "the Plague is not to be avoided by those that converse promiscuously in a Town infected" (151).

Alternately engulfed in and frightened by the soundscape of the plague, H.F. appears to retreat from memories of the frightening oral-aural world to the safe distance of his written text. His narrative is characterized by long passages of immersion in different types of oral discourse followed by a sudden emphasis on his writing. In one instance, he recalls how he came upon a poor disconsolate man who had been rendered nearly "mute" by grief. The gentleman was brought to Pye Tavern, but there a "dreadful Set of Fellows" assailed him with "impudent Mocks and Jeers," "taunt[ing] him with want of Courage to leap into the great Pit." H.F. dwells on the dreadful fellows' "ill Language and Oaths," "profane, and even blasphemous Expressions," and "cursing and swearing in a dreadful Manner," noting that he tried to intervene but that "so far from putting a Checque to their horrid Way of speaking . . . it made them rail the more." But the technology of writing will enable him to selectively erase what he has already partly forgotten about the past: "nor if I could remember, would I fill my Account with any of the Words, the horrid Oaths, Curses, and vile Expressions, such, as at that time of the Day, even the worst and ordinariest People in the Street would not use" (56–58).

H.F. sharply distances himself from vulgar oral street culture, even as he records this culture in great detail. In a memorable set piece on superstitious oral discourse, he claims that "the People . . . were more addicted to Prophesies, and Astrological Conjurations, Dreams, and old Wives Tales, than ever they were before or since" (21). It is significant that the trigger for this set piece is a step back in time in H.F.'s account. For Defoe, vulgar oral discourse is always associated with a backward past. H.F. says, "I must go back again to the Beginning of this Surprizing Time, while the Fears of the People were young" (20). At this point the plague has not yet arrived in London, but rumors of its impending arrival are circulating. The most superstitious forms of oral street culture appear to flourish (or is it that H.F.'s heightened state of anxiety suddenly makes these omnipresent voices more audible?). Religious enthusiasts "run about the Streets, with their Oral Predictions," and mountebanks and quack doctors hawk magical remedies. These retailers of superstitious oral discourse are not merely foolish but villainous: "Oracles of the Devil" who "bewitch'd the poor common People" (22, 27, 29). ("Oracle" stems from the Latin *orare*, "to speak.") The "common People" run about "to Fortune tellers, Cunning-men, and Astrologers, to know their Fortune, or, as 'tis vulgarly express'd, to have their Fortunes told them." These trades grow "so generally practised, that it became common to have Signs and Inscriptions set up at Doors; here lives a Fortune-teller" (26). Trade signs depict legendary women and men associated with prophetic speech, such as Mother Shipton, the cunning-woman of English folklore, or Roger Bacon, a medieval magus reputed to have possessed a brass head that could talk. Disembodied and brainless yet still able to exercise influence through foolish speech, "Fryar Bacon's Brazen-Head" was for Defoe an apt symbol for the superstitious oral discourse of the common people, who turned "mad, upon their running after Quacks, and Mountebanks, and every practising old Woman, for Medicines and Remedies" (26, 29).

The cultural response to this superstitious oral discourse is socially stratified: "the midling People, and the working labouring Poor . . . threw away their Money in a most distracted Manner" (27). The response is also gendered, for old women are the most superstitious. The "Heavens" are full of portents that can be read without literacy, and old women play a central role in this type of interpretive work: "the Dreams of old Women: Or, I should say, the Interpretation of old Women upon other Peoples Dreams . . . put abundance of People even out of their Wits" (22). H.F. does not reject the possibility that God could speak through portents; rather, he prides himself on being a cautious observer, and he especially mistrusts these women as interpreters of divine signs.[32] Under their guidance or misguidance, the people are "poreing continually at the Clouds," seeing "Shapes and Figures, Representations and Appearances," such as "Coffins in the Air" (22–23). H.F. sees a "Crowd of People in the Street" and discovers his fellow citizens

> all staring up into the Air, to see what a Woman told them appeared plain to her, which was an Angel cloth'd in white, with a fiery Sword in his Hand, waving it, or brandishing it over his Head. She described every Part of the Figure to the Life; shew'd them the Motion, and the Form; and the poor People came into it so eagerly, and with so much Readiness; YES, *I see it all plainly*, says one. (23)

As I have suggested in chapter 1, Defoe himself often associated the telling of fortunes, fables, legends, and "merry Tales" with old women. In his treatise on the occult, *A System of Magick* (1727), he observes, "We have abundance of merry Tales scatter'd abroad in the Oral Tradition of antient times, and among those antient things called *Old Women.*"[33] It is no accident that he uses the word "antient" here twice, for as I have suggested, he ideologically associated even living oral tradition with a backward past. In the *Journal*, H.F.'s association of old women and superstitious oral discourse is so strong that when men participate without caution in these conversations, H.F. calls them "*old Women* too":

> A blazing Star or Comet appear'd for several Months before the Plague, . . . the old Women, and the Phlegmatic Hypocondriac Part of the other Sex, who I could almost call *old Women* too, remark'd . . . that those two Comets pass'd directly over the City, and that so very near the Houses, that it was plain, they imported something peculiar to the City alone. (20–21)

(We have seen this gesture in the *Applebee's* issue attributed to Defoe, where the writer, addressing the problem of the women searchers, refers to the careless male clerks who recorded or invented their verdicts as "not above half a Degree better old Women than the Searchers" themselves.)

The theme of this section is the apparent explosion of erroneous oral discourse, but there is also a sharp increase in certain kinds of cheap print. H.F. condemns first oral modes and then print genres (such as almanacs) that he sees as linked to superstitious oral discourse. Of the people's addiction to "old Wives Tales," he remarks, "Whether this unhappy Temper was originally raised by the Follies of some People who got Money by . . . printing Predictions, and Prognostications I know not; but certain it is, Book's frighted them terribly; such as Lilly's Almanack, Gadbury's A[stro]logical

Predictions; Poor Robin's Almanack and the like" (21). Elsewhere, he works to distinguish between mere oral "Stories" and purportedly credible print, but at moments like this one, the reality of mutual interaction asserts itself against the proposed divide. The government tries to suppress these superstitious print genres, just as it tried to shut down dangerous sites and practices of public oral discourse (coffeehouses, taverns, the singing of ballads). But they too prove impossible to contain: "Some Endeavors were used to suppress the Printing of such Books as terrify'd the People, and to frighten the dispersers of them, some of whom were taken up, but nothing was done in it. . . . The Government being unwilling to exasperate the People, who were, as I may say, all out of their Wits already" (25). The government then attempts to counter illegitimate oral discourse with authorized print: "having seen the foolish Humour of the People, in running after Quacks, and Mountebanks, Wizards, and Fortune-tellers. . . . The Lord Mayor . . . order'd the College of Physicians to publish Directions for cheap Remedies, for the Poor." But, significantly, these directions printed "by Authority" turn out to be no more credible than "old Wives Tales": "the very Physicians were seized with [the plague]" (33–34).

After relating stories of oral street culture for thirteen pages, H.F. suddenly exclaims, "I might spend a great deal of Time in my Exclamations against the Follies, and indeed Wickedness of those things. . . . But my Memorandums of these things relate rather to take notice only of the Fact" (32). Emphasizing that he is writing, not telling, a story, he brings this set piece on illegitimate oral discourse to a close by pointedly announcing the arrival of the plague: "I am supposing now, the Plague to be begun" (33). The structural organization suggests a causal relation: the people's addiction to "old Wives Tales" seems to trigger the arrival of the plague. Abruptly moving on—as if to put the escaped oral back in its place—he then immediately reprints the 1665 Orders for the containment of the contagion (36–43). Structurally creating a before and after of superstitious oral discourse and would-be authoritative print, H.F. temporarily displaces this unsettling outburst of popular oral discourse with the printed dictates of a would-be ordered city.

And, in fact, in H.F.'s account the arrival of the plague seems to kill off oral street culture. H.F. claims that none of the superstitious strategies that the people turned to worked: "the poor People found the Insufficiency of those things, and . . . many of them were afterwards carried away in the Dead Carts" (32). At least three times he mentions the "silen[cing]" of superstitious oral discourse. It is not clear whether this silencing really happens or whether it is his wishful thinking. In one instance, he speculates that "the Hand of Divine Justice" has struck down the offending parties:

One thing I cannot omit here, and indeed I thought it was extraordinary, at least, it seemed a remarkable Hand of Divine Justice, (*viz*) That all the Predictors, Astrologers, Fortune-tellers, and what they call'd cunning-Men, Conjurers, and the like; calculators of Nativities, and dreamers of Dreams, and such People, were gone and vanish'd, not one of them was to be found: . . . *now they were silent* [my emphasis] . . . some have been critical enough to say, that every one of them dy'd; I dare not affirm that, but this I must own, that I never heard of one of them that ever appear'd after the Calamity was over. (141–42)

Later he again models the silencing of erroneous oral discourse: "As for Quackery and Mountebank, of which the Town was so full, I listened to none of them, and have observ'd often since with some Wonder, that for two Years after the Plague, I scarcely saw or heard of one of them about Town." Yet this phoenix-like culture again proves itself not really dead: "*Solomon Eagle* the naked Quaker . . . prophesy'd evil Tidings every Day" (186, 187). Oral culture is never really displaced; rather, the text repeatedly models its disappearance.

H.F. struggles to reject mere oral "Stories" in favor of empirical evidence and written records. Yet, as he himself notes, even the printed texts to which he turns to reconstruct the plague—the bills—are built on the foundation of oral reports. Although he strives to be modern in the face of older ways of seeing and coping (at least after he too tries to read the "Signs of the Heavens"), in the end he reaffirms certain traditional ways of seeing the world. John J. Richetti suggests that "H.F.'s narrative is the unfolding of a mystery and its reduction to facts—statistics, measurements, causes and effects."[34] But ultimately, H.F. concludes that the plague is not wholly explicable in empirical terms. In the end, he relies on both natural and supernatural explanations of the plague, and at the conclusion of his narrative it is the mystery that is given the prime place. In keeping with my argument that Defoe attempted to make print more credible by modeling it as separate from certain types of oral discourse, H.F. associates the opposition between suspect oral discourse and reliable writing with that between supernatural and empirical or natural explanations: "If I should say, that this is a visible Summons to us all to Thankfulness . . . perhaps it may be thought by some . . . an officious canting of religious things, preaching a Sermon instead of writing a History" (191–92). Again, media forms that are in reality copresent and interdependent are modeled as in some sense competing with each other. H.F.'s ultimate turn to supernatural explanation will, he fears, expose him to the charge of cant (yet another variety of the corrupt oral discourse that he has tried hard to dissociate himself from throughout the *Journal*).

In the final sentence of his narrative, H.F. explicitly reconnects himself to written record, referring again to the "Memorandums" on which his account is based. But then, in an unexpected move, he concludes in verse: "a coarse but sincere Stanza of my own, which I plac'd at the end of my ordinary Memorandums, the same Year they were written":

> A dreadful Plague in London *was,*
>> In the Year Sixty Five,
> *Which swept an Hundred Thousand Souls*
>> *Away; yet I alive!*
>
>   H.F. (193)

While Defoe was an accomplished poet, his saddler character pointedly is not. Today the hauntingly awkward verse with which H.F. concludes his narrative may serve as a timely reminder of the uneven development of literacy and access to written and printed texts in early modern England and so as a caution against narratives of the displacement of orality by writing and/or print. H.F.'s narrative began with an oral rumor, and it ends with a hybrid form indebted to both orality and literacy: a written ballad. His "coarse Stanza" is a traditional ballad stanza (alternating iambic tetrameter and trimeter lines rhyming *abcb*), a poetic form historically inseparable from oral expression but here also indebted to the visual organizing structures of the written or printed page. Throughout the *Journal*, H.F. has worked to rewrite the past of a culture still plagued by unruly orality in the new, idealized image of a print-oriented civic order, and his modeling of a binary divide between "those Days" and "now" is indicative of Defoe's larger contribution to evolutionary models of orality and literacy. But the endings of Defoe's fictions typically reject easy binaries, and H.F.'s hybrid stanza reminds us that binary models of media shift have never done justice to the complexity of actual lived experience. What we see at such moments is that there is no real divide between orality and literacy as H.F. would have it—only the eighteenth-century emergence of an enormously influential progressive narrative of media shift that would remodel a reciprocal, living relation as a historical fiction of "then" and "now."

CHAPTER FOUR

Oratory Transactions:
John "Orator" Henley and His Critics

Preach on, Great Orator, but Printing dread:
Thy Jargon spoke seems sense; 'tis nonsense read.
—*Grub-Street Journal* 63 (18 March 1731)

Glowing over the sales figures of the *Spectator* (1711–14), Joseph Addison enthused: "It was said of *Socrates*, that he brought Philosophy down from Heaven, to inhabit among Men; and I shall be ambitious to have it said of me, that I have brought philosophy out of Closets and Libraries, Schools and Colleges, to dwell in Clubs and Assemblies, at Tea-Tables, and in Coffee-Houses."[1] Like Addison, this chapter is concerned with the travels of philosophy across the sometimes-daunting distances of social rank, gender, and, especially, literacy. But whereas Mr. Spectator memorably described himself as a "Silent Man" who preferred to "write [him]self out,"[2] this chapter considers another early eighteenth-century author who developed a new commercial venue for *oral* exchange while also exploiting print. As Addison's comment on "Clubs and Assemblies" and "Coffee-Houses" suggests, the early eighteenth century saw the proliferation of new venues for oral discourse. It also saw the reign of their feminized, domestic counterpart, the "Tea-Table," which inspired Eliza Haywood's imitation of the *Spectator*, the *Tea-Table* (1725). But while these polite venues have received substantial attention from scholars, another new venue for oral discussion and debate remains neglected: the "oratory." As a few pioneering historians have suggested, the later eighteenth century saw a rage for public debating societies: "rational entertainments" where men (and sometimes women) of limited formal education paid a small entrance fee to hear and share views on religion, politics, and society.[3] This chapter, by way of contrast, considers an individual who I argue was of central importance to the emergence and institutionalization of these societies—an individual who was famous in his time but is now almost completely neglected by scholars.

This individual is John "Orator" Henley (1692–1756), a notorious preacher-cum-entrepreneur who for thirty years ran a public oratory in the heart of working London. Henley was an ordained minister of the Church of England, but in 1725 he openly broke with the church in order to pursue a grand scheme of setting up a new kind of religious and educational institution in the metropolis: "a New Institute of ye Sciences, School Learning & ye Classicks" that would "have a larger Compass than any other Institution of ye Kind that has been set on foot."[4] In 1724, before his secession from the church, Henley preached a sermon that anticipated his later nickname as "the Restorer of Antient Eloquence." This sermon, printed as *The History and Advantages of divine Revelation with the Honour, that is due to the Word of God; especially in regard to the most Perfect Manner of delivering it, form'd on the Antient Laws of Speaking and Action* (1725),[5] began as a conventional account of revealed religion, but it developed into a discourse on "the oratory of the pulpit"—and, remarkably, into an advertisement for a project to advance a new Baconian "system" of effective public speaking. Henley argued that to spread the "Word of God" effectively, Anglican preachers needed to pay greater attention to the oral delivery of their sermons. In addressing the topic of "pulpit eloquence," he followed in the footsteps of authors such as Addison and Richard Steele in the *Tatler* (1709–10) and the *Spectator*, who debated the propriety of the use of "action," or gesture, in the pulpit.[6] But Henley took a far greater risk than Addison and Steele did when he stood *in* a pulpit and suggested that the Church of England and the universities that trained (or failed to train) its ministers had neglected their duty. Effective oral delivery, he proposed, must now be treated as "a distinct science." Aspects of oral communication such as tone, pitch, motions of the body, and glances of the eye must be coordinated with "mathematical" precision, because "the precise fitness of one certain sound and movement of the . . . person, even to a line of the countenance, to one certain thing . . . [is] as demonstrable, as any proposition in the Mathematicks."[7]

About eighteen months after Henley preached this sermon marketing a "science" of oral delivery, he opened the Oratory in a rented room on the top floor of the Market House at Newport Market. For the next three decades, he supported himself by means of this unique freelance operation and a host of coordinated print publications. Taking advantage of the Toleration Act, which allowed the legal right of private worship to Protestant Dissenters under specified conditions, he registered the Oratory as a place of worship.[8] Henley always understood the Oratory to be a religious institution, but critics argued that he had taken advantage of the new laws to license an entirely new kind of public forum: one more aptly described as a "Temple of Rebellion" or "farce-house" than a church. Henley responded that he was a "Restorer," not a renegade: a restorer not only of the arts of "Antient Eloquence" but also of the "Primitive Church." The Church of England had strayed too far from the primitive church of the apostles, and he was merely working to restore it to its original, purer path. In justifying his break with the church, he argued that it was the Anglican episcopacy, not himself, that was guilty of "schism": "when I subscrib'd to the Church of *England*, I did it as far as I thought her Primitive; I am still the same; and I now dissent from her, only as she dissents from her self, and the Primitive Church."[9]

Henley also envisioned the Oratory as an educational institution. Fired with a passion for teaching public speaking, he proceeded with a Baconian confidence in the ability of new methodologies to transform society at every level. At a time when there was little, if any, support for government-sponsored public education, and literacy was by no means considered a universal good, he argued that there was a need for a new kind of educational establishment in the metropolis: one that would be available to a much broader spectrum of the population. His planned "Universal Academy" would be "beneficial to the public, to every rank of mankind."[10] Over the years, the Oratory offered a weekly program of sermons, "academical lectures," "conferences," and "disputations" on topics so diverse as to anticipate a modern university. Henley argued that there was no real separation between "religious" and "profane" subjects; accordingly, discussion of subjects such as mathematics, natural philosophy, logic, rhetoric, and belles lettres was within the scope of an ostensibly religious institution. "This is an ecclesiastical institution," he explained, "but, since the holy Bible and theology cannot be understood without all the other arts and sciences, it will also take in, on a religious footing, an academy of the sciences and languages."[11]

Predictably, given the Oratory's initial location above a meat market, satirists depicted Henley as the "Billingsgate and Butcher's Champion" and the "BULL BEEF ORATOR," preaching to meat porters who "rang Peals of *Marrow-Bones* and *Cleavers* to their Orator's Praise" and "greasy butchers [who] snore for pence" (as well as to hungry "dogs [who] snarl Amen").[12] Today Henley is remembered as the butt of Alexander Pope, who similarly suggested that Oratory audiences consisted of blaspheming butchers: "But fate with butchers plac'd thy priestly stall, / Meek modern faith to murder, hack, and maul."[13] But as Graham Midgley—Henley's only dedicated scholar to date—insists, despite Pope's skewering of him in the *Dunciad*,

"Henley was no obscure . . . dunce. . . . He was a famous figure in his day, a constant talking-point in London for thirty years, a prominent part of the life of the metropolis. Chat in a coffee-house, read a newspaper, visit a pamphlet shop, and, sooner or later, Orator Henley would crop up."[14] It is significant that Henley was satirized not only by Pope but also by most of the major English literary authors of his time. In 1730 Henry Fielding prominently featured Henley as "Dr. Orator" in his play *The Author's Farce*. Twenty years later, poet Christopher Smart took to the London stage in women's clothing, at once satirizing and imitating Henley's multimedia methods in his own oratorical venue, "The Old Woman's Oratory, or, *Henley in Petticoats*" (1751–52), and his coordinated periodical *The Midwife: Or, The Old Woman's Magazine* (1750–53).

Henley's Oratory experiment also brought him to the attention of powerful political and religious authorities. From the venue's opening days, church and government leaders (including the bishop of London, the attorney general, and the secretary of state) worked to shut it down. Henley's beliefs grew more and more heterodox over the years, and his Oratory programs grew explicitly politicized. Although he initially castigated "Deism," he came to approve some arguments that we would now label as "Deist." By the mid-1740s he was openly challenging the credibility of scripture and the validity of any kind of episcopal authority and holding advertised public debates on topics such as whether "there ever was such a Person as Jesus Christ."[15] By 1729 a popular feature at the Oratory was its Friday night "Chimes of the Times," a satirical event in which Henley commented orally on political news as reported in the weekly newspapers. (In so doing, he spread the contents of these papers to illiterate and literate persons alike.) Part of the Oratory's attraction was its medley of religion, politics, education, and entertainment. Henley defended his right to free political expression. As he observed in a manuscript lecture note, "ye Pulpit has always been a Warlike Place."[16] He argued that the teaching of the established church that Christ had "left Civil Government as he found it" and that, therefore, British subjects should do the same was an ideological tactic "to bite and bully ye people—to cheat them into order."[17] The separation of religion and politics was a fiction—one that currently favored the status quo.

Henley's development from a "Restorer" of the primitive church to a vocal religious, political, and social radical who ultimately came to reject all episcopal authority and supernatural tenets of the faith deserves far more attention than I can give it in this book devoted to examining the relationship of print commerce and the "invention of the oral." His liminal position as a self-exile from the church who continued to wear clerical habit even as he made a living excoriating "the coercive power of the church . . . over the bodies, lives, and fortunes of men"[18] allows us to see what happened to the more tentative theorizing of some of his more cautious (and better connected) contemporaries when these ideas were handled at the popular (and commercial) level. The Oratory served as a test case for the Toleration Act. Henley was arrested at least twice, but the government struggled to find laws that would allow them to shut down the Oratory permanently. On a third occasion, the Grand Jury of Middlesex found a true bill against Henley, but this time, the authorities did not take him into custody. Instead, they took the unusual step of printing the presentment against him in the public newspapers—presumably in the hope that by declaring the Oratory to be "an Offence to all serious Christians, . . . an Outrage upon civil Society, and of dangerous Consequence to the State"[19] they would frighten away audiences from this new forum. Not surprisingly, this plan backfired. With each new confrontation with the government, Henley's notoriety grew—and he grew angrier and more outspoken.

But it was not so much Henley's "dangerous," "blasphemous," and "licentious" ideas in themselves that most alarmed his contemporaries. Rather, I argue, it was the radically public, semi-institutionalized venue in which he expressed those ideas on a regular basis, and the multimedia methods that he devised to do so. It was Henley's institutional and media experiment, and the coordinated program of orations and print publications that he developed to reach across social divisions of rank, sex, and literacy, that made him a threat to the status quo in his own time—and make him of renewed interest and importance to us today. Henley treated freethinking as a methodology—"a rational process by which truth is discovered"[20]—and he attempted to build a new kind of public forum around this methodology: a space for religious, political, and educational debate that would be open not only to educated gentlemen but also to persons of both sexes, all ranks, even all "capacities."[21] His aspiration to foster truly public debate on religious, political, and social matters gave rise to his innovative methods—and these methods, in turn, directed new attention to the tool of oral communication. Between 1712 and 1756, Henley experimented with print formats and genres too numerous to list here. His publications include histories and translations, a ten-volume "Universal Grammar," a book-length epic poem, and at least three periodicals: *Oratory Transactions*, the *Oratory Magazine*, and the long-lived weekly *Hyp-Doctor* (1730–42) (which is undeservedly neglected today). But in the realm of print publication, he arguably grew most famous for his innovative use of printed newspapers to advertise the Oratory's oral offerings. Henley published literally hundreds of advertisements, written in what I contend was a purposely eye-catching, idiosyncratic style. Partly in response to this onslaught of advertisements, Henley's print nemesis, the satirical *Grub-Street Journal*, advised him to "Preach on, Great Orator, but Printing dread: / Thy Jargon spoke seems sense; 'tis nonsense read." This remark is obviously intended to be insulting, but it nonetheless provides us with a valuable clue to understanding Henley's modus operandi and his remarkable notoriety. For to read Henley's print publications without also reconstructing his oral career, I argue, is to risk seriously misunderstanding the nature and extent of his contemporary influence and enduring importance.

Henley's contemporaries commented widely on his highly physical manner of preaching. He was spreading his ideas orally and corporeally, as well as in print, and he was doing so in his own charismatic style. At the same time, he was delivering lectures on topics such as "the Art of moving the Passions" and "the general principles of Speaking" and offering to teach the ancient art of elocution to distinctly *new* social groups. His efforts to market effective public speaking as a new tool of power for tradesmen and shopkeepers (and their wives) helped to make his Oratory one of the most talked-about (and alarming) inventions of his generation. In the long term, the success of the Oratory attracted wide-scale public attention to the question of oral discourse: not only its unique characteristics and power but also its new possibilities when used in tandem with the increasingly accessible tool of the press. Only by comparing Henley's print publications to his widely remarked oral-corporeal performances, I suggest (insofar as we can reconstruct those performances from manuscript, print, and visual sources), can we begin to understand why "the Restorer of Antient Eloquence" and his legacy matter.

"FETTERS OF THE FREE-BORN MIND"

Born in 1692, Henley set out to follow in the footsteps of his father and both grandfathers by becoming ordained as a clergyman. In 1709 he was admitted on a fellowship to St. John's College, Cambridge, and four years later he graduated with a bachelor of arts, having learned little, in his opinion, that was of any real use to his chosen profession: "tho' he was brought up for a Clergyman he was not instructed to preach, or pray, or read Prayers, or speak, or catechise, or confer, or resolve a Case of Conscience, or understand the Scriptures."[22] For the rest of his life, Henley reflected critically on his university education. Forty years after leaving Cambridge, he described St. John's as "ye *College* where I had ye *Stupidity* to be educated."[23]

In the inaugural issue of his periodical *Oratory Transactions*, Henley asserted that it was at Cambridge that he began to be

> impatient, that Systems of all Sorts were put into his Hands, ready carv'd out for him, and that he incurr'd the Danger of losing his Interest, as well as incurring the Scandal of Heterodoxy and ill Principles, if (as his Genius led him) he freely disputed all Propositions, and call'd all Points to Account, in order to satisfy and convince his own Reason: It shock'd him, to find that he was *commanded* to believe against his Judgment, in Points of Logic, Philosophy, and Metaphysicks, as well as Religion. . . . He was always impatient under these Fetters of the free-born Mind, and privately resolv'd some Time, or other, to enter his Protest against any Persons being bred like a Slave, who is born an *Englishman*.[24]

As this rousing rhetoric suggests, Henley's critique of "the usual academical Education" was also fundamentally a critique of the Church of England. He criticized the church for its failure to provide practical training to future ministers; more dangerously, he lambasted it for mandating subscription to a "System" rather than teaching critical thinking or even the key issues at the heart of the Christian faith:

> The Examination for Orders was very short and superficial, . . . it is not necessary to conform to the Christian Religion in Order to the Deaconship, or the Priesthood, but to subscribe (whether you have study'd the Matter, or believe it, or no) to the System of the Church; and the Expence of your Education is lost, if you do not subscribe.[25]

Throughout his career, in his orally delivered sermons and lectures as well as his printed texts, he excoriated the "enslaving of youth to subscriptions, tests, and forms, which they neither understand, nor believe, nor approve."[26]

But Henley evidently managed to satisfy prospective employers that he had, in fact, been given a good education, for he never had any trouble finding employment. Immediately after he was ordained, he returned to his birthplace in rural Melton Mowbray and was hired as a minister at the Church of Saint Mary and as a teacher at the local grammar school. In educational matters a reformer rather than a "Restorer," he instituted various changes. He rejected the customary practice of rote learning and drills, preferring instead to require students to give oral reports of their progress so as to develop their speaking skills. According to a later biographical narrative (1729), he "establish'd . . . a Practice of improving Elocution by the public

Speaking of Passages in the Classicks . . . as well as Orations, *&c* . . . . [H]e
likewise settled a Method of making every Scholar learn and give an Account of his Studies, without the Necessity of . . . being examin'd by
particular Questions."[27] In language studies, his preference for showing
languages at work (rather than drilling students on grammar paradigms) influenced one of his earliest publications, *The Compleat Linguist. Or, An
Universal Grammar Of all the Considerable Tongues in Being. In a Shorter,
Clearer, and more Instructive Method than is extant. . . . To be published
Monthly* (10 parts, 1719–26). This series of grammars is the sort of ambitious eighteenth-century publishing endeavor that is easy to satirize now.
But Henley's work has since been described by a modern historian of linguistics as "the first systematic attempt at a polyglot grammar published in
England."[28] Furthermore, his goal of producing a grammar series aimed at
the growing sector of the reading public with limited time and funds fore-
shadows his lifelong commitment to expanding educational opportunities for those without access to elite educational institutions. Henley was
far more learned than contemporary satires (and modern neglect) suggest,
but he was always at heart a popularizer who aspired to make learning ap-
proachable (and indeed possible) for a broad spectrum of the population. In
the case of his *Universal Grammar*[s], he managed to publish ten volumes
priced at one shilling each. Later, after moving to London, he commented
on the difficulty of supervising a regular print publication from outside the
metropolis. In a statement that shows him conceptualizing "the Press" as
an emergent institution as well as a "Machine" or tool, he blamed "the Press,
a fantastical Machine, which no Writer can command" for "those [Errors]
of my Grammars formerly publish'd . . . occasion'd by my great Distance
then from *London*."[29]

Henley's envy of the resources available to "Men of Enquiry" in the
metropolis appears to have influenced his next steps, for in 1721 he "freely,
without Compulsion . . . gave up his Benefice and Lecture"[30] in Melton Mowbray and moved to London. The fact that he once again immediately earned
a number of positions suggests that he was already a talented preacher.
He was appointed as an assistant preacher at Saint John's Chapel, Bedford
Square (1721); reader at Saint George the Martyr, Queen Square (1721);
rector of Chelmondiston in the county of Suffolk (1723); and lecturer at
Saint Mary Abchurch (1723). Most intriguingly, and in need of investigation
by others, in 1722 he was appointed chaplain to Robert, 1st Viscount Moles-
worth, a powerful Whig politician with close associations to the notorious
freethinker John Toland (who died that year).

But in 1723 Edmund Gibson was appointed bishop of London (fl. 1723–48), and Henley's hopes of a London benefice were suddenly cut off. We will never know the initial cause of Gibson's hostility toward Henley, but two things we do know. First, after Henley opened the Oratory, Gibson worked relentlessly to shut it down. Second, Henley loathed Gibson with a passion all his life. In 1748, when Gibson died after holding sway as bishop of London for twenty-five years, Henley virtually crowed about his death.[31] Henley held that Gibson was a powermonger who was outraged by his lack of submissiveness to episcopal authority and jealous of his youthful "Popularity" as a preacher: "This Popularity, with his enterprizing Spirit, and introducing regular Action into the Pulpit, were the true Causes, which some obstructed his rising in Town, from Envy, Jealousy, and a Disrelish of those who are not qualify'd to be compleat Spaniels."[32]

Realizing that further advancement in the Church of England was now barred to him, Henley took the dramatic step of setting out to learn the potential consequences of secession from the church. His choice of advisers here is striking: he wrote to William Whiston (1667–1752), the theologian and mathematician who succeeded Isaac Newton as Lucasian Professor of Mathematics at Cambridge but who was deprived of his professorship and banished from the university for suspected heresy in 1710. Whiston advocated a return to "Primitive Christianity" in his *Primitive Christianity Reviv'd* (5 vols., 1711–12), and it was his primitivism (rather than his Arianism) that attracted Henley. By the time that Henley wrote to him in the 1720s, Whiston was lecturing on astronomy in London halls and coffeehouses. Henley asked the older man what kinds of civil and ecclesiastical consequences he should expect to face if he chose to separate from the Church of England:

> *Reverend* Sir,
>   I Would beg the Favour of you to resolve me, 1. What Power the University has, or in Fact exercises, on Church of *England* Priests, openly separating from that Church? 2. What Processes and Censures Ecclesiastical, and Civil Penalties He incurs by it? 3. What are the most proper Defences to each.[33]

We do not know how Whiston responded, but we do know that the two men corresponded for a time, before their epistolary relationship developed into an ugly public quarrel. For despite Whiston's suspected heresy, he was in fact less unorthodox than Henley. Both men embraced the idea of a return to

the primitive church, and in 1726 Henley published an alternative liturgy, the *Primitive Liturgy* (rev. ed., 1727). But Henley was a far more outspoken critic of episcopal government, and beginning in 1727, Whiston worked
to distance himself from the younger man by publishing an attack on him
and confronting him at the Oratory. Whiston published *Mr. Henley's Letters
and Advertisements, Which concern Mr. Whiston. Published by Mr. Whiston*
(1727), and Henley responded by preaching and printing against Whiston for
the remainder of their long lives. Twenty years after their initial conflict,
Henley compared Whiston to Mother Shipton, the legendary female soothsayer of popular culture: "Mthr. Wh——ton, the ingenious Rival of Mthr.
Shipton."[34]

Henley's *Primitive Liturgy* shocked many of his contemporaries, but it
is not impious; rather, the scandal lay in Henley's positioning in relation to
the established church. Henley's call for a return to the "Primitive Church"
of the apostles was a challenge to the accreted rituals, doctrines, and practices of Anglicanism. In Henley's view, these accretions were without apostolic authority and therefore invalid. On 23 April 1726 the *London Journal*
and other papers announced that Henley had resigned his preferment in the
Church of England. Henley named as his specific ground for registering as
a Dissenter his objection to the practice of infant baptism. The baptizing of
infants who had not yet attained to reason, he declared, was but one egre-
gious example of "the coercive power of the church . . . over the bodies, lives,
and fortunes of men."[35] On 3 July 1726 he preached his first sermon at the
Oratory, and immediately, church and government leaders began trying to
shut it down. Surviving correspondence indicates that Bishop Gibson wrote
to Attorney General Philip Yorke sometime in July alerting him to Henley's
activities. Yorke drafted a response on 1 August, and on 8 September, Gibson
wrote to the secretary of state, Lord Viscount Townshend, pressuring him to
take immediate punitive action. Gibson urged that Henley was not only dangerous in himself but also a dreadful example for others: "if Henley were able
to carry his point in the Metropolis of ye K[in]gdom, we shall quickly see a
Henley in every diocese."[36]

Gibson accused Henley of "turning Religious Assemblies into Theatres
and Stages, to which people repair . . . only for curiosity and amusement."
He added, "this is a new sort of Conventicle, and . . . deserves ye Consideration of ye Government." He suggested that the government might be able
to arrest Henley for violating the Toleration Act, which specified that Dissenting meetings could be held only behind unlocked doors. Gibson advised
the secretary of state that "Mr. Henley's Meeting house is neither locked
nor barr'd nor boulted [*sic*], but . . . there is an inner door kept shut and

guarded by two or three men, who hinder every body from coming in, but such as will give money or bring tickets as subscribing to the Design." Upon receiving this information, Townshend wrote to Yorke inquiring what could be done to silence Henley. But in a letter dated 22 September 1726, Yorke responded to Townshend, giving him the same advice he had already given to Gibson. Unfortunately, there was no longer any convenient law by which the government might shut down Henley's operation. Accordingly, it would be better not to make Henley a martyr by prosecuting him, as the government might lose its case, and a failed prosecution would only add to the Oratory's popularity: "I think it my duty not to advise the Administration to engage in a Prosecution . . . ye Event of which might rather encourage than restrain ye mischief it was intended to suppress."[37]

THE ORATORY

Henley opened the Oratory at Newport Market in a room with a history of use as a meetinghouse or Huguenot chapel. The room already had benches and a pulpit, but Henley made two changes that startled his contemporaries: he hired a doorman and installed a paybox at the door. A critic complained that this made the Oratory appear "more like a Theatre than a place of Worship: For first of all, when we come up, there is a Bar much after the same manner as in a Play-House: Secondly, a Hatch spiked: And Thirdly, a Man to take Money, otherwise, you say, we are not intituled to a seat."[38] Regardless of such complaints, the Oratory was so successful that the Newport Market venue quickly became too crowded. Within less than a year, Henley advertised his plans for a larger venue at the corner of Lincoln's Inn Fields near Clare Market. In February 1729 this site would become the home of the "Clare-Market Orator"[39] for the next twenty-seven years.

Contemporary satiric prints depict the Clare Market venue as a grand room with high ceilings, large windows, and three distinct areas for the audience: rows of pews and standing room behind them on the ground level, and additional standing room on an elevated platform (figs. 4.1 and 4.2). Contemporaries were flabbergasted by Henley's pulpit. Henley's "gilt tub," as Alexander Pope punningly called it in the *Dunciad*, was an imposing piece of architecture with a clerk's desk beneath it and a large sounding board above. As Pope commented, "the pulpit of a Dissenter is usually called a Tub; but that of Mr. Orator Henley was covered with velvet, and adorned with gold" (2.2n). Satiric prints show that Henley eventually had to separate the pulpit from the congregation with a railing. One print, *Oratory Chappel* (1746), depicts Henley's clerk standing beneath the pulpit with a club,

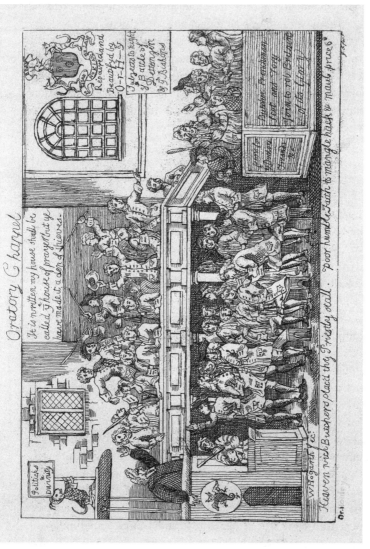

Fig. 4.1. *Oratory Chappel.* Attributed to William Hogarth but probably engraved by Jane Ireland. From Samuel Ireland, *Graphic Illustrations of Hogarth* (London, 1794), vol. 1, opposite 138. It depicts Henley's Oratory some time after the Battle of Culloden (16 April 1746), most likely after his December arrest for expressing outrage at British military reprisals against the Scots. Photograph: © The Trustees of the British Museum.

Fig. 4.2. *Temple of Rebellion* (1746), engraver unknown. Photograph:
© The Trustees of the British Museum.

prepared to fend off overly excited auditors and participants in debates. Admission to the Oratory was by a tiered system of payment. Standing room in the gallery could be purchased for sixpence, while a shilling bought standing room on the ground floor or a seat in the pews. It is difficult to determine what auditors actually paid for admittance. Some contemporaries accused the doorman of arbitrarily charging well-heeled patrons higher fees, while others satirized Henley for bulking up his audience by admitting the poor for free. Prices were sometimes raised for special lectures (such as a 1730 "Elogium on Masonry," discussed below). Clearly, though, admission fees were not prohibitive for the tradesmen and craftsmen who made up the bulk of his regular audience. Henley claimed that in comparison to Anglican ministers, he did "more for sixpence then any of them for six hundred pounds."[40]

As an alternative to cash payments at the door, patrons could purchase a season (or lifetime) pass in the form of "Oratory Medals." These medals cost three to fifteen guineas, and they came with various rights. A surviving copy of Henley's sermon *Deism Defeated, And Christianity Defended* (1731) with a manuscript note in his handwriting records that he sold the "Copyright" to a subscriber. One Mr. Wilson purchased a lifetime pass to the Oratory's theological offerings for himself and his family, and in so doing he earned the right to choose the dedicatee of the printed version of this "Lecture":

> Mr. Wilson bought of me a Medal called perpetual of ye Oratory, that is, for every Sunday, for himself and Family, while he lived, he preserving and shewing ye same, or receiving, as a Consideration, ye Copy-right of this Lecture, with Liberty of dedication, ye Medal to be forfeited, if others us'd it, and ye Copyright also.[41]

Despite the relatively high cost of these Oratory medals, enough people bought them that Henley continued this subscription program for several decades. Twenty-seven years after the Oratory opened, he advertised that "a new Beautiful Impression of the Oratory Medals is struck."[42]

The size of Oratory audiences varied according to the season and the topic. In its early years, the enterprise flourished: one 1729 advertisement asked genteel patrons arriving in sedan chairs to arrive early to avoid the crowds.[43] As the years went by, a smaller but steady audience continued, with occasional crowds for popular or controversial topics. Satiric prints always show a crowded house, but these prints were typically published at politically tumultuous moments when attendance may have been larger than was typical. Figures for Henley's "take" are almost nonexistent, but Midgley has calculated that over the course of one fourteen-month period in 1743–44, Henley collected approximately 196 pounds for seventy-one performances. This was long after the Oratory was "news," and as Midgley observes, "with such takings, and the income from his book sales and private teaching, he was richer than he would have been in his country living, and nearly as well off as if he had gained the coveted City church."[44]

It is also difficult to determine the socioeconomic makeup of Henley's audience. As I have suggested, contemporary satirists proposed that Henley's audience consisted chiefly of neighborhood butchers and their dogs—or, in one variant, butchers and their whores: "Clare-Butchers, mix'd with Saints of Drury-lane, / Astonish'd heard the learned, lofty strain."[45] Henley did, in fact, "cultivate" neighborhood butchers, in more ways than one. In 1729 he preached a special "Butcher's Lecture" that he also printed in *Oratory*

Transactions. This lecture serves to illustrate his lifelong faith in the liberating potential of education and his efforts to reach out to neglected groups. In addressing the butchers, he argued for the dignity of all trades and suggested that "Men of low Callings might have been qualify'd for the first Stations, the Differences of Men arising chiefly from Education, and what is call'd Fortune, but is really Providence." More pointedly, he remarked that "the meanest Trades have been the Original of many eminent Persons and Families." Henley was unwavering in his goal of spreading "academical literature" "to the meanest capacity." Challenging the assumption of the "elegant World" that butchers must necessarily be brutes, he pointed out the hypocrisy of this assumption coming from "elegant" persons who ate meat: "if it be cruel to kill it, it is the same to eat it, as the Receiver and the Thief are Terms equivalent."[46]

As his "Butcher's Lecture" suggests, Henley reached out to laboring people. At the same time, though, he was quick to defend the Oratory to the "elegant World." He insisted that "some of the Greatest Persons in Church and State, have been frequent Auditors at the Oratory."[47] In several of his newspaper advertisements, Henley thanked members of the peerage for approving his orations. He also claimed that learned persons of diverse faiths and professions had participated in Oratory "Disputations": "Professors of most Parts of Literature, many Clergymen, Students from both the Universities, Poets, Counselors, Physicians, Dissenters of all sorts, Romish Priests, Carmelites, Jesuits, Dominicans, Benedictines, Gentlemen of all Ranks, ingenious Artists, have maintain'd publick Disputations there."[48] Supporting Henley's claim of university student participation, one critic lamented the numbers of "Students either of *Divinity* or *Law*" who "run so often to . . . [the] *Newport-Market Oratory*."[49] In a pamphlet addressed to Alexander Pope, Henley asserted that Pope and his friend Henry St. John, 1st Viscount Bolingbroke, had visited the Oratory. (This pamphlet also states that Pope's works were the subject of numerous debates.)[50] In 1747 Henley recalled that Voltaire had attended the Oratory in 1728. Although there is no other record of Voltaire having made this excursion, he was in London at the time, and given his interest in English sects and politics, his attendance at the Oratory seems quite likely. Two decades later, Henley still remembered that "on Jan. 3rd., 17[2]8, in my Oratory, Mon. Voltaire, who perhaps now may forget it, told me that my Plan might be encourag'd by the King of France if I propos'd it as an improvement on the French Academy." Perhaps most remarkably, though, the Oratory consistently attracted a socially diverse female audience. Contemporary prints always show women in attendance, in all categories of admission: not only in the standing-room-only areas but also in the pews. In his advertisements, Henley thanked "the Ladies . . . who did me the Honour to be present." He also acknowledged his female support-ers' cash donations: "an Angel is 10s. but 6d. more from four fine Women makes them more than Angels."[51]

Henley stated that the educational goal of the Oratory was "to supply the want of an university, or universal school in this capital, for the equal benefit of persons of all ranks, professions, circumstances, and capacities." He observed that the majority of the population had neither the funds nor the "Leisure" necessary for a traditional gentleman's university education. Accordingly, his "academy of literature" would "diffuse a taste of literature and just thinking among persons of all ranks and capacities, without the profusion of time and expence, which must attend a more formal applica-tion." He aspired to

> teach indifferently Persons of all Ranks, Ages, Conditions and Circum-stances, either singly, or in Classes, in Proportion to their Genius and Application . . . what they desire to learn in all Parts of divine and hu-man Knowledge, Languages, Arts and Sciences. . . . This scheme will bring home to any Person all the Benefit of Schools, Universities, Tutors, Academies and Professors . . . not only to Gentlemen . . . but they who want Leisure, Opportunity, or Ability to take other Methods.[52]

In keeping with this populist vision of education, one of his targets was the obfuscation of learned language. He argued that

> great scholers, with all that air of Gravity and Importance, are ye most Errant Triflers in Nature: Distinctions without a difference, proposi-tions without Sense, Reasoning without connection, and Sounds with-out meaning, are almost a Compleat body of arts and Sciences: Remove these, and many a well-siz'd folio would sink to ye Modesty of a Pam-phlet . . . and ye Transition would not be altogether so Wide from ye haughty Supercilious Critic to ye poor illiterate Vulgar.

And he questioned by what "Design . . . Learned Men, ye Instructors of ye World, have Generally affected to Express themselves in a Dialect, which cannot be easily known by those they would instruct."[53]

In 1667 Thomas Sprat published *The History of the Royal Society of London, For the Improving of Natural Knowledge*, in which he offered a "History of The Institution, Design, and Progress, of the Royal Society of

London" and critiqued the "metaphorical" style of learned language. Many of Henley's foundational statements for the Oratory echo Sprat's *History*, and the title of *Oratory Transactions* echoes the *Philosophical Transactions of the Royal Society* (1665–). In the inaugural issue of his periodical, Henley echoed Sprat in offering "An Explanation of the Design" of his own "Institution." In addition, just as Sprat had published "A proposal for erecting an English Academy,"[54] so Henley envisioned the Oratory as an "English Academy."[55] In one section of his *History*, Sprat critiqued learned language and declared: "now I am warm'd with this just Anger, I cannot with-hold my self, from betraying the shallowness of all these seeming Mysteries; upon which, *we Writers*, and *Speakers*, look so bigg." Sprat called for a plain style of language that he modeled as a "return back to the primitive purity . . . when men deliver'd so many things, almost in an equal number of words." He praised members of the Royal Society for "bringing all things as near the Mathematical plainness, as they can: and preferring the language of Artizans, Countrymen, and Merchants, before that, of Wits, or Scholars."[56] Like Sprat, Henley raged against the obfuscation of learned language and called for a return to "primitive purity." He argued that "the most learned, or technical Language, without Reason, is mere sound."[57] Henley's call for a new plain style of learned discourse might seem at odds with his aspiration to restore "Antient Eloquence," but he was a populist who aimed to harness the ancient arts of oratory to radically new social purposes. His day-to-day population at the Oratory was precisely the "Artizans" and "Merchants" whose language Sprat had admired from a distance, and his Oratory was an attempt to put into practice Sprat's call for a more democratic mode of intellectual exchange.

In designing his course of offerings at the Oratory, Henley drew on and departed from the model he had experienced at Cambridge University. In the scholastic curriculum, the disciplines of the undergraduate program were divided into "Arts" and "Sciences," while in the graduate program "theology was . . . the all-important field."[58] In comparison, speech and performance genres at the Oratory included "Academical and Theological Lectures," "Sermons and Orations," and participatory "Disputations" and "Conferences." Sunday programs included a sermon and sometimes a celebration of the liturgy in the morning, followed by a lecture in the afternoon on "the critical, historical, speculative, or literary parts of [theology]." Henley's theological lectures occasionally addressed conventional topics such as the interpretation of passages of scripture or the ideas of Christian theologians, but he was wildly unconventional, to say the least, in his aspiration to "do . . . justice to all other religions, to examine their several pleas and pretensions in their full force, and without the least prejudice in favor of our own."[59] At a time when even Protestant Dissenters were objects of fear and sometimes violence, Henley offered to teach the history and beliefs not only of "the Jewish Religion" but also "the same in any different Religion, for the Instruction of Persons professing each Religion, or of others."[60]

Following the division of the scholastic curriculum into "Arts" and "Sciences," Henley's "academical lectures" addressed subjects such as rhetoric, logic, ethics, philology, and "Belles Lettres," on the one hand, and mathematics, optics, and natural philosophy, on the other. But Henley also collapsed this division—as when he proposed that "the art of publick speaking and gesture" must be seen as "a distinct science."[61] I shall consider Henley's efforts as "the Restorer of Antient Eloquence" in detail, but it is also worth noting his interests in mathematics and science. Henley expressed frustration that "a Course of the Mathematicks was the least (if any) Part of the usual academical Education."[62] Henley was a vocal admirer of Isaac Newton at a time when Newton's theories were controversial. In 1711, when Henley was at Cambridge (where Newton was Lucasian Professor of Mathematics), one Dr. Green had objected to Newton's theories, and Henley responded by publishing *Sir Isaac Newton's Principles of Natural Philosophy vindicated, from the Objections of a late System*. This work does not appear to have survived, but contemporary catalogs list it among his published writings.[63] On 29 March 1727, shortly after Newton's death on 20 March, Henley delivered a lecture at the Oratory "In Honour to the Memory and Character of Sir I. Newton, the Rise, Progress, Principles, and Usefulness of the Mathematicks."[64]

Henley also shared with his generation an interest in new scientific discoveries. In his "First Sermon at the Oratory," he noted his plan to lecture on "the discoveries and experiments of the moderns."[65] In the aforementioned "Butcher's Lecture," he referenced scientific discoveries to support his arguments. In addressing the assumption of the "elegant World" that butchers were brutes, he countered by noting, "there is not a Leaf of a Tree, a Blade of Grass, nor a Fruit, that does not abound with living Inhabitants without number, as Microscopes inform us. . . . [N]one can subsist on Milk, Water, Fruits or Herbs, without devouring Thousands of living Creatures."[66]

Along with lectures on mathematics and microscopes, Henley offered lectures on "Belles Lettres" in which he addressed both ancient and modern authors. His lectures on living authors such as Swift and Pope long predate Adam Smith's "Lectures on Rhetoric and Belles Lettres," delivered in Glasgow in 1762, now often held to be the first to introduce the subject of

"English Literature" into the university curriculum. Henley addressed topics such as the idea of "the Belles Lettres" (14 September 1726), "Poesy, the Judgment, Delight, and Beauty of it" (21 September 1726), and "Shakespear, and the Tragick Muse" (20 December 1727).[67] Responding to Pope's satiric portrait of him in the *Dunciad*, he observed that Oratory debates and lectures had addressed Pope's pastorals, his translation of Homer, his "Ethical Epistles," and even his *Dunciad*.[68] More appreciatively (and to be discussed later in this chapter) Henley lectured on "the History and Philosophy of Ridicule, from Democritus to Dean Swift" (31 January 1728).

Along with lectures "theological" and "academical," other speech genres of the Oratory included "disputations" and "conferences." In designing these participatory forums, Henley once again drew on and departed from the Cambridge model. The three chief scholastic exercises at Cambridge were lectures, disputations, and declamations. Significantly, Henley did away with declamations, the most hegemonic and text-based forum, and added a new forum that allowed for multiple participants and the impromptu, dialogic exchange of ideas. Henley envisioned "conferences" as collaborative endeavors fostering genuine intellectual discussion. At once idealistic *and* aware of religious, political, and social constraints on free speech, he declared that the "design of a conference, is to search the truth of one single proposition, by a mutual free communication of sentiments in an amicable manner, *as far as the church and state have thought fit to allow the search of truth.*"[69] Conferences involved as many as twelve discussants, with Henley serving as the moderator. These participatory events took place after Henley's lecture or sermon, with their subject arising from the preceding discourse, and Henley used the weekly newspapers to advertise topics in advance. He published the rules for disputations and conferences in *Oratory Transactions*,[70] and he required that these rules be read aloud before each event (thus involving illiterate, as well as literate, auditors). Whatever happened in reality, Henley's rules of protocol emphasized fair argument, civility, and order: "nothing that is prejudic'd or passionate, ill-bred, malicious, sophistical, or equivocating; no jests, puns, turns of wit, drollery, ridicule; nothing but what belongs strictly to the point, shall be allow'd." This idealistic vision of polite public disputation of controversial subjects was a goal not easily achieved. Henley's advertisements of 1742–43 repeatedly warned disputants and auditors of penalties for misbehavior and raucous noise. But Henley always insisted that the goal of these exchanges was "not contention for victory, decision or malice, but truth only."[71] And while they lasted, these innovative oral forums trained participants and auditors

in critical thinking and exposed a socially diverse audience to different—
and sometimes radical—views.

Perhaps most remarkably, the audiences for these debates included women,
and on at least one occasion a woman seems to have participated as a dis-
putant. Henley's paper, the *Hyp-Doctor*, records a debate on 22 July 1735 in
which three Quaker men and one woman debated whether or not Quaker
women had a Gospel-call to preach. Contemporary satirists depict Henley
encouraging "pious dames" to participate in debates:

> H—l—y the rostrum mounts displays his hand——
> Settles his scarf——and well adjusts his band——
> With front elate surveys the pious dames——
> Then——challenges them all,——t'oppose his themes——[72]

Whether or not any other woman participated as a speaker, it is certain that
Henley cultivated women as patrons, students, hearers, and readers. As we
have seen, he thanked various "Angels" for supporting his cause, and in
January 1728 he delivered a lecture addressing ideas for improving women's
education. He praised Anne Dacier (1654–1720), the distinguished French
classicist, advertising the topic of his lecture as "Madam *Dacier* a Pattern
to her Sex, and the Idea of a Study for them [women]."[73] Two years later, he
dedicated *The Lord, He is God* (1730) to the Baroness of Ockham, envision-
ing her as a patron of his educational projects. He concluded his dedication
by explaining that his plan for public education was inspired by his reading
of John Locke's *Essay Concerning Human Understanding* (1690) and *Some
Thoughts Concerning Education* (1693).[74] Henley also cultivated women as
political allies. One of his most outspoken critiques of the English government is addressed specifically to "Ladies" as well as "Gentlemen":

> *The Victorious Stroke For Old England . . . occasion'd by a Case, inter-
> esting every Man in Britain, of a Preacher [i.e., Henley] in London, here
> fully clear'd and vindicated, and the Rights of the Country concisely
> demonstrated: Necessary to be perus'd, not only by all Preachers, but
> Magistrates, Jury-men, Lawyers, Evidences, Political Writers, Scholars,
> and all Gentlemen and Ladies, who would form an exact Idea of what
> is strictly meant by Writing or Speaking for or against the Government
> of a Free Nation.* (1748)

Published shortly after his 1746 arrest for excoriating the English government's brutal treatment of the Jacobite rebels, this satirically titled text

aims to enlist all thinking persons, male or female, in the cause of freedom of "Writing or Speaking for or against the Government," and it encourages "Ladies," as well as "Gentlemen," to understand and defend their
"Rights."[75]

As his dedication to the Baroness of Ockham suggests, Henley conceived of his educational project as a truly "public Undertaking." In the
mid-1730s, he began advertising a new kind of educational offering: private
tutorials and small group seminars, offering instruction in "such parts of
universal Knowledge, Theoretical and Practical, as others will not, or dare
not teach."[76] Readers could consult the *Hyp-Doctor* for course offerings,
and prospective students could purchase subscription plans. Because our
primary source of information about these offerings is Henley's advertisements, it is difficult to know what actually went on, but we do know that
between 1736 and 1743 he carried on a steady trade in popular education.
Among his offerings was an unprecedented course of "Academical Literature for Ladies of Quality and Condition."[77] In the later eighteenth century,
the rapid growth of lecture programs and self-educational study groups responded to a huge demand for such programs among women and men deprived of formal education yet eager to expand their knowledge. Henley's
Oratory helped to generate this demand and to pave the way for these developments after his death.

"RESTORER OF ANCIENT ELOQUENCE"

In 1702, when Henley was a student at grammar school, French Protestant
clergyman Michel Le Faucheur's *Traitté de l'action de l'orateur; ou, de la
Prononciation et de geste* (Paris, 1657) was anonymously translated as *An
Essay Upon the Action of an Orator; As to His Pronunciation and Gesture.
Useful both for Divines and Lawyers, and necessary for all Young Gentlemen, that study how to Speak well in Publick. Done out of French* (London,
1702). Today, many scholars date the origins of the elocution movement in
Britain to the late 1750s or 1760s, when Thomas Sheridan began delivering
lectures on the art of speaking in urban centers such as London, Dublin,
and Edinburgh, then published his *Course of Lectures on Elocution* (1762).
But I agree with historian of rhetoric Wilbur Samuel Howell, who suggested
that "the date of the first publication of this translation [*An Essay Upon
the Action of an Orator*] is to be regarded as the moment when the English
elocutionary movement formally began."[78] Furthermore, I argue that it is
John "Orator" Henley who should be seen as the crucial link between the
publication of *An Essay Upon the Action of an Orator* (1702) and Sheridan's

transformation of Henley's Oratory endeavors into a national movement. As I will suggest in chapter 5, it is no coincidence that Sheridan published his inaugural elocutionary manifesto, *British Education: Or, The Source of the Disorders of Great Britain*, the same year that Henley died (1756).

Today, historians of the elocution movement acknowledge "Orator Henley" briefly (if at all) before moving on to politer territory. But it is an indisputable fact that by the 1730s, Henley was already so well known as "the Restorer of Antient Eloquence" that Ephraim Chambers referred to him by this title in his entry for "Pronunciation" in his frequently reprinted *Cyclopaedia* (2nd ed., 1738). Chambers suggested that Henley almost single-handedly shifted the popular understanding of "Pronunciation." He observed, "Some writers, particularly Mr. Henley, confound [pronunciation] with elocution, which is a very different thing. That author, when he styles himself restorer of the ancient elocution, means of the ancient pronunciation."[79] In singling out "Mr. Henley" in this way, Chambers implicitly acknowledged his centrality to the elocution movement—as well as his role in shifting the direction and goals of modern rhetorical training.

In Ciceronian rhetoric, there are five main parts or procedures: *inventio, dispositio, elocutio, memoria,* and *pronuntiatio* (or *actio*). But in eighteenth-century Britain, the elocutionists collapsed *elocutio* (which originally referred to compositional style) and *pronuntiatio* (or *actio*) and focused on pronunciation and action (what they called "elocution") above the other parts. In outlining the parts of rhetoric, Chambers observed that *"Pronunciation* is the same with what we otherwise call action," but he also noted that the meaning of "pronunciation" had shifted in contemporary use. Two hundred years later, Howell commented on Chambers's reference to Henley, noting that "it is no small accomplishment for a man in middle life to be mentioned in this special way in an important reference work, even with a rebuke implied." As a scholar of classical rhetoric (rather than, say, a social historian) Howell was largely dismissive of the eighteenth-century elocution movement, which he viewed as reducing the complex ethical art of rhetoric to a shallow matter of mere performance. But even Howell admitted that "the so-called 'Restorer of Antient Eloquence'" "attracted more attention to the elocutionary movement than did anyone else of his time."[80]

Shortly after the appearance of *An Essay Upon the Action of an Orator*, Steele and Addison devoted several issues of the *Tatler* and *Spectator* to the subjects of "Eloquence and graceful Action." As I have suggested, eighteenth-century Anglicans from Addison to Jane Austen debated the role of "pulpit eloquence" in spreading the Word of God. While some authors held that such concerns were better left to actors in the playhouses, others argued that neglect of the art of oral delivery was failing to do justice to an important cause. Almost all these authors, however, agreed that Anglican pulpit oratory had fallen to an all-time low. "The Clergy of *Great Britain*," Steele observed in the *Tatler*, "are . . . the most learned Body of Men now in the World," but regrettably, "this Art of Speaking, with the proper Ornaments of Voice and Gesture, is wholly neglected among them." (For Steele, as for most of his Anglican contemporaries, the "Art of Speaking" in a clerical context included both extempore speaking and the art of oral delivery in reading the liturgy: "the well Reading of the Common Prayer.")[81] This neglect was problematic in itself, but even more urgently, it was providing dangerous new opportunities to sectarian groups such as the Methodists, who were known for their more energetic styles of preaching.

Addison lamented that "in England we very frequently see People lulled asleep with solid and elaborate Discourses of Piety, who would be warmed and transported out of themselves by the Bellowings and Distortions of Enthusiasm." A commonplace of these debates was that Anglican services were putting people to sleep, while "enthusiastic" Dissenting preachers were arousing "ordinary Minds . . . wholly govern'd by their Eyes and Ears."[82] William Hogarth depicted a soporific Church of England preacher in his engraving *The Sleeping Congregation* (1736) (fig. 5.2). Later, in a sharply contrasting work titled *Credulity, Superstition, and Fanaticism* (1762) (fig. 5.3), he depicted an "enthusiastic" Dissenting preacher inspiring his congregation with all of the *wrong* passions. Henley too employed this trope of snoozing Anglicans. Defending his use of "action" in the pulpit, he asserted, "Since many Pulpits are appointed to administer Spiritual Opium to their Hearers, and preach the People to a Lethargy, there may, surely, be tolerated, one Pulpit to awaken them, to prevent the Enemy sowing Tares, while they sleep."[83] If we look closely at what Henley is saying here, we see that he associates not his own lively preaching style but the failure of the Anglican Church to train its ministers with "the Enemy sowing Tares."

Like his contemporaries, Methodist leaders John Wesley (1703–91) and George Whitefield (1714–70), Henley had a sense of the oral opportunities that were being missed by the Church of England to engage the minds and emotions of the common people through effective preaching. Henley admired Whitefield and (especially) Wesley, and he admired the Methodist practice of "field-preaching," or preaching in the open air. But significantly, he viewed both of these Dissenting leaders (especially Whitefield) as too subservient to the government and the established church. In a manuscript lecture note he wrote, "*Whitfield,* who is a Circumambient Preacher, is so far commendable, supposing our Laws wrong—but he is *no Patriot*: he does not tell ye Govt and ye higher Powers their Faults: but compounds with them, if they will let him preach; he will let them cheat and oppress."[84]

As we have seen, in 1725 Henley published his sermon *The History and Advantages of divine Revelation,* in which he advertised his plan for a new Baconian "system" of public speaking. In 1729 he reprinted this sermon in *Oratory Transactions* with a new title, "The Discourse on Action in the Pulpit." The same issue of *Oratory Transactions* includes a thirty-nine page catalog of lectures delivered at the Oratory between 3 July 1726 and 30 August 1728, divided into "Theological, or Lords-Day Subjects" and "Academical, or Week-Day Subjects." From the Oratory's opening days, this catalog shows, Henley attempted to put into practice his system for teaching the "arts of public speaking and gesture." Over this period of roughly two years, he delivered at least two dozen different lectures addressing the practical, moral, and social benefits of effective public speaking "in the Senate, at the Bar, in the Pulpit, and in all the remarkable Places, States, and Circumstances of Humane Life."[85] Representative topics included "The History of Preaching, or the Rhetorick of the Pulpit in all Ages and Dispensations," "The general Principles of Speaking," "The general Principles of Action," "The Harmony of the Voice," "On the Attitude . . . of the Body, in Action," "The Action of the Eye and Features," and "The Action of the Hands." As we shall see, Henley's own style of preaching entertained, baffled, and alarmed his contemporaries. Pope depicted Henley as "Preacher at once, and Zany of his Age," linking his performative style to that of mountebanks and fairground hucksters (*Dunciad,* 3.206). (A "zany" was a merry-andrew, or clown.) But Henley was far more threatening than these showmen, for he not only performed his system of elocution but also offered to teach it to anyone who would pay. Henley was an ordained minister with a Cambridge degree who offered to teach the arts of oratory to new social groups—and to do so far outside a traditional university setting.

In 1727, only a few months after Henley opened his Oratory, an enterprising publisher decided that the time was ripe for a second edition of the English translation of Le Faucheur's *Traitté de l'action de l'orateur.* Strikingly, when this edition was published later that year, it had a revised title and a new "Introduction," both explicitly referring to Henley: *The Art of Speaking in Publick: Or An Essay on the Action of an Orator; As to his Pronunciation and Gesture. Useful in the Senate or Theatre, the Court, the Camp, as well as the Bar and Pulpit. The Second Edition Corrected. With an Introduction relating to the Famous Mr.* Henly*'s present Oratory*. In less than a year, Henley had reached celebrity status ("*the Famous Mr.* Henly"), and for the author of the "Introduction and Apology for this Edition," this was a problem that needed to be addressed. The "real and true Occasion" for this new edition of a seemingly obscure manual on rhetorical action, this author stated, was Henley's "alarm[ing]" success. By purchasing this book, readers could compare for themselves how far "the *Newport Market* Orator's Gestures" and "Gesticulations" departed from the "Rules":

> The Town having been of late very much alarm'd at the *Reverend* and *ingenious* Mr. *Henly*'s extraordinary Performances and Attemps [*sic*] to revive the antient Manner of Speaking in Public . . . several Pamphlets have appear'd . . . and particularly one, written by Mr. *Wood*, which mightily condemns Mr. *Henly*'s Gestures, comparing them to the absurd and indecent Gesticulations of a *Merry-Andrew* or *Harlequin*. Mr. *Wood** lashing the *Newport Market* Orator's Gestures so satyrically, and at the same Time referring his Readers to the following Sheets, whereby they might judge how different Mr. *Henly*'s Gestures were from the Rules laid down in them; great Demands were made for them, which is the real and true Occasion of their appearing abroad once more in public Print.[86]

Contrary to "the *Newport Market* Orator's" practice, this critic asserted, "*Eloquence* does not consist in the Hands, nor *Rhetoric* in *Frisking* and *Gesticulating*, in *Catering* or cutting *Phiz*; but in the Reverse; a *grave, just*, and *becoming Frame* of the *Voice, Aspect* of the Eye and cast of the *Countenance*, together with a genteel regular Motion of the Body."[87] As this anxious remark suggests, oral communication is rooted in the body (the lips, tongue, vocal cords, lungs, and so on) and in the relationship between bodies. To understand what we might call oral agency, it is necessary to begin at the level of individuals, while also seeking to understand the power of the spoken word to affect social groups. Eighteenth-century elocutionists devoted extensive attention to theorizing the physical nature of oral communication, yet at the same time they intensified existing efforts to patrol the boundary between "modest" and "immodest" actions in public speaking. A virtuous orator, Le Faucheur and his followers advised, should never clap his hands, beat his breast, or make "indecent" movements associated with "a *Merry-Andrew* or *Harlequin*"—or, now, with a "Famous" figure such as John "Orator" Henley himself.

CHIMES OF THE TIMES:
HENLEY AND THE ORAL-PRINT NEXUS

The editors of the *Grub-Street Journal* satirized Henley as the "Restorer of Antient Elocution." They accused him of "learning the action of the ancients from a modern player." In one squib, they foregrounded his use of his "limbs," "arm," "lungs," "mien," and "visage" to persuade his audience. They suggested that Henley's oral discourse was so intimidating that it provoked critics to respond in print, for "None dares the Champion face to face oppose":

> Say, envious GRUB, why thus is H——y blam'd,
> For *Elocution* and for *Action* fam'd?
> You see, he daily challenges his Foes:
> None dares the Champion face to face oppose.
> Nor wonder, since his voice, and limbs, and mien
> All terrible to all, when heard, or seen.
> When ancient *Elocution* he restores,
> Action reviv'd inforces what he roars.
> And should his lungs, or voice, or visage fail,
> His brawny brandish'd arm must needs prevail.[88]

A few months later, the editors printed an elaborate engraving titled "The Art and Mystery of *Printing* Emblematically Displayed," with an extensive commentary satirizing Henley (fig. 4.3).[89] The engraving depicts a printing house with various creatures setting type, inking forms, pulling at the press, and hanging up freshly printed sheets of paper to dry. The fictional editor of the journal, Mr. Bavius, offers an "Explication of the picture," in which he suggests that one creature, a Janus-faced figure looking in two directions, could be interpreted as signifying Henley. Acknowledging Henley's dual identities as an oral *and* print entrepreneur, Mr. Bavius suggests that this figure

> represents [Henley] in his present two double capacities; in the one of
> which he appears with his theological or sundays, and his satyrical or
> wednesday's face, either as a JACK PRESBYTER or a JACK PUDDING:
> in the other he is represented as Orator and Hyp-Doctor. If we look upon
> him in the former character, we may suppose him to be teaching variety
> of action to three pupils in a private room: if in the latter, we may imag-
> ine him to be in a printing house.

The Grub-ſtreet Journal.

NUMB. 147.

Thursday, OCTOBER 26. 1732.

The ART and MYSTERY of *Printing* Emblematically Diſplayed.

Devil with Devil damn'd
Firm concord holds : Men only diſagree.
Of creatures rational.   *Paradiſe Loſt*, B. II. 496.

Mr. BAVIUS,

AS I was going the other day into Lincoln's-inn, under the great gate-way, I met ſeveral lads and boys of different ſizes, loaded moſt of them with great bundles of news-papers, led by a luſty fellow, who turned round and ſtopped them in the paſſage. They were all exceeding black and dirty; and made ſo very odd a figure, that I could not but ſtop myſelf to gaze upon them. Some that lagged behind and brought up the rear, I ſaw come out of the Stamp-office: from whence I rightly inferred, that they were Printers Devils, carrying from thence the returns of unſold news-papers, after the ſtamps had been cut off. I thought ſomething comical would enſue: nor was I deceived in my expectation by the following Dialogue; which I committed to writing, as ſoon as I returned to my lodgings. The Dialogiſts I have diſtinguiſhed by names, with as great propriety as I could, either from the appearance the perſons themſelves made, or from the information of others. I have kept as near as poſſible to the thoughts and expreſſions of theſe black gentry; at both which I was not a little ſurprized at firſt. But when I conſidered, that many perſons in higher life, without ever reading at all, acquire, ſolely by converſation, a faculty of talking, with great fluency, upon variety of ſubjects, tho' they neither underſtand them, nor the language in which they talk; I did not think it ſo ſtrange, that theſe gentlemen, tho' moving in a lower ſphere, yet having conſtant opportunities of reading the weekly works of our politeſt authors, or at leaſt of hearing them read, ſhould obtain, in ſome degree, their way of thinking and ſpeaking. Thus what they generally carry on the outſide, might get into the inſide of their heads; from whence it proceeded in the following manner.

POCK-FRETTEN STUMP. Devils, Gentlemen, and Brethren. Let us ſtop here, and lay down our burthens for a

while — upon the ground, ſince the bulk is ſhut off, and we are violently debarred from our property. Our property, I ſay; for tho' we at firſt took poſſeſſion of it by force; yet ſince no body oppoſed us at that time, we may juſtly be ſaid to have had the tacit conſent of every body. And from that time to this, thouſands of paſſengers have given us their expreſs conſent by a laughter of applauſe. — Nor was this to be wondered at, ſince the uſe to which we put this place, was of the ſame nature with that to which it ſerved before, and was a greater improvement of it. It had been for a long while a receptacle of unſaleable hiſtory, politics, and poetry; and therefore a very proper place for us to eaſe our ſhoulders of the weight of all thoſe, which lay ſo heavy upon them. And what company could be more ſuitable to moſt of the preſent writers, under whoſe works we ſweat, than that of PRYN, DEFOE, and OGILBY? — and therefore our title to this place has been confirmed to us by long poſſeſſion; and no one can pretend, that we have abuſed it; why are we thus unjuſtly excluded? I ſhould be for breaking their locks, and demoliſhing theſe ſhutters directly, were not the lawyers much more terrible at the Old Baily, than here in Lincoln'sinn. But they are always on the ſtrongeſt ſide, and thereby make it the legal. Wealth and power, I have heard ſquire STONECASTLE ſay, like two vicious horſes, hurry on the chariot of the law, through thick and thin, through fair and foul ways and weather, juſt as they pleaſe; while the coach-man in his black livery, ſitting in the box, as it were, for form's ſake, unable to ſtop their career, encourages them in it, with thoſe reins which ought to reſtrain them. Hence we ſometimes ſee thoſe in a coach, who ought to ride only in a cart; which is frequently aſſigned to honeſter men, who are driven up Holborn-hill by ſome legal coachman. On which account, I think, it will be better for us to acquieſce under the preſent injurious excluſion, and patiently to lay our burthens down on the ground, than by forcibly re-entring upon our right, expoſe ourſelves to be taken, and, perhaps, tucked up. — If you do not expreſs your diſſent to what I have ſaid, I ſhall look upon your ſilence as a token of your concurrence in the ſame opinion with myſelf.

JEREMY TRUNCK. I am heartily glad you are aſk of my

mind: and aſſure you, had you been of another, as ſoon as ever you had begun your work, I ſhould have ſlipp'd my neck out of the collar, and ſhewed you a fair pair of heels. I think my maſter APPLEBEE, who was the firſt great inventer of *Weekly Journals*, has taken the wiſeſt courſe. As politics is a ſubject which has grown more and more dangerous to meddle with, he has for a long while lived it aſide; and is become a much more famous biographer than Mr. CURL himſelf. It is no ſmall conſolation to thoſe heroic, but unfortunate gentlemen, who make their exit at the Oratory at Tyburn, where all are firmly admitted, that a faithful account of their lives and tranſactions, written or dictated by themſelves, ſhould be printed in a Weekly Journal. It is likewiſe of great advantage to the living in general, as well as to my maſter in particular, to publiſh the dying ſpeeches of theſe Orators; which are much more inſtructive to the publick, than copies of laſt wills and teſtaments, which are always added to the CURLEAN Lives and Memoirs, only to ſwell the volume. Theſe Speeches or Orations may be juſtly called Lectures or Sermons, but moſt properly Poſtils: and I have heard, that ſeveral eminent divines have declared, that they contain more ſound divinity, in better language, than any of thoſe delivered at the Coffee-houſe near Clare-market. — But, notwithſtanding all this, I am heartily glad, that you deſiſt from breaking of locks: for ſhould a load of the laſt dying ſpeeches of any of you, my brethren, be ever layed upon my back, I ſhould doubly groan under it, as the moſt ſad and heavy burthen I ever carried in my life. — But I beg your pardon, Mr. Preſident, for this long interruption: for you ſeem to have ſomething of great importance in your countenance.

POCK-FRETTEN STUMP. Tho' my ſeniority, who have been Devil to the Daily Poſt, London Evening Poſt, and Univerſal Spectator, ever ſince their exiſtence; and my ftature, which is much ſuperior to yours, might ſeem to give me ſome ſort of right to this Preſidentſhip; yet I acknowledge the honourable title you have conferred upon me, by a free unbribed election, as a mere inſtance of your favour, tho' undeſerved, yet not altogether unexpected. For it ſeems a natural conſequence of the reſpect you have always ſhewn me, in not taking one cancelled page

Fig. 4.3. "The Art and Mystery of *Printing* Emblematically Displayed." From *Grub-Street Journal* 147 (26 October 1732). Photograph: By permission of the Folger Shakespeare Library.

As this commentary suggests, Henley's "two double capacities" as oral and print entrepreneur ("Orator and Hyp-Doctor") were fundamental to his modus operandi. For Henley, oral entrepreneurialism and print commerce worked together. Henley printed his most successful sermons, and for his customers, the originally *oral* occasion of these sermons was important. The title page of *The History and Advantages of divine Revelation* (1725) advertises this printed text as a transcript of "A Sermon Preach'd in the Church of St. George the Martyr, London, On Sunday; Nov. the 15th. 1724" and notes that it was "Publish'd at the Request of many of the Audience." Similarly, the title page of "The Butcher's Lecture" notes that it was *"Preach'd at Newport-Market, On Easter-Day . . . April 6. 1729. And on Low-Sunday following, at the Oratory, remov'd from Newport-Market to Lincoln's-Inn-Fields"* and claims that it was "publish'd at the Desire of both Auditories." Printed sermons, like printed play texts, were marketed as records and reminders of prior oral occasions. Henley also used the imprints of his publications to remind readers of the location(s) of the Oratory and so to direct them to future oral/aural events.

Henley's earliest publications were book length, but after he opened the Oratory, he shifted his focus to cheaper formats such as pamphlets and newspapers. Henley always aimed to reach a broad audience, and he knew that his turn to "cheap print" had social and political implications. Whereas books typically sold for about two to three shillings for a duodecimo or octavo and ten to twelve shillings or more for a folio, Henley's *Oratory Transactions* sold for only sixpence per issue—about the same price as an almanac or chapbook.[90] The fact that even the "Dregs of the Multitude" could purchase his periodical issues and pamphlets (as well as gain access to his Oratory) would have significant implications when he began using these platforms as a populist court of law.

By the 1720s newspapers were part of everyday life in London. Henley's involvement with the newspaper press was extensive: in addition to the hundreds of advertisements that he placed in newspapers, he was the sole author of *Oratory Transactions*, the *Oratory Magazine*, and, especially, the *Hyp-Doctor*, published weekly from 15 December 1730 to 20 January 1742. Henley's move to London coincided with the reappointment of Robert Walpole, a Whig, as First Lord of the Treasury in 1721. By 1730 Walpole was the undisputed leader of the cabinet, and the same year, Henley began publishing the *Hyp-Doctor*. The editors of the leading Tory paper, the *Craftsman*, suggested that Henley was in the pay of Walpole, and this charge quickly spread. (For Pope's contribution to these rumors, see my discussion below.) But it is not surprising that Henley, a lifelong Whig, defended the Whig administration. Furthermore, the *Hyp-Doctor* is not merely a pro-Walpole vehicle, as many modern critics now assume.[91] In the eighteenth-century print marketplace, no periodical lasted for eleven years without a wide readership. To read the *Hyp-Doctor* now, in my view, is to (re)discover a periodical that is, as its title proposes, a cure for the spleen ("hyps"): a lively miscellany that is at once imaginative, witty, populist, and (sometimes) erudite.

Taking advantage of the ever-growing thirst for news, Henley added a new feature to the Oratory in 1728. At Friday evening events that he called "Chimes of the Times," he delivered satirical *oral* commentaries on the printed news. These satirical and burlesque commentaries on the weekly news grew to be one of the Oratory's most popular (and imitated) programs. (As we shall see later in this chapter, Christopher Smart's imitation of Henley's Oratory in his own "Old Woman's Oratory" foregrounded this feature.) As the government immediately recognized, this "Chimes of the Times" feature was a new kind of public forum for oppositional politics disguised as harmless entertainment. When Henley came into conflict with the law in 1729, the Grand Jury of Middlesex listed among its charges against him his "Diversions under the Title of Voluntaries, *Chimes of the Times*, Roundelays, College Bobs, Madrigals & Operas, &c." (my emphasis). The grand jury accused Henley of using satire and burlesque to make "base and malicious Reflections upon the established Churches of England and Scotland, upon the Convocation, and almost all Orders and Degrees of Men; and upon particular Persons by Name, and even those of the highest Rank." The presentment also highlights Henley's use of newspapers, both his oral commentary on the printed news in his "Chimes of the Times" and "his Advertisements in the publick News Papers." But ironically, in taking the unusual step of printing their presentment against Henley in the "publick News Papers,"[92] the grand jury followed in his footsteps in recognizing that newspapers were a useful tool for bringing one's case before the "publick."

Ironically, too, the category of printed texts that Henley was most recognized for in his lifetime consisted of his most "ephemeral" productions: the newspaper advertisements that he placed to advertise Oratory events. Henley was fascinated by the book trade as a "Craft" and a business. In January 1728 he lectured on book-trade-related topics such "the History, and Secret of Book-Craft," "Characters of Booksellers and Authors," "the Trade and Furniture of Books," "Subscriptions and Dedications," and "the Advantage of the Oratory to Booksellers, in advertising for them."[93] As the latter topic suggests, Henley had a special interest in the still-new phenomenon of print advertisements. In the eye-catching advertisements that he placed in the

London Daily Post and the *Daily Journal*, he developed his own unforgetta-
ble style, earning himself the satiric title of "PUFFERUS PRIMUS."[94] From
these advertisements alone, one might conclude that Henley was a mere
mountebank of the print realm (or a lunatic). But as Midgley suggests, his
eccentric advertisements "were a calculated effort at mystification, to stim-
ulate curiosity and to draw crowds. . . . He[nley] succeeded, through them,
in keeping his name always on the lips of the London public."[95] In a telling
remark, the editors of the *Grub-Street Journal* contrasted Henley's eloquent
speaking style and the "nonsens[ical]" style of his printed advertisements.
They advised, "Preach on, Great Orator, but Printing dread: / Thy Jargon spoke
seems sense; 'tis nonsense read."[96] Henley's advertisements became an easily recognized comic interlude in the typically mundane space of the classified section of the news.

   For about seven years of its existence (1730–37), the *Grub-Street Journal*
parodied Henley's activities on a regular basis: "hardly a month went by
without some note or verse mocking and insulting him, and many a month
he received a weekly stab."[97] Henley then answered the *Grub-Street Journal* in the *Hyp-Doctor*, setting up a cycle of invective that was a form of
mutual publicity. The editors of the *Grub-Street Journal* were fascinated
by Henley's multimedia methods (as their attention to his "two double capacities" suggests). They noted his coordinated use of oral and print genres
and the way that he crafted different personae in each. On the one hand,
Henley's oral delivery was making him famous (and the *Grub-Street Journal*
editors "envious"): "Say, envious GRUB, why thus is H——Y blam'd, / For
Elocution and for *Action* fam'd?" On the other hand, his construction of an
immediately recognizable persona in his print advertisements was cultivating an audience for his Oratory performances. The *Grub-Street Journal*
editors imitated Henley's style in responding to his competitors (including
the *Craftsman*, *Fog's Journal*, and the *Grub-Street Journal* itself). They commented on the "oratorical . . . manner [in which] my *Hyp Doctor* writes, in
answer to the *Craftsman*, *Fog*, and *Grub-street*. 'Calebite, Fog-pate, Tory,
Tantivee, Saucy Puppy, Skip-kennel, Tatterdemalion, Ragamuffin, Pygmies,
Monkey-Vermin, Rats, Moles, Weazles, Tom-tits, Griggs, Stickle-backs,
Newts, Minikins.'" In discussing Henley's "weekly advertisements, setting
forth the arguments or contents of his frantick harangues," they noted that
"all of these, both puffs and advertisements, died immediately after birth."
In a play on the officially published Bills of Mortality and on Henley's dual
identities as "the Orator" and the author of the *Hyp-Doctor*, they printed
"A bill of Hyp-oratorial mortality for the year 1732" in which they tal-
lied up Henley's recent advertisements: "Hyp puffs, 60. Oratorial ditto, 62.

In all, 122.——Hyp-advertisements, 65. Oratorial ditto, 83. In all, 148.——
Sum total of puffs and advertisements, 270."[98] The *Grub-Street Journal* editors recognized that in using ephemeral newspaper advertisements to advertise his oral forum, Henley was using print in a new way. Instead of aspiring
to immortality through print publication, he was consciously taking advantage of the seriality and ephemerality of particular print genres to advertise
his even more fleeting Oratory performances. Readers needed to act fast,
these puffs implied, for just as newspaper advertisements "died" quickly, so
the Oratory offered one-time-only topics and events.

ARGUMENTS AND ARRESTS

On 8 February 1728 the *London Journal* announced that Henley had been
arrested. Henley later recorded that the same week, "all Mr. *Henley*'s Writings were seiz'd to be examin'd by the State. *Vide Magnam Chartam, &
Engl. Lib.*"[99] After having been bound over to appear at the Court of King's
Bench, he was released on bail, and eleven months later, on the last day of
the term, he appeared at King's Bench as required and was discharged.[100]
Two months after this discharge, he was faced with another government effort to shut down the Oratory. On 9 January 1729 the Grand Jury of Middlesex found a true bill against him and signed a presentment. On this second
occasion it is not known whether Henley was actually arrested, but we do
know that on 18 January, the grand jury took the unusual step of printing
their presentment against him in the public newspapers. They warned readers that his enterprise was an "Offence to all serious Christians, . . . an Outrage upon civil Society, and of dangerous Consequence to the State."[101] But
the government's plan to frighten off Henley's audience backfired completely.
By printing their charges in a public newspaper, the grand jury in effect appealed to the public as a court of law, and the public responded by flocking
to the Oratory to investigate and judge for themselves. One week later, the
London Evening Post reported: "We hear that the Reputation of Mr. Henley's Discourses and the Number of his Assemblies is encreas'd by the late
Bug-bear, design'd . . . to thin his Oratory."[102] The grand jury's printing of the
presentment in the newspapers also gave Henley a widely available document that he could refer to and use to advance his own case. Characteristically, he did not let the matter drop. Instead of allowing the presentment
to silence him, he reprinted it in *Oratory Transactions*, then responded to
the jurors' charges one by one. The brazen title of this special issue of *Oratory Transactions* makes it clear that he had no intention of apologizing to
anyone (especially the unidentified "*Mr. H——s*"):

Milk for Babes: Or, A Hornbook For That Able Divine, Eminent Lawyer, and Honest Politician, Mr. H——s, and his Disciples; by way of Answer to his Godly and Conscientious Scruples relating to the Oratory. Being No. V. of Oratory Transactions, all enter'd in the Hall-Book, according to Act of Parliament.

Milk for Babes consists largely of "*The* Presentment of the Grand-Jury of Westminster, Jan. 9. 1728–9, *answer'd Word for Word.*" A sense of Henley's defiance may be gathered from his counterinterrogation of the government: "am I of Consequence to endanger the State? Pity that a Plan for the utmost Encouragement of Reason, Liberty, Commerce, Learning, and Wit, should be against the State."[103]

Both orally and in print, Henley defended the legal status of the Oratory. Indeed, judging from its contents, one of the primary reasons why Henley published *Oratory Transactions* was to give himself a print venue in which to defend his oral activities. The first issue of Henley's periodical includes "A Defence of the Oratory, against Objections, in an Academical Discourse, deliver'd at *Newport*-Market, being One of the Three Hundred Discourses, that were seiz'd and acquitted by the State."[104] In Henley's view, the lawfulness and moral purpose of the Oratory were closely intertwined. The "fundamental authority of it as a Church," he wrote in his "Plan of the Oratory," "will be the same . . . [as] that of all the modern Churches, i.e. a legal liberty of private judgment in religion." "All local right of exercising sacred functions is from the crown, so that the right of the Oratory is equal to any episcopal authority in this realm."[105] Independent critical thought was the fundamental right of a freeborn Englishman and the moral duty of a Christian. From its opening sermon—reprinted in *Oratory Transactions*—the Oratory rang with rousing rhetoric: "Assert your selves, my fellow Christians: In learning and religion, see with your own eyes, think with your own judgments: what is more beautiful than truth? What is dearer than liberty?"[106] The "greatest sign of the Truth of any Religion, is the being permitted to ask Questions concerning it, and suffering the Tenets to be examined and disputed upon."[107] The goal of the Oratory was to "promote the justest turn of free impartial thinking on all occasions." "Free impartial thinking" leads *toward* truth, not away from it: "the freest Reasoning can be no Injury, but a Service, to the Interest of Truth; and without it, Truth can never be found."[108]

What were critics' main concerns about Henley? Why did the Oratory cause such great alarm? Many critics were concerned by Henley's "Action in the Pulpit," which they felt was immodest or improper. Others feared his specific religiopolitical ideas. They accused him of being a deist or an Arian or of attempting to set up a "new Sect." But all of his critics were concerned by two of his innovations: first, his regularly scheduled oral appeals to a socially heterogeneous audience and, second, his collapsing of an ideological dividing line between "sacred" and "profane" spaces and topics. As one author complained, the Oratory seemed "more like a Theatre than a Place of Worship."[109] Another pamphlet noted the location of the Oratory above a meat market, or "Shambles," and compared Henley's tactics to those of a "Jack-Pudding," or mountebank's zany:

> He set up a public Stage in the Shambles; mounted it, and hung up the shameless Flag of Defiance against the Law, against Virtue and Decency, while he impiously mock'd his God, and ridicul'd the Religion of his Country, together with the whole Druidical Order. He drew the Dregs of the Multitude after him by his Ribaldry, and cracking obscene Jokes, like a Jack-Pudding in Bartholomew Fair, at the same Time that he was clad in the venerable Vestments of the sacred Order, and with the volume of Salvation in his hand; while his dirty Auditory, crying Smoke the Parson, rung Peals of Marrow-Bones and Cleavers to their Orator's Praise.[110]

Henley's mixing of "a Church and a Farce-house" and "Ribaldry" with clerical vestments was unprecedented. Even the *Grub-Street Journal*, itself a satiric medley, critiqued his generic mixing of different kinds of spaces, topics, and purposes: his "unparallell'd [*sic*] profanation of sacred things, by his monstrous jumble of divinity and buffoonery, or a Church and a Farce-house, of a *Bartholomew*-fair booth and the Sacrament."[111] To compare Henley's Oratory to a Bartholomew Fair booth was to critique its vulgarity and to note its popularity. Henley's ludic style was all too effective in maintaining the attention of his "dirty Auditory." In 1729 the Presentment of the Grand Jury of Middlesex listed among its charges against Henley his having made improper use of the room that he had registered as a site of worship: "he made use of the said Room for purposes very different than those of Religious Worship, and . . . he has there discoursed on several subjects of Burlesque and Ridicule . . . contrary to the Intention of the . . . Act of Toleration." With even greater specificity, the grand jury recorded that on 12 December 1728, he had advertised a performance in which "he would pronounce King Lear's Oration in an Apology for Madness, on which Evening he did in the said Room (call'd by him the Oratory) in the Habit of a Clergyman of the Church of England, repeat a Speech out of the Tragedy of King Lear, acting in such Manner and with such Gestures as are practised in the Theatres."[112] But of course, the intentions of the grand jurors backfired: these details about Henley's performances acted as advertising for future Oratory events.

For many commentators, Henley's use of humor in discussing religious matters was the ideological equivalent of casting pearls before swine. To be sure, Anthony Ashley Cooper, 3rd Earl of Shaftesbury, had argued in *Characteristics* (1711) that humor and ridicule could in certain circumstances be a legitimate way of discovering religious truth. But Shaftesbury was an aristocrat writing to a learned audience, and he was referring chiefly to humor in written texts circulated chiefly among aristocratic men. Henley, by way of contrast, was putting his doctrine of "burlesque teaching" into *public oral practice on a regular basis*. It was Henley's innovation to rouse laughter orally and physically from the pulpit—and from an audience potentially far more socially diverse than the readers of elegant written texts.

Henley defended his use of "burlesque" as a teaching tool. He argued that "to burlesque Error, Vice, and Folly is part of my Religious Persuasion, as a Teacher, in my Place of Worship; it is doing Honour to Religion."[113] In a lecture "On the History and Philosophy of Ridicule, from Democritus to Dean Swift," he pointed to a long line of distinguished predecessors (from ancient philosophers to modern clergymen) who used humor as a teaching tool.[114] He also published a number of texts addressing this issue, such as "A Dissertation on Nonsense" and "An Oration on . . . Serious Buffoons."[115] He pointed to Erasmus as an admired predecessor: "*Erasmus* was one of the first Lights of the Reformation; read in Schools, and esteem'd by all Persons . . . his Praise of Folly is a refin'd Piece of *Buffoonery*." More strikingly, because immediately contemporary, he also praised "the Burlesquing Pen of Dean *Swift*."[116] In defending himself against the charges of the Grand Jury of Middlesex, he alluded to Swift's "Apology" to *A Tale of a Tub*, in which Swift defends his text against charges of impiety. Henley suggested that he was consciously adopting the dean's satirical methods: "My Burlesque flings a Tub before a Whale, that might toss the Ship of the Common-Wealth."[117] For Henley, "Serious Buffoon" was an honorary title—one that he earned at a cost. In answering the charges of the grand jury, he responded with a rhetorical question that flaunted his success at attracting an audience through his satiric methods, however scandalous: "I love, and would rather chuse the Serious, but will the Town chuse it, or my Enemies daily come to it?"[118]

The most threatening aspect of the Oratory, though, was its combination of religion, disputation, and publicity: the new idea of organized public debate of religious "Truths." Less than a year after the Oratory opened, an anonymous author assailed Henley in a pamphlet titled *A Letter To The Celebrated Orator*, expressing horror at "that Impious Ridicule and Insult, which . . . you have been now suffer'd too long Weekly to put upon our Holy Religion." In this author's eyes, it was not so much any particular doctrine that Henley was espousing that was the problem. Rather, it was the public, disputational nature of the venue that he had created and the way that he put the questioning of religious truths at the center of his ostensibly religious institution—thus "exposing our Blessed Lord and his Holy Religion to the Ridicule and Scorn of Libertines and Atheists." The author compared the Oratory to another institution frequented by a cross-spectrum of the (here, mostly male) population, "Figgs' Amphitheatre." James Figgs (d. 1734) operated a boxing school in London that featured prize fights, bearbaiting, and, sometimes, female boxers. The author of the *Letter* suggested that Henley encouraged disputants at the Oratory to "digladiate" holy truths like gladiators in a ring:

> When the Apostle gravely advises not to hold *doubtful Disputations* before *such as are weak in the Faith*, dare you, sitting in the Chair of the Scorner, before a profane multitude bring those Momentous Truths into Question, to be digladiated by fictitious Combatants, as in *Figgs' Amphitheatre*! Thus *throwing that which is holy unto dogs, and casting pearls before your Swinish* herd of Epicureans, Deists and Atheists assembled with you, who will be sure *to trample them under feet, and turn again and rend them*!

The "Celebrated Orator" was successfully attracting a socially broad audience across barriers of rank, literacy, and gender—an audience consisting of butchers and fishwives, "Epicureans, Deists and Atheists"—in short, "the worst part of Mankind."[119] But what comes across most clearly in critiques such as this one of Henley's "dirty Auditory" is the vigorous engagement of that audience in Oratory proceedings. These are not passive "auditors" but engaged participants who are being entertained *and* intellectually challenged by the bringing "into Question" of "Momentous Truths."

FROM "RESTORER" TO RADICAL

Although Henley initially saw himself as a restorer of the "Primitive Church," he eventually came to question not only the apostolic authority of the Anglican Church but also episcopal authority altogether. He initially offered an alternative liturgy at the Oratory, but this aspect became less and less important to the Oratory's programs, and he eventually dropped it altogether. Furthermore, from the Oratory's opening days, he emphasized that "we propose the [Apostolic] Constitutions . . . [but] we do not impose them: We recommend them by Reason and Persuasion, not by a high Hand, by calling on ecclesiastical Officers, or the secular Arms, to put them into Practice."[120] The Oratory would be organized around inquiry, not indoctrination. Nothing would be forced when it came to religious views. Influenced by the arguments of Benjamin Hoadley, bishop of Bangor, whose sermons provoked the Bangorian controversy (1716–) by denying that it was necessary for men to belong to any external church in order to obtain salvation, Henley eventually came to reject altogether "the claims of Apostolicity, the organized clergy, and the ruling episcopacy, the creeds and canons and articles of the Church . . . [and] temporal power and possessions."[121] By the late 1730s Henley was citing Hoadly's arguments and proclaiming that "God alone being the legislator of the Conscience . . . Subscription to the *Articles of the Church* is discretionary, political, judicial."[122] By 1750 he was even more blunt, describing the Church of England as a humanly established political institution and no more: "I can subscribe to ye Church of England, as a political system, by Law established; wch. is all I can make of it."[123]

Henley's lifelong "questioning of authority" eventually led him to interrogate the historical truth of the scriptures.[124] By 1740, he was advertising public debates on topics such as "Whether Law and Prejudice apart, the Story of the Nativity be true" and "The Greek Testament spurious?"[125] Sermons like Hoadly's metaphorically enthroned individual judgment in the place of the church, but Henley took matters further in attempting to put the exercise of reason into a new kind of institutional practice in Oratory debates. Holding views that were similar in some ways to those of deists, yet never openly endorsing deism, Henley held that reason, a God-given gift, should be exercised in assessing the scriptures as historical texts and as guides to belief. In his will, he defiantly declared: "Tell my notorious Enemies I dye a Rationalist."[126] Ultimately, his religious views were organized around a methodology—a method of inquiry—rather than a particular doctrine. In this sense, he more closely resembled freethinkers than deists.

Henley also grew more outspoken against English government practices and policies in general (i.e., as distinct from the policies of the Anglican Church). Outraged by English military and legal reprisals against the Scots after the defeat of Charles Edward Stuart at the Battle of Culloden, he was taken into custody on 1 December 1746 for preaching in support of the

Jacobite rebels. The following day, a newspaper reported that Henley was examined by His Majesty's justices of the peace for Oratory remarks "tending to alienate His Majesty's Subjects from their Duty and Allegiance."[127] Three weeks later, on 20 December, he was released on bail, and six months later, on 19 June 1747, he appeared at the Court of King's Bench and was discharged.[128] As with Henley's earlier conflicts with the law, this prosecution brought renewed attention to the Oratory and gave rise to a flurry of pamphlets and satiric prints. The aforementioned *Oratory Chappel* depicts Henley defiantly wearing the Scottish plaid, preaching to an audience including plaid-wearing Jacobites and a Scottish terrier raising a signboard labeled "Politicks & Divinity" (fig. 4.1). An energetic mob of Jacobites gesticulates in a pew labeled "Butcher Frenchman Scot and Tory Join to rob Britain of its Glory." Another aforementioned print, depicting the Oratory as the *Temple of Rebellion* (fig. 4.2), accuses Henley of "Blasphemy & Treason"—the latter an especially inflammatory charge in the heated political context of 1746.[129] Accompanying these prints was a flood of pamphlets authored by Henley and his critics. The title page of *An Epistle to O——r H——nl-y* (1746), accuses him of "Gross and Insolent Misrepresentations of the King's Government," "Virulent Invectives against the Ministry and all other Officers of State both Civil and Military," "Insolent Misrepresentations of the Protestant Religion, as establish'd in these Kingdoms," and defending the Jacobites "during the late National Troubles."[130] Characteristically, Henley responded by publishing even more outspoken arguments: not only against the English government's brutality but also, increasingly, for the universal right to freedom of speech. Henley's mock praise for "Old England" in the satirical title of the following pamphlet did little to disguise his fury at the government:

> *The Victorious Stroke For Old England . . . occasion'd by a Case, interesting every Man in Britain, of a Preacher in London* [Henley], *here fully clear'd and vindicated, and the Rights of the Country concisely demonstrated: Necessary to be perus'd, not only by all Preachers, but Magistrates, Jury-men, Lawyers, Evidences, Political Writers, Scholars, and all Gentlemen and Ladies, who would form an exact Idea of what is strictly meant by Writing or Speaking for or against the Government of a Free Nation.* Printed for PRIMATE REASON, Esq; 1748. Price 6 d.

Similarly, Henley's use of a mock imprint, "Printed for PRIMATE REASON," did little to disguise this pamphlet's oppositional nature. As the pamphlet's mocking title suggests, Henley held that the "Right" to freedom of

"Writing or Speaking for or against the Government" was an issue of urgent concern for both "Ladies" and gentlemen. Furthermore, the pamphlet's low cost of sixpence ensured that it was accessible to men and women across a wide spectrum of social ranks.[131] As with the earlier issue of *Oratory Transactions* in which he systematically quoted and responded to each of the charges of the "Presentment of the Grand-Jury of Westminster, . . . *Word for Word*,"[132] Henley here repeated and responded to each of the government's charges. The cumulative effect of repeating these charges—such as the charge that he had accused English soldiers of butchery at Culloden—was to repeat his "Virulent Invectives" against the government: but this time, to do so by quoting the government itself. *The Victorious Stroke* also mentions and summarizes a number of critical "Discourses" presumably already delivered at the Oratory. These discourses include lectures such as the "Third Discourse: A Protestant Dissenter's Liberty, of Preaching in his own way, asserted" and the "Fifth Discourse: Free Speaking on Trustees of Government no Sedition." Always alert to media tactics, Henley commented on the government's multimedia onslaught against his reputation, noting the "innumerable Methods taken to destroy a Preacher [Henley], by Advertisements, and Letters in the Publick Papers, by Prints, Images, Pamphlets, Paragraphs, Outrages, Lies, and Abuses." He argued for the right to liberty of conscience and freedom of speech: "Free-speaking is a principal Sign of a Free Government." Finally, for now, he concluded by asserting that "if speaking freely on Matters of State be call'd *seditious*, it ought to be considered what *Sedition* is."[133]

SATIRIZING "DR. ORATOR"

Henley's most famous critic was Alexander Pope, who satirized him at length in the *Dunciad* (1728–43). In one of many references to Henley, Pope depicts him as follows:

> But, where each Science lifts its modern type,
> Hist'ry her Pot, Divinity his Pipe,
> While proud Philosophy repines to show,
> Dishonest sight! his breeches rent below;
> Imbrown'd with native bronze, lo! Henley stands,
> Tuning his voice, and balancing his hands.
> How fluent nonsense trickles from his tongue!
> How sweet the periods, neither said, nor sung!
> Still break the benches, Henley! with thy strain,

While Sherlock, Hare, and Gibson preach in vain.
Oh great Restorer of the good old Stage,
Preacher at once, and Zany of thy age!
Oh worthy thou of Aegypt's wise abodes,
A decent priest, where monkeys were the gods!
But fate with butchers plac'd thy priestly stall,
Meek modern faith to murder, hack, and mawl;
And bade thee live, to crown Britannia's praise,
In Toland's, Tindal's, and in Woolston's days.

The Dunciad in Four Books (1743), 3.195–212

Pope devotes a third of this passage to Henley's status as the "Restorer of Ancient Eloquence." He depicts Henley's performative style of preaching, and he suggests that his action in the pulpit was better suited to the stage. Significantly, he represents Henley as a competitor to several Anglican divines who were renowned for their preaching but who now "preach in vain": Thomas Sherlock (d. 1761), Francis Hare (d. 1740), and Henley's enemy, Edmund Gibson (d. 1748). Like other critics, he noted Henley's populist appeal ("fate with butchers plac'd thy priestly stall") and his confusion of a church and a stage. Most remarkably, though, Pope not only linked Henley with some of the most "infamous" English freethinkers of the era—John Toland (1670–1722), Matthew Tindal (1657–1733), and Thomas Woolston (d. 1733)—but also represented Henley as potentially the *most* dangerous of these thinkers to "Meek modern faith": as "crown[ing] Britannia's praise, / In Toland's, Tindal's, and in Woolston's day."

From the *Dunciad Variorum* (1729) on, a lengthy prose note accompanied this portrait of Henley (see 3.199n). This note describes the layout of the Oratory and Henley's procedures, and it provides information cribbed from the biographical "Narrative" of Henley published earlier that year (see *Oratory Transactions* 1). Henley himself was convinced that most of the gossipy notes to the *Dunciad Variorum* were drafted by Richard Savage in return for meals at Pope's Twickenham estate: "*Richard Savage . . .* was [Pope's] *Provider . . .* he rambled about to gather up *Scraps of Scandal,* as a Price for his *Twickenham Ordinary . . .* no Tittle-tattle, no Dinner."[134] By 1729 Savage was certainly familiar with Henley; that year, he published his own satire on the business of authorship, *An Author to be Lett,* in which he noted the relocation of the Oratory to Clare Market and linked Henley's entrepreneurialism to that of two of the best-selling authors of the 1720s, Daniel Defoe and Eliza Haywood. Whoever wrote the notes to the *Dunciad Variorum* was fascinated by Henley's strategies for supporting himself

outside the usual channels of social advancement in church and state (channels of advancement that were also unavailable to Pope as a Catholic Dissenter). The note at 3.199 describes the payment options for admission to
the Oratory, whether by cash at the door or by subscription: "each auditor
paid one shilling. . . . This wonderful person [also] struck Medals, which he
dispersed as Tickets to his subscribers." The note also speculates that Henley's *Hyp-Doctor* was subsidized by Walpole: "This man [Henley] had an
hundred pounds a year given him for the secret service of a weekly paper . . .
called the Hyp-Doctor." Despite the lack of any hard evidence—and, more
importantly, the fact that the *Dunciad* is a satire (rather than, say, a court
transcript)—these damaging assertions about Henley have shaped critical
assumptions about "Orator Henley" ever since.

There is no evidence that Henley provoked Pope before this portrait appeared in the *Dunciad*, but he responded to Pope's satire with characteristic
energy. His best-known printed response took the form of a pamphlet with
a sensational title that may have attracted purchasers but today gives little
sense of the work's sometimes-thoughtful contents: *Why* How now, *Gossip Pope? Or, The Sweet Singing-Bird of Parnassus taken out of its pretty
Cage to be roasted. . . . Exposing the Malice Wickedness and Vanity of his
Aspersions on J. H. in that Monument of His Own Misery and Spleen, the
Dunciad* (1736; 2nd. ed., 1743). Now neglected by critics, this pamphlet
offers shrewd insights into Pope's adept manipulation of the literary marketplace, and it was popular enough to go into a second edition. Irked by
Pope's self-representation as a gentleman-amateur author who was above
the sordid fray of the commercial literary marketplace, Henley responded to
Pope: "the Bulk of what you possess was gained by *writing for Booksellers;
their solid Sterling has built your enchanted Castle.*"[135] As Claudia Thomas
has suggested, "from Henley's perspective, Pope is merely another entrepreneur in the literary marketplace, whose methods are . . . less genteel
than his own."[136] Deploying the same gendered stereotypes against Pope
that Pope deployed against others, Henley compared Pope's print strategies
to stereotypically feminine varieties of oral discourse. He described Pope
as "one that can only use *the Old Woman's Weapon of malicious Gossip-
ing, venomous Scandal,* and *lying Chit-chat*" and accused him of borrowing his techniques from foul-mouthed Billingsgate fishwives: "Your *whole
Piece* is only refining on the low Jests of *Porters* and *Fish-Women,* as you
live by the Water-side; or dressing the *insolent Scurrility of Link-Boys* and
Hackney-Coachmen in something (not much) genteeler Language." More
surprising, however, is Henley's response to Pope's grouping of him with

perceived religious radicals such as Toland, Tindal, and Woolston, all of whom were accused of being freethinkers, if not deists. (Woolston had just been tried for blasphemy in 1729.) For instead of aligning himself against this trio (as he had, in fact, aligned himself against Toland earlier in his career), Henley responded by suggesting that Pope, a fellow Dissenter, was not only a hypocrite but also ignorant of the true nature of these "valuable Men": "*Toland, Tindal, Woolston*, were better and more valuable Men, than any Saints in *your Kalendar*, or *any Wits* of your Acquaintance."[137] Both in publications such as *Why* How now, *Gossip POPE?* and in Oratory debates on Pope's writings and ideas, Henley suggested that "Gossip Pope" was woefully ill-informed.[138]

A more conflicted satirist of Henley, and in many ways a more intriguing one, was Henry Fielding, who satirized Henley as "Dr. Orator," a central character in his play *The Author's Farce* (1730). In the printed version of this play, Fielding attributed its authorship to "Scriblerus Secundus," and today many scholars align Fielding with the cluster of authors now commonly called the "Scriblerians" (including Pope). But as Ashley Marshall has suggested, in 1730, "no such group existed in the public imagination."[139] On 30 March, when the *Author's Farce* debuted at the Haymarket, Fielding was a relatively unknown playwright who was desperate for a hit.[140] Although no Fielding scholar has closely examined Fielding's portrait of Henley as "Dr. Orator" (and regrettably, space prevents me from doing so here), I would argue that a case could be made that in 1730, Fielding was in fact fascinated by Henley's performance experiments and multimedia methods (and, of course, envious of his rise to fame).

The *Author's Farce* begins as a conventional sentimental comedy (albeit with musical interludes in the form of "Airs"), but the third act of this three-act drama consists of a highly unconventional play within a play: a "puppet show" performed by human characters. The characters depicted include the Goddess of Nonsense and a motley assortment of individuals representing types of contemporary entertainment, such as Mrs. Novel, Monsieur Pantomime, Punch and Joan, Signior Opera, and "Dr. Orator." Fielding allies Dr. Orator with the Goddess of Nonsense, but he also acknowledges Henley's tremendous commercial success. The lead character of the play, an out-of-work playwright named "Luckless," is advised by his friend Witmore to "set up an Oratory and preach Nonsense, and you may meet with Encouragement enough."[141] (The name "Dr. Orator," coined by Fielding, indicates his observation that Henley had successfully made the Oratory a "profession.")

As Charles B. Woods has observed, "John Henley . . . as Dr. Orator receives—at least as far as space goes—more attention than anyone else in the
last act."[142] (The actor who plays Dr. Orator also speaks the prologue of the
play.) At the beginning of act 3, the curtain is drawn up, revealing "the Orator, in a Tub," surrounded by the other characters who form his audience.
Dr. Orator is greeted by the Goddess of Nonsense, who announces, "Dr. Orator, I have heard of you."[143] Dr. Orator sings several rounds of a catch that
Fielding calls "Chimes of the Times." The third round is sung to a tune with
the refrain "When I was a bold Orator" (air 15). Dr. Orator also sings a duet
with Punch (air 16), then a debate between these two entertainers ensues.
The subject of the debate is the Muggletonians, a radical sect founded in
the seventeenth century and still active in the 1730s. (However facetiously,
Fielding appears to have linked Henley with radicalism, as Pope did.) In
Fielding's farce, the debate ends happily and is followed by a dance. Henley
is also the subject of the last line of the epilogue (and so of the play itself).

The topicality of Fielding's satire on Henley is striking. Fielding references immediately contemporary lectures at the Oratory; in fact, Henley may have delivered one of these lectures less than ten days before the
Author's Farce debuted.[144] Furthermore, this topicality was reciprocal. On
24 April 1730, Fielding debuted his farce *Tom Thumb* as an afterpiece to the
Author's Farce, and two weeks later, Henley referred to *Tom Thumb* in his
own advertisements for the Oratory.[145] Fielding parodied the eccentric style
of Henley's newspaper advertisements, but significantly, he also made use
of the same newspapers that Henley did to "puff" his own plays. Although
his pseudonym "Scriblerus Secundus" positions him as a *satirist* of scrib-
blers, better-known authors such as Pope and Swift would have perceived
Fielding as something of an upstart, for at this stage his career as an author was a work in progress (as his semiautobiographical character "Luckless" suggests). Significantly, the *Grub-Street Journal* mocked *both* Henley
and Fielding for their cultural and social aspirations and their practice of
"puffing" their own works.[146] Both of these entrepreneurs were associated
with fairground entertainments—and in Fielding's case, the association
was not unmerited, for later that summer adaptations of the third act of
the *Author's Farce* were performed in fairground booths. The proprietors of
these booths advertised these adaptations in the same newspapers in which
Henley advertised his Oratory. On one occasion, an advertisement for a fairground performance of Fielding's play appeared immediately adjacent to a
stylistically similar advertisement for an upcoming lecture at Henley's Oratory. The fairground performance of Fielding's play was puffed as follows:

At REYNOLDS's
GREAT THEATRICAL BOOTH,
. . . a celebrated Operatical Puppet Show, call'd
PUNCH'S ORATORY:
OR,
The PLEASURES of the Town.
Containing several diverting Passages; particularly, a very
elegant and learned Dispute between Punch and
another great Orator . . . No Wires, all alive.[147]

This puff appeared alongside an advertisement for the next day's program at the Oratory and the latest set of *Oratory Transactions*. The similarity of the typographical layout and tone of the two advertisements is striking, but most noteworthy for our purposes is the foregrounding of the "great Orator" (i.e., Henley) and "Punch's Oratory" as the central attraction of this fairground adaptation of Fielding's play. In 1730 it was a promised depiction of the "great Orator," rather than the mention of Fielding's name, that was more likely to draw a crowd.

As L. J. Morrissey has observed, "Fielding's most exciting and most successful plays financially are all almost plotless salads in which songs, dances, verbal parody, and vignette scenes, attacking corrupt politicians or stupid theatre managers or obtuse physicians, are jumbled together."[148] Although no Fielding scholar has made this connection (or owned to it), this description of Fielding's "most exciting and most successful plays"— his farces—could also function as a description of Henley's "Chimes of the Times" events. Throughout his career as a dramatist, novelist, and periodical writer, Fielding was far more interested in Henley than Henley was in him. A decade after depicting Henley as Dr. Orator, Fielding mentioned him in *Joseph Andrews* (1742). In a scene in which Parson Adams falls asleep as Joseph delivers a lecture on charity, the narrator suggests that if the reader would charitably recall how long it had been since Adams slept, "he will not wonder at his repose, though even *Henley* himself, or as great an Orator (if any such be), had been in his Rostrum or Tub before him."[149]

Another conflicted commentator on Henley was Christopher Smart (1722–71). It is a little-known fact that this devout religious poet also dressed up in women's clothing and performed in a variety show advertised as "The Old Woman's Oratory, or, *Henley in Petticoats*."[150] Smart opened "The Old Woman's Oratory" on 3 December 1751 at the Castle Tavern in Paternoster Row, and he continued to deliver performances irregularly until 1754. Some of these performances took place at the Little Theatre in the Haymarket, the site of Henry Fielding's theatrical experiment satirizing Henley. (Smart was a friend of Fielding's.) But Smart's Oratory was a less high-minded endeavor than Henley's. Like Fielding, he appears to have targeted for imitation one element of Henley's program, his weeknight feature, "Chimes of the Times." Christopher Mounsey describes Smart's "Old Woman's Oratory" as "an evening's entertainment of comic speeches on current political events interspersed with musical interludes."[151] (This description recalls L. J. Morrissey's description of Fielding's "most successful plays," quoted above.) But whereas Henley's Oratory was a one-man endeavor, Smart was assisted by a panoply of characters such as Monsieur Timbertoe, a one-legged dancer; by acrobats and animal entertainers; and by musicians playing native instruments such as a hurdy-gurdy and a salt-box. Furthermore, whereas Henley dressed in his clerical habit and always spoke as himself (whether in his capacities as preacher, educator, or political commentator), Smart adopted the costume and the character of a midwife, "Mrs. Mary Midnight."

On one level, Smart's gossipy female persona was chosen for comic effect, as his frequent stereotypical jokes about the "fair sex" suggest. Mary Midnight justifies her enterprise as follows: "since *Oratory* is no more than the *Art of Speaking*, and consequently depends chiefly upon the *Exercise of the Tongue*; Women are allow'd to be the best qualified for it by the universal Consent of all Mankind."[152] But on another level, Smart's adopted persona Mary Midnight was a strategy for veiled political speech: one that illustrates Smart's debt to the career and writings of political scandal writer Delarivier Manley (c. 1670–1724).[153] Manley structured her best-selling political satire, *The New Atalantis*, as an oral exchange among four female speakers, one of them the gossipy midwife "Mrs. Nightwork." For a time, Smart got away with oppositional political commentary in his show because it was ostensibly Henley's Oratory—rather than the Pelham administration—that was the target of Mary Midnight's satire. The Old Woman's Oratory was "merely entertainment" and he was "only a woman."

Smart followed Henley, too, in linking his Oratory performances to a print periodical, *The Midwife: Or, The Old Woman's Magazine* (1750–53). He used the *Midwife* to advertise his Oratory performances, and he placed advertisements in other papers as Henley had done. Smart assumed that his readers were familiar with Henley's advertisements. On one occasion, he satirized Henley's advertising style by printing "a Specimen directly in *his Taste*, and exactly in *his Manner*." A small sample of this satirical "Specimen," published when Henley was recouping his finances after his 1747 appearance at King's Bench for preaching against English government atrocities, reads: "*Argument——Oration——Declamation——Dissertation——Declaration . . . Poverty turn'd Dives, and my Court Debt a Hundred and Forty Thousand Pound . . . This is the True Oratory——Fact——Proof——Reason——Demonstration——Evidence——Conviction——Certainty and Probability*" (and so on).[154]

Smart's *Midwife* frequently refers to Henley, describing him as "the *Stentorian* Orator" (i.e., one known for his thunderous, declamatory tone) and as "my bawling Adversary of Clare Market." Acknowledging Henley's aspirations as an educator, Smart satirized the Oratory as "the University of *Clare-Market*." Smart also associated the Oratory with noise: the "Temple of *Noise* and *Nonsense*." In 1751 Smart published the "Inauguration Speech of Mrs. *Mary Midnight*, at the opening of her Oratory."[155] This speech was a parody of Henley's inaugural sermon at the opening of his Oratory, "The First Sermon Preach'd at the Opening of the Oratory . . . On the Design, and Reasons, of the Institution," published in *Oratory Transactions* 1 (1728). The fact that Smart expected his audience in 1751 to understand this parody of a sermon originally delivered in 1726 suggests the remarkable longevity of Henley's operation and the status of this inaugural issue of *Oratory Transactions* as a "collectible" that someone preserved for twenty-five years.

Smart assumed that his readers and hearers had attended Henley's performances and read his papers. Referring to Henley's oral and print endeavors, he wrote: "you all have been *both* Eye and Ear Witnesses of these Things." Smart commented on the multimedia nature of Henley's enterprise and on his Oratory as an experiment with institutional genres. Henley's mixture of "a Church and a Farce-house," to recall a familiar critique, combined existing institutions into something new. It was therefore difficult to decide whether Henley was "the best Poet, Philosopher, Chymist, Merry Andrew, Fiddler, or Divine." Like Fielding, Smart seems to have admired Henley's bravado, originality, and energy. Again acknowledging the heterogeneity of Henley's project—its "moral, political, literary, critical, civil, religious, [and] miscellaneous" aspects—he commented on Henley, now an old man who would die only a few years later, that

> there is something very singular in his Manner, something peculiarly his own and unborrow'd; so that he can't be charged with Imitation for that he never copied; or with Plagiarism for what he never stole. . . . [W]hether we consider the Orator, in a moral, political, literary, critical, civil, religious, or miscellaneous Light, we may justly say as Hamlet says of his Father,——Take him all in all we shall never behold his like again.[156]

The same combination of bewilderment and begrudging admiration can be seen in the *Grub-Street Journal*'s satiric declaration two decades earlier that Henley's ambitions, innovations, and energy made him "a species by himself."[157]

CONCLUSION: THE ORATORY LEGACY

Henley's Oratory also had high-minded imitators of considerable importance to historians of the Enlightenment. The eighteenth century saw the rise of new associational practices such as clubs, debating societies, and alternative educational institutions and programs. Henley was an early member of the Freemasons, and a promoter of all things Masonic. The Freemasons were dedicated to egalitarian principles and religious toleration, and like Henley, they argued against the hegemony of the universities and their official teachings. The first Grand Lodge was established in London in 1717, and in June 1730 Henley was initiated as a Mason. This event was deemed sufficiently newsworthy to be reported in several London newspapers; two months later, across the Atlantic, Benjamin Franklin announced it in the *Pennsylvania Gazette* (13–20 August). (The following year Franklin himself became a Mason.) Henley involved local Freemasons in the activities of the Oratory. On 13 June 1730 he advertised a special "Elogium on Masonry," with the Fraternity of Freemasons to be in official attendance in their Masonic regalia. Three years later, in June 1733, he advertised a similar event at the Oratory, with a special admissions fee of two shillings.[158] The *Grub-Street Journal* recorded that Henley delivered a "harangue on Free Masonry" on 28 June.[159] Henley also reached out to the Freemasons in his publications, even changing the name of the *Hyp-Doctor* to the *Free Mason* for fifteen issues between late 1733 and early 1734.[160] Writing in his dual identities as Orator and Freemason, he addressed papers to the grand master, described Masonic rituals and customs, and defended the Freemasons against attacks by papers such as the Tory *Craftsman*. Ten years later, in March 1743, the *St. James's Evening Post* reported that Henley had been rewarded for his loyalty: that year, he was elected chaplain of the London Grand Lodge.[161]

Henley was also an early member of the Robin Hood Society "for free and candid Enquiry," which met regularly in Butcher Row from some time in the mid-1740s to 1779.[162] As with the Oratory, so with the Robin Hood Society, a group of workingmen (tradesmen, craftsmen, clerks, and, no doubt, butchers) assembled to hear and share views on religion, politics, trade, and law. But while Henley supported other like-minded public fora, he grew angry when these societies plagiarized his forum. In 1751 one especially close imitator, the Philosophical Society, advertised "lectures of Natural

Philosophy, Natural Religion, and Rational Christianity," available "to all candid Enquirers and Philosophers" for an admission fee of three pence. Henley charged them with usurping the "Priest's Office," and the society's response to Henley is telling, for it suggests the way that eighteenth-century debating societies increasingly modeled themselves as *secular* institutions (as distinct from Henley's initial model of the Oratory as an alternative "ecclesiastical institution"). In an advertisement for "a course of Lectures on Dr. [Samuel] Clarke's Divine Attributes," the Philosophical Society responded to Henley's objections by declaring, "We do not usurp the Priest's Office and Authority . . . No Devotion or Worship being perform'd in this Place. We only philosophize. Therefore Mr. H[enley] might have spared his Reflections last Saturday."[163] Henley understood his Oratory to be a religious institution, but in the long run, his establishment was an important model for a variety of later eighteenth-century societies whose members understood their purposes to be fundamentally nonreligious. In Britain, I would suggest, public debating societies were an outgrowth of new fora for Dissenting worship. Ostensibly religious institutions such as Henley's played an important (and, today, relatively neglected) role in the formation of the "secular" public sphere that we associate with modernity. Henley's enterprise also offers an avenue for future investigation into the links between various radical movements of the seventeenth and early eighteenth centuries and the ideological upheavals of the 1780s and 1790s. Oratory offshoots such as "amicable societies" and debating clubs allowed persons of diverse backgrounds to meet, air their views, and develop their intellects— that is, until 1795, when the British government suppressed most public assemblies in response to the events in France.

Henley died in 1756, and three years later his manuscripts were put up for auction. The catalog of these manuscripts, published by auctioneer Samuel Paterson, was forty-two pages long, and it lists hundreds, if not thousands, of "Sermons," "Discourses," "Essays," "Lectures," and other Oratory genres written by Henley: *A Catalogue of the Original Manuscripts, and Manuscript Collections, Of the Late Reverend Mr. John Henley, A.M. Independent Minister of the Oratory in Lincoln's-Inn Fields* (1759). Following "Dr. Orator," mid- and later eighteenth-century elocutionists set out to harness "ancient eloquence" for an even wider variety of modern purposes. In the next chapters, we will examine Thomas Sheridan's successful spinoff of Henley's Oratory in his *Course of Lectures on Elocution* and related print publications. We will also investigate the "Billingsgate rhetoric" that "polite" elocutionists such as Sheridan defined their own elocutionary endeavors against.

CHAPTER FIVE

How to Speak Well in Public:
The Elocution Movement Begins in Earnest

In 1747 William Hogarth published a series of engravings titled "Industry and Idleness." This series depicts the careers of two London apprentices, Francis Goodchild and Tom Idle, whose hard work or lack thereof shapes their fates. In the final plate, plate 12, Goodchild rides in a coach in the Lord Mayor's Procession, having been elected the lord mayor of London. In the penultimate plate, plate 11, Tom Idle rides in a cart to the gallows to be hanged (fig. 5.1). Plate 11 depicts a crowd gathered at Tyburn to watch the hanging. In the center front, staring directly at the viewer, a hawker uses her booming voice to advertise cheap print. Like the other female street vendors to her left and right, this loud and noticeably strong woman is not a person one would wish to engage in a verbal or physical battle. Lugging a child on her hip and wearing ragged clothes and ill-fitting shoes, she cries broadsides titled *The Last Dying Speech & Confession of Tho. Idle.*

On a direct vertical axis above the street crier is the official figure who stands to profit most from her labors: the chaplain, or "Ordinary," of Newgate Prison, who rides in a closed coach ahead of Tom. With sales of prisoners' "Last Dying Speeches" sometimes running into the thousands, the right to print these texts was a significant perquisite of the Ordinary's position. It was the Ordinary's duty to provide solace to condemned persons and to encourage their salvation. But instead of preaching and saving souls, this Anglican clergyman is passively profiting from cheap print.

In Hogarth's image, the Ordinary is strikingly separated from both the prisoner and the populace: he is barely visible through the window of his coach. In sharp contrast to this silent and aloof Anglican clergyman, a Methodist preacher sits next to Tom in the open cart, preaching energetically and gesturing toward heaven. The Methodist preacher's efforts to encourage Tom's spiritual reform appear to be succeeding, for the young man is using

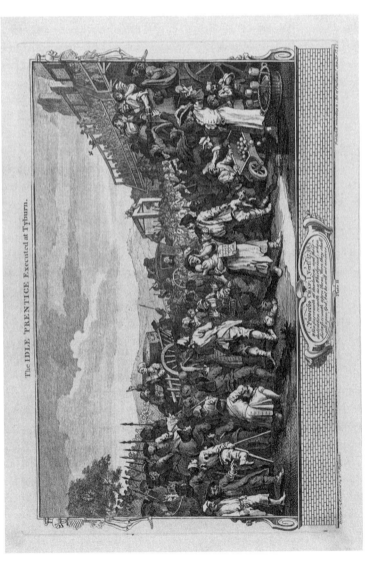

The IDLE 'PRENTICE Executed at Tyburn.

Fig. 5.1. William Hogarth, *The Idle 'Prentice Executed at Tyburn*, pl. 11 of "Industry and Idleness" series (1747). Photograph: Courtesy of the Lewis Walpole Library, Yale University.

the last minutes of his life to read a book (presumably a Bible or a psalm book). Along with the foregrounded female hawker, this "enthusiast" preacher is one of plate 11's most commanding figures. Not coincidentally, both of these socially marginal figures are depicted with wide open mouths. It is *their* voices, not the Anglican clergyman's, that are being heard.

In my next two chapters—this one on the elocution movement and chapter 6 on Billingsgate fishwives and the rhetorical topic of "Billingsgate" discourse—I argue that Dissenting preachers and female hawkers (especially fishwives) were the two dominant figures of loud, unruly, "impolite," and threatening noise in eighteenth-century British literature and art. Furthermore, I contend that the seemingly omnipresent depiction of these culturally central, yet socially marginal figures' powerful voices in satiric prints, periodical papers, poetry, drama, novels, and rhetorical texts was to a significant degree a product of widespread cultural reflection by eighteenth-century authors and artists on the spread and implications of print commerce. In this chapter, I begin by examining English contributors to the elocution movement after Henley, along with their French precursor, Michel Le Faucheur. I then turn to the nation-building projects of Irish elocutionist Thomas Sheridan and to the later eighteenth-century transformation of the movement. I conclude with a brief consideration of late eighteenth-century assessments of the movement's legacy and social, political, and moral implications. While rhetorician Hugh Blair warned of Britons' new "absurd rage for Public Speaking," and Sheridan's son, Richard Brinsley Sheridan, satirized women's participation, Jane Austen spotlighted her contemporaries' *diverse* motives for heightened attention to "good [oral] delivery"—now construed, significantly, as "the art of reading."[1]

In eighteenth-century Britain, almost everybody participated in some form of public worship. Sermons were a print phenomenon as well as an auditory one, but far more people *heard* sermons than read them, and almost everybody discussed them. Sermons played an enormous role in shaping public opinion, especially political opinion.[2] In one of his political sermons at the Oratory, John Henley observed shrewdly, "ye Pulpit has always been a Warlike Place."[3] As I have suggested in earlier chapters, authors and auditors were deeply concerned with the *delivery* of sermons as well as with their ideological contents: they were intensely aware that preaching was an oral and visual performance. While some sermons were delivered extempore, most involved some reading from notes or printed texts, and Anglican services routinely included the reading aloud of the liturgy and the scriptures. In the *Tatler* and the *Spectator*, Isaac Bickerstaff, Mr. Spectator, and their contributing readers discuss the "eloquence of the pulpit," including "the well Reading of the Common Prayer."[4]

For virtually all commentators, the ideal sermon was neither "enthusiastic" nor soporific. Addison and Steele satirized the extremes of contemporary preaching styles and suggested that the goal was somewhere in between. Steele complained that "a great Part of the learned Clergy of Great Britain . . . deliver the most excellent Discourses with such Coldness and Indifference, that 'tis no great Wonder the unintelligent Many of their Congregations fall asleep." After the Toleration Act granted freedom of worship to Protestant Dissenters, auditors could choose the preacher they wished to listen to. Accordingly, Addison and Steele hinted, Anglican clergymen needed to pay greater attention to their delivery, or they would lose followers to "enthusiastic" and "warm[ing]" preachers: "we very frequently see People lulled asleep with solid and elaborate Discourses of Piety, who would be warmed and transported out of themselves by the Bellowings and Distortions of Enthusiasm."[5] Jonathan Swift also acknowledged the problem of dull sermons. In his sermon "On Sleeping in Church," he warned his parishioners against falling asleep in a sacred space. Swift took as his scriptural text Acts 20:9, a verse that relates how Eutychus fell asleep while Saint Paul preached. Swift began his sermon with a wry warning to his parishioners: "I have chosen these Words with Design, if possible, to disturb some Part in this Audience of half an Hour's Sleep, for the Convenience and Exercise whereof this Place, at this Season of the Day, is very much celebrated."[6]

In his engravings *The Sleeping Congregation* (1736) and *Credulity, Superstition, and Fanaticism* (1762), Hogarth thematized the undesirable extremes of contemporary preaching (figs. 5.2 and 5.3). In *The Sleeping Congregation*, he depicts an Anglican clergyman using a magnifying glass to read his sermon from a book. Despite the grandeur of the church, with its lofty ceilings, elaborate stained-glass windows, and imposing pulpit, most of the parishioners are snoozing. The preacher's sermon text is Matthew 11.28: "Come unto me, all ye that labor and are heavy laden, and I will give you rest." Beneath the pulpit, a clerk also has a book open before him (in his case, a large folio). Like the preacher, the clerk is unable to read the text without an ocular instrument (he holds spectacles). Furthermore, instead of actually *reading* the book, he ogles the breasts of a woman nearby. For Hogarth, as for so many eighteenth-century commentators, dull preaching was far more than a matter of professional ineptitude: it jeopardized the salvation of souls. Thirty years later, Hogarth advanced this argument even more powerfully. Whereas *The Sleeping Congregation* depicts an Anglican preacher putting his audience to sleep, *Credulity, Superstition, and Fanaticism* depicts an "enthusiast" preacher (most likely a Methodist) rousing

Fig. 5.2. William Hogarth, *The Sleeping Congregation* (1736).
Photograph: Courtesy of the Lewis Walpole Library, Yale University.

his crowded congregation to dangerously heightened passions. Behind the
preacher, a gigantic thermometer measures the intensity and range of their
emotions. The scale on the thermometer moves downward from low spirits
to sorrow, agony, grief, despair, madness, and suicide and upward from love-
heat to lust, ecstasy, convulsions, fits, and madness. Behind the preacher, a
gigantic open mouth bawls "Blood Blood Blood."

Fig. 5.3. William Hogarth, *Credulity, Superstition, and Fanaticism* (1762).
Photograph: Courtesy of the Lewis Walpole Library, Yale University.

A central concern of eighteenth-century debates on preaching was the question of "Action" in the pulpit. As I have stated, *actio*, or *pronuntiatio*, was traditionally *one* of the five parts of rhetoric (the others being *inventio, dispositio, memoria*, and *elocutio*, with the latter referring to compositional style), but in the eighteenth century, action became the most important part. *Actio* referred to precepts of voice and gesture, but in this period it came to be known as "elocution." In eighteenth-century Britain and America, Wilbur Samuel Howell observes, "the term was to dominate all other[s] . . . and was even to become the term for the entire art of rhetoric."[7] While the elocutionists continued to think of themselves as rhetoricians, they focused almost exclusively on delivery: that is, on the question of how to speak well in public.

In their papers addressing "Eloquence and graceful Action," Addison and Steele argued that Anglican preachers made insufficient use of "Action" in the pulpit: "our Orators are observed to make use of less Gesture or Action than those of other Countries. Our Preachers stand stock-still in the Pulpit, and will not so much as move a Finger to set off the best Sermons in the World." "[T]he Clergy of *Great Britain* . . . are . . . the most learned Body of Men now in the World; and yet this Art of Speaking, with the proper Ornaments of Voice and Gesture, is wholly neglected." Action is a crucial tool for speakers, for by communicating the speaker's "passion[s]," it triggers a sympathetic corporeal response in his audience:

> Proper Gestures and vehement Exertions of the Voice cannot be too much studied by a Public Orator. . . . [T]hey keep the Audience awake, and fix their Attention to what is delivered to them, at the same time that they shew the Speaker is in earnest, and affected himself with what he so passionately recommends to others.

Addison asserted that rhetorical action was especially powerful in influencing the ladies, for women are particularly susceptible to a "moving Preacher," and their passions are triggered by oratorical action even when they cannot hear a word the preacher says: "Nothing is more frequent than to see Women weep and tremble at the sight of a moving Preacher, though he is placed quite out of their Hearing." As an example of the "Power of Action," Steele depicted "little Parson Dapper, who is the common Relief to all the lazy Pulpits in Town." This "smart Youth" fixes the attention of his congregants by his delivery rather than his doctrine: by his "good Memory . . . quick Eye . . . clean Handkerchief" and "decisive Air."[8]

But as Steele's example of Parson Dapper suggests, action in the pulpit was also considered suspect, for it threatened to turn the church into a stage. A preacher must not be overly theatrical, thumping the pulpit or haranguing his auditors, for "as harsh and irregular Sound is not Harmony; so neither is banging a Cushion, Oratory. . . . [I]n a Religious Assembly, it gives a Man too Warlike, or perhaps too Theatrical a Figure, to be suitable to a Christian Congregation." But Addison and Steele were convinced that the potential benefits of "Action" in oratory made it worth the risk of impropriety, for "the force of Action is such, that it is more prevalent, even when improper, than all the Reason and Argument in the World without it." Nevertheless, they emphasized that a virtuous orator uses the time-honored "Arts of Speaking" "honest[ly]": "he never attempts your Passions, till he has convinced your Reason."[9]

Addison and Steele acknowledged that Anglican orators now competed with Dissenting preachers. They foregrounded the immediacy of this threat when they suggested that "if our [Anglican] Preachers would learn to speak . . . within Six Months Time we should not have a Dissenter within a Mile of a Church in *Great Britain*." Whereas Dissenting preachers spoke "*Extempore*," Anglican preachers too often read their sermons from written and printed texts. In so doing, they failed to employ sufficient action, or attention to the "Graces of Voice and Gesture":

> If Nonsence [*sic*], when accompanied with such an Emotion of Voice and Body, has such an Influence on Mens Minds, what might we not expect from many of those admirable Discourses which are Printed in our Tongue, were they delivered with a becoming Fervour, and with the most agreeable Graces of Voice and Gesture?

If the established clergy would "recommend Truth and Virtue in their proper Figures . . . it is not possible that Nonsense should have so many Hearers as you find it has in Dissenting Congregations, for no Reason in the World, but because it is spoken *Extempore*: For ordinary Minds are wholly govern'd by their Eyes and Ears." Addison and Steele tactfully suggested that the "Indifferency" of the Anglican clergy to the "Graces of Voice and Action" might stem from their endeavor to avoid "the Imputation of Cant." (Cant was associated with affectation and with "bawling" and "whining Tones.") At the same time, though, while they critiqued Dissenting preachers' "Cant," they acknowledged with dismay the "great . . . Effect" that their "improper" styles of speaking had "on the People."[10]

Addison and Steele directed their critiques of enthusiasm against Quakers, Baptists, Familists, and others, but after the Methodist movement gained headway in the 1730s, Anglican critiques increasingly focused on Methodist preachers. In the early years of Methodism, critics commonly lumped together Methodists and Dissenters—despite the fact that the founders of Methodism, John Wesley (1703–91) and George Whitefield (1714–70), always considered themselves members of the Church of England, and Wesley, in particular, worked to distance Methodism from Dissenting sects. Early Methodists benefited greatly from the Toleration Act granting Protestant Dissenters freedom of worship, but Wesley and Whitefield were wary of Dissenters' "refusal to conform to the requirements of Anglicanism and its hierarchical governance." In shaping Methodism as a distinct *branch* of Protestantism, they adapted some practices employed by Dissenters and others employed by Anglicans. They selected tactics and material from multiple traditions and used them to different ends.[11]

The same year that Henley left the established church (1725), Wesley was ordained an Anglican deacon. Wesley preached in Anglican churches for about a decade, but in the later 1730s he began open-air preaching. While he was initially wary of this practice due to its associations with Dissent, he came to think that its benefits outweighed the risks. Open-air preaching allowed him to reach new audiences and enormous crowds. By 1739 Wesley was "preaching in and around London to crowds that numbered 12,000 to 20,000 listeners."[12] After Whitefield was ordained in 1736, his tireless preaching and powerful voice made him a celebrity. Benjamin Franklin heard Whitefield preach in Philadelphia and estimated that his voice reached an enormous crowd of 30,000 people.[13]

Wesley's and Whitefield's negotiation of their relationship with the established church can be better understood by contrasting their self-positioning with that of Henley. Like these men, Henley was ordained an Anglican clergyman, but unlike them, he openly left the church, and for the next two decades, he used his speech and print to critique particular aspects of Anglicanism as oppressive. Henley associated Methodism with freedom of speech, populism, and the "right[s]" of "ye people," and he admired Wesley and Whitefield (especially Wesley). In Henley's view, there were important *class* implications to what these gentlemen were doing. Of Wesley, he wrote approvingly: "Was every preacher in England to be as free & righteous as that Gentleman . . . ye people wd. be more able to right themselves, by knowing their Strength."[14] As an innovator himself, Henley was intrigued by Methodist open-air preaching. In one of his own sermons, he memorably described Whitefield as a "Circumambient Preacher." By the 1730s open-air preaching was neither illegal nor wholly new. But it was still highly singular, and Henley rightly recognized that Whitefield's systematic embracing and organization of this practice constituted a significant innovation. But although Henley praised Wesley as "free & righteous," he questioned his politics and tactics. He critiqued Wesley for toeing the line of the government whenever it suited his purposes, and he openly scoffed of Whitefield, "if they will let him preach, he will let them cheat and oppress."[15]

Like Henley, Wesley and Whitefield made extensive use of print publication in tandem with preaching. In 1749 Wesley published a twelve-page practical guide for Methodist lay preachers titled *Directions Concerning Pronunciation and Gesture*. Three things are worth noting about this pamphlet. First, it was aimed at humble readers and was priced accordingly (one penny); second, it focused exclusively on delivery rather than doctrine; and third (and seldom recognized or acknowledged today), substantial parts of it were taken almost verbatim from the English translation of Michel Le Faucheur's *Traitté de l'action de l'orateur* (Paris, 1657). To understand early Methodist preaching—and the significant social threat that it represented—it is helpful to have some familiarity with Le Faucheur's treatise. In 1702 the *Traitté* was published in London as *An Essay Upon the Action of an Orator; As to His Pronunciation and Gesture. Useful both for Divines and Lawyers, and necessary for all Young Gentlemen, that study how to Speak well in Publick. Done out of French*. In borrowing from this work, Wesley would most likely have used the second English edition, *The Art of Speaking in Publick: Or An Essay on the Action of an Orator*, with its new *Introduction relating to the Famous Mr. Henly's present Oratory* (1727).[16] By the end of their careers, Wesley and Whitefield were as media savvy as anyone else in Britain. They made extensive use of manuscript correspondence networks as well as print, and they were pioneers in the cause of teaching the poor to read. But in the case of *Directions Concerning Pronunciation and Gesture*, Wesley made use of cheap print to teach lay preachers how to use voice and gesture to reach the minds and souls of the common people.

As the full title of *An Essay Upon the Action of an Orator* suggests, Le Faucheur focused on gesture, which he called the "Eloquence of the Body."[17] One of the longest chapters "Lays down Particular Rules for *Gesture*" (chap. 13), for "*Gesture* . . . is the *Life* of all *Speech*."[18] Echoing Le Faucheur, Wesley called gesture "this silent Language of your Face and Hands."[19] In teaching rhetorical action, both men recommended the example of the ancient Greek orator Demosthenes (384–322 BCE). Demosthenes was known for his emphasis on action in public speaking: he viewed action as "the *First, Second*, and *Third* Faculty of Eloquence, all in *one*."[20] But what made Demosthenes especially useful for teachers of elocution was his excellence as an example of self-help and of overcoming obstacles.²¹ Demosthenes was the son of a slave, he was orphaned at seven years old, and he suffered from a speech impediment. According to Le Faucheur, he was born with "a *weak Voyce*, an *Impediment* in his *Speech*, a *Short Breath*," and a "*Tongue* . . . so *Gross*, that he could not speak his words Plain and Distinct, nor pronounce some Letters at all."²² But despite these challenges, this enterprising young man taught himself to speak clearly and powerfully by making use of free natural resources such as pebbles and waves. He practiced speaking with rocks in his mouth and while competing with the sound of the ocean. Le Faucheur, Wesley, and, later, Thomas Sheridan all held up the "example of this prince of orators" as "afford[ing] the highest encouragement, to all men who labour under imperfections of speech, to endeavour their cure."²³

Le Faucheur and Wesley observed that Demosthenes practiced his gestures in front of a mirror: "He had a great *Looking-glass* made him, where he might see all his *Shapes* at once in full *Proportion* and *Symmetry*; and know how to correct every *Motion* or *Posture* of his *Body*, which transgress'd the *Rules* of Art."²⁴ Wesley advised Methodist preachers to practice their gestures in front of a mirror (or a friend), for "a Man may hear his own Voice, but he cannot see his own Face: Neither can he observe the several Motions of his own Body; at least but imperfectly. To remedy this, you may use a large Looking-glass, as *Demosthenes* did, and thereby observe and learn to avoid every disagreeable or unhandsome Gesture."²⁵ Le Faucheur made no attempt to deny that there were strong links between practicing one's gestures and learning to act for the stage. He observed that Demosthenes took speech lessons from an actor: "*Demosthenes*, who had naturally a very *short Breath*; finding that he had need of a very *long one* . . . gave *Neoptolemus* the *Stage-player*, and a great *Actor* of *Comedy*, a thousand *Drachms* to teach him this *Art*."²⁶ But in eighteenth-century Britain, rhetoricians and elocutionists worked to distinguish "Action" in oratory from the low "tricks" of actors. While they celebrated Demosthenes's determination and self-help methods, they were wary of his crowd-pleasing style, and they warned contemporary orators not to let the "vulgar" be their guides. Of Demosthenes's overdependence on his auditors, David Hume complained that "the lowest vulgar of Athens were his sovereigns."²⁷

While Le Faucheur acknowledged the links between oratory and acting, he nonetheless worked to distinguish the correct use of gesture in oratory from all that "smells [sic] of the *Juggler* and the *Mountebank*." He cautioned that some of the "Actions" of the great ancient orators would be out of "Vogue" in the "*Age*" we live in." Quintilian, for instance, "teaches up several Fondnesses and Foppish *Actions*; as of beating his Brow, his Head, his

Breast, his Thigh; of Stamping and such like: Which in *his time*, were decent enough perhaps; but they are very unbecoming, disagreeable and *antick* motions in *ours*, and quite out of Countenance and Vogue now." Orators should "take great care to avoid imitating those *Actions* which are *Base*, *Filthy*, and *Dishonest.*" One's body parts and "Motions" should be kept under tight control at all times:

> The *Orator* must manage his *Gesture* so nicely, that there may be nothing, if possible, in all the *Dispositions* and *Motions* of his *Body*, which may offend the *Eyes* of the *Spectators*; as well as take care that his *Pronunciation* have nothing in it, which may grate and disoblige the *Ears* of the *Hearers.*

Unlike eighteenth-century British elocutionists, who tended to be politely circumspect in discussing such matters, Le Faucheur actually indicated what actions were *"Base, Filthy,* and *Dishonest."* He detailed proper versus improper movements of the *"Head," "Breast," "Shoulders," "Face," "Eyes," "Eye-lids," "Eye-brows," "Mouth," "Lips," "Tongue," "Belly," "Elbow," "Arms," "Hands," "Knees,"* and *"Feet."* Anticipating Addison and Steele, he advised preachers: you "must never *clap* your *Hands,* nor *thump* the *Pulpit,* nor *beat* your *Breast."* He especially advised that one's hands should be kept under tight control, for hands had a language of their own, and excessive movement was mere "babbling of the Hands."[28] Echoing Le Faucheur, Wesley cautioned Methodist preachers, "Your Hands are not to be in perpetual Motion: This the Ancients call'd, The Babbling of the Hands."[29] Like Le Faucheur, too, Wesley provided specific guidance as to how orators should use their bodies so as not to offend polite audiences. Vulgar body parts such as "the Mouth," "Lips," "Shoulders" and "Elbows" should be monitored closely: "the Mouth must never be turn'd awry: Neither must you bite or lick your Lips, or shrug up your Shoulders; or lean upon your Elbow; all which give just Offence."[30] Methodist preachers should avoid clapping or thumping the pulpit (if they had one). They should avoid a thundering, ranting delivery, and above all, they should avoid "Speaking with a Tone," for "whining," "whimsical," and "Theatrical Tone[s]" were associated with Dissenters and evidently also with women:

> [T]he greatest and most common Fault of all, is, the Speaking with a Tone. Some have a Womanish, squeaking Tone: Some a singing or canting one: Some an high, swelling, Theatrical Tone, laying too much Emphasis on every Sentence: Some have an awful, solemn Tone; others an odd, whimsical, whining one, not to be exprest in Words.

Le Faucheur also advised that orators should preserve distinctions of social rank. One's "*Movements* and *Countenances*" should be tailored to the "Quality" of one's auditors, "so as to show . . . a *Gravity* and an *Authority* in speaking to . . . your *Inferiors*; but *Submission, Humility* and *Respect* to your *Betters.*"[31] Similarly, Wesley advised Methodist preachers to "look with Gravity on your Inferiors, on your Superiors with Boldness mixt with Respect." At the same time, though, Wesley fine-tuned Le Faucheur's advice to the different situation of socially marginal lay preachers. He advised even preachers of the lowest orders to be "Bold."[32]

Like Henley, who admired Wesley's work with the poor, Samuel Johnson praised Whitefield for "devot[ing] himself to the lower classes of mankind." But like Alexander Pope in the *Dunciad*, who depicted Whitefield's preaching as exemplifying the "wond'rous Pow'r of Noise," Johnson compared Whitefield to a "mountebank" and criticized his style of preaching as "familiarity and noise":

> Whitefield never drew as much attention as a mountebank does; he did not draw attention by being better than others, but by doing what was strange. . . . I never treated Whitefield's ministry with contempt; I believe he did good. He had devoted himself to the lower classes of mankind, and among them I believe he did much good. But when familiarity and noise claim the praise due to knowledge, art, and elegance, we must beat down such pretensions.

Johnson distrusted action in rhetoric; he held that one used "action" on "brutes" (animals), not men. While Johnson was skeptical, James Boswell admired the "power of rhetorical action," and he made this shrewd observation about human nature: "I thought it extraordinary, that [Johnson] should deny the power of rhetorical action upon human nature. . . . Reasonable beings are not solely reasonable. They have fancies which may be pleased, passions which may be roused."[33] Even reasonable men, Boswell knew from plentiful personal experience, had "passions which may be roused."

SHERIDAN, PRINT, AND THE "POWERS OF [THE] LIVING VOICE"

The same year that John Henley died (1756), an unemployed Irish actor, Thomas Sheridan (c. 1719–88), published *British Education: Or, The Source of the Disorders of Great Britain. . . . With An Attempt to shew, that a Revival of the Art of Speaking, and the Study of Our Own Language, might contribute . . . to the Cure of those Evils.* Thomas Sheridan Jr. was the son of Dr. Thomas Sheridan, a Dublin clergyman and schoolteacher who died in 1738, leaving his family in straitened circumstances. Thomas Jr. found work as an actor and theater manager in Dublin and London, but by 1755 he was broke and exploring the possibility of a new career as an elocution-ist. He spent that winter writing *British Education,* in which he outlined an ambitious plan "to revive the long lost art of oratory, and to correct, ascertain, and fix the English language."[34] Over the next decade, he would deliver lectures on "Elocution" in major cities in England, Ireland, and Scot-land. In 1762 he published *A Course of Lectures on Elocution: Together With Two Dissertations on Language; And Some Other Tracts Relative to Those Subjects.* In an appendix to this work, he outlined his proposal for an "ENGLISH SOCIETY instituted for . . . the establishment of the Art of Elocution."[35] Not surprisingly, given his many manifestos and advertise-ments, Sheridan is now often assumed to be the founder of the elocution movement in Britain.[36] But in my view, the 1702 English translation of Le Faucheur's *Traitté* triggered the movement, and Sheridan took over where John "Orator" Henley left off. It is no accident that Sheridan published *British Education* the year that Henley died, and in the following pages, I will show how Sheridan capitalized on and extended Henley's innovations. Sheridan was neither more important nor more innovative than Le Fau-cheur or Henley, but Howell is correct that Sheridan was "much luckier than Le Faucheur's translator . . . or Henley in getting himself remembered by posterity."[37] As Paul Goring observes, too, the fact that "Sheridan was able to base the latter half of his career on the business of promoting polite eloquence . . . testifies to the immense public interest that surrounded the subject by the mid century."[38]

In the 1740s Sheridan was a struggling actor at Drury Lane Theatre in London. Given the proximity of Henley's Oratory to Drury Lane and Sheri-dan's strong interest in performance, it seems likely that he would have attended the Oratory. Henley was the talk of the town, discussed weekly in newspapers, and Sheridan would certainly have known who he was. But whereas Henley was tied to the physical location of his Oratory, Sheridan took his lecture series on the road. He traveled between London, Dublin, Edinburgh, Bath, Oxford, Cambridge, and other major towns in England, Scotland, and Ireland, and for the remainder of his life he never really set-tled down. Henley developed a new market for training in public speaking, but Sheridan expanded that market, tying it to the goal of nation building in Britain after the political union of England and Scotland in 1706/7. Whereas Henley was forced by his fixed location to come up with an endless array of new ideas and topics, Sheridan recycled his lectures to different audiences. He then reached out to further audiences through print. Both speakers attracted socially diverse audiences, and both were satirized for appealing to "persons of the meaner sort." But in reality, the cost of Sheridan's lectures was far beyond the means of most small tradesmen (let alone laborers and the poor). As Goring observes, Sheridan's "subscription fee of a guinea per head for the London lectures" was "a substantial amount. . . . And the published version of the lectures was sold by subscription at half a guinea (in boards)." As we shall see, too, whereas Henley critiqued Wesley for conceding to the authority of the government and the established church, Sheridan was intensely concerned with gaining the approval and collaboration of those in power. He was also successful at gaining their acceptance. As Goring observes, that Sheridan "should lecture by invitation in the universities of Oxford and Cambridge as he did in 1758 and 1759 (and indeed be awarded an honorary MA) testifies to the degree of establishment approval [that] he gained."[39]

In advancing his plan for the teaching of elocution, Sheridan proclaimed that "a general inability to read, or speak, with propriety and grace in public . . . shews itself in our senates and churches, on the bench and at the bar."[40] He argued that training in oratory would promote excellence in these great traditional arenas of British oratory and, furthermore, that the "powers of [the] living voice" would promote the nation's political and economic interests abroad. To illustrate his claims, Sheridan pointed to a well-known public figure who had recently distinguished himself by his *voice*: Prime Minister William Pitt, who had resigned in 1761 after leading the British government during much of the Seven Years' War.[41] Sheridan described Pitt as a man who "by the mere force of cultivating the [spoken] language . . . raised himself to the sole direction of affairs in this country: and not only so, but the powers of his living voice shook distant thrones." Access to the press, he suggested, was now relatively cheap and easy, yet this great man owed his fame to his voice rather than to print. In contrast to the example of Pitt, he lamented, "some of our greatest men have been trying to do that with the pen, which can only be performed by the tongue; to produce effects by the dead letter, which can never be produced but by the living voice, with its accompaniments." Sheridan even went so far as to hypothesize that if Pitt *had* made greater use of print genres such as polemical pamphlets and newspapers—as so many other politicians were now doing—he would have failed miserably in his glorious cause. If Pitt's powerful speeches had "been sent out into the world in a pamphlet; they would probably have produced less effects upon the minds of a few readers, than those of some hireling writers."[42]

Eighteenth-century elocutionists were concerned with several different kinds of "speaking" in public, including the reading aloud of manuscript and printed texts. Sheridan implicitly included both extempore speech and reading aloud when he lamented that "a general inability *to read, or speak*, with propriety and grace in public . . . shews itself in our senates and churches, on the bench and at the bar."[43] In *Speaking Volumes: Women, Reading, and Speech in the Age of Austen*, Patricia Howell Michaelson argues that "for all of his emphasis on the 'living' voice, Sheridan's advice (like that of all the elocutionists) concerns not oratory, but reading—not debate nor impromptu speech." But Michaelson's study focuses on the "Age of Austen" (1775–1817), and earlier in the eighteenth century, I would argue, elocutionists were much less likely to equate oratory and reading aloud.[44] Early eighteenth-century elocutionists looked back to the ancients as their models of oratorical excellence, and as Sheridan himself emphasized, ancient orators relied on "the great volume of society" rather than on books. (In the days of Cicero and Demosthenes, he remarked, "there was no press agoing at that time.")[45] Printed texts were far more readily available in Austen's day than they were in Addison and Steele's. In 1774 the House of Lords ruled that perpetual copyright was illegal in England and Scotland, and Austen's era saw a sharp rise in the number of anthologies, abridgements, and adaptations published. Elocutionists were among those who immediately took advantage of the changing commercial contexts of print. (It is no accident, for instance, that elocutionist William Enfield published *The Speaker*, his best-selling anthology of extracts for oral recitation, in 1774.)[46] It was only in the *nineteenth century* that recitation was institutionalized in public schools in Britain and America, and I would argue that this later phenomenon has distorted—or even prevented—our full understanding of the earlier eighteenth-century elocution movement.[47]

Sheridan made a career out of celebrating the power of the spoken word. While he regularly printed his own works, his texts are full of provocative statements praising speech at the expense of writing and print. In contrast to the still commonly held view that writing was God's gift to mankind, he wrote: "we have in use two kinds of language; the spoken, and the written. The one, the gift of God; the other, the invention of man." Arguing for elocutionary training in schools, he lamented "an early false bias given to us in our system of education. . . . I mean that extravagant idea entertained of the power of writing, far beyond what in its nature it can ever attain." He suggested that "the vanity of ingenious men [had] prompt[ed] them to think, that they can do that by writing, which is beyond the power of writing to accomplish; and . . . readers shall continue to search for that in books, which it is beyond the power of books to teach." Statements like these are highly memorable (and quotable), and it is not surprising that many scholars have assumed that Sheridan was chiefly concerned with theorizing the effects of *writing* in general. But I would argue that Sheridan's elocutionary projects, both oral and printed, were more significantly motivated by his thinking about print commerce. At once critiquing *and* attempting to capitalize on the still-new tool of the press, he made extensive use of printing while deploring its "abuse" by others: "the invention of printing . . . thro' the abuse of it . . . has done more harm than good." It was not writing per se but "the invention of printing, and the consequential application to book language only" that in his view contributed most to the "loss of the language of nature." Strikingly, Sheridan defined ancient Greece by its lack of print—and, more particularly, its lack of "low," polemical genres such as "pamphlets": "There was no press agoing at that time, to furnish pamphlets for, or against any measure."[48] Sheridan's constant sniping about "low" print genres and "hireling writers," and his complaints about hard times for literary "men of genius," support my larger argument in this book that the eighteenth-century reevaluation of oral communication was triggered in large part by reflection on the consequences and implications of the commercial press.

Sheridan did not deny that print was a valuable tool. He extolled the opportunities introduced by the "invention of printing," especially when combined with "general commerce, and a free press." He especially noted the class implications of the wider availability of texts: "the invention of printing has given us an amazing advantage over the ancients. . . . [A]mongst us, . . . there are hardly any so low who may not acquire knowledge by the eye, as well as by the ear." The pulpit and the press were two key advantages that Britain had "over other nations, both ancient and modern." Both of these could (and should) be put to work teaching elocution: "By means of these, an uniformity of pronunciation might with ease be diffused through the whole land." But the press was a powerful force for bad as well as good: "as the press is in constant action, it must constantly diffuse either a good or bad taste thro' the people."[49]

Sheridan was typical of literary gentlemen of his day in his belief that his era was a time of great changes with respect to literacy. He claimed that "reading . . . by means of the press, is become almost universal amongst us." In actual fact, reading was far from "universal," but the perception or assertion is revealing nonetheless. In the past, Sheridan suggested, the ability to read was a mark of great distinction. It was a way to set oneself apart from—and exercise power over—the lower ranks: "reading, in its infancy, was looked upon as a supernatural gift; and the few who were masters of that

art, considered by the vulgar in the light of magicians." But now, he suggested, the situation had changed. Literacy was no longer a mark of real distinction, and this shift was due not so much to the technology of writing per
se as it was to the spread of print commerce: "the press, and the cheapness
of books . . . has made the art of reading . . . familiar to the lowest people."
The press and the "cheapness of books" were profoundly affecting class
relations in Britain: "by means of the press all ranks of people are taught to
read, throughout the most distant parts of these countries."[50] Reading and
writing were now "common," and in this new era of widespread reading it
was learning how to *speak* well in public, rather than to read or write, that
would make a gentlemen stand out from the crowd. Eloquence, Sheridan
argued, was a new tool of distinction in an increasingly literate age.

Anticipating some of Sheridan's arguments, Samuel Johnson playfully
proposed that too much reading could undermine one's oral abilities. In an
issue of the *Rambler*, Johnson depicts one "Vivaculus," a university graduate who inherits a fortune and determines to devote his life to books: "I
furnish'd a large room with all conveniences for study; collected books of
every kind." Vivaculus reads for several years, only to discover that his oral
skills have deteriorated. He now finds himself "bewildered," "disconcerted,"
and "overwhelmed" in any kind of oral dispute: "my quickness of apprehen-
sion, and celerity of reply, had entirely deserted me; when I delivered my
opinion, or detailed my knowledge, I was bewildered by an unseasonable
interrogatory, disconcerted by any slight opposition, and overwhelmed and
lost in dejection, when the smallest advantage was gained against me." Determined to restore his oral skills, Vivaculus resolves "for a time to shut my
books, and learn again the art of conversation." He travels to London, whereupon one of his "academical acquaintances" introduces him to "the little
societies of literature which are formed in taverns and coffee-houses." One
of these societies consists of a "company of curious men" who meet every
week to compare their collections of print ephemera (pamphlets, gazettes,
old prints, and texts in Gothic letter). But Vivaculus discerns that, like himself, these print-obsessed gentlemen have lost the oral talents that they
once possessed. Their "conversation" is "fretful and waspish," and he leaves
them to their print collections, "without any intention of returning."[51]

Johnson never seriously believed that reading undermined one's speaking skills. He was, after all, a renowned conversationalist as well as an avid
reader and prolific author. But in contrast to Johnson, Sheridan posited a
causal connection between extensive reading and lost oral arts, and he made
this connection the raison d'être of his elocutionary program. Somewhat
incongruously, given his status as a published author, he argued that too

much reading—whether silent reading or reading aloud—was detrimental to modern elocution: "happy had it been for the state of modern elocution, that the art [of reading] had still remained unknown." Reading aloud from texts undermined "natural" eloquence: "with respect to extemporaneous speaking in public, I have not known many instances in my life in which the artificial manner, got from a bad habit of reading, or imitations of others, has not supplanted the natural manner of speaking." Furthermore, "attention to written language will never in the least improve the faculties of speech, or talents of delivery, but rather impede than bring them forwards, as bookish men are observed to be more defective than others on those points."[52] In contrast to the elocution of bookish men, Sheridan suggested, "the natural manner of delivery" of "rude" or "illiterate" orators had its own special kind of "force."[53]

Today elocution is often confused with pronunciation or articulation. But for eighteenth-century elocutionists, delivery involved far more than the mere utterance of words. For Sheridan, "a just delivery" included the "graceful management of the voice, countenance, and gesture":

> A just delivery consists in a distinct articulation of words, pronounced in proper tones, suitably varied to the sense, and the emotions of the mind; with due observation of accent; of emphasis, in its several gradations; of rests or pauses of the voice, in proper places and well measured degrees of time; and the whole accompanied with expressive looks, and significant gesture.[54]

Like Le Faucheur and Henley, Sheridan devoted extensive attention to the arts of gesture. Gesture was the "hand-writing of nature," yet the effective use of gesture could not be taught by printed texts, for the most "essential articles to a good delivery"—tone, accent, emphasis, and gesture—"have been wholly left out of the graphic art."[55] Gesture was also difficult to teach in an age of polite decorum. "Offensive" gestures must be avoided, but how were such gestures to be known? Whereas Le Faucheur, Henley, and Wesley provided some specific examples of "indecent" action (such as the overuse of elbows), by Sheridan's day it was considered improper even to *mention* "vulgar" body parts in polite prose. Accordingly, Sheridan seldom discussed specific body parts. He focused almost entirely on the eyes and hands rather than on vulgar or highly sexualized body parts such as the mouth or lips, and he relied on vague adjectives to depict tasteful delivery. A speaker's gestures must be "graceful," "harmonious," "delicate," and "refined."

As we have seen, Addison and Steele focused their critiques of indecent action on the "extravagant gestures" of Dissenters. As we have seen,
too, Henley's "Action in the Pulpit" earned him comparisons to actors and
mountebanks. Immediately after Henley opened his Oratory, "several
Pamphlets . . . appear'd in the World . . . which mightily condemn[ed] . . .
Mr. *Henly*'s Gestures, comparing them to the absurd and indecent Gesticulations of a *Merry-Andrew* or *Harlequin*."[56] But by the 1740s, the spread
of Methodist lay preaching meant that mid- and later eighteenth-century
elocutionists were forced to contend with a new array of "unbecoming"
orators and the threat that these speakers collectively represented to the existing social order. Sheridan noted with dismay that the "wild uncultivated
oratory" of Methodist preachers was "seducing . . . flocks" of parishioners
away from the established church. He remarked "the wonderful effects
which have been produced by the . . . oratory of our methodist preachers."
At the same time, he proposed that the established clergy might learn something from these powerful speakers. Despite their "nonsense," the "extravagant gestures" of Quakers and of "other religious sects" produced "powerful effects on the imagination of hearers." He observed that "we have many
flagrant instances in our methodist preachers, of the power which words
acquire, even the words of fools and madmen, when forcibly uttered by the
living voice."[57] "Enthusiastic" preachers and speakers were gaining "advantages" over the established clergy, who relied on polite, passionless reading
of books and "notes" to address their flocks:

> The fancied operations of the spirit, in the people called Quakers, mani-
> fested by the most unnatural signs; and in some other religious sects, by
> a certain cant, and extravagant gestures, produce powerful effects, on the
> imaginations of such hearers. . . . This sort of language of emotions . . . is
> well calculated to make enthusiasts, but not believers. . . .
>
> Sure I am, that the advantages which the Methodist teachers, have
> obtained over the regular clergy, in seducing so many of their flocks from
> them, have been wholly owing to this. For were they to read their non-
> sense from notes, in the same cold, artificial manner, that so many of the
> clergy deliver rational discourses, it is to be presumed, that there are few
> of mankind, such idiots, as to become their followers.[58]

In persuading their congregations of their "rational" arguments, Anglican
clergymen needed to use their "hearts" to "move" their audiences. They
needed to exploit the "language of the emotions":

He who is utterly without all language of emotions . . . is not to be classed at all amongst public speakers. . . . And this, it is to be feared, is too much the state of the pulpit elocution in general, in the Church of England. . . . [T]here never was perhaps a religious sect upon earth, whose hearts were so little engaged in the act of public worship as the members of that Church. . . . The Presbyterians are moved; the Methodists are moved; they go to their meetings, and tabernacles, with delight. The very Quakers are moved. Fantastical, and extravagant as the language of their emotions is, yet still they are moved by it, and they love their form of worship for that reason.

If the established clergy could imitate the Quakers, Methodists, and Presbyterians and learn to preach with "force and energy, upon righteousness and judgment to come," then "the greatest and mightiest among us [might] be made to tremble."[59]

But despite the importance of gesture in his elocutionary program, Sheridan is remembered today chiefly for teaching pronunciation, and especially, for his role in spreading the notion of a standard English. Writing half a century after the political union of England, Wales, and Scotland in 1706/7, Sheridan depicted Britain's continuing linguistic diversity as a problem that needed to be solved. He observed that "not only the Scotch, Irish, and Welsh, have each their own idioms . . . but almost every county in England, has its peculiar dialect. Nay in the very metropolis two different modes of pronunciation prevail, by which the inhabitants of one part of the town, are distinguished from those of the other." Traveling throughout Britain delivering his lectures, he aspired to distribute "an uniformity of pronunciation . . . through the whole land."[60]

Sheridan capitalized on the linguistic insecurities of his countrymen. Scottish philosopher David Hume, for instance, suffered lifelong anxiety about his Scots dialect. In a 1754 letter to John Wilkes, Hume described his "Tongue" as "totally desperate and irreclaimable," despite "all the Pains, which I have taken in the Study of the English Language."[61] As an Anglo-Irishman himself, Sheridan was intensely aware "that speaking, rather than writing, was more likely to betray an unwanted provincialism."[62] He dreamed of a kind of equalization through linguistic homogenization, and he understood his elocutionary project as a democratic one. His scheme for teaching the "English Tongue" would "put an end to the odious distinction kept up between subjects of the same king, if a way were opened, by which the attainment of the English tongue in its purity . . . might be rendered easy to all inhabitants of his Majesty's dominions" in Britain, Ireland, and the colonies. Along with male foreigners, colonists, and provincials, he explicitly included British women in his plans. At a time when there was little support for the idea of public education, and a significant proportion of the population could not read, he proposed that by his "method . . . all children of these realms, whether male or female, may be instructed from the first rudiments, in a grammatical knowledge of the English tongue, and the art of reading and speaking with propriety and grace." Oral delivery was best taught in person, but instruction in pronunciation would be greatly assisted by the sale of books: "if a method of acquiring a just pronunciation by books, as well as conversation, were established, the acquisition would . . . lie open to all British subjects wherever born, as well as to all foreigners." Sheridan concluded *A Dissertation on the Causes of the Difficulties, Which occur, in learning the English Tongue. With a Scheme for publishing An English Grammar and Dictionary, Upon a Plan entirely New* by representing the English language as a once-common property that had been wrongfully subjected to enclosure, or privatization:

> Thus might the rising generation, born and bred in different countries, and counties, no longer have a variety of dialects, but as subjects of one king, like sons of one father, have one common tongue. All natives of these realms would be restored to their birthright in commonage of language, which has been too long fenced in, and made the property of a few.[63]

According to Sheridan's (somewhat twisted) metaphor in this passage, his project of teaching a standard English would be the equivalent of making a now-private property—"proper" English—once again "common" to all.

Sheridan's *Scheme for publishing An English Grammar and Dictionary, Upon a Plan entirely New* was published as an appendix to his *Course of Lectures* (1762). Implicitly critiquing Johnson's monumental *Dictionary of the English Language*, published seven years earlier, Sheridan argued that Britons needed a new kind of dictionary that taught them how to *pronounce* the English language rather than merely spell it: "the written language . . . is by no means a guide to right pronunciation of the English tongue. To the truth of this, not only all foreigners, but the Irish, the Scotch, the Welsh, the inhabitants of the several counties of England, nay of the very metropolis itself, can bear testimony." Appealing to potential subscribers, he proposed to publish "a Dictionary, in which the true pronunciation, of all the words in our tongue, shall be pointed out." He suggested that such a work (with a corresponding grammar) would have a large, ready-made market in schools: "if such a Grammar and Dictionary were published, they must soon be adopted into use by all schools professing to teach English."[64] Two decades later, Sheridan published *A General Dictionary of the English Language* (2 vols., 1780), the first dictionary in English in which "pronunciation was the leading feature."[65] While Sheridan aimed to mitigate, not exacerbate, the social ramifications of linguistic difference, his efforts to democratize the language by promoting the idea of a "standard" or "pure" English had the effect of further stigmatizing the way that most Britons actually spoke. His focus on pronunciation, in particular, drew more attention to accent as a marker of social difference. As Lynda Mugglestone suggests, it was only in the late eighteenth and nineteenth centuries that accent "came to be conceived as a *primary* marker of . . . class distinction."[66]

In eighteenth-century Britain, elocution became a means for gaining access to polite society *and* for consolidating that society in contradistinction to excluded groups. Elocution served as a marker of shared interests among members of the gentry and professional orders and well-to-do tradespeople *and* it served to distinguish this new (and tenuous) alliance of orders "from a 'vulgar' class of laborers, servants and 'cits.' "[67] Immediately after Sheridan published *A Course of Lectures*, dramatist and theater manager Samuel Foote satirized this ex-actor's grand ambitions. In two farces, *The Orators* (1762) and *The Mayor of Garrett* (1764), Foote satirized the class implications of Sheridan's proposal and the special appeal of his agenda to the Scots. Foote depicts one Ephraim Suds, a "soap-boiler in the city," who wants to "learn to make speeches" on the advice of his wife, Mrs. Suds, and another character, a lowborn Scot named Donald, who has learned to "speechify" by attending Sheridan's lectures. Betraying his thick Scotch dialect and bumpkin status, Donald announces the "topick" of his oration as follows: "Dunna heed man—the topick I presum to haundle, is the miraculous gifts of an orator, wha, by the bare power of his words, he leads men, women and bairns as he lists."[68] Donald's focus on the "bare power of [the orator's] words" echoes Sheridan's implicit argument that effective oratory was a tool of power for nonelite speakers and other members of disenfranchised groups. But as Foote rightly recognized, the political implications of Sheridan's projects were ambiguous, and Sheridan himself seemed to vacillate between populist rabble-rouser and would-be member of the ruling class.

BLAIR'S *LECTURES* AND THE "ABSURD RAGE FOR PUBLIC SPEAKING"

While Sheridan extended Henley's oratorical program beyond the capital, it was Scottish clergyman and rhetorician Hugh Blair (1718–1800) who played the greatest role in institutionalizing a new kind of rhetoric in English-speaking universities (and, eventually, colleges and grammar schools). After obtaining his MA at the University of Edinburgh, Blair began preaching in the Church of Scotland. In 1759 he began lecturing at his alma mater, and in 1762 he was appointed Edinburgh's first Regius Professor of Rhetoric and Belles Lettres. For the next twenty years Blair delivered an annual course of lectures, and upon his retirement he published these as *Lectures on Rhetoric and Belles Lettres* (2 vols., 1783; rev. ed., 3 vols., 1785). Blair's *Lectures* became a staple of instruction for the English-speaking world. It was widely read and used not only in colleges and universities but also in literary societies, clubs, and domestic settings.

Yet while Blair played a key role in the institutionalization of the new rhetoric, his modern editors rightly note that "little if any of the theoretical material in [his] Lectures is original."[69] Blair was a student of Adam Smith's, who began lecturing on rhetoric at Edinburgh in 1748, and Blair was also greatly indebted to Sheridan. In a footnote to his lecture "Pronunciation, Or Delivery," Blair praised "Mr. Sheridan's Lectures" and acknowledged that "several hints are here taken from him." Blair was chiefly a synthesizer and developer of the work of others. Like his predecessors, he "recognized that some of the old categories [of rhetorical training] no longer worked and needed to be supplemented by . . . new ideas." Following Sheridan, he praised the unique power of the human voice and argued that "Spoken Language has a great superiority over written Language, in point of energy or force. The voice of the living Speaker, makes an impression on the mind, much stronger than can be made by the perusal of any Writing." Gestures, in particular, constitute a universal language: one "which nature has dictated to all, and which is understood by all."[70] Printing presses made impressions on paper, but gestures, tones, and glances made impressions directly on one's audience, and the "impression" made by these nonverbal aspects of communication "is frequently much stronger than any words can make."

Blair worked to adapt classical rhetoric from its originally oral context to a commercial print society. His awareness of print commerce and the spread of books and reading shaped virtually everything that he wrote. In an age when reading was increasingly common, he asserted, powerful orators were now rare: "we have Historians, we have Poets of the greatest name; but of Orators, or Public Speakers, how little have we to boast?" As a clergyman, Blair especially commented on the implications of print for preaching. He argued that the regrettable practice of "reading Sermons instead of repeating them from memory . . . has done great prejudice to Eloquence." Yet Blair also celebrated the virtues of writing, and like Henley, Sheridan, and Methodist leaders, he made extensive use of print. He published his sermons, lectures, critical dissertations, and other works, and (perhaps as a counter to Sheridan's critique of writing) he bluntly declared, "Writing is, beyond doubt, the most useful art which men possess. It is plainly an improvement upon Speech."[71]

Blair theorized that "the Language of the first ages" was "passionate and metaphorical." "In the infancy of societies," men's "passions have nothing to restrain them. . . . As their feelings are strong, so their language, of itself, assumes a poetical turn."[72] Like Adam Smith, he proposed that the language of "savages" was picturesque, hyperbolical, and characterized by the heavy use of rhetorical tropes and figures. He acknowledged that this association of figures and tropes with "rude orators" might seem counterintuitive: "figures are commonly considered as artificial modes of speech, devised by orators and poets, after the world has advanced to a refined state." But he argued that "the contrary of this is the truth. Men have never used so many figures . . . as in . . . [the] rude ages."[73] He proposed that "in the progress of society," something is lost as well as gained: "language advances from . . . fervour and enthusiasm, to correctness and precision. Style becomes more chaste, but less animated."[74] In modern commercial print societies, he implied, something valuable had been lost.

Blair's statements about the unrestrained "passions" of rude orators are an example of eighteenth-century authors' increased attention to the passions (emotions).[75] A century before Blair, Le Faucheur advised public speakers to appeal to their listeners' "Passions" as well as to their "Understanding" and "Will." Le Faucheur suggested that the passions were fundamentally corporeal in nature, and that powerful oratorical appeals to the passions set up a sympathetic circuit between the speaker and his audience, for "the *String* sounds as it is touch'd."[76] Forty years later, the work of another influential French author, the art theorist and painter Charles Le Brun, was posthumously published and translated into English. In his study of the physiognomy of the passions, *A Method to learn to Design the Passions* (in French, 1698; trans. 1701), Le Brun theorized that the passions were corporeal and that their effective expression triggered a powerful corresponding "Action" in the bodies of others: "Passion" is "an emotion of the Soul, residing in the sensitive part," and "whatever causes Passion in the Soul, creates also some Action in the Body." As a painter, Le Brun was interested in the visual depiction of the passions as rendered in the subject's facial expressions: "Expression . . . intimates the emotions of the Soul, and renders visible the effects of Passion." In one of his *shortest* descriptions of a particular passion, he suggested that a painter might depict as follows the corporeal signs of "Contempt":

CONTEMPT is expressed by the Eye brows knit and lowering towards the Nose, and at the other end very much elevated; the Eye very open, and the Pupil in the middle; the Nostrils drawing upwards; the Mouth shut, with the corners somewhat down, and the Under-Lip thrust out further than the Upper one.[77]

British elocutionists, actors, and artists drew on Le Brun's *Method to learn to Design the Passions*. Sheridan, for instance, frequently observed that "the passions and the fancy have a language of their own . . . independent of words," and he regretted that this language is "wholly neglected by us."[78]

Teaching his students "a method to learn to design the passions," Blair advised these young gentlemen that it was not enough to *persuade* one's audience; one must also *move* them. A speaker "must address himself to the passions . . . and touch the heart." Blair depicted a hierarchical scale of three different "degrees of Eloquence." The "first, and lowest degree of Eloquence" "aims only at pleasing the hearers," and a "second and higher degree" occurs "when the Speaker aims not merely to please, but also to inform, to instruct, to convince." But the "third and highest degree of Eloquence" is "the offspring of passion." Impassioned oratory inspires a passionate response in one's audience: "a greater power is exerted over the human mind; by which we are not only convinced, but are interested, agitated, and carried along with the Speaker; our passions are made to rise together with his."[79]

The "highest attainment of Eloquence," then, was to unite "the strength of reason, with the vehemence of passion." But as Adam Potkay has observed, the eighteenth century was "an age that did not want its passions inflamed."[80] (Recall Hogarth's giant thermometer for measuring the inflamed passions of religious enthusiasts in *Credulity, Superstition, and Fanaticism*.) Blair emphasized that his arguments in favor of appeals to the passions must be "understood with certain limitations and restraints, which it will be necessary to point out distinctly, in order to guard against dangerous mistakes." However "fired by his subject," a speaker must "lay a decent restraint upon his warmth, and prevent him from carrying it beyond certain bounds." Blair followed Addison, Steele, Swift, and others in suggesting that Dissenting preachers' "popular manner of preaching" played a key role in fomenting the upheaval of the Civil War period and Interregnum. Dissenters' problematic preaching styles continued to have dangerous influence long after the monarchy was restored: "the sectaries and fanatics, before the Restoration, adopted a warm, zealous, and popular manner of preaching; and those who adhered to them . . . [after the Restoration] continued to distinguish themselves by somewhat of the same manner." Blair also blamed Dissenting preachers for the decline of *Anglican* preaching after the Restoration: "the odium of these sects drove the established church from that warmth which they were judged to have carried too far, into the opposite extreme of a studied coolness, and composure of manner." According to this argument, the "dry and unpersuasive . . . character of English sermons" in the established church was an epiphenomenon of Dissenting preaching:

> As the Dissenters from the Church continued to preserve somewhat of the old strain of preaching, this lead [*sic*] the established Clergy to depart the farther from it. Whatever was earnest and passionate, either in the composition or delivery of Sermons, was reckoned enthusiastic and fanatical; and hence that argumentative manner, bordering on the dry and unpersuasive, which is too generally the character of English Sermons.

Blair rejected both the "warm" manner of Dissenting preachers and the "cool reasoning" of the "established Clergy." He argued that the goal of "preaching is to be popular; not in the sense of accommodation to the humours and prejudices of the people . . . but, in the true sense of the word, calculated to make [an] impression on the people; to strike and seize on their hearts." Although Blair sometimes aligned "the common people" with "good sense," he taught his students and readers that it was "a dangerous mistake" for a would-be virtuous orator to let himself be guided by the "humours and prejudices of the people."[81]

The eighteenth century saw the rise of new associational practices and venues such as clubs, societies, and coffeehouses. (Johnson's aforementioned reference to "little societies of literature . . . formed in taverns and coffee-houses" springs to mind.) This period also saw the spread of "academical associations." As we have seen, Henley envisioned one branch of his Oratory as a new kind of "Academical Association." Whereas Blair's teaching career was spent in a prestigious university setting, Henley aspired to set up a "Weekdays Academy" that would "bring Home to any Person all the Benefit of Schools, Universities, Tutors . . . not only to Gentlemen . . . but [to persons who] want Leisure, Opportunity, or Ability to take other Methods."[82] Blair's reactions to the flourishing academical associations and debating societies of his time were distinctly mixed. He argued that although the Parliament of Great Britain was "the most august Theatre" for eloquence, lesser degrees of eloquence could now be witnessed at "meetings . . . of less dignity. . . . [W]herever any number of men are assembled for debate or consultation, there, in different forms . . . Eloquence may take place." These assemblies included "those academical associations where a moderate number of young Gentlemen, who are carrying on their studies . . . assemble privately, in order to improve one another." These meetings of "Gentlemen" were "laudable institutions; and, under proper conduct, may serve many valuable purposes."[83] But in sharp contrast to these "private" academical associations, he argued, the new "public . . . Societies" that were springing up in towns throughout the nation were "not merely . . . useless, but . . . hurtful." In contrast to Henley, who explicitly aimed to make his academical association accessible to all ranks of people, Blair excoriated the societies that were indiscriminately bringing together people of the lower classes for no other apparent reason than "an absurd Rage for Public Speaking":

> As for those public and promiscuous Societies, in which multitudes are brought together, who are often of low stations and occupations, who are joined by no common bond of union, except an absurd rage for Public Speaking, and have not other object in view, but to make a show of their supposed talents, they are institutions not merely of an useless, but of an hurtful nature. They are in great hazard of proving seminaries of licentiousness, petulance, faction, and folly.

Blair judged these public societies seminaries of sin and social disorder. In the mouths of persons of "of low stations and occupations," he argued, the arts of "Eloquence . . . may prove dangerous."[84]

Blair warned his students against effeminacy in public speaking. He rejected "loose and frothy Declaimers" in favor of "an air of manliness and strength, which is a powerful instrument of persuasion."[85] Whereas Blair lectured to an exclusively male student body, Sheridan and Henley offered lectures to women as well as men. As we have seen, in proposing his scheme for teaching elocution, Sheridan suggested that by his methods, "all children of these realms, whether male or female, may be instructed from the first rudiments, in . . . the art of reading and speaking with propriety and grace." At the same time, though, whatever promise Sheridan envisioned for the future of British girls, he had nothing but disdain for the "old women" who were now teaching in Britain's grammar schools. The task of teaching children, he observed, was currently left to "old women, or the lowest and most ignorant of mankind." These "miserable drudges" neglected to teach children "the art of speaking." Instead, they focused "only" on teaching them to read and write: "the first master (or rather mistress, as this charge is generally consigned to old women) . . . is utterly ignorant of all rules, with regard to the art of speaking, or pronunciation. These miserable drudges profess only to teach the written alphabet."[86]

As the satiric character of "Mrs. Suds" in Samuel Foote's *The Orators* suggests, though, some women of the middling ranks attended Sheridan's lectures and otherwise supported his various projects. Sheridan's son, Richard Brinsley Sheridan, followed his father into the theater business, and in his comedy of manners *The Rivals* (1775), he satirized female participation in the elocution movement. Perhaps his best-known character, Mrs. Malaprop (from the French *mal à propos*, "inappropriate"), is a ridiculous older woman who prides herself on her vocabulary and pronunciation yet misstates almost everything that she says. Outlining her view of the ideal education for her niece, Lydia Languish, Mrs. Malaprop notes that training in orthography and elocution are essential:

> I would have her instructed in geometry, that she might know something of the contagious countries; but above all, Sir Anthony, she should be mistress of orthodoxy, that she might not mis-spell and mispronounce words so shamefully as girls usually do; and likewise that she might reprehend the true meaning of what she is saying.[87]

Much like Thomas Sheridan's "old women" teachers of grammar schools, who are "utterly ignorant of all rules, with regard to the art of speaking, or pronunciation," Mrs. Malaprop (a "weather-beaten old she dragon") is depicted as dispensable and indeed detrimental. Whereas Mrs. Malaprop is a *failed* elocutionist, Richard Brinsley Sheridan appears to have mastered his father's elocutionary training. After a career as an actor as well as a dramatist, he went on to participate in what his father called the "most august Theatre" for eloquence, the "Parliament of Great Britain." Elected a member of Parliament in 1780, Richard Brinsley Sheridan became one of the most renowned orators of his generation.

As the character of Mrs. Malaprop suggests, by 1775 elocution was no longer neglected in Britain. W. Benzie observes that "R. C. Alston's *Bibliography of the English Language* from the invention of printing to 1800 shows that five times as many works on elocution were published between 1760 and 1800 than prior to 1760, and most of the prominent texts went through a large number of editions within a short space of time."[88] A century after Addison and Steele addressed "the eloquence of the pulpit," a provincial rector's daughter, Jane Austen, commented on this topic in her novel *Mansfield Park* (1814). In a drawing-room discussion, Henry Crawford, a visitor to Mansfield Park, engages Edmund Bertram, the younger son of Sir Thomas

Bertram, in a conversation on the art of reading aloud the scriptures. The two gentlemen discuss the importance of "good delivery" while Sir Thomas Bertram's pious niece, Fanny Price, listens intently (and silently). Edmund, a newly minted Anglican clergyman, suggests that while these arts have been neglected in the past, "it is different now":

> [T]he two young men . . . talked over the too common neglect of the qualification, the total inattention to it, in the ordinary school-system for boys, . . . the want of management of the voice, of proper modulation and emphasis, of foresight and judgment, all proceeding from the first cause, want of early attention and habit. . . .
>
> "Even in my profession"—said Edmund with a smile—"how little the art of reading has been studied! how little a clear manner, and good delivery, have been attended to! I speak rather of the past, however, than the present.—There is now a spirit of improvement abroad. . . . It is different now. The subject is more justly considered. . . . [I]n every congregation, there is a larger proportion who know a little of the matter, and who can judge and criticize."[89]

Henry asks Edmund's opinion (then delivers his own) as to "the properest manner in which particular passages in the service should be delivered." He opines that "a sermon, well delivered, is more uncommon even than prayers well read. . . . It is more difficult to speak well than to compose well. . . . There is something in the eloquence of the pulpit, when it is really eloquence, which is entitled to the highest praise and honour."[90] At this point, we begin to question Henry's motives for participating so passionately in this discussion. Is he sincere in these beliefs, or is he merely a seductive charmer who is attempting to impress Fanny Price by repeating now-fashionable clichés? A shallow cad whose immorality has not been fully revealed at this point in the story, Henry is intrigued by the pious Fanny primarily because she is not interested in him. For a moment, his effort to reform his rakish reputation in Fanny's eyes appears to be having some success, for her body language suggests that she agrees with him on the praise due to "the eloquence of the pulpit." But shortly afterward, when Henry seduces Maria Bertram (who is married to another man), his dissoluteness is revealed. Significantly, in addressing the popularization of the elocution movement by 1814, Austen put Addison and Steele's sentiments concerning the importance of "pulpit eloquence" into the mouth of a heartless rake. In so doing, she gave her contemporaries' now-widespread discussions of the importance of oral "delivery" an entirely new (and, for us, revealing) valence.

CHAPTER SIX

"Fair *Rhet'ric*" and the Fishwives
of Billingsgate

There foam'd rebellious *Logic*, gagg'd and bound,
There, stript, fair *Rhet'ric* languish'd on the ground;
His blunted Arms by *Sophistry* are born,
And shameless *Billingsgate* her Robes adorn.
—Alexander Pope, *The Dunciad in Four Books*, 4.23–26

In 1711 Joseph Addison devoted an issue of the *Spectator* to the subject of "Female Orators." He observed that "*Socrates* was instructed in Eloquence by a Woman," and he noted that he himself had often looked upon the "Art [of Eloquence] as the most proper for the Female Sex." He suggested that "the Universities would do well to consider whether they should . . . fill their Rhetorick Chairs with She Professors." He then proposed:

> Were Women admitted to plead in Courts of Judicature, I am persuaded they would carry the Eloquence of the Bar to greater heights than it has yet arrived at. If any one doubts this, let him but be present at those Debates which frequently arise among the Ladies of the *British* fishery.[1]

The "Ladies of the *British* fishery" were fishwives. In London, Billingsgate was the most important market for fish. The term "fishwives" typically referred to street criers. These women did not own shops or stalls but instead relied on their *voices* to attract customers and sell their goods. The distinctive harangues of fishwives and oyster wenches were among the most familiar of the London Cries (a print genre as well as oral form). In the eighteenth century, these cries were thematized in poetry, periodical essays, novels, and satiric prints. "Billingsgate" came to signify a type of discourse that was held to be characteristic of fishwives: a style of linguistic or rhetorical activity distinguished by obscenities, slang, hyperbole, and an occupational argot not fully comprehensible by outside groups (like the cant language of the criminal underworld). In satirizing the modern literary marketplace in the *Dunciad*, Alexander Pope depicted *"Billingsgate"* and "Bawdy" as the "daughters dear" of Dulness (2.307). In his apocalyptic vision of the takeover of Britain by Dulness, he portrays "shameless *Billingsgate*" wrestling "fair *Rhet'ric*" to the ground. "Shameless *Billingsgate*" suggests total disregard for polite norms of linguistic and bodily decorum; meanwhile, "fair *Rhet'ric*" suggests a form of discourse that is at once aesthetically pleasing and "fair" in the sense of consistent with the rules. By the later eighteenth century, "Billingsgate" was a general term of abuse. Nonetheless, the idea of Billingsgate discourse retained its link to the characteristic activities and voices of Billingsgate market. Samuel Johnson assumed that his readers would understand his link between language and location when he observed that "the style of Billingsgate would not make a very agreeable figure at St. James's."[2]

This chapter is the first detailed analysis of the omnipresent but largely unremarked satiric topos of "Billingsgate eloquence" in Restoration and eighteenth-century poetry, periodical essays, novels, rhetorical discourse, and satiric prints. A short list of authors who drew on this rhetorical topos would include such diverse figures as Aphra Behn, the Earl of Rochester, John Dryden, William Wycherley, Jonathan Swift, Alexander Pope, Daniel Defoe, Henry Fielding, Eliza Haywood, Tobias Smollett, and Adam Smith. During the French Revolution, Edmund Burke and Hannah More lamented that the fishwives of Paris had brought down the king of France. I am especially interested in the relationship between the idea of "Billingsgate" discourse and the voices and bodies of actual fishwives. After providing historical background on the fishwives of Billingsgate, I examine satiric representations of these laboring-class women's voices in visual and verbal texts. The association of fishwives and foul language dates back at least to Plato: "as early as classical Greek times 'to swear like a fishwife' was a common expression."[3] But in eighteenth-century Britain, I will argue, "Billingsgate eloquence" became a rhetorical commonplace, and authors and artists from Behn to Smith drew on this topos to do new kinds of creative, didactic, and ideological work (especially, to comment on implications of the expanding world of print commerce).[4]

The label "Billingsgate" came to denote the transgression of polite style. Yet intriguingly, in eighteenth-century visual and verbal satire, fishwives are typically depicted as *achieving* their rhetorical ends (whether their goal was the intimidation of reluctant customers or the bringing down of the king of France). In innumerable anecdotes and images, fishwives humiliate literate gentlemen with their powerful lungs and brawny bodies. Authors and artists alike suggested that these plebeian women's quick wit, improvisational repartee, and energetic use of gesture beat out book learning and logic on the streets. In his periodical the *London Spy* (1698–1700), Ned Ward more than once depicted his bookish narrator as frightened by fishwives' voices. After seven years of reading in a "country hut," Ward's narrator ventures to London to see what can be learned outside of books. Strolling by the Thames, he and a male companion are browbeaten and driven off by fishwives who subject them to a volley of verbal abuse. The aggressive orality of fishwives was also thematized by visual artists. The caption to one popular print, *The Views and Humours of Billingsgate* (1736), explicitly foregrounds fishwives' "Elocution." It warns visitors to Billingsgate market to exercise "Prudence" and "cautio[n]" when bargaining for fish: "beware, when you your Board would grace, / To rouse the Elocution of that place." Other prints, such as *Poll Dab a Match for the Frenchman* (mid-1770s), pointedly depict fishwives humiliating men of a higher social standing. (A dab is a type of fish.) John Collet's print *The Female Orators* (1768) depicts two female vendors, a fishwife and a fruit seller, engaged in a verbal battle that is about to come to blows. Yet this print too is characteristic of depictions of fishwives in that it highlights the effects of these women's voices on the *men* around them. (Here, both a book-learned lawyer or judge and a scowling street musician are disgruntled by the female vendors' noise.)

Why are there so many orally aggressive fishwives in eighteenth-century British literature and art? Why are there so many depictions of loud, foul-mouthed fishwives publicly disturbing (and shaming) gentlemen with their powerful tongues? Certainly, these representations express long-standing anxieties pertaining to gender roles and women's oral discourse. These street vendors are loud, "masculine" women humiliating men. These satiric depictions of verbally victorious fishwives also participate in a long tradition in European popular culture of depicting witty plebeian women and their verbal jesting.[5] The images and texts that I discuss also share some characteristics with the French literary genre of *poissarde*. But in eighteenth-century Britain, fishwives are routinely depicted as overpowering *gentlemen*: men of superior social rank, learning, and culture (never porters or fishermen). Why?

I will argue here that eighteenth-century British authors and artists used the topic of Billingsgate eloquence to work through newer anxieties pertaining to media shift and to politeness. They used representations of *oral* discourse to comment on the expanding world of *print*. The eighteenth-century fascination with fishwives' voices is another example of what I have argued is this period's intensified interest in the power of oral communication. But examining the rhetorical topic of Billingsgate fishwives' *voices* can also help us to better understand eighteenth-century authors' efforts to come to terms with the spread of *print commerce*. A surprising number of these representations suggest a special anxiety having to do with the "consequences" of literacy—particularly traditionally elite oratorical skills supposedly being surrendered through negligence to "vulgar" (and sometimes threatening) social groups. In the new age of print and politeness, gentlemen were increasingly likely to be out of practice with the arts and tools of oral delivery (such as the arts of gesture that I discussed in chapter 5). In neglecting these oral arts, they risked being cowed by the very "Billingsgate rhetoric" that they condemned.

As Pope's female wrestling match between "fair *Rhet'ric*" and "shameless *Billingsgate*" suggests, examining the relationship between Billingsgate and fishwives' burly bodies can also help us to understand this topos in eighteenth-century "*Rhet'ric*." Rhetoricians such as Adam Smith linked Billingsgate not only to "low" and "vulgar" discourse but also, more surprisingly, to the excessive use of rhetorical tropes and figures. How are we to account for this seemingly counterintuitive link between fishwives and figures of speech? Much can be learned about what I call the eighteenth-century "invention of the oral" by attending to the efforts of rhetoricians, elocutionists, and others to distance their own genteel oral projects from Billingsgate rhetoric. At the same time, though, these polite commentators on the arts of public speaking were forced to grapple with the paradoxical *power* of "shameless *Billingsgate*." Commentators from Addison to Hugh Blair acknowledged with dismay (and, occasionally, a hint of envy) that the "energetic and forcible manner"[6] of "rude orators" had its own special kind of force.

As we have seen in chapter 5, elocutionist Thomas Sheridan argued that "the invention of printing, and the consequential application to book language only" contributed to the "loss of the language of nature."[7] In his own time, he believed, the spread of printing and reading was undermining "natural" eloquence. Book-learned gentlemen now spoke less "forcibly" than the "meanest" of the "illiterate vulgar":

> ELOCUTION . . . has been in a much worse state since the introduction of letters, than it could have been before, when left wholly to nature. The emotions then, however rudely, were still forcibly expressed, borrowing their power from feeling, unsophisticated by art. Of this we have instances at this day amongst the illiterate vulgar; the meanest of whom, when impassioned, delivers himself better than our most eminent

orators; I do not mean in choice of words, but in the use of their concomitant signs, tones, looks, and gesture.[8]

"Illiterate" speakers were more likely than learned gentlemen to exploit the
communicative resources of the body. The "illiterate vulgar" used "signs,
tones, looks, and gesture," while bookish men "confine[d] . . . [themselves]
to the mere utterance of words." Paradoxically, in limiting themselves to
"mere . . . words," literate orators disqualified themselves as public speakers. Sheridan argued that "he who . . . confines himself to the mere utterance of words, without any concomitant signs, is not to be classed at all
amongst public speakers. The very worst abuse of such signs, is preferable
to a total want of them; as it has at least a stronger resemblance to nature."
Eighteenth-century gentlemen's increasing reliance on *texts*, many authors
agreed, was undermining rather than enhancing their speaking skills. Sheridan observed that "bookish men are generally remarkable for the worst
[oral] delivery."[9] Not coincidentally, I would point out, Addison and Steele
represented their fictional persona Mr. Spectator as an exceptionally learned
gentleman who is also nearly mute. In the inaugural issue of the *Spectator*,
Mr. Spectator boasts that "there are very few celebrated Books, either in the
Learned or the Modern Tongues, which I am not acquainted with." But he
also admits that when he attended university, "I distinguished my self by a
most profound Silence: For, during the Space of eight Years, excepting in the
publick Exercises of the College, I scarce uttered the Quantity of an hundred Words; and indeed do not remember that I ever spoke three Sentences
together in my whole Life."[10]

As we have seen in the previous chapter, a central concern of the elocution movement was the effective use of the body in public speaking. Elocutionists from Michel Le Faucheur to Sheridan discussed not only the vocal
and auditory apparatus (ears, lips, and tongues) but also the body parts and
positions involved in gesture (hands, arms, eyes, and stance). Polite speakers needed to monitor their body language carefully. We have seen Le Faucheur, John Henley, and John Wesley, for instance, advise against "babbling
of the hands." At the same time, though, to stand motionless before one's
audience was a mistake, for oral communication is inescapably rooted in
the body, and the body is a powerful (and universal) communicative tool.
Genteel speakers must control their bodies, yet in the new age of print and
politeness, they must also learn to use them effectively. Ironically, when
it came to "polite" oral delivery, the bodily self-control that was formerly
viewed as the epitome of politeness was also coming to be seen as something of an Achilles' heel.

For female speakers issues of bodily decorum were paramount.[11] As Pope's startlingly physical representation of Billingsgate suggests, Billingsgate eloquence is a topos that borrows its power from the reality of unruly female plebeian bodies. Eighteenth-century representations of fishwives invariably link their powerful lungs and burly bodies. In poetry, novels, drama, and rhetorical discourse, the link between *orality* and *corporeality* is foregrounded in surprising (and illuminating) ways. We need to be wary of recent critical generalizations about the position of women and "the feminine" in eighteenth-century rhetoric. To be sure, the elegant discourse of genteel ladies was sometimes represented as the epitome of politeness. (As we have seen, Pope depicted "fair *Rhet'ric*" as female.) But at the same time, the occupational argot of Billingsgate fishwives was held up as the *antithesis* of politeness. From Addison onward, representations of "the Ladies of the *British* Fishery" functioned to delimit oratory as a *male* activity. Furthermore, as Addison warned in his satire on "Female Orators," if "women of the better sort" did not control their "Passions" (and their tongues), their speech and body language too might quickly deteriorate into the "shameless *Billingsgate*" of "the Ladies of the *British* Fishery."

BILLINGSGATE AND THE CRIES OF LONDON

Since at least the thirteenth century, Billingsgate was London's most important fish market. The sale of fish was a complex business, tightly regulated by government and guild. The Fishmongers' Company was one of the great London livery companies, and members of the company fought to maintain their privileges. Throughout the early modern period, there were ceaseless efforts to regulate the sale of fish: where, when, how, what types, and by whom. The principal fishmongers worked to "secure . . . for themselves the pick of the catch," but they "allow[ed] what they did not want . . . to go to lower fishmongers, stallholders and hawkers who represented the retail section."[12] Certain kinds of fish swim in shoals, resulting in gluts in certain seasons, and these "common and . . . cheap fish were taken straight to market without any attempt to control sales." Common and "inferior" fish included mackerel, herrings, sprats, sole, plaice, and flounder and certain kinds of shellfish, especially oysters. Women who cried fish in the streets were typically selling the cheapest types of fish. One reads, for instance, of "mackerel women" and "oyster wenches" but seldom of street sellers hawking salmon or trout.

Fishwives were at once inside and outside the trade of fish marketing. Some were related to fishermen, while others were not, and most had no particular ties to the fishmongers' guild. Although they were essential to the sale of this highly perishable commodity, "Fish-women" were perennially targets of hostility by fishmongers and stallholders. A typical petition, *The Case of the Free Fishmongers* (1699), castigates the "lewd and disorderly Women, called Fish-women," who in this case were perceived to be undermining the fishmongers' trade.

At the same time, though, fishmongers needed fishwives to move their products: hence the prominence of fishwives' voices in the oral and textual genre(s) known as the "London Cries." In addressing the Cries of London, we need to distinguish between three main types: the oral cries of street vendors, the textual representation of these cries in literary texts, and the visual and verbal print genre of the "Cries of London" (hereafter distinguished as *Cries*). First and foremost, the Cries were an *oral genre* with distinct subgenres: the different cries that different kinds of vendors used to advertise their goods. There were three main types of street vendors: (1) hawkers of perishable goods such as fish and milk, (2) providers of services (such as knife grinders and chimney sweeps), and (3) criers who entertained audiences to promote their wares (such as balladmongers, who sold broadsides, or mountebanks and quacks, who hawked medicines and other cures). Besides individual differences between criers, each type of crier had a characteristic "Song," "Tune," "Tone," or "Accent" that distinguished their variety of goods or services even at a distance. In the *Tatler*, Steele reported a citizen's complaint that "Oysters are . . . neither cry'd; sung, nor said; but sold, with an Accent and Tone neither natural to Man or Beast."[13] An oyster seller or fishwife could be aurally distinguished from a milkmaid, even when her *words* could not be heard.

As this example from the *Tatler* suggests, the Cries of London were a frequent topic of discussion in periodicals. In an issue of the *Spectator*, Addison notes the "particular Songs and Tunes" of the pastry seller "Colly-Molly-Puff." In another issue, he records "the Decease of Cully Mully Puff of agreeable and noisy Memory." Mr. Spectator deems Mr. Puff's cries "agreeable," but most commentators were less sanguine about criers' "noise." In a *Spectator* issue devoted to the Cries of London, Mr. Spectator prints a letter that he has received from one "Ralph Crotchett." Mr. Crotchett complains that certain types of criers advertise their goods "in Sounds so exceedingly shrill, that it . . . sets our Teeth an edge." Crotchett notes that the Cries of London are currently "under no manner of Rules or Discipline," and he proposes that city governors should appoint a "Comptroller general of the *London* Cries." Volunteering for the job, he offers to train hawkers to cry their wares in pleasing tones: "it should be my Care to sweeten and mellow the Voices of these

Four for Six pence Mackrell.
Maquereux quatre pour Six Sols
Quatro Sgombri p̃ sei Soldi

Mauron delin:

P Tempest exc:
Cum Privilegio

42

Fig. 6.1. Marcellus Laroon, *Four for Six pence Mackrell.* From *Cryes of the City of London drawne after the Life* (1687). Photograph: Courtesy of the Lewis Walpole Library, Yale University.

itinerant Tradesmen, before they make their appearance in our Streets."[14] As in literary works like the *Spectator* and *Tatler*, so in visual texts the Cries of London are a recurring theme. In Hogarth's satiric engraving *The Enraged Musician* (1741), for instance, the music of a genteel violinist is drowned out by a milkmaid's cries and other kinds of plebeian "noise."

Finally, for now, the Cries were also a print genre. From about 1500, booksellers sold broadsides, gatherings of leaves, and, later, chapbooks and larger collections illustrating the personnel of London streets. The most sophisticated and influential collection, Marcellus Laroon's *Cryes of the City of London drawne after the Life* (1687), immortalizes more than seventy vendors. Of these, six are sellers of fish and oysters, suggesting the prevalence of this type of crier. One of the most powerful images, *Four for Six pence Mackrell*, depicts an old woman, blind in one eye, wearing a worn coat and battered hat (fig. 6.1). This fishwife's clothing is bulky, layered, and carefully mended—suggesting that she may be wearing everything that she owns. While fishwives often carried their fish in baskets on their heads (hence their nickname "flat-caps"), this older woman is too weak to carry a heavy load. Instead, she stands motionless, in her patched coat and supported by a stick that she uses as a cane. Contrary to the sentimental depictions of street criers in Victorian chapbooks, Laroon's mackerel woman reminds us that most fishwives, like most criers, "belonged in the last [category] of Defoe's sevenfold classification of England's population: 'The Miserable, that really pinch and suffer Want.'"[15] Later in this chapter, I discuss depictions of fishwives in satirical prints. Art historian Diana Donald rightly observes of similar prints that "confronted with these ebullient bruisers, it is difficult to recall . . . the historical evidence for [street criers'] experience of extreme poverty . . . in one of the lowest and most uncertain kinds of labor open to women in eighteenth-century London."[16] As Laroon's unsentimental depiction of a half-blind, elderly fishwife should remind us as we proceed, fishwives' voices were often the *only* tool of agency that these women had.

FISH, FEMALE BODIES, AND THE "ANATOMY OF A WOMAN'S TONGUE"

To understand the cultural work done by eighteenth-century representations of fishwives and oyster wenches, it is helpful to review some contemporary assumptions about the female body. Fishwives and oyster wenches are often depicted as highly sexualized, and understanding assumptions about women's bodies can help to explain why this is so. In early modern Europe, the dominant physiological paradigm was the Galenic theory of the four humors. According to humoral theory, women's bodies were "moister than men's and cyclically controlled by that watery planet, the moon."[17] Body fluids shaped one's temperament, and the wet, spongy nature of women's bodies made them "lustful, irrational, and emotional."[18] The association of women's bodies with fluids and with lust may help to explain why in popular lore Venus was the goddess of bawds and fishwives. According to one English almanac, *Poor Robin* (1719):

> The fifth *Planet* is *Venus*, a feminine *Planet*, but very unconstant as other Females are, for sometimes she is a Morning and sometimes an Evening *Star*, so that you know not where to have her. She is Governess of *French Taylors*, *Ale-wives*, *Fish-wives*, *Nurses*, *Tripe-women*, Cryers of *Oranges*, and . . . *Herrings*, *Whores* and *Bawds*. (n.p.)

Also in keeping with humoral theories about women's wet, spongy bodies are the aquatic feminine seductresses pervading European culture: mermaids, sirens, and other creatures who have the upper bodies of women and the lower bodies of fish.[19] Still more common was the everyday association of fish and female body parts. In his dictionary of early modern slang, Eric Partridge defines "*fish, n.*" as "a girl or women, viewed sexually. . . . indubitably allusive to the female genitals. A fish is slimy."[20] Women's genitals (and sometimes breasts) were compared to fish and oysters; also, certain kinds of fish were named after women. A "maid" was a type of fish *and* a young unmarried women. Even today, a prudish or sexually passive woman is referred to as "a cold fish."

The association of fish, oysters, and female body parts turns up repeatedly in Restoration and eighteenth-century gentlemen's private writings. Antiquarian John Aubrey recorded in his miscellany a "filthy rhyme" that he claimed to have heard sung by girls: "When I was a young Maid, / And wash't my Mothers Dishes / I putt my finger in my Cunt / And pluck't-out little Fishes."[21] Aubrey's contemporary, John Wilmot, Earl of Rochester, repeatedly associated women's genitals with fish and oysters. In "A Ramble in St. James's Park," he compared a woman entering a coach with her male admirers to a "Bitch" attracting a pack of male dogs by the "scent" of her "Salt-swolne Cunt":

> And with these Three confounded *Asses*,
> From *Park*, to *Hackney-Coach*, she passes,
> So a proud *Bitch* does lead about,
> Of humble Currs, the Amorous rout;

Who most obsequiously do hunt,
The sav'ry scent of Salt-swolne Cunt. (ll. 81–86)

In "The Imperfect Enjoyment," Rochester links oyster sellers, beggars, and whores as his "Common" sex objects. Infuriated by his impotence during a sexual encounter with a woman of a higher social rank, he demands of his flaccid penis: "What *Oyster-Cindar-Beggar*-Common *Whore* Didst thou e'er fail in all thy Life before?" (l. 50). Another Restoration author, William Wycherley, thematized this association of oyster wenches, fish, and female genitals in his little-known poem "*To a Pretty* Young Woman, *who opening Oisters said,* / She wou'd open for Her, and Me too; since 'twas for her Plea-sure. *A Song.*" Wycherley depicts his male speaker bargaining with a "Pretty Young Woman" to buy her oysters. But the commodity that the speaker desires most is the "Juicy, Salt Commodity" of the girl's vagina (l. 21). He pleads with the oyster seller as she opens oysters for customers: "If a good Op'ner you wou'd be, / Wou'd please your self, ease me of Pain; / Open your Legs, not Shells for me" (ll. 9–12). Drawing on the association of Venus with fishwives, oyster wenches, and lust, he argues that in triggering his lust, the oyster wench has surpassed the talents of the goddess Venus, whom he com-pares to a "Fish-Wife": "*Venus,* that Fish-Wife yet ashore, / Who, some say, from the Sea, did spring, / Cou'd never raise Men's Vigour more" (ll. 13–15).[22]

The most written-about body parts of early modern women, though, were not their genitals but their tongues. In polite society, the very act of opening one's mouth was potentially problematic. Lord Chesterfield advised his nephew never to laugh out loud in public, for this practice was "low and unbecoming," due to the "disagreeable noise" and the "shocking distortion of the face that it occasions."[23] For a woman, laughing, yawning, or even singing with a wide open mouth put one's sexual reputation at risk. In the *Dunciad,* Pope depicts Billingsgate and Bawdry as the "yawning daughters" of Dulness, and in a parody of divine inspiration, he depicts Dulness's take-over of Britain as a gigantic openmouthed yawn that puts all thinking per-sons to sleep. Billingsgate and Bawdry applaud and imitate their mother and cry for more: "and all thy yawning daughters, cry, *encore*" (4.60). Singing in public could also be risky for a woman. As Defoe observed, it was almost impossible for a painter to portray a *virtuous* woman singing, for a "Lady" depicted with "her Mouth open" was likely to be mistaken for a scold—or a whore:

[T]he most difficult thing in the Limners Art is, to represent a Person singing; suppose it be the picture of a young Lady, the utmost he can do is, to shew her Countenance bright, the Company listening, and appearing pleased; but alas towards the Sound, towards the Charm of her Voice, and the Beauty of her Judgment, he can do no more than paint her with her Mouth open, which is the meanest Posture she can, with Decency, be shewn in; and unless the other Passions discover it, she may as well be supposed to be swearing, scolding, sick, or anything else, as well as singing.[24]

To depict a "Lady" of "Judgment" and "Charm" with "her Mouth open" was to depict her in "the meanest Posture she can, with Decency, be shewn in." Admittedly, some eighteenth-century artists depicted fresh-faced country girls crying milk and other goods. (See, for instance, Hogarth's unfinished watercolor experiment "The Shrimp Girl.") But the youthful sexuality of these openmouthed girls is nonetheless implied by their bold gazes and blushing cheeks.

Just as humoral theory posited a physiological explanation for women's mental, physical, and emotional characteristics, so Addison questioned whether there might be a physiological explanation for female "Loquacity." After discussing "Female Orators" and "the Ladies of the *British* Fishery," he went on in the same *Spectator* paper to offer an "Anatomy of a Woman's Tongue." Drawing on the popular subgenre of the "Anatomy of a Woman's Tongue,"[25] as well as on contemporary developments in natural philosophy, he speculated that if a female cadaver was dissected, clues to women's ceaseless "Tattle" might be found in the "Tongue," "Fibers," "Muscles," "Channels," "Head," and "Heart":

[A] Friend of mine, who is an excellent Anatomist, has promised me . . . to dissect a Woman's Tongue, and to examine whether there may not be in it certain Juices which render it so wonderfully voluble and flippant, or whether the Fibers of it may not be made up of a finer or more pliant Thread, or whether there are not in it some particular Muscles, which dart it up and down by such sudden Glances and Vibrations; or whether, in the last place, there may not be certain undiscovered Channels running from the Head and the Heart, to this little Instrument of Loquacity, and carrying into it a perpetual Affluence of animal Spirits.

Addison's depiction of the human vocal apparatus reflects his contemporaries' growing interest in the physiology of oral communication. At the same time, though, his "Anatomy of a Woman's Tongue" goes beyond an amateur's interest in natural philosophy. For in fact, Mr. Spectator continues with this theme for several paragraphs, recounting gruesome stories from ancient and modern authors about female decapitation and severed tongues. In all these anecdotes, women's tongues continue to "cry out" long after they are severed from the women's bodies. Addison jovially recounts, for instance, that "*Ovid* . . . tells us that when the Tongue of a beautiful Female was cut out, and thrown upon the Ground, it could not forbear muttering even in that posture."

After quoting this violent passage from the *Metamorphoses* (6.556–60), Addison goes on to recount a modern version of this anecdote. He tells the "Story of the Pippin-Woman," about a hawker of apples who was decapitated when she fell through the frozen Thames, yet whose severed head continued to cry her goods as it rolled along the ice. Five years later, perhaps inspired by Addison's gruesome story, John Gay offered his own version in *Trivia: Or, the Art of Walking the Streets of London* (1716). In Gay's poem, the violence and misogyny of the anecdote are even clearer:

> The cracking crystal yields, she sinks, she dyes,
> Her head, chopt off, from her lost shoulders flies;
> Pippins she cry'd, but death her voice confounds,
> And pip-pip-pip along the ice resounds.

Gay explicitly compares the female hawker's severed head to that of the legendary poet and prophet Orpheus, whose still "warm Tongue" continues to "cry" for his beloved Eurydice after he is torn to pieces by the female followers of Bacchus.[26] (Gay's linking of the apple seller to Orpheus underlines the way that hawkers were known primarily by their *voices*.) Addison insists that in recounting stories of female dismemberment his purpose is purely didactic. In reality, he says, he is "charmed with the Musick of this little Instrument" (i.e., a "Woman's Tongue"); all that he aims to do is "to Cure it of . . . disagreeable Notes." But as Addison's diction here suggests, for many eighteenth-century commentators on female speech, a "Woman's Tongue" was ideally a "charm[ing]" "Music[al] . . . Instrument" rather than a powerful, "disagreeable" tool.

In the same issue of the *Spectator*, Addison groups "Female Orators" into four different subcategories: "the Censorious," "the Coquet," "Gossips," and women "who are employed in stirring up the Passions." In satirically referring to Billingsgate fishwives as "Ladies of the *British* Fishery," Addison's point is not that fishwives can be "Ladies"; rather, his point is that "Fine Women" will sink to the status of fishwives if they fail to control their "Passions." The association of women and the passions is as old as

Augustine, and it continued to thrive in humoral theory, as we have seen. But eighteenth-century authors repeatedly warned women readers of the dangers of succumbing to their passions, and in so doing, they compared women's language to that of fishwives. In her novel *A Spy Upon the Conjurer* (1724), Eliza Haywood raises the specter of fishwives as a warning to her polite readers. She depicts a genteel lady who is transformed by her passions and begins to resemble a fishwife: "She had quite forgot all Decorum; . . . her Cheeks bloated with Fury; her Lips trembled; every Feature was distorted; her voice was big, hoarse, and masculine; and her Expressions such as are ordinarily made use of by Fish-Wives."[27] In describing this formerly decorous lady, Haywood underlines the corporeality of oral discourse: "her Cheeks bloated with Fury; her Lips trembled." Her "big, hoarse, and masculine" voice disfigures her entire "Person."

Like Haywood, Henry Fielding depicted would-be polite ladies' language deteriorating into "Billingsgate" when their wrath was triggered. In *Tom Jones* (1749), Mrs. Western's language degenerates into Billingsgate whenever she falls into a "violent passion." In one scene, Squire Western and his sister (a woman of "masculine Person") engage in a verbal battle that Fielding compares to the altercations of Billingsgate market. Mrs. Western "fell . . . into the most violent Passion, and so irritated and provoked the Squire, that . . . there ensued between them both so warm a Bout at Altercation, that perhaps the Regions of *Billingsgate* never equaled it." In another scene, Mrs. Honour, Sophia's maid, bursts into a room at an inn "in a most outrageous Passion." In a lengthy epic simile, Fielding compares Mrs. Honour's discourse to the harangues of Billingsgate fishwives (and the noise of yelping dogs). He then compares Billingsgate fishwives to the classical Naiads, legendary female creatures who presided over fountains, rivers, and streams. Merging jest book culture and allusions to classical mythology, he suggests that Mrs. Honour makes

a Noise, not unlike, in Loudness, to that of a Pack of Hounds just let out from their Kennel . . . or, indeed, more like . . . those Sounds, which, in the pleasant Mansions of that Gate [Billingsgate], which seems to derive its Name from a Duplicity of Tongues, issue from the Mouths, and sometimes from the Nostrils, of those fair River Nymphs, ycleped of old the *Naiades*; in the vulgar Tongue translated Oyster-Wenches; For when, instead of the ancient Libations of Milk and Honey and Oil, the rich Distillation from the Juniper-Berry [i.e., gin], or, perhaps, from Malt, hath, by the early Devotion of their Votaries, been poured forth in great Abundance, should any daring Tongue with unhallowed License profane; i.e., depreciate, the delicate fat *Milton* Oyster, the Plaice sound and firm, the Flounder as much alive as when in the Water, the Shrimp as big as a Prawn, the fine Cod alive but a few Hours ago, or any other of the various Treasures, which those Water-Deities, who fish the Sea and Rivers, have committed to the Care of the Nymphs, the angry *Naiades* lift up their immortal Voices, and the profane Wretch is struck deaf for his Impiety.[28]

Fielding alludes to Billingsgate as a type of discourse *and* as a widely recognized location. At Billingsgate market, he suggests, any "Wretch" who dares to question the freshness of fishwives' shrimp, plaice, cod, or flounder will be "struck deaf" with these women's "immortal Voices." Like many of his contemporaries, Fielding depicts fishwives as heavy drinkers. But instead of "Libations of Milk and Honey and Oil," modern fishwives "pour forth in great abundance" the cheapest kinds of liquor available, gin and beer: "the rich Distillation from the Juniper-Berry" and "Malt." By means of the topos of "Billingsgate eloquence," Fielding links women regardless of their social rank, geographical location, or historical era (fictional or otherwise). Polite persons might aspire to contain, even transcend their bodies (the seat of the passions), but women's physiological makeup, he suggests, makes them constitutionally unable to control their "outrageous," "violent" passions.

"SHAMELESS *BILLINGSGATE*" AND THE "BOOKISH" GENTLEMAN

Fielding depicts a poor "wretch" who is publicly shamed by Billingsgate fishwives. For rhetoricians and elocutionists, two key ends of training in oratory were obtaining power and avoiding shame. From Le Faucheur to Hugh Blair, rhetoricians conjure up trauma-inducing images of worthy, but ill-trained speakers being shamed by their moral, intellectual, or social inferiors in oral confrontations. Le Faucheur depicts public speaking as a battle between an "Orator" and his "Adversary": "the *Orator* holds his *Auditor* . . . by the *Eyes* as well as by the *Ears* and absolutely engages both his *Attention* and his *Reason* at once: and if he speaks *thus* to an *Adversary* not so well qualified, he dashes him out of Countenance, he confounds him with *fear*, and overcomes him with *shame*."[29] The scenes that he depicts anticipate Pope's verbal wrestling match between "shameless *Billingsgate*" and "fair *Rhet'ric*," whereby one speaker "confounds," "overcomes," and "shame[s]" another and metaphorically "dashes" her opponent to the ground. Le Faucheur argues that speakers must "arm" themselves for competition by perfecting their pronunciation and gesture, for "the *best Cause* in the world may soon be lost for want of *Action*," and "the *good* at least ought to be as well arm'd as the bad."[30]

Writing a century after Le Faucheur, in a more developed print society, Sheridan provided his own version of this traumatic scene so often depicted by rhetoricians. In the new age of print commerce, he suggested, "bookish men" were especially at risk of being publicly shamed by their "inferior[s]":

> [B]ookish men are remarkable for taciturnity. . . . [S]uch men find it difficult, through want of practice, to express their thoughts with freedom, and therefore avoid speaking, as painful. . . . Whilst on the other hand a superficial man of the world, by being habituated to conversation, shall be always ready to express his thoughts with volubility and ease, though infinitely inferior to the studious man both in knowledge of things and words.

In Sheridan's elocutionary writings, "bookish men" is a classification. He repeatedly observed that "bookish men, make in general the poorest figure in conversation."[31] As I shall go on to demonstrate now, eighteenth-century literary texts and satiric engravings also commonly depict bookish or artistic gentlemen publicly shamed by the powerful oratory of their social inferiors (especially fishwives). As Pamela Allen Brown suggests, in "the culture of jest" women appear not only as the butts of jokes but also as *agents*. In popular ballads, comic drama, and other genres of print and performance, "jesting women do not get hauled off to court or the cuckstool for shutting someone's mouth with their wit, which these brief narratives often represent as devastatingly effective." While "official culture" praised submissive woman, "jesting culture often applauded the satiric shrew."[32]

In the *London Spy*, Ned Ward depicts his male narrator intimidated and silenced by fishwives' voices. After seven years of study in the country, the narrator puts down his books and ventures to London to learn through empirical observation. After strolling through Billingsgate market, he and his male companion seek refreshment at a nearby tavern in a narrow lane. Inside the tavern, they encounter a "litter" of fishwives warming themselves by the fire, each with a "nipperkin of warm ale and brandy." Again, fishwives are represented as heavy drinkers (and as animals). As Brown notes, "early modern drinking places have been treated as male-dominated milieus that were off limits and off-putting to 'respectable' women," but "in fact, tens of thousands of women ran alehouses or worked in them," while others routinely gathered there at the end of their day's work.[33] Ward depicts Billingsgate fishwives as regulars in this dockside tavern. These women frequent this tavern so often that they claim all the best seats by the fireside as their own, and their presence en masse intimidates the two "outside" guests. Ward also describes the fishwives as "promiscuously engaged in a mess of tittle-tattle." Their "tittle-tattle" is lewd, satiric, and scornful of these relatively elite male outsiders. Unnerved by the fishwives' discourse, the narrator's companion warns him that "these saucy-tongued old whores will tease us to death." When one fishwife overhears this insulting remark, she explodes in a volley of oral abuse. Ward depicts the fishwives' language as characterized by figures of speech such as metaphor and hyperbole. (In the later eighteenth century, we shall see, Adam Smith also associated "the Billingsgate language" with the use of figures.) The insulted fishwife roars back at the narrator's friend, "You white-livered son of a Fleet Street bum-sitter, begot upon a chair at noonday between Ludgate and Temple Bar! . . . Who is it that you call whore?" Confronted by this powerful plebeian female orator, the two gentlemen are rendered speechless and unable to defend themselves. Their book learning and superior social rank are useless, and they have no choice but to exercise prudence and retreat to another, less desirable part of the tavern. In his own highly figurative language, Ward describes his narrator slinking away from the fishwives. Employing one of his many animal metaphors for these women, he writes: "Away slunk my friend and I into another room . . . thankful to Providence we escaped so imminent a danger, as if delivered from the rage of so many wild cats."[34]

As the *London Spy* suggests, fishwives were commonly associated with lewdness and bawdy language. (In the *Dunciad*, not coincidentally, "Bawdry" and "Billingsgate" are sisters.) A City of London mayoral proclamation of 1590 describes fishwives as "women not onely of lewde and wicked life and behaviour themselves but procurers and drawers of . . . servaunts and suchlike to sundry and wicked accions."[35] Yet while fishwives' discourse is represented as bawdy and lewd, these women are also represented as quick to engage in verbal or physical combat to defend their sexual honor. This characterization appears to have had some basis in reality. Historian Laura Gowing finds that riverside women such as sailors' and fishermen's wives were relatively common plaintiffs in court records of litigation over sexual insult:

> In one particular occupational area, circumstances combined to produce the highest level of women's participation [in the church courts] in London. East London parishes, like the fast-growing, crowded industrial area of Wapping, were mostly riverside neighborhoods where as much as three-quarters of the male population might be sailors, absent for long

periods. Their wives were both open to accusations of illicit sex and bastardy in their husbands' absence, and well prepared to fight cases alone.[36]

These litigious women call to mind Ward's insulted fishwife who immediately and fearlessly responds to a male stranger of a higher rank by confronting him and demanding, "Who is it that you call Whore?"

The next morning, Ward's narrator and his friend leave the tavern. Walking along the riverside, they encounter fishwives hard at work sorting sprats. Like the first encounter, this confrontation concludes in a failure of male courage. Ward depicts his narrator as an urban Odysseus, forced to make his way past a grotesque, "grunting" version of Scylla and Charybdis. But whereas the classical she-monsters devoured Odysseus's sailors, Ward's "hungry," "snarling" fishwives (or "flat-caps") assault him with their "ill tongue[s]":

> We turned into a crowd of thumb-ringed flat-caps, from the age of seven to seventy, who sat snarling and grunting at one another over their sprats and whitings, like a pack of domestic dogs over the cook-maid's kindness, or a parcel of hungry sows at a trough of hog-wash. Every one looking as sharp as a strolling fortune-teller, I feared they would have picked my pocket with their eyes or have brought me under an ill tongue before I could have shot this dangerous gulf, where the angry surges of a tempestuous tittle-tattle ran mountain-high, dashing into my ears on every side. I was as glad when I had weathered this storm of verbosity.

In Ward's representation, the fishwives' aggressive orality ("snarling," "grunting," "tattling") links them to beasts rather than to humans: "hungry sows," "wild cats," and "dogs." Once again, the narrator and his male companion slink away as quickly as they can: happy to have "weathered this storm of verbosity."[37]

Along with literary representations such as Ward's, satiric prints showcase the powerful voices of fishwives. These visual depictions of fishwives suggest some of the ways that oral discourse is thematized in eighteenth-century art. Arnold Vanhaecken's *The View and Humours of Billingsgate* (1736) foregrounds fishwives' "Elocution," against which the would-be consumer must exercise caution (fig. 6.2). Vanhaecken's engraving depicts a chaotic scene, with hawkers vending fish and oysters from baskets and carts. Surrounding the market are stately classical buildings; their orderliness contrasts with the energy of the crowd. On the far right are buildings with shop fronts opening up to the market: these stalls function as

Fig. 6.2. Arnold Vanhaecken, *The View and Humours of Billingsgate* (1736).
Photograph: © The Trustees of the British Museum.

permanent display areas for the sale of fish. On the far left is a tavern—one
of many such establishments that hard-drinking fishwives were reputed to
retreat to daily. (The arms of the Vintners' Company are displayed over one
of the tavern doors.) In the center of the print, a dog with a liquor flask tied
to its tail knocks over a fishwife's basket. Meanwhile, a gentleman buys
oysters while a boy attaches a fish to his wig. The caption to the print foregrounds the fearsome oratory of Billingsgate fishwives, warning the visitor
to exercise "Prudence" when bargaining for provisions:

> You may, if Prudence is your cautious guide
> Procure the produce of the oceans Pride
> But Ah! beware, when you your Board would grace,
> To rouse the Elocution of that place

For else, while bargaining for Prawns & Shrimps,
You'll hear your self proclaimed a thousand Pimps.

Like Ward (and, as we shall see, Adam Smith), Vanhaecken associates Billingsgate discourse with obscenities and the frequent use of figurative language. These orally adept fishwives, as Ward, Vanhaecken, and others suggest, have a "thousand" different ways to proclaim that an irritating outsider is a "Pimp," a "son of a Fleet Street bumsitter," or "a son of a whore."

Another satirical print, John Collet's *The Female Orators* (1768), is a close-up of two female vendors. Collet depicts a fishwife and a fruit seller who are engaged in a heated oral dispute (fig. 6.3). Both women have their mouths wide open, with all the connotations that I have suggested such depictions entail (vulgarity, sexuality, and noise). But their oratory is not limited to what Sheridan called "the mere utterance of words": it also involves the use of posture, stance, facial expressions, and gestures. The fishwife is squared off aggressively against the fruit seller, with her hands on her hips

Fig. 6.3. John Collet, *The Female Orators* (1768). Photograph: Courtesy of the Lewis Walpole Library, Yale University.

and her legs braced apart. Meanwhile, the fruit seller's facial expression, bodily stance, and hand gesture also speak eloquently without words. With a little "bookish" help, we can decipher the fruit seller's hand gesture even today. By consulting John Bulwer's 1644 manual of gestures, *Chirologia: or the Natural Language of the Hand*, we can identify her two outstretched hands as making a gesture that Bulwer calls "*Indignor.*" *Indignor* means "to be indignant, offended; to resent." As is typical of satiric prints depicting fishwives, this engraving shows not only the women's oral and physical confrontation but also the effects that their voices have on the *men* around them. On the left side of the print, a gentleman in a wig and gown plugs his ears and grimaces as he emerges from a sedan chair. Significantly, this gentleman's clothing suggests that he is a lawyer or a judge (a "bookish" man with rhetorical training). His back is turned to the women, and he seems eager to get away from their noise. On the right, a musician (a fiddler or violinist) scowls as the women's voices drown out his art. (This vignette is reminiscent of Hogarth's print *The Enraged Musician* [1741], which also depicts the effects of plebeian noise on genteel art.) A third male gestures toward a broadside posted on a wall. Not coincidentally, this text advertises a performance of Ben Jonson's comic drama *Epicoene, or the Silent Woman* (1609). Print, performance, voice, and gesture are linked by the thematizing of plebeian women's oral discourse.

In Collet's *Female Orators*, women take center stage and men react to them. Along with several other satiric prints of the 1760s and 1770s, Collet's depiction of orally aggressive fishwives and their effects on the men around them exemplifies heightened concerns in these decades about male "effeminacy." In 1757 clergyman John Brown's treatise *An Estimate of the Manners and Principles of the Times* brought such concerns to the level of a national debate. Addressing the ills of advanced commercial societies, Brown argued that "vast Wealth naturally produces Avarice, Luxury, or Effeminacy." In a section of *An Estimate* discussing "the Effects of Commerce on Manners," he proposed that in modern Britain, the sexes had swapped gender roles: "the one sex [have] . . . advanced in boldness, as the other have sunk into effeminacy."[38] Brown's text stimulated a broad discussion of gender roles in modern commercial society, and perhaps not coincidentally, a flurry of prints appeared depicting "masculine" fishwives beating down, intimidating, or otherwise disturbing effete gentlemen (especially macaronis and foppish Frenchmen). Between 1756 and 1763, Britain was engaged in the Seven Years' War with France, and another factor in these depictions of fishwives was intensified nationalism and xenophobia at a time of war. Some of these prints side with the fishwives and represent them as patriotic Britons. In this regard, they anticipate similarly patriotic prints of the 1780s and 1790s wherein "hawkers are made to personify British pluck and ferocious retaliation against injury or slight, particularly from the French or the Frenchified."[39]

A pair of anonymous mezzotints published in London in the mid-1770s by the Bowles family of printsellers links feisty fishwives to the cause of nationalism. The titles of these prints, *Sal Dab giving Monsieur a Reciept* [*sic*] *in full* and *Billingsgate Triumphant, or Poll Dab a Match for the French-man*, suggest their anti-Gallic sentiments. The first print depicts a combat between two fishwives and a Frenchman in front of the "Good Woman" tav-ern (fig. 6.4). The tavern signboard foregrounds the theme of female voices: it depicts the "Good Woman" as a body without a head (and so a tongue). One of the fishwives boxes the Frenchman, while the second holds a lob-ster's claws to his buttocks. A second Frenchman watches the proceedings, horrified and disgusted, while the English host of tavern looks on and laughs. Another sign on the tavern advertises "Wilkes Cordial," a liquor named after John Wilkes, who was elected a member of Parliament in 1757 on a platform of representative government. The presence of this political advertisement implicitly links the fishwives' aggressive plebeian orality (and physicality) to protodemocratic developments in popular political culture.

The second image in this pair of mezzotints, *Billingsgate Triumphant, or Poll Dab a Match for the Frenchman*, depicts another verbal and physical battle between fishwife and Frenchman, once again before a tavern (fig. 6.5). (Again, fishwives are associated with taverns and drinking.) This time, the tavern is called the "The Fighting Cocks." In this print, the bloodied Frenchman is so terrified that he is defecating in fear. A second Frenchman looks on in horror, holding his countryman's coat. The host and patrons of the tavern look on in amusement and laugh. Another fishwife squats on the ground beside her basket of fish. Her mouth is wide open, shouting (with all the connotations that a wide open mouth implies).

A third mezzotint of the same period, Philip Dawe's *The Enraged Maca-roni* (1773), also published by the Bowles family, depicts yet another burly fishwife, this time thrusting a fish into an effete, foppishly dressed gentle-man's face (fig. 6.6). Like Vanhaecken's *View and Humours of Billingsgate*, this image features a caption that foregrounds the power and poison of fishwives' "vip'rous Tongue[s]":

> The Billingsgate with rude and cutting Jokes
> The Macaroni in fierce Rage provokes:
> Who threatens Blood and Wounds with glaring Eyes,
> But she with vip'rous Tongue his Rage defies.

The Good Woman

Wilkes's Cordial
and Purl
all the Year

Sal Dab giving Monsieur a Reciept in full.

London, Printed for R.Sayer & J.Bennett No. 53 Fleet Street, as the Act directs 29 May 1776.

389

Fig. 6.4. *Sal Dab giving Monsieur a Reciept* [sic] *in full* (c. 1775). Hand-colored mezzotint.
Photograph: © The Trustees of the British Museum.

Fig. 6.5. *Billingsgate Triumphant, or Poll Dab a Match for the Frenchman* (c. 1775).
Hand-colored mezzotint. Photograph: © The Trustees of the British Museum.

Fig. 6.6. Philip Dawe, *The Enraged Macaroni* (1773). Photograph: Courtesy of the Lewis Walpole Library, Yale University.

Like so many other gentlemen before him, this "Macaroni" is beaten by "the Billingsgate" and humiliated by her "rude and cutting Jokes" (despite the fact that this man is carrying a sword).

A century after Addison held up the "Ladies of the *British* fishery" as an example of "Female Orators," author, artist, and incipient ethnographer Rudolf Ackermann published his lavishly illustrated work *The Microcosm of London* (3 vols., 1808–10). In a chapter devoted to Billingsgate market, Ackermann describes Billingsgate as a "renowned school of *British oratory*" where many members of Parliament and lawyers have polished their debating skills. Describing an illustration titled *Billingsgate Market* that is similar but not identical to Vanhaecken's *View and Humours of Billingsgate*, Ackermann writes:

> The accompanying print represents . . . a scene in this renowned school of *British oratory*, an academy from which many illustrious orators, both of the bar and the senate, have derived that energetic and forcible manner, which, in honour of the original seminary, is so emphatically termed *Bilingsgate*.

Foregrounding the fishwives' "eloquence" and "forcible manner," and imitating Fielding in linking modern-day fishwives to the ancient Naiads, Ackermann continues:

> The power of their eloquence has raised such a tempest and whirlwind of passion in the gentle bosoms of two fair disputants, that, forgetting or laying aside the native softness and delicacy of their sex, they have engaged in furious combat. . . . Their sister *Naïads* on either side encourage and foment the immortal strife: one of them has fallen with inconceivable fury on a wretch, who is possibly a Frenchman and a fiddler, and has probably raised this storm by either undervaluing the fair one's fish, or having made some *mal-à-propos* observation on its degree of freshness; . . . he seems to be nearly in as bad a situation as *Orpheus*,
>
> > "When, by the rout that made the hideous roar,
> > > "His goary visage down the stream was sent,
> > "Down the swift Hebrus to the Lesbian shore."
>
> It appears probable that the ladies who used poor Orpheus so cruelly, were *Grecian Bilingsgates* . . . . [C]ertain it is, that the English *poissardes* are as jealous devotees of the jolly god [Bacchus], as the Grecian

Maenades could be for their lives, and quite as apt to be quarrelsome in their cups.[40]

As we have seen, Fielding depicted the fishwives and oyster wenches of Billingsgate "lift[ing] up their . . . Voices" and striking deaf a "Wretch" who dared to question the freshness of their fish. Along similar lines, Ackermann speculated that the Naiads, who ripped Orpheus to shreds, were fishwives. (This contrasts with Gay's use of Orpheus mentioned earlier, where Gay compares the "shrilling Strain" of the decapitated apple seller to the "cry" of the murdered poet's tongue, rather than to the "hideous roar" of the murderous Bacchantes.)[41] Like other eighteenth-century authors, Ackermann suggested that the "energetic and forcible manner" of rude orators such as street sellers has its own kind of power. Gentlemen must not take the potency of oral delivery for granted, for the adept use of voice and gesture by one's opponents, however "low," could be disabling. Ackermann also represented English fishwives as drunkards. He observed that "the English *poissardes* are as jealous devotees of the jolly god [Bacchus], as the Grecian *Maenades* could be for their lives, and quite as apt to be quarrelsome in their cups."

Eighteenth-century verbal and visual representations of Billingsgate fishwives depict these women as "masculinized" by their powerful rhetoric, and they increasingly portray that rhetoric as intimidating to "bookish" men. Of course, not all these representations exemplify concerns about media shift. As I observed earlier, satiric representations of fishwives as loud and intimidating long predate the 1695 explosion of the press. This is especially true of depictions of fishwives and oyster sellers in popular culture. In an undated broadside ballad, *An excellent new Ditty . . . Which proveth that women the best Warriors be*, the voices of fishwives and oyster sellers frighten the devil himself back to hell. The devil has returned to earth to corrupt mankind, and he successfully buys the souls of men and women of diverse social ranks and occupations. But when he encounters "the poore women / that cry fish and Oysters," he is unsuccessful—and terrified. The voices of these plebeian women, who "flock" in "clusters" and squawk like geese, frighten him more than eternal damnation itself. Confronted with their powerful voices, he makes a hasty retreat, exclaiming, "I must from them, / for, should I stay here, / In pieces, among them, / my body they'l teare." By exercising prudence—as Vanhaecken's *View and Humours of Billingsgate* recommends—the devil escapes the fate of Ackermann's Orpheus, whose body is ripped to shreds by "*Grecian Bilingsgates*." Significantly, it is the fishwives' powerful *voices*, rather than their burly bodies, that frighten away the devil himself.

English depictions of fishwives also share some characteristics with the French literary tradition of *poissarde*. From about the 1640s, the term *poissarde* was used in France to describe the language of fishwives, and later, a fishwife persona was created in popular theater, song, and verse. In the mid-eighteenth century, *poissarde* became "a bona fide literary genre."[42] In pamphlets and theatrical productions, elite authors imitated the discourse of fishwives for parodic purposes. In her chapter on French *poissarde* plays and verse of "the prerevolutionary period," Carla Hesse describes the contribution of Jean-Joseph Vadé in the 1740s:

> [A] minor royal official, Jean-Joseph Vadé, . . . created the most lasting model of *poissarde* literature as a kind of fictionalized scripting of an ethnographic record of popular speech. He did this through the construction of a myth of the male author as a mere scribe of female speech, a man of letters who haunted marketplaces, taverns, and cafes . . . recording eloquent street disputes.

Vadé's persona resembles Ward's in the *London Spy* forty years earlier. Later in the eighteenth century, *poissarde* plays and verse "cast the male writer as the butt of the fishwife's wit. Her natural eloquence trumps his literary pretensions."[43]

FISHWIVES AND FIGURATIVE LANGUAGE

At the same time that Pope depicted "shameless *Billingsgate*" as the daughter of Dulness, he hurled accusations of Billingsgate rhetoric at his enemies and critics. By the 1720s in Britain, Billingsgate came to refer to a style of language, and authors of all kinds tossed back and forth charges of "Billingsgate" print. Defending his satire against charges of excessive harshness, Pope argued that his critics' Billingsgate discourse obligated him to respond in kind in print: "the politest men are sometimes obliged to swear, when they happen to have to do with porters and oyster-wenches." He pointed to a "Billingsgate paper" and to "whole volumes of Billingsgate against Dr. Swift and Mr. Pope."[44] The same year that Pope published *The Dunciad Variorum* (1729), Richard Savage capitalized on the success of Pope's poem by publishing his own work satirizing hack writers, *An Author to be Lett* (1729). Like Pope, Savage drew on the dual meanings of Billingsgate as a fish market *and* a style of discourse when he described political journalist Benjamin Norton Defoe as "*Daniel*'s Son of Love, by a Lady who vended Oysters," and suggested that this "Grub Street" author would have been better off dealing "in a *Fish-Market*, than . . . in dealing out the Dialects of *Billingsgate*" in newspapers and essay journals such as the *Flying Post*. John "Orator" Henley initially refrained from responding in print to Pope's portrait of him in the *Dunciad* (i.e., with the exception of a short doggerel poem titled "Tom O'Bedlam's Dunciad: or Pope Alexander the Pig" [1729]). But in 1736 he published a rejoinder, *Why* How now, *Gossip POPE?*, in which he proposed that the source of Pope's verbal creativity was "Billingsgate! an unexhausted Spring, / Whence we our Flights and Witticisms bring." Alluding to Pope's riverside estate at Twickenham, he accused the poet of "refining on the low Jests of . . . Fish-Women, as you live by the Water-side."[45] Charges of Billingsgate language were familiar to Henley. In 1727 the anonymous author of *A Letter to the Celebrated Orator* accused him of "Billingsgate discipline." Henley's critic drew on the dual meanings of Billingsgate as a fish market and a type of discourse when he advised Henley: "as for the Fineness of your Oratory . . . we shall not think it worth our while to give you a Shilling to hear it, since by spending a Penny at *Billingsgate* in Oysters, we can hear . . . much more delicately scurrilous in its Kind."[46]

In the more refined realm of university lectures, eighteenth-century rhetoricians also employed the topos of Billingsgate discourse. In his Glasgow University Lectures on Rhetoric and Belles Lettres (1762–63), Adam Smith cautioned his students against the overuse of tropes and figures. He warned these young gentlemen, "there is nowhere more use made of figures than in the lowest and most vulgar conversation. *The Billingsgate language is full of it.*"[47] Smith acknowledged that figures of speech were commonly held to "give the chief beauty and elegance to language." But he argued that to the contrary, the most forceful expression occurs when the speaker expresses his sentiments "in a neat, clear, plain and clever manner."[48] "Plain" language was the most elegant and persuasive (in contrast, oddly enough, to what he implicitly suggested was the *less* plain language of Billingsgate). Smith was not the first author to associate Billingsgate with figurative language. As I suggested earlier, the caption to Vanhaecken's print *View and Humours of Billingsgate* represents fishwives' discourse as highly figurative ("while bargaining for Prawns & Shrimps, / You'll hear your self proclaimed a thousand Pimps") while Ward's *London Spy* depicts fishwives lambasting the narrator and his friend with multiple variants of "son of a whore."[49] Billingsgate discourse by definition violates polite behavioral norms of detachment and reserve; it is passionate and without restraint (fig. 6.7). We might

Fig. 6.7. James Gillray, *Billingsgate Eloquence* and *Pulpit Eloquence* (1795).
Photograph: Courtesy of the Lewis Walpole Library, Yale University.

therefore expect Billingsgate to be associated with hyperbole, but why other tropes and figures? Why did eighteenth-century authors associate illiterate fishwives with tropes?

The association of fishwives and figurative language can be partly explained by the "plain style" movement in Britain. As we have seen in chapter 4, after the 1662 founding of the Royal Society of London for Improving Natural Knowledge, the first historian of the society, Thomas Sprat, outlined the members' preferred "manner of Discourse."[50] He recommended that the language of learned exchange be brought "as near the Mathematical plainness [as possible] . . . preferring the language of Artizans, Countrymen, and Merchants, before that, of Wits, or Scholars."[51] Plain style advocates recommended what they called a "middle style" of language. In theory, it was the language of "Artizans . . . and Merchants," but in reality, the ideal middle style was closer to that of an author like Addison—a university-educated gentleman who was schooled in the literary arts.[52] Plain style advocates vilified the use of tropes and figures. On the one hand, they linked these devices with aristocrats and their supposedly ostentatious language; on the other hand, they linked figures with the passionate, unrestrained language of "vulgar," "illiterate," and "savage" speakers. Writing in the immediate aftermath of the Civil War period and Interregnum, Sprat associated the overuse of tropes and figures with dangerous oratorical appeals to men's passions rather than their reason. "This vicious abundance of Phrase, this trick of Metaphor," could be "fatal to peace and good manners." The common people were believed to be especially susceptible to the deceptions of figurative language, and Sprat connected the use of figures to "Noise" and "volubility of Tongue." Despite his association of tropes and figures with dangerous passions, Sprat admitted that he himself was roused to "indignation" and "Anger" by the "mists and uncertainties" brought on by "Tropes and Figures."[53] But unlike the illiterate vulgar, who were dangerously misled by figurative language, the very thought of tropes and figures put *him* on guard against the deceptions of rhetoric.

One hundred years after Sprat's attack on "Tropes and Figures," Scottish rhetoricians were discussing this topic with fervor. Smith associated tropes and figures with Billingsgate, and Hugh Blair linked them with savages and "the infancy of man." The same year that Smith was delivering his Lectures on Rhetoric and Belles Lettres (1762–63), Blair published *A Critical Dissertation on the Poems of Ossian* (1763). James Macpherson had published *Fragments of Ancient Poetry* (1760), claiming to have recovered the poetic legacy of an ancient Highland bard, and in defending the authenticity of this poetry, Blair attempted to account for the Ossian poet's highly figurative language. Working to counter the assumption that "figures are . . . artificial modes of speech, devised by orators and poets, after the world . . . advanced to a refined state," he argued that in fact, "men never have used so many figures of style, as in . . . rude ages," when "their passions [had] nothing to restrain them."[54] Returning to this theme twenty years later in his *Lectures on Rhetoric and Belles Lettres* (1783), Blair taught his University of Edinburgh students that "the Language of the first ages [w]as passionate and metaphorical" and that "all Languages are most figurative in their early state." Although Smith and Blair cautioned their students against the overuse of figures, Blair nonetheless admired what he took to be the powerful style of savage orators, stating that "an Indian chief makes a harangue to his tribe, in a style full of stronger metaphors than a European would use in an epic poem."[55] Meanwhile, across the English Channel, a very different author was also theorizing the oratorical style of the "noble savage" and linking figurative language with the earliest "stages" in the development of man. In his *Essay on the Origin of Languages* (wr. c. 1762–63), Jean-Jacques

Rousseau argued that "as man's first motives for speaking were of the pas-sions, his first expressions were tropes. Figurative language was the first to be born. Proper meaning was discovered last."[56]

We will never know which came first: "savages" or figurative language. But either way, it is clear that in eighteenth-century Britain, debates about figures of speech and "the Billingsgate language" were closely intertwined. By the 1770s Scottish rhetoricians' discussions of Billingsgate discourse and its overreliance on tropes and figures had spread beyond university class-rooms to the pages of the popular novel. In 1771 another Scot, Tobias Smol-lett, satirized rhetoricians' obsession with "the tropes and figures of Bil-lingsgate" in his epistolary novel *Humphry Clinker*. In a letter to a friend, Jery Melford, an Oxford student, describes a tearoom ceremony at Bath and the chaos that ensues when dessert is served. Confronted with a lavish spread of tea and cakes, the formerly polite patrons lose all self-discipline:

> There was nothing but jostling, scrambling, pulling, snatching, strug-gling, scolding, and screaming. . . . Some cried; some swore; and the tropes and figures of Billingsgate were used without reserve in all their native zest and flavour; nor were those flowers of rhetoric unattended with significant gesticulation. Some snapped their fingers; some forked them out; some clapped their hands, and some their back-sides; . . . and everything seemed to presage a general battle.

The tea table disputants employ all the "tropes and figures of Billingsgate" in an effort to fulfill their gustatory desires, and their Billingsgate discourse is accompanied by "significant gesticulation."[57] Like Billingsgate fishwives before them, these formerly genteel ladies and gentlemen now also make effective use of their "fingers," "back-sides," and "hands."

PRINT, PLEBEIAN DISCOURSE, AND POLITICAL CHANGE

Thirteen years before Addison published his satire on "Female Orators," a book genuinely commemorating great female orators, *Les Femmes illus-tres ou les Harangues héroiques* (Paris, 1642), was translated into English and published in Edinburgh as *Les Femmes Illustres: Or, Twenty Heroick Harangues Of the most Illustrious Women of Antiquity* (1681). Attributed to "Monsieur de Scuddery [*sic*]," this defense of female oratory was most likely written by novelist and woman of letters Madeleine de Scudéry (1607–1701), who published under the name of her brother Georges. A collection of fictional speeches attributed to exemplary women of history, myth, and legend, *Les Femmes Illustres* begins with an "Epistre aux Dames," which argues for women's right to be educated and, sometimes, to exercise political authority. In 1662 another woman of letters, Margaret Cavendish, Duchess of Newcastle, published *Orations of Divers Sorts*. In a section on "Female Orations," she addressed the question of elite women's participation in oratorical traditions.

To contrast seventeenth-century celebrations of "Female Orations" with eighteenth-century satires of "Female Orators" is instructive. Like Addison, poet, periodical writer, and performer Christopher Smart (1722–71) satirized the idea of female orators in *The Midwife: Or, The Old Woman's Magazine* (1750–53).[58] Smart also developed an oral offshoot of his periodical, a variety show titled "The Old Woman's Oratory." One of his advertisements for this enterprise describes it as "Henley in Petticoats." Like Henley, whose Oratory was in operation until 1756, Smart employed print and oral venues together, and he used satire as a vehicle for commenting on political, topical, and social issues. But whereas Henley encouraged women to attend his Oratory and participate in its debates, Smart satirized the idea of female orators as ridiculous. Adopting the persona of "Mrs. Mary Midnight" (recalling "Mrs. Nightwork," the garrulous female narrator of Delarivier Manley's political scandal chronicle *The New Atalantis* [1709]), he satirically proposed that "since *Oratory* is not more than the *Art of Speaking*, and consequently depends chiefly upon the *Exercise of the Tongue*; Women are allow'd to be the best qualified for it by the universal Consent of all Mankind." He then listed examples of great female orators, ancient and modern, that were meant to be amusing to his audience, such as "Queen *Elizabeth* instructing her Senate, or animating her Soldiery, with the *Pathos of Cicero*, and *Vehemence of Demosthenes*."[59]

The existence of texts such as de Scudéry's *Les Femmes Illustres* hints at early modern efforts to recover a tradition of elite women's oratory, but attempting to recover the everyday discourse of *common* women is another kind of endeavor entirely. Today, one of the best places to find relatively direct transcriptions of plebeian women's oral discourse is in legal records. These transcriptions were produced by literate clerks, but they nonetheless shed light on cases of women's oral discourse causing them to be examined by the authorities for disturbing the peace. In the Middlesex County Records, we find plebeian women taken up and examined for seditious words. One Deborah Hawkins is recorded to have boasted to another woman, Mary Bennett, that she was ready to "put on breeches [her]self" to support the efforts of James, 1st Duke of Monmouth, to depose his uncle, King James II:

Deborah Hawkins spinster . . . maliciously intending to . . . rouse ill feeling against the said Lord the King . . . audaciously . . . uttered, in the course of conversation with Mary Bennett spinster . . . these wicked and seditious words, to wit, "Before the King . . . shall be crowned, this head of mine shall goe off, and before that day comes there will be a greate deal of bloodshed," and also spoke . . . these words in contempt of the said king, to wit, "Hee is noe King but an Elective King, and if there were warrs as I believe there will be, I will put on breeches myself to fight for the Duke of Monmouth."[60]

In a separate incident the same year, one Mary Sleet was sent to London Bridewell for declaring that "the King was the son of a whore and . . . the Duke of York was a bastard and . . . the Duke of Monmouth was a true born child."[61] Of course, legal records do not allow us to recover unmediated oral discourse. But they do help us to recover the *contexts* of that discourse—as well as the community's response. In this case, the recording clerk classified Mary Sleet as a "beastly drunkard and a common beggar," and the government sentenced her to hard labor at London Bridewell. As the examples of Deborah Hawkins and Mary Sleet suggest, legal records often provide a strikingly different view of women's oral discourse than do printed texts (especially literary texts such as novels). Compare, for instance, the oppositional political statements of Hawkins and Sleet to Samuel Richardson's representation of his working-class heroine's oral discourse in *Pamela; Or, Virtue Rewarded* (1740). To what extent, we must ask ourselves, has our focus on printed texts (especially literary sources such as novels) distorted as much as enhanced our understanding of nonelite women's oral discourse?[62]

As I discussed in the introduction, Hogarth's engraving *Beer Street* (1751) depicts a fishwife pausing momentarily from her labor to enjoy a pint of ale (figs. 0.1 and 0.2). As we have seen in the current chapter, fishwives were associated with heavy drinking and disruptive behavior, but Hogarth pointedly depicts *this* fishwife as hardworking (and sober). Even more strikingly, he depicts her as *literate*: she is reading aloud or singing a broadside ballad. As we shall see in chapter 7, ballads were traditionally an oral genre, but Hogarth shows this fishwife reading a printed ballad to another laboring woman. As we have seen amply demonstrated in the current chapter, fishwives were associated with aggressive oral discourse—but strikingly, Hogarth depicts this fishwife reading (*and* voicing) a text. Hogarth's *Beer Street* and its companion engraving, *Gin Lane*, are openly ideological works. Published in support of legislation to control the sale of gin, they portray

beer as healthful and invigorating and gin as socially and morally destructive. Hogarth's illustration of a literate, well-behaved fishwife sharing the
contents of a printed text with another laboring woman is also ideological.
This may not be the reality now, Hogarth suggests, but for better or worse,
it is what *may* happen if wholesome malt rather than gin ("the rich Distillation from the Juniper-Berry," to recall Fielding's phrase) becomes plebeian
women's beverage of choice.

The gap between Hogarth's literate, well-behaved fishwife and conventional representations must surely have struck contemporary viewers. What
would happen, this image seems to ask, if fishwives were able not only to
read texts but also to disseminate their contents further by means of their
notoriously powerful oral discourse? In early modern society, a plebeian
woman who could read was potentially a force for social change, since she
"could act as a cultural bridge between her mostly illiterate milieu and
the world of print." As we have seen, Ward depicted Billingsgate fishwives
gathering in a tavern at the end of their workday to discuss political news.
He depicted these women as hostile toward elite male outsiders and as expressing oppositional political sentiments and antielite views. At times of
political instability, a laboring-class woman who could read appeared "that
much more dangerous as a . . . neighborhood agitator who combined the
knowledge of print with the power of speech." Hesse suggests that in Old
Regime France, fishwives "gathered daily in neighborhood wine bars . . . and
held forth on the political issues of the day. Wine bars were . . . key nodes in
the oral networks of Parisian neighborhoods: It was here that political news
was transmitted in an illiterate world." Hesse describes a politicization of
the literary genre of *poissarde* in revolutionary France: "the *poissarde* pamphlet genre . . . exploded as (mostly) male authors took on the voice of the
fishwife to heighten their claims to popular legitimacy."[63] Similarly, Diana
Donald notes that some British artists of the 1780s and 1790s encouraged
support for popular causes by depicting market women besieged by the authorities, yet vocally defending their customary rights. (A number of these
prints show fishwives' and fruit sellers' baskets and carts being overturned
by government soldiers on the march.)[64] But the political prospect hinted at
in *Beer Street* is different. Whereas Hesse notes elite male authors' *mimicry*
of fishwives' voices to advance their own political arguments, and Donald
describes artists' sympathetic depiction of street vendors so as to critique
government oppression, Hogarth's engraving hints at the politicization of
the common people through expanding literacy and greater access to printed
news. Tellingly, Hesse notes that at the same time the literary genre of *pois-*

sarde "exploded" during the revolutionary period, "fear of actual women speaking on the streets grew."[65] It was one thing, I would emphasize, for literate gentlemen to adopt fishwives' voices to advance their *own* causes. It was another thing for plebeian female orators such as fishwives to take to the streets and speak for themselves.

In July 1789 "fishwives were central participants in the Parisian crowd that brought down the Bastille." In October, "processions of market women led the massive march to Versailles that brought the King and the royal family back to Paris and ensured the ratification of the Declaration of the Rights of Man."[66] Learning about these events, British author Hannah More was horrified. In a letter to Horace Walpole, she wrote that "the throne of the grand monarque has been overturned by fishwomen."[67] In *Reflections on the Revolution in France* (1790), Edmund Burke similarly sympathized with Louis XVI and his family when he portrayed the "royal captives . . . moved along, amidst the horrid yells, and shrilling screams, . . . and all the unutterable abominations of the furies of hell, in the abused shape of the vilest of women."[68] Despite Burke's vilification of market women and their voices, the political activism of these plebeian women attracted at least one British sympathizer. In *A Vindication of the Rights of Men* (1790), Mary Wollstonecraft responded disdainfully to Burke's representation of street vendors as "the vilest of women." She wrote, "probably you mean women who gained a livelihood by selling vegetables or fish, who never had any advantages of education."[69] Wollstonecraft sympathized not with the royal captives but with the female street vendors who participated in a crowd revolt.

As these competing representations suggest, for eighteenth-century British commentators, fishwives and other female vendors were objects of revulsion, fascination, and sometimes fear. For many authors and artists, the "harangues" of hawkers were the epitome of intimidating urban noise. In *The Prelude* (1805), book 7, "Residence in London," William Wordsworth describes how in venturing to London as a young man he at first "sang / Aloud, in Dithyrambic fervour" (l. 6). (A dithyramb is a pagan chant in honor of Dionysus.) But the song of Wordsworth's youthful narrator is "short-lived," for he is overwhelmed by the "Babel din" (l. 157) of London streets. Wordsworth was deeply affected by, and initially sympathetic to, the French Revolution. But like Ward's "London Spy" a century earlier, Wordsworth's narrator is alternately fascinated, dazed, intimidated, and horrified by the sights and sounds of London. Eventually, overwhelmed, he darts into an "unsightly Lane" and then a private courtyard: "Meanwhile the roar continues, till at length, / Escaped as from an enemy, we turn / Abruptly into some

sequestered nook" (ll. 184–86). But even in such "private" places, the young
gentleman cannot escape the "shrillest of all London Cries," the intimidating sound of the "female Vendor's scream":

> . . . . Private Courts,
> Gloomy as Coffins, and unsightly Lanes
> Thrilled by some female Vendor's scream, belike
> The very shrillest of all London Cries,
> May then entangle us awhile,
> Conducted through those labyrinths unawares. (ll. 196–202)

In these lines, "thrilled" (l. 198) does not mean "delighted." The verb "to
thrill" means "to cause to move tremulously, vibrate, quiver." The impli-
cation is that the "unsightly Lanes" and "Private Courts" of London (and
perhaps also the narrator's body) are made to quiver or shake by the hawker's voice. Like the "shrilling screams" of Burke's revolutionary fishwives
and fruit sellers, the "shrillest of all London Cries," the "female Vendor's
scream," can be heard throughout the modern city. Like the powerful voices
of Billingsgate fishwives, this "female Vendor's scream" at once unnerves
the eighteenth-century author and generates his art.

CHAPTER SEVEN

"The Art of Printing Was Fatal":
The Idea of Oral Tradition in Ballad Discourse

In a series of lectures delivered in 1964, Walter J. Ong observed the way that a sudden awareness of media shift in one generation seemed to trigger groundbreaking insights into parallel historical moments:

> Awareness of the succession of the media stages and wonder about the meaning of this succession are themselves the product of the succession. . . . [O]nly as we have entered the electronic stage has man become aware of the profundity of differences, some of which have been before his eyes for thousands of years, namely, the differences between the old oral culture and the culture initiated with writing and matured with alphabetic type.[1]

Ong suggested that new insights into "oral culture" in the late 1950s and early 1960s were the unexpected consequence of (hu)man's entrance into the latest phase of their communications development, the "electronic stage." A Jesuit priest, he expressed concern that the "great but distracting boon" of "artificially contrived media" (electronic devices such as radio and television, but also writing and print) was threatening to displace "the word . . . in its original and still natural habitat, the world of voice, of sound."[2] Exactly two hundred years earlier, in 1764, clergyman and scholar Thomas Percy (1729–1811) drafted "An Essay on the Ancient Minstrels in England." This essay would be appended to his anthology, *Reliques of Ancient English Poetry: Consisting of Old Heroic Ballads, Songs, and Other Pieces of Our Earlier Poets, Together With Some Few of Later Date* (3 vols., 1765). Percy collected his "reliques" entirely from textual sources, but in his ambitious seventy-page "Essay," he represented the "Old Heroic Ballads" in his collection as the "select remains of our ancient English bards and minstrels," "oral itinerant poet[s]" who "probably never committed [their rhymes] to writing."[3] He suggested that these minstrels were at one time generously rewarded by those in power for the important sociocultural function that they served, but that by "the end of Queen Elizabeth's reign [1558–1603] ... the genuine old minstrelsy seems to have been extinct." Attempting to account for this extinction, he postulated a nearly literal confrontation between these dignified "oral ... poets" and "a new race of ballad writers ... an inferior sort of minor poets, who wrote narrative songs merely for the press."[4] Like Ong, Percy modeled historic communications developments as in some ways devolutionary. In his scenario, ancient minstrels and their successors, modern balladmongers, are not participants in one continuous artistic tradition; rather, the institutionalization of the commercial press contributed to the disappearance of an earlier (and superior) cultural practice based on voice. Percy's harshest critic, ballad collector Joseph Ritson (1752–1803), virulently disagreed with Percy's theories of "ancient minstrelsy," but he nonetheless concurred that the sixteenth-century spread of print was responsible for the decay of minstrelsy. In his "Observations on the Ancient English Minstrels," prefaced to his collection *Ancient Songs, From the Time of King Henry the Third, to the Revolution* (1790 [sic; recte 1792]), Ritson declared: "The art of printing was fatal to the Minstrels who sung; people began to read, and, unfortunately for the Minstrels, their compositions would not bear reading."[5]

Eighteenth-century Britain saw the emergence of an extensive print discourse about ballads (a discourse that was itself a product of the expanding print marketplace). In prefaces to printed collections, in essays printed in these collections, in commentaries in periodicals, and elsewhere, a wide variety of authors commented positively and negatively on balladry as a hybrid oral and textual practice. These commentators had diverse (and sometimes competing) agendas, but almost without exception, in writing about ballads they explicitly addressed the phenomenon of print commerce. While a few early eighteenth-century authors celebrated the press as contributing to "British Manufacture and Trade," most later commentators concurred that the nexus of print, commerce, and balladry had produced a "great quantity of sad trash."[6]

Today, many ballad scholars follow the great nineteenth-century scholar Francis James Child (1825–96) in dividing ballads into two principal categories—traditional (or "popular") and broadside ballads—but in the early eighteenth century this conceptual division did not exist. As Albert B. Friedman observes:

The traditional ballads ("Sir Patrick Spens," "Edward," and the like), those canonized in Professor Child's monumental collection . . . [were] not even tentatively differentiated from other ballads until well along in the eighteenth century. Before that time, a ballad, so far as either men of letters or plain citizens were concerned, was a doggerel poem written to a familiar tune, printed on a folio sheet or long slip, and sold at book-stalls or hawked about the streets by ballad-singers.[7]

Ballads still circulated widely in manuscript and by voice, but they were now almost routinely associated with "cheap print."[8] Over the course of the century, however, the polite ballad revival and especially the rise of ballad scholarship would forge significantly new ways of conceptualizing ballads. Whereas early eighteenth-century commentators such as Joseph Addison largely took for granted the multimedia nature of balladry (oral, written, printed), later eighteenth- and nineteenth-century ballad scholars increasingly modeled a distinct "oral tradition" of balladry that was threatened or displaced by commercial *print*, and they represented themselves as working to "rescue" this tradition before it was too late.

Percy's "Essay" implicitly asks, when did ballads first become a major category of commercial print in England? The present chapter, by way of contrast, asks when did ballads first come to be especially valued by scholars as "oral tradition"? Thirty years ago, Dianne Dugaw observed that many folklorists were reluctant to relinquish their conception of ballads as "unwritten" and noncommercial: "they contend that an unwritten song, a song from oral tradition, differs in some intrinsic way from one in print."[9] Today, most ballad scholars reject binary (or tripartite) models of balladry. As Adam Fox observes of "Chevy Chase," for which printed copies date back to 1624 and manuscript transcriptions to c. 1557–65, "it is difficult to know whether to describe such a ballad as the product of oral, scribal, or print culture."[10] But as Fox's phrase "oral, scribal, *or* print culture" here suggests (my emphasis), it is easier for us to agree that rigid binary (or tripartite) models of transmission are unsatisfactory than to move beyond them. The especially problematic "displacement" model of print and orality that I focus on here, whereby print is imagined as having displaced an earlier, more valuable oral tradition, has arguably been replaced by what Dugaw has identified as a still-problematic "metaphor of cross-pollination": "oral and printed, folk and commercial" traditions are still modeled as fundamentally distinct entities, each "exert[ing] their influences upon each other in turn."[11] Both "displacement" and "cross-pollination" models are predicated on an initial conceptual separation between oral and textual (especially printed) balladry. But where did this conceptual separation come from? When did ballad scholars first begin to forge a sharp distinction between printed (especially broadside) ballads and another set of practices they defined as "oral"?

As I suggested in chapter 1, the concept of oral tradition is not timeless and universal. For most English authors writing in 1700, this term would have first brought to mind the Catholic idea of the superior reliability of the unwritten tradition of the church as "the rule of faith." Throughout the century, the dominant understanding of tradition remained theological, but one increasingly sees this concept explored in an ethnographic context. Travel writings were a major category of the British book trade, and the diffusion through print of European accounts of "savages" in the New World and elsewhere offered Britons previously unknown information about sophisticated societies wherein genealogies, laws, customs, and arts were passed down through tradition (oratory, ceremonies, music, and dance). The later eighteenth century saw landmark arguments for oral tradition. In 1760 James Macpherson published *Fragments of Ancient Poetry, Collected in the Highlands of Scotland, and Translated from the Gaelic or Erse Language,* notoriously claiming that he had reconstructed the oral art of a great Highland bard, Ossian, passed down from the third century chiefly by word of mouth.[12] Macpherson's claims were considered scandalous by many, but they triggered extensive research into Celtic and Gaelic cultures and brought these debates concerning "oral tradition" to a very wide audience. Meanwhile, antiquarian Robert Wood advanced the first detailed case for Homeric orality in his *Essay on the Original Genius of Homer* (1769; rev. ed., 1775).[13] Wood's suggestion that Homer was unable to read or write was greeted with scorn, but it influenced the German classicist F. A. Wolf, whose *Prolegomena ad Homerum* (1795) later influenced the twentieth-century Homer scholar Milman Parry. By the end of the eighteenth century, we see an epochal shift in ideas of (and attitudes toward) oral tradition.

Percy's conjectural account of minstrels as "oral itinerant poet[s]" greatly spurred interest in the notion of oral tradition. Twenty-three-year-old ballad collector John Pinkerton (1758–1826), enthralled by his reading of *Reliques,* prefaced his collection *Scottish Tragic Ballads* (1781) with a lengthy "Dissertation on the Oral Tradition of Poetry."[14] In the nineteenth century, ballad collectors such as Walter Scott and William Motherwell worked to trace what they saw as a still-living "oral tradition" of balladry. In preparing his anthology *Minstrelsy, Ancient and Modern* (2 vols.; Glasgow, 1827), Motherwell increasingly aspired to collect ballads directly from oral performance and recitation rather than from texts. Motherwell's collecting practices differed dramatically from Percy's, but significantly for our purposes, he never-theless followed Percy and Ritson in positing an epochal sixteenth-century displacement of "ancient minstrelsy" by commercial print. In the Eliza-bethan period, Motherwell concurred, minstrel compositions were "super-seded in vulgar affection" by (inferior) broadside ballads. By the end of the nineteenth century, this now-naturalized "displacement" model of oral bal-ladry versus print balladmongering would evolve into Child's profoundly influential classificatory (and evaluative) distinction between traditional and broadside ballads. Child defined "traditional" ballads as those stemming from more authentic oral traditions. He suggested that in contrast to more valuable (and still traceable) traditional ballads passed down through voice, "the vulgar ballads of our day, the 'broadsides' which were printed in such huge numbers in England and elsewhere in the sixteenth century or later," belong to an entirely "different genus."[15]

This chapter argues that eighteenth- and early nineteenth-century bal-lad critics, responding to the perceived dramatic spread of print in their own time, contributed significantly to the emergence of our modern secular con-cept of "oral tradition." Whereas early eighteenth-century commentators tended to understand the oral and print dissemination of ballads as working in tandem (with positive or negative consequences), later commentators increasingly posited a distinct "oral tradition" of balladry that was anti-thetical to and threatened by commercial print. One way to denaturalize binary models of oral and textual balladry, I propose, is to understand where this conceptual separation came from in the first place. By comparing early eighteenth-century discussions of balladry, wherein ballads are assumed to be oral *and* printed, commercial *and* culturally influential, with later eighteenth- and nineteenth-century discussions, I will show the central role of ballad scholarship in shaping the idea of "oral tradition." Ballad schol-ars increasingly forged a sharp conceptual (not actual) separation between "oral" and "printed" ballads. In so doing, they contributed to the binary model of "orality and literacy" through which we now almost inevitably comprehend ballads.

"SOMETHING . . . TO HIT EVERY TASTE"

The dichotomy between ancient minstrels and modern balladmongers that structures Percy's "Essay on the Ancient Minstrels in England" is completely absent from Joseph Addison's papers on ballads in the *Spectator* (1711).[16] Mr. Spectator makes no attempt to theorize an especially valuable "oral" tradition of balladry that is separable from print. He expresses his "Delight in hearing" ballads and his "exquisite Pleasure" in reading broadsides. Even the fact that broadsides are often found in "despicable Circumstances" (such as pasted on the walls of country houses) does not lessen the satisfaction he takes in reading these "Printed Paper[s]" that he associates with "the Rabble of a Nation" (nos. 70, 85). Addison introduced ballads into the *Spectator* in order to make a point about polite *writing*. While his ballads papers are often read separately today, they were originally part of an ongoing discussion of "true and false wit." Addison held up two carefully selected examples of ballads—the heroic, patriotic "Chevy Chase" and the sentimental "Two Children in the Wood"—in order to illustrate the virtues of simplicity of style and thought in literary composition and to advance a case against "the Gothick [i.e., baroque] Manner in Writing." He assumed that the ballads he was discussing were originally "written" (e.g., "At the Time the Poem we are now treating of was written"),[17] and he neither conceptualized nor valorized something we might now label "popular oral culture."

Eleven years later, the editor of *Applebee's Original Weekly Journal* published a letter from one "Jeffrey Sing-Song," titled "The Ballad-maker's Plea."[18] While Mr. Sing-Song's own name emphasizes the oral aspects of balladry, his "Plea" argues for the centrality of ballad "Manufacture" (i.e., the printing of broadside ballads) to British trade. Like Mr. Spectator, Mr. Sing-Song implicitly associates ballads with broadsides. He does not see oral and print balladry as competing, and he certainly does not see valuable oral practices of balladry (what he wittily calls "Lingua-facture") as "lost." Mr. Sing-Song identifies himself as "by Trade a British Manufacturer." Convinced of the virtue, not degradation, of print commerce, he laments that the "Trade" of balladry is "of late . . . under a sensible Decay." He notes that a well-known ballad "Manufacturer" has been arrested: "the greatest Merchant in that kind of Goods has been taken up lately for something done *in his Way*, a little out of the Way, &c." Mr. Sing-Song does not specify this "Manufacturer's" name or alleged crime, but it appears that he has been taken up for printing Jacobite ballads. Mr. Sing-Song concludes his "Plea" with a veiled threat, offering to "furnish" some protest ballads should the merchant and his "Fellows" be hanged for treasonous publication:

[S]hall the jolly Fellows that may chance to Swing upon this Occasion, have never a *Passing Song* for them, as well as they have a *Passing Bell* at *St. Sepulchre's*?

Never fear it, I can furnish you with something suitable to every Occasion, and you shall perhaps have a Test of my Performance very speedily.

Mr. Sing-Song is proud, not condemnatory, of the links between ballads and print commerce (and here, popular political expression). Both ballad "Manufacturers" (printers) and "Lingua-facturers" (singers) are, unashamedly, "Merchants of Goods," and "it is by the Success of our Manufactures that our Nation is made happy, rich, powerful and great."[19]

One year after Mr. Sing-Song published his "Plea," an anonymous editor published the first two volumes of *A Collection of Old Ballads. Corrected from the best and most Ancient Copies Extant. With Introductions Historical, Critical, or Humorous, Illustrated with Copper Plates* (3 vols., 1723–25). The genesis of this collection remains uncertain. It was published by James Roberts, a trade publisher who typically published works on behalf of others, and it has recently been suggested that the collection was "a reprint commissioned by the then intellectual property owners made from printed versions held in their Ballad Warehouse."[20] But the most noteworthy aspect of the *Collection* is arguably neither the mystery of its publication nor the 159 ballads it contains (most of them already in print), but the way that these ballads are presented to the reader. In a series of three lively prefaces, the editor foregrounds his economic motives for publishing these ballads, but like Mr. Sing-Song, he does so without suggesting that economic concerns necessarily preclude "higher" motives. He praises the historical, educative, and entertainment value of ballads, and he works to elevate their status by constructing an extraordinarily dignified lineage. The frontispiece to the first volume of the *Collection* depicts busts of ancient poets such as Homer, Pindar, and Horace alongside the highly esteemed modern poets Abraham Cowley and Sir John Suckling, and in a statement whose significance we shall appreciate in a moment, the editor asserts that "the very Prince of Poets, old *Homer*," was "nothing more than a blind *Ballad-Singer*, who writ Songs of the Siege of *Troy*."[21] Admittedly, the tone of these prefaces is unstable. The editor sometimes seems to satirize his own high-minded attempts, but at other moments, he appears to abandon his self-satirizing style to assert the "real value" of ballads: "our old Songs I think ought to be preserv'd, and some of them are really valuable." Ultimately, both the editorial framing and the contents of the *Collection* suggest an entrepreneurial desire to attract readers and so maximize sales. The editor makes little (if any) attempt to rank different types of ballads. As the full title of the *Collection* makes clear, he especially values "Old Ballads" printed from "Ancient Copies." But contrary to what we might expect, he is surprisingly uninterested in preserving "Old Ballads" for their own sake. Indeed, he notes that he has omitted "a great number of old Songs" because they were "written in so old and obsolete a stile that few or none of my Readers wou'd have understood

'em." While he argues for the usefulness of old ballads as sources of historical information, he does not privilege historical ballads over other types. In
fact, he assures the reader that "those who have no Relish for these antique
Pieces, may, in the other half of the Book, meet with Variety of Entertainment; there are serious and humourous Ballads, *Scotch* Songs; and something I hope to hit every Taste." In comparison to later scholarly collections
of ballads—such as Percy's dignified anthology of "Old Heroic Ballads"—
the *Collection* is most striking for its miscellaneity and playfulness. Alongside historical narratives such as "The Battel of Agincourt" and sentimental
favorites such as "The Children in the Wood," one finds courtship songs
and "Drinking songs" such as "The Praise of Sack" and "The Answer of
Ale." Furthermore, like Addison and Mr. Sing-Song, the editor of the *Collection* makes no attempt to theorize an especially valuable "oral" tradition
of balladry that is separable from print. Indeed, this editor associates ballads so closely with texts that he touts the usefulness of ballads in teaching
children to read: "The Use of these Songs too is very great. I have known
Children, who never would have learn'd to read, had they not took a Delight
in poring over *Jane Shore*, or *Fair Rosamond*."[22]

The year 1723 also saw the publication of the first volume of *The Tea-
Table Miscellany: A Collection of Choice Songs, Scots and English* (4 vols.;
Edinburgh, 1723–37), edited by Scottish wigmaker-turned-author Allan
Ramsay (1684–1758). A native of Edinburgh, Ramsay's first publications
were broadside ballads, sold for a halfpenny or penny each; encouraged
by his success, he opened a bookstore and began publishing longer works.
Rather like Jeffrey Sing-Song, who depicted ballads as the products of "Manufacture and Lingua-facture," Ramsay represented the production of verse
as a kind of "manufact[ure]." Appealing to his fellow Scots, he argued that
Edinburgh, in particular, "is the Scene of many Adventures, which may be
proper Subjects for both Poet and Philosopher: But the Humour of under-
valuing *home-manufactory* discourages publication."[23] Ramsay's goal as a
bookseller and print author was sales, but in the long run, his collections
greatly encouraged interest in "Scots songs" and the Scottish vernacular,
and they were widely read by later ballad editors such as Percy, Motherwell,
and Scott, and by authors such as Robert Burns (1759–96).[24]

"A BLIND *BALLAD-SINGER*, WHO WRIT
SONGS OF THE SIEGE OF *TROY*"

In attempting to show the "Antiquity" of balladry, the editor of the *Collection* suggests that Homer was an itinerant ballad singer: "the very Prince of

Poets, old *Homer*, if we may trust ancient Records, was nothing more than a blind *Ballad-Singer*, who writ Songs of the Siege of *Troy*, and the Adventures of *Ulysses*; and playing the Tunes upon his Harp, sung from Door to Door." It was not until after Homer's death, he proposes, that an ancient Greek ballad collector "thought fit to collect all his Ballads, and by a little connecting 'em, gave us the *Iliad* and *Odyssey*, which since that Time have been so much admired."[25] In asserting that Homer's works were not linked together into epic poems until after his death, this editor echoes the views of the classical scholar Richard Bentley (1662–1742), who suggested that the man named "Homer" was a relatively lowly entertainer, or rhapsode:

[Homer] wrote a sequel of Songs and Rhapsodies, to be sung by himself for small earnings and good cheer, at Festivals and other days of Merriment; the *Ilias* he made for the Men, and the *Odysseis* for the other Sex. These loose Songs were not connected together in the form of an Epic Poem, till *Pisistratus*'s time about 500 years after.[26]

The eighteenth century saw a major reevaluation of Homeric poetry. Whereas neoclassical commentators valued what was universal and timeless in Homer and saw him as a divinely inspired "genius," later scholars increasingly understood this poetry as the work of multiple individuals and as the product of a unique historical and geographical environment. In the 1730s Scottish classicist Thomas Blackwell reopened an ancient debate concerning Homeric literacy in his *Enquiry Into the Life and Writings of Homer* (1735). He proposed that Homer was a blind "stroling indigent Bard" who had little learning: that is, "such Learning as we get from Books."[27] In 1769 another classical scholar, Robert Wood, pushed these suggestions further, asking "how far the use of Writing was known to Homer." Anticipating "the Reader's astonishment" at such a question, he reminded his readers, "We are not far removed from the age, when great statesmen, and profound politicians, did not know their alphabet." Wood proposed that before the spread of writing, valuable knowledge was passed down across generations by "bards" who were "entrusted with the whole deposit of Law, History, and Religion, till the art of Writing introduced a more easy, faithful, and comprehensive method of recording things."[28]

Ossian "translator" James Macpherson and his supporters drew on (and helped to shape) these debates concerning Homeric literacy. (Wood, for instance, suggested that Homer might have been indebted to later authors, just as Ossian was indebted to "the ingenious Editor of Fingal," or Macpherson.)[29] Macpherson was a student at Marischal College, Aberdeen, where

Blackwell was principal; he also came under the influence of Edinburgh clergyman and rhetorician Hugh Blair (1718–1800). Blair probably wrote the preface to Macpherson's *Fragments*. Although the preface does not ascribe these works to an entirely oral society, it asserts that "such poems were handed down from race to race; some in manuscript, but more by oral tradition."[30] In 1763 Blair published his immensely influential *Critical Dissertation on the Poems of Ossian*. (He published an expanded edition with an "Appendix" in 1765.) Blair famously labeled Ossian the "Homer of the Highlands," but he insisted that the status of Celtic bards was far superior to Homer's: "the Bards continued to flourish; not as a set of strolling songsters like the Greek . . . Rhapsodists, in Homer's time, but as an order of men highly respected in the state."[31] Even more influentially, he proposed that "until the present century, almost every great family in the Highlands had their own bard, to whose office it belonged to be master of all the poems and songs of the country." These poems were thus part of a still-traceable *native* oral tradition. In a gentlemanly gesture toward "fieldwork"—an endeavor not systematically practiced until Motherwell's labors in the 1820s—he proposed that reputable gentlemen should collect these works, recovering "oral tradition" by comparing "different oral editions of them" (i.e., oral performances) with existing manuscript transcriptions and printed texts. He appealed to his fellow clergymen to "make enquiry in their respective parishes" concerning persons who might be able to recite Ossianic poetry from memory, and he referenced the "testimony" of respected gentlemen who believed that they had heard such poetry, such as "Sir James Macdonald of Macdonald, in the Island of Sky, Baronet," who claimed that "he had lately heard several parts of [Ossian's poems] repeated in the original . . . with some variations from the printed translation, such as might naturally be expected from the circumstance of oral tradition." Blair's *Dissertation* triggered extensive research in part by assuming the existence of "oral tradition" and positing a set of characteristics that "might naturally be expected."[32] But in his view, it was not the living song practices themselves but the testimony of literate gentlemen concerning them that ultimately authorized these practices as "tradition."[33]

"THE ART OF PRINTING WAS FATAL"

Four decades after the publication of *A Collection of Old Ballads* (1723–25), Percy drew on it as one of his chief sources in assembling his *Reliques of Ancient English Poetry* (1765). In contrast to the miscellaneity and playfulness of the *Collection*, the *Reliques* proclaims its own selectivity and high seriousness. Published by James Dodsley, a major literary publisher rather than a trade publisher, and edited by a learned curate who assured his readers that "great care has been taken to admit nothing immoral and indecent," Percy's *Reliques* definitively established *certain types* of balladry as worthwhile objects of genteel appreciation and scholarly study.[34] It cannot be overemphasized that Percy only *selectively* valorized ballads. In his view, only select ballad traditions were worthy of being saved. One does not find here the type of oppositional political ballads alluded to by Mr. Sing-Song or the "Drinking Songs" touted by the editor of the *Collection* as likely to appeal to many readers' tastes. Instead, Percy favored "Old Heroic Ballads" such as "The Battle of Otterbourne" and "Chevy Chase." He extensively revised the language of many ballads to make them acceptable to polite taste, and he later described these rewritings as "conjectural emendations . . . without which the collection would not have deserved a moment's attention."[35] As is well known, Percy's most valued source was his fortuitously found "old Folio M.S. Collection of Historical Ballads &c.," which he especially treasured because it was not commercial. But Percy also consulted huge numbers of broadside ballads. In 1761 he visited Cluer Dicey, the most prolific ballad printer of the day, who had graciously promised to "romage into his Warehouse for every thing curious that it contains." Dicey presented him with more than eighty ballads, but Percy never publicly acknowledged Dicey's assistance in the *Reliques*. Although both men were involved in the publishing of ballads, Dicey was in Percy's view a mere balladmonger—a huckster of commodities rather than a scholar. In a letter to a genteel friend, Percy described Dicey as "the greatest printer of Ballads in the kingdom"—but also, significantly, as "an Acquaintance . . . of a much lower stamp."[36] Percy also greatly downplayed the extent of his debt to archival collections of broadside ballads. Although he acknowledged his debt to the Pepys Collection of broadside ballads at Cambridge University, he scorned the group of ballads that would later form part of the Roxburghe Collection as "Such as are still sold on stalls; not one in a hundred of them fit to be republished."[37]

In his "Essay on the Ancient Minstrels in England," Percy sought to link the history of English song to nobler origins than a printer's warehouse. He hypothesized that his "relics" were the written traces of originally oral compositions dating back to a sophisticated feudal society before commercial print. He especially modeled a "great divide"[38] between ancient minstrels and the degenerate modern distributors of broadside ballads. Like Blair distinguishing Celtic and Gothic bards from the "strolling songsters" of ancient Greece, Percy represented ancient minstrels as far more than mere entertainers. In his view, these men were the chroniclers of their times. These esteemed bards recorded honorable feats and aristocratic genealogies and were supported by a culture of patronage in a society where poetry and music were cherished by those in power: "their skill was considered as something divine; their persons were deemed sacred; their attendance was solicited by kings; and they were everywhere loaded with honours and rewards." As late as the reign of Henry VIII, the minstrels' situation was "honourable and lucrative." But by the end of the sixteenth century, he suggested, "this profession had fallen into such discredit that it was considered in law as a nuisance." What caused this relatively rapid "extinc[tion]" of an ancient cultural practice in Percy's view? Not coincidentally, as we have seen, Percy traced the decline of minstrelsy to the reign of Queen Elizabeth, immediately after the Worshipful Company of Stationers received its royal charter of incorporation (granted by Queen Mary in 1557 and ratified by Elizabeth in 1558). The same period to which Percy dated the disappearance of "the genuine old minstrelsy" also saw the institutionalization of commercial printing and a steep rise in the number of printed books. Percy's "Essay" ends abruptly with the royally authorized retailing of cheap printed goods: "little miscellanies, under the name of Garlands." With their royally granted privileges and their ephemeral products circulating "in such abundance," it was members of the Stationers' Company, not worthy "oral itinerant poets," who now had a "lucrative" situation. Percy concluded his narrative with the sixteenth-century decay of minstrelsy, but not without pausing to assert that the situation of contemporary ballad singers was even worse. Even the Elizabethan minstrels, who had "lost much of their dignity, and were sinking into contempt and neglect . . . still sustained a character far superior to anything we can conceive at present of the singers of old ballads."[39]

The *Reliques* established Percy's reputation as a scholar. It was also a huge commercial success. Yet Percy suffered tremendous anxiety about printing his work. In the preface, he was careful to portray himself as a disinterested gentleman rather than a Grub Street compiler. Of his exhaustive labors and 1,200-page anthology, he stated, "To prepare it for the press has been the amusement of now and then a vacant hour amid the leisure and retirement of a rural life."[40] For Percy, and for virtually all learned ballad collectors after him, redefining balladry as a fit object of study meant separating scholarly collections from mere vendible commodities. As I have suggested, Joseph Ritson virulently disagreed with Percy's theories of minstrelsy. Yet in publishing his own collections, such as *A Select Collection of English Songs* (3 vols., 1783) and the aforementioned *Ancient Songs* (1792), Ritson, too, conceived of his work as "impelled by no lucrative or unworthy motives." Both men drew heavily on printed (especially broadside) ballads. But even Ritson, who valued broadsides, emphasized that he had braved the swelling tide of print anthologies only to rescue ballad "pearls":

> So long as these beauties, this elegance, continue to be . . . buried alive, in a multitude of collections, consisting chiefly of compositions of the lowest, and most despicable nature; one or more being annually hashed up (*crambe repetita*) by needy retainers to the press . . . the greater part of this inestimable possession must, of course, remain altogether unknown to the generality of readers. . . . Every one who wishes to possess a pearl, is not content to seek it in an ocean of mud.[41]

Ritson was ambivalent about print commerce just as Percy was, yet he was unwilling to adopt the latter's idealizing theories of minstrelsy. In his own ambitious essays, such as "An Historical Essay on the Origin and Progress of National Song" prefaced to the *Select Collection* or the aforementioned "Observations on the Ancient English Minstrels," he suggested that there were much stronger links between "ancient minstrels" and modern ballad-mongers than Percy was willing to admit.[42] The primary function of *both* minstrels and ballad singers was entertainment, and their chief audience was the "illiterate vulgar."[43] Ritson quoted Percy's statement that the minstrels "continued down to the reign of Elizabeth; in whose time they had lost much of their dignity," only to scoff, "As to dignity; it is pretty clear they never had any to lose."[44] He agreed that broadside ballads displaced earlier minstrel traditions, but he saw this as a shift to celebrate rather than lament. For Ritson, the institutionalization of the press marked the welcome "origin of the modern English song; not a single composition of that nature, with the smallest degree of poetical merit, being discoverable at any preceding period."[45]

Ritson suggested that the majority of Percy's "reliques" were never separate from commercial print: "That these ballads were originally composed for public singers by profession, and perhaps immediately for printers, booksellers, or those who vended such like things, is highly probable." Tracing the history of "modern English song" not only to "the earliest ages of mankind" but also to seventeenth-century "writers by profession of amusing books for the populace," he named as "famous ballad-makers about this period" several authors whom many of his contemporaries would have considered Grub Street hacks (such as Martin Parker, Thomas Deloney, and Aphra Behn).[46] Even more provocatively, he expressed a preference for broadside ballads over "minstrel compositions." He suggested that even in the Elizabethan period, "minstrel songs," with "their wild and licentious metre," did not stand a chance against the products of the press. Broadside ballads, with their relative regularity and simplicity, were thought by the masses to be more poetical than earlier forms, and "though critics will judge otherwise, the people at large were to decide, and did decide: and in some respects at least not without justice." Significantly, these printed ballads were the "favourite compositions" of "the people at large" because they could be easily sung: "the songs used by the ballad-singers . . . were smooth and regular, were all printed, and, what was much more to their advantage, were generally united to a simple but pleasing melody, which . . . any one could sing."[47] Like etymologist Nathan Bailey, who defined "ballad" as "a Song *commonly sung* up and down the Streets,"[48] Ritson understood balladry as a *living* oral practice (though *not* necessarily as "oral tradition"). In a groundbreaking move in scholarly ballad collecting, he included the "airs" to the songs he reprinted whenever they were known.[49]

But although Ritson endorsed the verdict of "the people at large" in valuing ballads, it is important to understand that neither he nor Percy possessed a concept anything like our modern idea of "folk authorship" or valorized what we might now call "popular oral culture." Neither of these gentlemen viewed "the illiterate vulgar" as a positive generative force. Ritson understood "the people at large" as assisting in the *preservation* of ballads rather than as significant creators, and Percy aligned his ancient minstrels with aristocratic courts. Furthermore, neither man advanced claims for oral tradition as a complex body of verbal art passed down across generations solely by word of mouth. Percy never proposed that minstrels were the product of wholly oral societies, and Ritson bluntly expressed his skepticism concerning claims being made by others for "oral tradition." He rejected Macpherson's Ossian "translations" as fraudulent, and he remarked of the proposition of still-extant "ancient" ballads: "it is barely possible that something of the kind may be still preserved in the country by tradition. The Editor has frequently heard of traditional songs, but has had very little success in his endeavours to hear the songs themselves."[50]

At the same time, though, Percy's romantic account of ancient minstrels as "oral itinerant poets" enthralled later eighteenth- and nineteenth-century readers and in so doing contributed significantly to the now rapidly growing interest in "oral tradition." Edinburgh native John Pinkerton's "Dissertation on the Oral Tradition of Poetry," prefixed to his *Scottish Tragic Ballads* (1781), exemplifies the cross-fertilization in this period between the Ossian debates, new theories of Homeric orality, and ballad scholarship. Pinkerton's "Dissertation" is deeply indebted to Blair's *Critical Dissertation*, but it also does something new. In explicitly titling his essay "A Dissertation on the Oral Tradition of Poetry" and prefixing it to a collection of *ballads*, Pinkerton foregrounded "oral tradition" as a central concern of ballad scholarship. Employing what I have identified as an increasingly familiar "devolution" model of balladry, as well as the terminology of "success[ion]" and "extinct[ion]," he lamented that the "successors of Ossian the first of poets were at length employed chiefly in the mean office of preserving fabulous genealogies, and flattering the pride of their chieftains at the expence of truth. . . . That order of men, I believe, is now altogether extinct." Whereas Percy's "Essay" had only gestured toward an evolutionary (or devolutionary) model of media shift, Pinkerton explicitly modeled an inevitable development whereby one stage "necessarily" succeeds another. He proposed to give an "account of the utility of the Oral Tradition of Poetry, in that barbarous state of society which *necessarily* precedes the invention of letters." Pinkerton's evolutionary model of media shift could not be more starkly confrontational: "In proportion as Literature [i.e., letters, writing] advanced in the world Oral Tradition disappeared."[51]

Pinkerton's "Dissertation" also made a genuine contribution to our understanding of the unique characteristics of oral poetry. Pinkerton discussed oral poets' mnemonic devices, or "retentive arts": the ways that oral poets used versification (sound effects such as alliteration, refrains, and rhyme) to "make their verses take such hold of the memory of their countrymen, as to be transmitted safe and entire without the aid of writing." He also exhibited new insights into the workings of what Milman Parry would later label "oral formulaic epithets." He proposed that repeated epithets, formerly held to be lapses of the poet's genius, in fact served as "land-marks" for the reciting poet: "in the view of which the memory travelled secure over the intervening spaces."[52] Pinkerton does not appear to have surmised that traditional epithets actually helped oral poets to *compose* works extemporaneously rather than merely memorize them. (This would be Parry's groundbreaking insight in the late 1920s.)[53] But the concluding sentence of his "Dissertation" gives a sense of the "wonder" with which later eighteenth- and nineteenth-century ballad scholars approached what seemed to them an exciting new idea of "oral tradition":

> When all the circumstances here hinted at are considered, we shall be less apt to wonder, that, by the concurrence of musical air, retentive arts in the composition, and chiefly of rime, the most noble productions of

former periods have been preserved in the memory of a succession of admirers, and have had the good fortune to arrive at our times.[54]

"PRINTED AS THEY ORALLY EXIST"

Percy's romantic narrative of ancient minstrels as oral itinerant poets contributed not only to growing interest in the idea of oral tradition but also to some later ballad editors' conviction that certain *living* practices of ballad singing were surviving traces of feudal oral traditions. Walter Scott (1771– 1832) seized on Percy's figure of the minstrel, developing it in his *Minstrelsy of the Scottish Border: Consisting of Historical and Romantic Ballads Collected in the Southern Counties of Scotland; With A Few of Modern Date Founded Upon Local Tradition* (3 vols.; Kelso and Edinburgh, 1802–3). Scott argued that until recently, a figure like Percy's "ancient minstrels" could be seen in the pipers of Scottish border towns. In a later essay, "Introductory Remarks on Popular Poetry" (1830), Scott echoed Percy in suggesting that minstrel ballads were an innately oral art form displaced by print— especially cheap print aimed at certain "class[es] of readers" and hearers:

> It is probable that the minstrels, seldom knowing either how to read or write, trusted to their well-exercised memories. . . .
>
> The press, however, at length superseded the necessity of such exertions of recollection, and sheafs of ballads issued from it weekly, for the amusement of the sojourners at the alehouse, and the lovers of poetry in grange and hall, where such of the audience as could not read had at least read unto them.[55]

Scott opened another essay of 1830 with an even more blunt statement exemplifying emergent evolutionary (and devolutionary) narratives of media shift: "The invention of printing *necessarily* occasioned the downfall of the Order of Minstrels."[56]

Like Scott, Glasgow journalist and civil servant William Motherwell (1797–1835) saw himself as preserving a still-living tradition of Scottish minstrelsy in his collection *Minstrelsy, Ancient and Modern* (2 vols.; Glasgow, 1827; repr., Boston, 1846). In his lengthy introduction to this anthology, Motherwell described his subject as "the Ancient Romantick and Historick Ballad [*sic*] of Scotland." But whereas Scott collected his ballads from textual as well as oral sources, Motherwell increasingly set out to recover a distinctly *oral* tradition of balladry. He opened his collection with the bold claim: "This interesting body of popular poetry, part of which, in point of antiquity, may fairly be esteemed equal, if not superior, to the most ancient of our written monuments, has owed its preservation principally to oral tradition."[57] Today known as the first systematic "field collector" of ballads, Motherwell transcribed songs from oral performance and recitation. Although he initially collected ballads from texts, he became interested in oral performance and transformed himself "from a culler of old volumes to a cultivator of old singers."[58] Motherwell focused on the oral aspects of balladry to a greater degree than any previous collector had done, and his attention to performance allowed him to advance our understanding of how oral tradition actually works. Ballad scholars such as Percy and Ritson had long observed metrical differences between the "ancient" and more modern ballads in their collections. But Motherwell's practice of *listening* to ballads led him to surmise that the metrical irregularity of the older ballads was linked to their originally oral nature: "they have throughout the marks of a composition not meant for being committed to writing, but whose musick formed an essential part."[59] Motherwell's introduction is an important (and neglected) contribution to oral formulaic theory.[60] Anticipating Parry (and recalling Pinkerton) he too theorized the workings of traditional epithets. Repeated epithets, he proposed, were "ingenious devices . . . whereby oral poetry is more firmly imprinted on the memory, more readily recalled to it, when partially obliterated, and, in the absence of letters, the only efficacious means of preserving and transmitting it to after times."[61]

Motherwell's practice of collecting ballads from oral sources led him to resituate authenticity in the voices of the "unlettered." In sharp contrast with the view of Samuel Johnson, who had argued in the preface to his *Dictionary* that written records are the only way to stabilize language, Motherwell argued:

> Language, which in the written literature of a country is ever varying, suffers no material changes nor corruptions among the lower and uneducated classes of society by whom it is spoken as their mother tongue. With them, primitive forms of speech, peculiar idiomatick expressions, and antique phrases are still in use. . . . It is not, therefore, with the unlettered and the rude that oral song suffers vital and irremediable wrong.

Motherwell contended that scholars looking to preserve "traditionary" ballads needed to rethink their editorial practices. It was the oral tradition of the "uneducated," not the corrupt texts of the lettered, that was in certain circumstances "a safe and almost unerring guide."[62] In a letter to Walter Scott, Motherwell shared his growing belief in the importance of printing

all significant variants rather than attempting to collate them into a "correct" version: "it is of some importance to preserve these remnants of ancient traditionary song in the exact state in which they pass from mouth to
mouth among the vulgar."[63] In a statement that ironically underlines the
multimedia nature of this type of ballad collecting, Scott urged Motherwell
to "print it exactly as you have taken it down."[64] Nonetheless, despite Motherwell's innovations, there are also telling continuities between his history
of balladry and Percy's "Essay on the Ancient Minstrels in England." Like
Ritson and Scott, Motherwell adopted Percy's model of a sixteenth-century
confrontation between oral balladry and print commerce. He quoted Percy's
argument that the "old minstrels" were displaced by "a new race of ballad-
writers," and he later reiterated this thesis with a telling citation:

> In the reign of Elizabeth and James the Sixth, the Minstrel ballads of
> England began to be superseded in vulgar affection by a more ambitious
> class of similar compositions, written purposely for the press, by sundry
> indefatigable small poets of that prolifick day. The chief balladmongers
> of said period have been enumerated by Percy and Ritson.[65]

Like virtually all scholarly ballad collectors after Percy, Motherwell defined
his collection in opposition to the "trash" of the print marketplace.[66] Of
the major archival collections of broadside ballads scrutinized by Percy and
Ritson, he observed:

> The editor regrets that he knows none of the collections now enumer-
> ated by personal inspection; but he believes that they contain few, very
> few, of what are the real ancient minstrel ballads of the country, and
> this opinion he forms from the great quantity of sad trash to be found in
> works whose materials are professedly derived from these sources.

But Motherwell was writing more than sixty years after Percy: in the 1820s
rather than the 1760s. As a working journalist, he knew that print commerce was here to stay. The nineteenth-century literary marketplace was
now flooded with ballad collections whose editors *all* professed worthwhile
motives. Accordingly, Motherwell warned that modern editors, in their
well-intentioned zeal, could be a force for the *destruction* rather than preservation of ballads:

> The tear and wear of three centuries will do less mischief to the text of
> an old ballad among the vulgar, than one short hour will effect, if in the

possession of some sprightly and accomplished editor of the present day, who may choose to impose on himself the thankless and uncalled-for-labour of piecing and patching up its imperfections, polishing its asperi-ties . . . and of trimming it from top to toe with tailor-like fastidiousness and nicety, so as to be made fit for the press.

While it would be possible to see this type of extensive rewriting of bal-lads as artistic *production* rather than *destruction* (a new mode of adapt-ing songs to make them "suitable to every Occasion"), Motherwell rejected such a view. Instead, he suggested that the exigencies of the literary market-place, enacted by overzealous editors, almost literally "tear and wear" "oral song." The editor looking to please "the tastes of the many" undermined the true value of ballads by polishing their language. Cataloging previous collections, he concluded with a crushing review of Allan Cunningham's *Songs of Scotland* (1826). He expressed outrage that a fellow Scot should have allowed the "humours of . . . [the] marketplace" to determine his edi-torial practice:

> The apology for this will be, that the work was meant to be popular; that the tastes of the many had to be consulted more than the sober appro-bation of the few; and above all, that special heed had to be paid to the humours of that great marketplace in which the principal commodity was to be vended.
>
> It was not, however, a mere book-making speculation, or a good vendible article, which Scotland was prepared to welcome from the pen of one of her gifted and patriotick sons.

Motherwell accused Cunningham of "hacking, and hewing, and breaking the joints of ancient and traditionary song" by rewriting ballads to suit "popular" tastes. Significantly, he aligned the "popular" with the masses and with indis-criminate *reading* (rather than with illiteracy or oral tradition). He suggested that instead of valuing the unique characteristics of oral song, Cunningham had catered to the "gross body of mere *song-readers*" (my emphasis). But the duty of a serious ballad collector was to print all significant variants exactly as they were sung. Contrasting his own editorial practice with Cunning-ham's, Motherwell stated that the songs in *Minstrelsy, Ancient and Modern* had been "printed precisely in the form in which they were remembered by the several individuals who sung or recited them." In a phrase we shall return to in a moment, he asserted that these songs had been "printed as they orally exist."[67]

Motherwell's editorial practices greatly influenced Francis James Child, who zealously worked to minimize what he viewed as the distorting effects of print on the orally circulating songs that he now explicitly categorized (and valorized) as "traditional" ballads. Child described his own earliest collection, *The English and Scottish Ballads* (8 vols.; 1857–58), as containing "all but two or three of the ancient ballads of England and Scotland, and nearly all those ballads which, in either country, have been gathered from oral tradition—whether ancient or not." Child published his earliest collection as part of a commercial reprint series. While he included many broadside ballads that may never have circulated in "oral tradition," he suggested that he had done so only to please his publishers: "as many ballads of this second class have been admitted as it was thought might be wished for, perhaps I should say tolerated, by the 'benevolent reader.'"[68] For the next ten years he apologized to the Danish ballad scholar Svend Grundtvig for having had to make this collection "tolerably saleable" to a general readership. He vowed, "I shall make no concession to such a consideration in the [collection] which I hope to make."[69] In a letter to Grundtvig, he echoed Percy's disdain for broadside ballads, describing both the Roxburghe and the Pepys Collections as "veritable dung-hills, in which, only after a great deal of sickening grubbing, one finds a very moderate jewel."[70] Child knew that many of the broadside ballads he consulted were older than the oral variants he had collected. But as Mary Ellen Brown observes, "he implies that the broadsides were later, corrupting the popular, orally transmitted version."[71] Over the course of his career, Child would forge a sharp conceptual distinction between "traditional," or orally circulating, ballads (which he favored) and "vulgar" broadside ballads (which he largely disdained). In his widely cited essay "Ballad Poetry" (1874), Child echoed ballad scholars from Percy onward in suggesting that the Elizabethan institutionalization of commercial printing was a key factor in the displacement of earlier oral traditions. But in Child's version of this now-familiar narrative, an earlier "displacement" model of oral minstrelsy versus print balladry evolved into a powerful classificatory (and evaluative) distinction between traditional and broadside ballads:

> The vulgar ballads of our day, the "broadsides" which were printed in such huge numbers in England and elsewhere in the sixteenth century or later, belong to a different genus; they are products of a low kind of *art*, and most of them are, from a literary point of view, thoroughly despicable and worthless.

In Child's schema, broadside ballads are not simply a *medium* of balladry; rather, they differ in kind from oral ballads. Broadside ballads are "a different genus." Furthermore, according to Child's influential classifications, many of the same broadside ballads that Ritson described as the "favourite compositions" of the vulgar were no longer to be seen as "popular" ballads: "the popular ballad is not originally the product or the property of the lower orders." Whereas Motherwell aligned the "popular" and the literary marketplace with the "gross body of mere song-readers," Child famously redefined "traditional" or "popular" ballads in such a way as to assert their fundamental incompatibility with "book-culture" and the art of printing. True "popular" ballads, he proposed, were those that had circulated in oral tradition and, indeed, typically originated under sociocultural conditions no longer extant in literate society: "the condition of society in which a truly national or popular poetry appears . . . is a condition in which the people are not divided by political organization and book-culture into markedly distinct classes." But "increased civilization, and especially the introduction of book-culture," undermined this social and political unity. The "popular" ballad, once a common inheritance, was abandoned by literate elites and fell to "*the people in the lower sense*" (my emphasis). In early modern Europe, Child suggested, "the art of printing" was a powerful force for the disintegration of communal traditions: "the diffusion of knowledge and the stimulation of thought through the art of printing . . . broke up the national unity." Media developments triggered correlating social, political, and cultural effects. For the oral tradition of balladry, the introduction of "book-culture" had tragic consequences: "the educated classes took a direction of their own, and left what had been a common treasure, to the people in the lower sense, the ignorant or unschooled mass."[72]

But Motherwell's impassioned call for "collections of [traditionary] ballads, printed as they orally exist," foregrounds the practical difficulty and conceptual contradiction of positing an "oral tradition" of balladry that is separable from print, then attempting to preserve this "orality" through a different medium. Print is not merely a form of archiving; it transforms oral discourse into something else. (As Marshall McLuhan put it, the medium is the message.) Today, scholars routinely note the impossibility of eliminating the "distorting" effects of print on ballads, and many also note that print may have done as much to preserve oral tradition as to destroy it. But as I hope to have shown, our modern secularized concept of "oral tradition" is itself inseparable from the eighteenth-century spread of print commerce. Ballad scholars' heightened reflection on the spread of print, I have argued,

triggered the *new* idea that valuable ballad traditions were innately *oral*.
Historicizing the *concept* of oral tradition helps us to see that it was only
at a particular moment in the history of ballad collecting that print began
to be imagined both as threatening ballads *and* as potentially saving them
from being lost. Dugaw is certainly correct that *"all* facets of [the ballad]
tradition—commercial and non-commercial, written, printed, and oral—
need to be thoroughly investigated and represented."[73] But we also need to
understand how ballad scholars contributed to the construction of these
conceptual separations in the first place. Ballads are not separable from
print but neither, paradoxically, is the very conceptual framework through
which we now understand the "orality" of ballads.

For early ballad scholars, defining balladry as a fit object of genteel or
professional study meant separating "worthwhile" oral practices from "vulgar" or subversive ones. These gentlemen's constructions of oral tradition
bore an antithetical relationship not only to print commerce but also to
what we might call "popular oral culture." Genteel collectors excluded entire categories of popular ballads from their collections. Well into the nineteenth century, for instance, the singing of socially or politically subversive
ballads such as those mentioned by Mr. Sing-Song was a still-vibrant oral
practice. But topical political ballads are almost never included in genteel
collections, for these so-called ephemeral productions, with their irreverent
and sometimes-seditious viewpoints, were not part of the legacy these gentlemen saw fit to preserve. Today, persons interested in the history of balladry need to be alert to the ways that eighteenth- and nineteenth-century
constructions of oral tradition have shaped our own assumptions about the
actual *diverse* oral practices of balladry. We especially need to be wary of
models that associate valuable "popular" practices of balladry solely with
stasis or the past and adaptive, urban, and/or printed ballad traditions with
"contamination" and decay. In eighteenth-century Britain, scholarly models of oral tradition were themselves a product of heightened reflection on
(and nervousness about) the spread of print commerce. As Mary Ellen Brown
urges, we need a "catholic perspective on the ballad . . . whether performed
at a given moment . . . or circulated in cheap print . . . popularity need not
be limited to the oral."[74]

CHAPTER EIGHT

Conjecturing Oral Societies:
Global to Gaelic

In 1711 Anthony Ashley Cooper, 3rd Earl of Shaftesbury, lamented that English gentlemen were engaged in "a wrong kind of serious reading." The "most ridiculous" kind of reading matter now in vogue, he suggested, was books of travels, geography, and what we might call ethnography: "barbarian customs, savage manners, Indian wars, and wonders of the *terra incognita*, employ our leisure Hours, and are the chief materials to furnish out a library."[1] Shaftesbury was right that these materials were wildly popular. "Travels" constituted a major category of the English book trade since the introduction of printing, and travel writing influenced virtually every kind of print and area of knowledge. By 1700 this sector of the print market had grown so vast that it needed its own bibliography. In 1704 booksellers Awnsham and John Churchill published a four-volume series, *A Collection of Voyages and Travels*, including a lengthy "Catalogue of . . . Books of Travels" in Latin, English, Italian, Spanish, and French. Throughout the eighteenth century, literary authors incorporated exotic settings and themes of travel into their works, and many also published accounts of their own travels. Jonathan Swift satirized travel books (and their readers) in *Travels into Several Remote Nations of the World, by Lemuel Gulliver* (1726). He also critiqued the legacy of travelers such as Gulliver's "cousin Dampier," the seaman and pirate William Dampier, whose *A New Voyage Around the World* (1697) contributed to his reputation as the greatest English explorer-adventurer between Sir Francis Drake and Captain James Cook. The print trade also saw a proliferation of geographies: a category that overlapped with travel writing and included accounts of the world's peoples, countries, climates, and natural resources. By the end of the century, William St. Clair observes, "books poured from the presses, on France, Italy, Germany, Spain, Russia, India, Egypt, Ottoman Turkey, Africa, China. . . . [T]here was no territory too remote or too barren, no period of the past too obscure, but it was of interest to the travellers, the historians, the archaeologists, the poets, and the readers of Great Britain."[2]

In this chapter I argue that the eighteenth-century proliferation of printed accounts of the world's peoples by explorers, missionaries, diplomats, and others profoundly—and permanently—changed ideas about oral tradition. I also argue that this explosion of print contributed to a distinctly new concept of oral societies. Writers (and readers) of travels show a growing interest in the question of oral tradition: they address its function and reliability in "primitive" and complex societies across the globe. In 1688 Paul Rycaut's *Royal Commentaries of Peru* taught readers that the Incas passed down complex histories, genealogies, customs, and laws over generations entirely by oral tradition. In 1690 William Temple's *Essay Upon the Ancient and Modern Learning* argued for the reliability of ancient, elite oral traditions in societies from China to Peru. In 1724 missionary Joseph-François Lafitau's *Customs of the American Indians* depicted eloquent native American orators who employed oral arts to preserve order and history among their peoples. I begin by discussing representative texts addressing oral tradition in a non-European context. I then show how these discussions of oral tradition and communication in ancient and modern societies across the globe influenced important intersecting debates in the world of letters. As I suggested in chapter 7, the eighteenth century saw the first printed arguments for Homer as an oral poet, and in the later eighteenth century, developments in Homer scholarship—combined with proliferating accounts of oral traditions across the world—triggered new interest in (and excitement about) the possibility of surviving oral traditions "at home." In 1763 Hugh Blair announced the discovery of a new "Homer of the Highlands": a polite primitive poet for modern times.[3] Blair's protégé, James Macpherson, published a series of books implying that he had "translated" the surviving works of a third-century Gaelic bard, passed down for centuries by tradition from "an age, when no written records were known."[4] The authenticity of Macpherson's "Ossian" poems was vehemently contested by Samuel Johnson and others, but Macpherson's texts and Blair's printed endorsements inspired generations of *readers* to imagine how oral tradition worked. In so doing, I suggest, these texts contributed to the popularization and, eventually, naturalization of the previously controversial idea of oral tradition.

Eighteenth-century British authors increasingly categorized different peoples according to their arts of transmission: a concept similar (but not identical) to our "modes of communication." Primitivists, philosophers, and others devoted considerable attention to tracing the development of human communication from the first savage cries and gestures, to oral tradition, to the invention and development of writing, and (sometimes) to the introduction and spread of print. In the mid- and later eighteenth century, a subset of moral philosophers retrospectively named "conjectural historians" developed a new temporal framework for relating all human societies. Confronted with new accounts of the diversity of the world's peoples, they attempted to make sense of this diversity by linking together all human societies into one evolutionary or developmental chain. Stadial or "four-stages" theorists such as Adam Smith argued that societies progressed naturally through a succession of stages, each with its own characteristic institutions, economy, and social arrangements (typically hunter-gatherer, pastoral, agricultural, and commercial societies). This sequence was typically (but not always) viewed as "progress." In his essays on Ossian, Blair associated different arts of transmission with different "ages," and he assigned Ossian to the earliest, "primitive" stage.

The methodology of conjectural history was partly a consequence of what we would now call orality. In some ways anticipating the situation of scholars of orality today, conjectural historians were forced to cope with a lack of written records for periods "before writing was invented." Edinburgh moral philosopher Dugald Stewart, who coined the term "conjectural history" in a lecture on Smith, addressed the challenge of writing histories of societies that lacked written records. While this methodological challenge was not new, eighteenth-century historians were—as I demonstrated in chapter 1—increasingly expected to support their claims with documentary evidence rather than "mere tradition," and accordingly, this challenge was deeply felt. Even the finest historians, Stewart lamented, were "under necessity of supplying the place of fact by conjecture," for "long before that stage of society when men began to think of recording their transactions, many of the most important steps of their progress have been made."[5] In the same lecture, Stewart addressed what he saw as the monumental implications for mankind of the "the art of writing" and "the art of printing." Conjectural historians conventionally linked stages of development to modes of sustenance (such as agriculture), but by the end of the century, I show, we begin to detect the idea of communications technologies as *themselves* triggering "stages" in the evolution of human societies. Stewart himself declared that the invention of printing "change[d] the whole course of human affairs."[6]

But the eighteenth century also saw critiques of the methodologies and abstract models of conjectural history, and these critiques sometimes come from unexpected places. In the second half of this chapter, I offer a new

reading of Samuel Johnson's *Journey to the Western Islands of Scotland*
(1775). Johnson's travel narrative begins as a conjectural history; he journeys
to the Hebrides expecting (indeed hoping) "to hear old traditions, and see
antiquated manners" (128) of a primitive or "rude" society. But he soon discovers that the type of society that stadial theory had prepared him to see no
longer exists. Johnson at once acknowledges and foregrounds his earlier "ignorance" about the true conditions in the Highlands. He especially mocks
his previous desire to witness for himself (rather than merely read about)
what Shaftesbury called "barbarian customs, savage manners, . . . and wonders of the *terra incognita*." "A longer journey than to the Highlands," he
observes, "must be taken by him whose curiosity pants for savage virtues
and barbarous grandeur."[7]

I read Johnson's *Journey* as an ethnographic account, a philosophical
meditation, and a complex political argument. Whereas the temporal frame-
works devised by conjectural historians enabled Enlightenment philosophers to account for the discrepancy between the Highlands and the Lowlands by assigning the Highlanders to an earlier, "primitive" stage of social
development, Johnson learned, as a result of his travels, to account for this
discrepancy in other ways. Having witnessed for himself the consequences
of the Act of Union (especially after the defeat of the Jacobites at Culloden
in 1745–46), Johnson used his text to redirect the attention of Ossian enthusiasts away from Scotland's ancient, mythic past to the urgent plight of
the Highlanders in the present. One of Johnson's central arguments in the
Journey is that despite the craze for Ossianic poetry, the true state of the
Highlands remained virtually unknown—not only to the English but also to
the Lowland Scots. Throughout the eighteenth century, printed travel narratives had an almost incalculable influence on Britons' ways of viewing parts
of the world beyond the seas. Johnson's travel narrative introduced readers to
terra incognita within Britain itself.

At the same time, Johnson's *Journey* exposes the political implications
of the new elite idealization of oral tradition at a time when as many as
half of the nation's people could not read or write. (In the Hebrides, Johnson
observes, "the greater part of the Islanders make no use of books" [65].) As
I suggested in the introduction, Johnson was deeply skeptical of contemporary appeals to "oral tradition," and as we shall see in this chapter, he
publicly disputed the authenticity of Macpherson's Ossianic works. But far
from dismissing oral tradition outright, I suggest, Johnson was energized
by the Ossian debate, and throughout his nearly four-month journey, he
made a concerted effort to learn for himself how the ancient oral tradition
of the Highlands actually worked. Departing from earlier interpretations, I

argue that Johnson's deep distrust of his literate contemporaries' valoriza-
tion of oral tradition was tied to his sense of the importance of literacy for
all people in the new "reading nation" of Great Britain—and, especially, to
his deeply personal conviction that in the new world of print commerce,
illiteracy and poverty would increasingly go together.

PRINTED TRAVEL NARRATIVES AND
THE IDEA OF ORAL TRADITION

In 1688 English diplomat and traveler Paul Rycaut published *Royal Commentaries of Peru*, a translation of *Commentarios Reales de los Incas* (1609)
by mestizo historian Garcilaso de la Vega. *Royal Commentaries* was commissioned by Jacob Tonson, a leading literary bookseller, and it was dedicated to James II. As we saw in chapter 1, the reign of this Catholic king
(1685–88) was a time when the question of oral tradition was of special national importance. Rycaut's dedication of his work to the king underlines
the immediate political context of his discussion of oral tradition. A lavishly
produced book adorned with plates, *Royal Commentaries* taught English
readers that the Incas passed down histories, genealogies, laws, and customs
entirely by oral tradition. Rycaut depicted Peruvian bards who excelled at
poetry and performance, and he offered detailed accounts of these singers'
training and oral feats. But even as he expressed admiration for the Incas'
means of preserving their history, Rycaut insisted on the greater reliability
of written records: "thus they remembered their history. But as experience
has shown, all these were perishable expedients, for it is letters that perpetu-
ate events."[8]

Two years after Rycaut published *Royal Commentaries*, Sir William
Temple asserted in *An Essay Upon the Ancient and Modern Learning* (1690)
that ancient peoples from Peru to China passed down genealogies, laws, and
customs "with care and exactness" via tradition. Temple's *Essay* addresses
the question "whether the Ancients or Moderns can be probably thought to
have made the greatest Progress in the Search and Discoveries of the vast
Region of Truth and Nature."[9] But in arguing for the superior achievements
of the ancients, he commented in detail about the functioning of tradition
"before the . . . use of Letters." As a proponent of the superiority of the
ancients, he could hardly avoid entertaining the possibility of reliable oral
traditions. But Temple was an Anglican statesman who published his work
in the immediate aftermath of the oral tradition debates of the 1680s and
the Revolution of 1688, and in this context, I suggest, he appears remarkably open-minded about the question of oral tradition. Informed by newly

printed ethnographic writings as well as by theological debates, he argued
for the reliability of learned oral traditions in ancient societies across the
globe. In an early example of comparative media studies, he discussed tradition not only in ancient Greece and Rome but also in Ireland, the Americas
(Mexico and Peru), and "Eastern Regions" such as Egypt, Ethiopia, Persia,
Syria, India, and China. Controversially, he proposed that the Greeks owed
"all the[ir] Learning" to their "Commerce" with Egypt, Phoenicia, and the
Far East. (In his own time, as readers of Swift's satires will recall, Temple
was considered ridiculous for his great admiration for the learning of "*Eastern* Regions.")[10]

For Temple, the reliability of tradition was not so much a matter of geography or even of religion as it was of social rank. Temple was concerned
with elite knowledge transmission by bards and priests who passed down
laws, histories, and genealogies in their otherwise-"rude" societies. The kind
of tradition that he was concerned with had nothing to do with those whom
he called "the generality of People." Anticipating the skepticism of his genteel readers, he wrote:

> It may look like a Paradox to deduce Learning from Regions accounted
> commonly so barbarous and rude. And 'tis true the generality of People
> were always so in those *Eastern* Countries, and their lives wholly turned
> to Agriculture, to Mechanicks, or to Trades; but this does not hinder
> particular Races or Successions of Men, the design of whose thought and
> time was turned wholly to Learning and Knowledge, from having been
> what they are represented . . . since among the *Gauls*, the *Goths*, and
> the *Peruvians* themselves, there have been such Races of Men under the
> Names of *Druids*, *Bards* . . . and other barbarous Appellations.

"Whether this was managed by Letters, or Tradition, or by both, 'tis certain
that the Ancient Colleges, or Societies of Priests, were mighty Reservoirs
or Lakes of Knowledge. . . . [N]othing was lost out of these Stores." As
Temple's reference to "Letters" *and* "Tradition" suggests, he was not necessarily looking to valorize a kind of oral tradition that was untainted by
writing or print. Unlike later folklorists and ballad collectors, he focused
on the question of the *reliability* of tradition rather than its purity, and he
emphasized that *both* oral and written tradition were subject to enormous
loss. Contrasting the continuity of oral tradition in ancient Peru with the
destruction of texts in Ireland after the dismantling of the early Christian
monasteries, he remarked "how much better the Records of time may be
kept by Tradition in one Country than Writing in another."[11]

Temple's interest in contextualizing the arts of transmission in their broad social and political contexts led him to understand oral tradition not merely as a means of communication or storage but rather as part of a "total way of life." An important part of his argument is that certain political structures effectively enable the preservation and transmission of valuable knowledge. Temple's theorizing of the sociopolitical function of oral tradition in ancient societies, I suggest, in some ways anticipates the later development of the ethnographic concept of cultural wholeness.[12] As a royalist and a man of letters, Temple valued powerful monarchies and empires for what he took to be these societies' support for the arts. He suggested that bards were professionally employed by rulers and by "Design of the Governments" to conserve and pass down "Knowledge and Story":

> there seems to have been a general Custom of the Priests in each Country having been either by their own Choice, or by Design of the Governments, the perpetual Conservers of Knowledge and Story. . . . [I]n *China* this . . . was committed particularly to certain Officers of State. . . . In *Ethiopia, Egypt, Caldea, Persia, Syria, Judea*, these Cares were committed wholly to the Priests.

As for the "Invention of Printing," Temple held that this much-celebrated modern technology had no *necessary* consequences for the advancement of human knowledge. He proposed that "Printing has not, perhaps, multiplied Books, but only . . . Copies." Whereas Defoe celebrated printing for multiplying opportunities for readership across the social spectrum, Temple held that more books did not necessarily mean better libraries (for gentlemen, at least). For Temple, it was not the number of books that mattered, but how many of them were worth reading and passing down. A good book was like an oral proverb, a distillation of knowledge and values tested by time: for "Books, like Proverbs, receive their Chief Value from the Stamp and Esteem of Ages through which they have passed."[13]

About a decade after Temple published his *Essay*, Louis Armand, Baron de Lahontan published *New Voyages to North-America* (2 vols., 1703).[14] A military officer and explorer, Lahontan depicted orderly Iroquois societies where knowledge and poetry were passed down through oral tradition. His portrait of Adario, an eloquent Huron Indian who associates Europeans and writing with corruption, greatly influenced Enlightenment authors such as Jean-Jacques Rousseau. But as Nicholas Hudson has observed, Lahontan's primary purpose in portraying a community of noble savages was "satiric rather than ethnographic."[15] Lahontan presented Adario's society, with its reliance on oral tradition, as a foil to European corruption rather than as a viable alternative to a literate society.

A text of yet another different kind, and one cited throughout the Enlightenment as a source on native Americans and oral tradition, is Joseph-François Lafitau's *Customs of the American Indians Compared with the Customs of Primitive Times* (*Mœurs des sauvages amériquains, comparée aux mœurs des premier temps* [Paris, 1724]). A Jesuit missionary who spent six years among the Iroquois near Montreal, Lafitau has been described as "a pioneer anthropologist of high caliber."[16] Today, his modern editors credit him with having founded comparative ethnology. They suggest that in "comparing the manners of savages with those of the peoples of antiquity, and vice-versa," he was "interested in building a science of culture."[17] Lafitau advanced the enlightened idea that peoples without writing might nonetheless have a highly developed system of laws, customs, and arts preserved through oral tradition. His grounding in Catholic theological notions of tradition helped to move him beyond the widespread assumption of European intellectuals that cultures without writing were lawless and barbaric. Lafitau depicted Iroquois leaders as eloquent orators and as wise governors of their people. Comparing these speakers to ancient Greek and Roman orators such as Cicero and Demosthenes, he suggested that in "public councils and solemn transactions," Iroquois orators were "brilliant" leaders:

> They alone speak . . . , their duty properly consisting in announcing all the business which has been discussed in the secret councils, in declaring the results of all deliberations and in bearing the news authoritatively in the name of the entire village and nation.
>
> This role is not easy to sustain. It demands a great capacity, the knowledge of councils, a complete knowledge of all their ancestors' ways, wit, experience, and eloquence.

Like the eighteenth-century elocutionists I discussed in chapters 4 and 5, Lafitau emphasized the use of gesture in oratory. He observed that Iroquois orators "speak with gestures as much as with the voice and act out things so naturally as to make them seem to take place under their audience's eyes."[18]

Lafitau did not advance a general argument for the reliability of oral tradition (as Temple did), but he represented the Iroquois as having a functioning oral tradition that effectively preserved their history, customs, and laws: "these people, without written laws, do not fail to have basically a strict system of justice." Like virtually all European authors who commented on what we might call "oral societies," he associated the absence of letters with the degeneration of tradition into "myths": "having no letters they have also no chronological tables and annals on which reliance can be placed. They have . . . a kind of sacred tradition which they are careful to conserve. . . . [T]his tradition, passing from mouth to mouth, changes as it is passed on, and degenerates into myths."[19] Lafitau's work was widely cited by theorists of oral tradition throughout the century. In *Reliques of Ancient English Poetry*, Thomas Percy drew on Lafitau's account to support his own conjectures concerning oral tradition. In "barbarous nations," Percy suggested, poetry and song "are the first rudiments of history. It is in this manner that the savages of North America preserve the memory of past events." Drawing on conjectural history and stadial theory, as well as on ethnographic accounts such as Lafitau's, Percy compared the use of oral tradition among the "ancient Britons . . . and the Gothic nations" to its use among native American tribes. In so doing, he situated these temporally and geographically distant societies at a comparable "stage" of development: one before "letters began to prevail."[20] Another ballad scholar, Joseph Ritson, disagreed with Percy in many ways, but he too cited Lafitau to support a stadial model of the development of modes of communication. Ritson characterized different "ages of mankind" according to their arts of transmission, and like Percy, he assigned *contemporary* native Americans to the "earliest age."[21] Ritson agreed with Percy that songs were an important means of passing down knowledge across generations before "the invention of letters." To support this argument, he pointed to the role of songs and oratory "among the savage tribes of America, at present; or at least before they were civilised—perhaps corrupted—by their commerce with Europeans."[22]

But not all readers of Lafitau's *Customs of the American Indians* were so receptive to his portrait of a civilized oral society. Two years after *Customs* was published, Jonathan Swift satirized the idea of oral tradition in *Gulliver's Travels* (1726). In book 4, he depicts a race of noble horses, the Houyhnhnms, who "have no Letters, and consequently, their Knowledge is all traditional." These rational horses pass down their laws, arts, and customs by tradition, for they "have not the least Idea of Books."[23] In contrast to the Houyhnhnms, who are peace loving and dignified, Swift's warmongering Lilliputians in book 1 are prolific producers of documents (inventories, proclamations, petitions, and so on). Some critics have interpreted this to mean that Swift condemned writing and printing as degraded supplements to speech.[24] But Swift was a prolific author himself, and like Lahontan's depiction of Adario, his primary purpose in portraying a civilized society without "Letters" or "Books" was to satirize European assumptions (and arrogance). In depicting an orderly society of rational horses whose laws, history, and arts are preserved entirely through tradition, Swift was satirizing European *pride* in writing rather than critiquing writing itself.[25] Swift critiqued the corruption of technologies such as writing and printing, but he never seriously suggested that mankind would be better off without them. Nor did he follow in the footsteps of his patron, William Temple, and seriously explore the possibility of complex, civilized oral societies. Nonetheless, it is remarkable that more than two decades after Swift satirized the *theological* concept of "oral tradition" in *A Tale of a Tub* (1704) (see chapter 2), he was sufficiently intrigued by new printed accounts of oral societies such as Lafitau's *Customs of the American Indians* that he once again addressed the idea of oral tradition (this time in a pointedly *secular* context).

The same year that Swift published *Gulliver's Travels*, Daniel Defoe published *An Essay upon Literature: or, An Enquiry into the Antiquity and Original of Letters*. In this little-known 127-page text, he surveyed the arts of transmission from Moses to modern times (oral tradition, writing systems, printing, and so on). Defoe attempted to merge scripture-based explanations of the origins of writing with a new stadial model of human development that made room for "progress" and for modern inventions such as printing. (In this regard, I shall suggest in the conclusion to this chapter, his *Essay* anticipates the stadial models of media shift devised by later eighteenth-century conjectural historians and philosophers.) Significantly, he devoted the bulk of his discussion of printing to a consideration of its consequences for oral tradition. Like so many eighteenth-century authors, he associated oral tradition with dangerous myths. In Defoe's view, the "Multitude and Cheapness of Books" enabled by print commerce—as distinct from the technology of printing—made it possible for human users of print to challenge oppressive "Fiction[s]" transmitted by tradition. Accordingly, in his history of mediation, printing is not only a superior mode of transmission but also a potentially liberating force.[26]

A little over a decade after Defoe published *An Essay upon Literature*, clergyman William Warburton published *The Divine Legation of Moses Demonstrated* (1738–41).[27] In this 1,300-page tome, Warburton rejected the notion that writing was a onetime gift from God to Moses at Mount Sinai. Instead, he placed all the world's writing systems along one developmental chain. (He argued, for instance, that New World pictograms were an early stage of writing, and that alphabetic writing was relatively late.) Warburton's theories of the historical development of worldwide writing systems influenced Enlightenment authors such as Condillac. As we shall see, in offering an evolutionary paradigm for understanding the development of different arts of transmission, Warburton's text indirectly contributed to the later development of an evolutionary model of "oral" and "written" societies.[28]

In considering the eighteenth-century "invention" of the idea of oral societies, another intersecting area of debate must be (all too briefly) taken into account. As I suggested in chapter 7, the eighteenth century saw a major shift in approaches to Homeric poetry, from a neoclassical approach emphasizing what was universal and timeless in "Homer's" works, to a new historical sense that Homeric poetry was the product of a particular environment and period of development, and that its characteristics could be explained only if the poet's "primitive" society was understood on its own terms.[29] Theories of Homeric orality date to the first century, when Jewish author Flavius Josephus, arguing for the superiority of Hebrew culture, suggested that Homer could not read or write. In the seventeenth century, the Homer question was revived as part of the Quarrel of the Ancients and Moderns. Francois Hédelin, abbé d'Aubignac, argued in his *Conjectures académiques ou Dissertation sur l'Iliade* (pub. 1715) that there was no single author "Homer." Instead, there was a series of rhapsodes, or professional poets, whose compositions were later collected and linked together into epic poems.[30] In 1713 English classicist Richard Bentley argued that there was a man named Homer but that he should be understood as a relatively lowly entertainer rather than a learned author.[31] In 1735 Scottish classicist Thomas Blackwell similarly asserted in *An Enquiry Into the Life and Writings of Homer* that Homer was an "indigent" rhapsode whose poverty "forced him to take up, and continue in the Profession of . . . [a] *Stroling Bard.*"[32] Homer was not a divinely inspired God; rather, he was a primitive bard whose "Poems are of *Human Composition*; inspired by no other Power than his own natural Faculties, and the Chances of his Education." Somewhat contradicting his emphasis on Homer's "indigence," Blackwell insisted on the high social status of ancient bards. He suggested that British scholars had failed to recognize the "Dignity" of ancient Greek bards because "we have no modern Character like it: For I should be unwilling to admit the Irish or Highland Runers to a share of the Honour." In contrast to "modern" Celtic and Gothic bards—let alone authors in the new era of print commerce—ancient Greek bards "were welcome to Kings and Courts . . . and were highly reverenced by the People." Blackwell may have been beginning to surmise the oral nature of Homeric poetry, for he proposed that Homer's "Poems were made to be recited, or sung to a Company; and not read in private, or perused in a Book, which few were then capable of doing." He also proposed that the many repeated phrases in the *Iliad* and the *Odyssey*, or what we now call oral formulae, were a product of oral performance, and that this repetition "cannot be understood in any other light."[33] But Blackwell never explicitly suggested that Homer was illiterate, and he did not share our modern understanding of oral poetry. As Kirsti Simonsuuri suggests, "oral tradition with its laws and conventions was an unknown concept to him, as it was to his contemporaries, and he did not rate a 'folk poet' very highly."[34]

Blackwell's insights were influential. (As I will suggest later in this chapter, they especially influenced Robert Wood, a pivotal figure in the discovery of Homer as an oral poet.) But most commentators in print continued to assume that the "father of Western poetry" was literate like themselves. In *Joseph Andrews* (1742), Henry Fielding jovially offered his own theory of Homeric composition and publication. Describing his novel as a "comic-epic poem in prose," he depicted Homer as a prototype of the modern market-oriented *print* author and, indeed, as the "Inventor" of publication by "Subscription." In a chapter entitled "Of Divisions in Authors" (i.e., the new practice of using chapter divisions in novels), he observed that "according to the Opinion of some very sagacious Critics," Homer maximized his profits by "divid[ing] his great Work into twenty-four Books," then "hawk[ing] them all separately, delivering only one Book at a Time."[35]

A NEW "HOMER OF THE HIGHLANDS": POLITE READERS AND THE POSSIBILITY OF ORAL POETRY

By the mid-eighteenth century, classicists were debating whether Homer was a literate poet. At the same time, stadial theorists were eager to find evidence for their postulates about primitive societies. These factors, combined with the political and social climate in Scotland after the defeat of the Jacobites in 1745–46, made the timing ripe for Macpherson's claim to have discovered and translated the epic poetry of a third-century Highland bard. Macpherson's and Blair's claims were viewed with suspicion by many (including some eminent Scots). But readers in Britain and beyond went wild for Macpherson's poetic prose and "Ossian's" stirring stories of heroic Highland warriors, tragic love, and a noble (yet dying) Celtic race. Between 1760 and 1765, Macpherson and Blair operated as an unlikely tag team, with Macpherson's poems providing subject matter for Blair's lectures at the University of Edinburgh, and Blair's lectures and essays generating enthusiasm (and respect) for Macpherson's works. As much as any other single factor, the commercial success of Macpherson's and Blair's *printed* works can be said to have popularized the debate about oral tradition. In so doing, these printed texts contributed to the eighteenth-century "invention" of the category of the oral.

Macpherson (1736–96) was born into a farming family in the Highlands. In the 1750s he attended classes at King's College and Marischal College in Aberdeen, where he may have encountered Blackwell's theories of Homer as a primitive bard. Returning to the Highlands, he began collecting Gaelic poetry, and in 1760 he published *Fragments of Ancient Poetry, Collected in the Highlands of Scotland, and Translated from the Gaelic or Erse Language*. The preface to this work, mostly likely written by Blair, opens with the assertion that "the public may depend on the following fragments as genuine remains of ancient Scottish poetry." It declares that the poems exhibit the "ideas" and "manners" of "the most early state of society" and that in Scotland "such poems were handed down from race to race . . . by oral tradition." The preface alludes to the possible existence of "a greater work" and calls for "encouragement" of its publication: "there is reason to hope that one work of considerable length, and which deserves to be styled an heroic poem, might be recovered and translated, if encouragement were given."[36] In 1762 Blair was appointed Regius Chair of Rhetoric and Belles Lettres at the University of Edinburgh, and Macpherson published the promised "work of considerable length," *Fingal: An Ancient Epic Poem in Six Books*. In 1763 he published *Temora: An Ancient Epic Poem in Eight Books*, and Blair published *A Critical Dissertation on the Poems of Ossian*. In this major essay, first delivered orally as lectures, then "enlarged and given to the publick," Blair compared Ossian to Homer, but strikingly, he judged the Celtic bard superior to the Greek in "dignity of sentiment" and in "humanity, magnanimity, virtuous feelings of every kind."[37]

Blair read Macpherson's Ossian poems as if they provided direct access to third-century Scotland. He used these *contemporary* literary texts as a historical source. Blair's *Critical Dissertation* is an example of stadial theory. Echoing a lecture delivered by Smith the previous year, Blair taught his own students (and later readers) that "there are four great stages through which men successively pass in the progress of society. The first and earliest is the life of hunters; pasturage succeeds to this; . . . next agriculture; and lastly commerce. Throughout Ossian's poems, we plainly find ourselves in the first of these periods of society."[38] In 1765 Macpherson published *The Works of Ossian* (2 vols.), including a revised and expanded version of Blair's *Critical Dissertation* and an additional "Appendix" by Blair. Together, these essays played a major role in "legitimating" the notion of "primitive" oral tradition, and since 1765 they have been reprinted in virtually every edition of "Ossian's" works.

In his "Appendix" to the *Works of Ossian*, Blair acknowledged that "the manner in which the originals of these poems have been preserved and transmitted" might seem "mysterious and inexplicable" to modern readers. But in Scotland, he claimed, "the whole country is full of traditionary stories derived from [Ossian's] poems, concerning Fingal and his race of heroes, of whom there is not a child but has heard."[39] Blair's arguments set off a voluminous oral, manuscript, and print debate, and I will not attempt to rehearse it here.[40] Suffice it to say that four decades after the publication of the *Works of Ossian*, the Highland Society of Scotland formed an official committee to investigate this question. In 1805 the *Report of the Committee* concluded that although the legends that Macpherson drew on were real, his version of the Ossian poems was essentially his own creative work.[41] The committee also sadly concluded that the question of what exactly Macpherson "found" in the Highlands would now never be answered, for forty years after his apparent discoveries, the oral tradition that he had evidently drawn on had disappeared.[42]

As I suggested in chapter 7, Blair called on literate gentlemen to collect and compare surviving "oral editions" of Ossianic poetry. In his "Appendix," he cited creditable gentlemen who could testify to the survival of oral tradition in the Highlands.[43] Blair's appeal to creditable witnesses suggests the influence of empiricist philosophy and scientific methods on assessments of tradition, and his call for further investigation triggered research into Celtic and Gothic oral traditions that is still being carried out today. Macpherson's imaginative creations and Blair's conjectural histories inspired generations of readers to imagine how oral tradition functioned in "rude societies." In so doing, these printed texts helped to forge a new literate concept of oral societies.[44]

At the same time, though, it is a mistake to overidentify the eighteenth-century Ossian phenomenon with all things "oral." Macpherson was a university-educated author who made a fortune by printing his works, and Blair was a university professor who was one of the most widely read print authors of the late eighteenth and nineteenth centuries. By 1815 the *Works of Ossian* "was translated into a dozen languages."[45] In 1764 Macpherson began working for the British government. He published pamphlets, journalism, and historical works, and he obtained an annual government pension of five hundred pounds for writing works such as *Original Papers; Containing the Secret History of Great Britain, from the Restoration, to the Accession of the House of Hannover* [sic] (2 vols., 1775). As a result of his astute navigation of print commerce *and* traditional literary patronage, Macpherson became a wealthy man. He acquired an estate and built an imposing mansion in Scotland; he was elected a member of Parliament for a constituency in Cornwall; and he was buried in London at Westminster Abbey. Today, even one of Macpherson's most appreciative critics acknowledges that he was extraordinarily ambitious and that "the extravagance of his later life reveals a great zest not only for material possessions but also for impressing people on a grand scale."[46] Meanwhile, Blair received fifteen hundred pounds for the copyright of his *Lectures on Rhetoric and Belles Lettres* (1783; rev. ed., 1785)—the highest amount ever paid for a work of rhetoric.[47] In the nineteenth century, Blair's *Lectures* and *Sermons* (pub. 1778–1800) were widely used in schools, churches, and literary circles, and with the establishment of public education in the nineteenth century, these books were excerpted in anthologies and textbooks, effectively "reaching . . . the whole reading nation."[48]

Given this extraordinary commercial success and public acclaim, then, it seems doubly significant that like Percy (whose *Reliques of Ancient English Poetry* was also a best seller) Blair idealized feudal bards as "highly respected" and generously supported by those in power. As we have seen in chapter 7, Percy argued in his "Essay on the Ancient Minstrels in England" that oral tradition was displaced by the spread of "letters," and he linked the decline of bards to the spread of print commerce. These formerly esteemed historians were now forced to cater to "gross and ignorant minds."[49] Like William Temple earlier in the century, Percy and Blair surmised that the continuity of tradition was dependent on larger social and political structures and on due "encouragement" for bards. Blair proposed that "until the present century, every Regulus or chief had his own Bard, who was considered as an officer of rank in his court" and that ancient bards were "supported by a publick establishment."[50] As these authors' emphasis on the high rank of bards suggests, it would be a mistake to confuse their praise for bards with the later eighteenth- and nineteenth-century celebration of the "folk." The societies that Temple, Macpherson, and Blair valorized were deeply hierarchical ones, and as Katie Trumpener has pointed out, many Romantic celebrations of the bard exhibit a barely concealed nostalgia "for a lost feudal order."[51] Macpherson brought Gaelic tradition to the attention of an international audience, but what he did with it brings to mind one critic's praise for Percy's *Reliques.* In 1782 Vicesimus Knox praised Percy, a fellow clergyman, for having "rescued" oral tradition "from the hands of the vulgar" by printing his own polite version of popular ballads: "the popular ballad composed by some illiterate minstrel, and which has been handed down by tradition for several centuries, is rescued from the hands of the vulgar, to obtain a place in the collection of the man of taste."[52] Percy's three-volume collection helped to transform "vulgar" ballads into genteel literary culture. Similarly, Macpherson's works elevated traditional materials by transforming "fragments" into the esteemed genre of epic poetry, then printing them in volumes with elaborate paratextual materials (prefaces, appendices, engravings, and so on) that "authorized" them as acceptable objects of polite taste.

The Ossian phenomenon greatly influenced Homer scholarship (and vice versa). In 1769, as readers were devouring the *Works of Ossian*, traveler and antiquarian Robert Wood published *An Essay on the Original Genius of Homer*. In a section entitled "Homer's Language and Learning," he suggested that "Homer could neither read nor write."[53] In theorizing Homeric orality, Wood was influenced by accounts of the New World such as Garcilaso de la Vega's history of the Incas. He pointed to "the Mexicans, . . . whose picture-writing on the leaves of trees was very insufficient for the purposes of history," but who "trusted to the memory of their Poets and Orators, from whose recitals the Spaniards wrote down the accounts which they have transmitted." Extrapolating from Mexican bards to Irish ones, he wrote, "in like manner the historians of Ireland have collected their materials from the lays of their Bards, and Fileas; whose accounts have been merely traditional." He then surmised that in Homer's society, too, "Memory" was "entrusted with the whole deposit of Law, History, and Religion, till the art of Writing introduced a more easy, faithful, and comprehensive method of recording things." Wood assumed that writing and printing were "ingenious" inventions, but he nonetheless believed that modern book culture had some drawbacks. For one thing, the proliferation of print was contributing to the decline of memory: "in a rude and unlettered state of society, the memory is loaded with nothing that is either useless or unintelligible; whereas modern education employs us chiefly in getting by heart, while we are young, what we forget before we are old."[54] Like Wood, Jean-Jacques Rousseau questioned whether Homer knew how to write. In his *Essay on the Origin of Languages*, drafted around 1762–63 but not published in his lifetime, Rousseau suggested that Homer's poems "remained for a long time written only in men's memories." But unlike Wood, who never questioned that writing and printing were in general highly beneficial, Rousseau advised his readers to set aside their books and study the book of nature. It was only "when Greece began to abound in books and written poetry," he proposed, "that all the charm of that of Homer came to be felt by comparison."[55]

Wood's arguments for Homeric orality were not widely accepted in his lifetime. Revealingly, in 1775 an expanded version of his *Essay* was printed with the new title *An Essay on the Original Genius and Writings of Homer*.

But Wood's theories influenced the German classicist F. A. Wolf, whose *Prolegomena ad Homerum* (1795) set the course for nineteenth-century Homer scholarship. Wolf argued with unprecedented rigor (and obvious exasperation) that Homeric poetry was clearly not the product of a lettered society: "the word *book* is nowhere, *writing* is nowhere, reading is nowhere, *letters* are nowhere; . . . there are no pacts or treaties except face to face."[56] In the nineteenth century, the idea of the unlettered poet was accepted, but for most theorists of "orality and literacy" today, it was Milman Parry's discoveries in the 1920s that marked the breakthrough moment in "the modern discovery of primary oral cultures."[57] Parry's electronic recordings of Serbo-Croatian bards allowed him to show that oral poets compose their works orally rather than merely memorize them. In *Orality and Literacy*, Ong briefly acknowledges the contribution of eighteenth-century Homer scholars, ballad collectors, and theorists of "folk culture" who "worked over parts of oral or quasi-oral or near-oral tradition more or less directly, giving it new respectability." But for Ong, Parry is "the prime mover in the orality-literacy universe." It was his research and vision, Ong suggests, that "fused" earlier insights "to provide a provable account of what Homeric poetry was."[58]

"WE . . . CAME TO HEAR OLD TRADITIONS": JOHNSON'S *JOURNEY TO THE WESTERN ISLANDS OF SCOTLAND*

In 1746 the Battle of Culloden saw the final defeat of the Jacobites by Hanoverian forces. The brutality of English soldiers both during the battle and in the months that followed was widely condemned by English authors as well as Scots.[59] In this context, Macpherson's stirring stories of Ossian, Fingal, and the defeat of an invading army by Celtic warriors offered a timely boost to Scottish morale. But there are problems with national myths, even inspiring ones, and Johnson's portrait of Scotland in *A Journey to the Western Islands of Scotland* was partly an attempt to counterbalance Macpherson's poetic portrait. Instead of focusing on Scotland's mythic past, Johnson's political travel narrative demanded his readers' attention to the nation's pressing problems and divisions in the present.[60] At the same time, Johnson's investigation of the question of oral tradition throughout his journey was related to his belief in the importance of history. Johnson associated oral discourse with ephemerality, and he believed that "in nations where there is hardly the use of letters, what is once out of sight is lost for ever" (65). The preservation of the history of the Hebrides, then, was a particularly urgent problem, for in this rapidly changing region, the "greater part" of the people "make no use of books" (65).

As I suggested in the introduction, Johnson's definition of "oral" marks a significant shift in dictionary definitions of this word. Whereas Nathan Bailey's popular *Universal Etymological Dictionary* (1721) defines "oral" as "delivered by the Mouth or Voice," Johnson defined "oral" as "delivered by mouth; *not written*" (fig. 8.1, my emphasis). Along similar lines, he defined "tradition" as "the act or practice of delivering accounts from mouth to mouth without written memorials." Johnson introduced an explicit binary opposition between "oral" and "written," and his usage examples are a showcase of Protestant skepticism concerning the reliability of oral discourse, oral testimony, and oral tradition. He cites authors such as Locke, who described "oral discourse" as fugitive and "fault[y]"; Addison, who emphasized that the "oral testimony" of the apostles can be trusted only because they were not ordinary men; and Hale, who stated that "Oral Tradition . . . were incompetent without written Monuments to derive to us the original Laws and Constitutions of the Kingdom."[61]

But while Johnson's sense of the comparative reliability of written and oral discourse was typical of authors of his era, his belief in the necessity of literacy for all ranks of society was not. As we turn to an examination of Johnson's *Journey*, it is worth recalling that throughout eighteenth-century Britain, there was little support for state-sponsored public education, and in rural areas as much as half the population could not read. Johnson consistently argued in favor of teaching the poor to read and write, but it was not yet taken for granted by everyone that literacy was an inherent good for all social groups. In 1757 Johnson reviewed Soame Jenyns's *A Free Inquiry Into The Nature and Origin of Evil*. Like Bernard Mandeville in *The Fable of the Bees* (1714), Jenyns argued that teaching the poor to read was a waste of time. The bulk of the population subsisted through agricultural labor, and accordingly, teaching the poor to read would be going against the divine plan. Widespread "Ignorance," Jenyns claimed, was in fact an "instance of the Divine Wisdom," for

> Ignorance, or the want of knowledge and literature, the appointed lot of all born to poverty, and the drudgeries of life, is the only opiate capable of infusing that insensibility which can enable them to endure the miseries of the one, and the fatigues of the other. It is a cordial administered by the gracious hand of Providence; of which they ought never to be deprived by an ill-judged and improper Education.[62]

Johnson reserved his greatest contempt for Christian moralists like Jenyns who argued that poverty and ignorance were irremediable aspects of the ßroyed *or* to ftand eternally?   *Burnet.*

He my mufe's homage fhou'd receive,
If I cou'd write *or* Holles cou'd forgive.   *Garth.*
Every thing that can be divided by the mind into two *or*
inore ideas, is called complex.   *Watts's Logick.*

2. It correfponds to *either* ; he muft *either* fall *or* fly.

3. *Or* is fometimes redundant, but is then more properly omitted.

How great foever the fins of any unreformed perfon are,
Chrift died for him becaufe he died for all ; only he muft reform and forfake his fins, *or* elfe he fhall never receive benefit of his death.   *Hammond's Fund.*

4. [op, *or* ape, Saxon.] Before ; *or ever*, is *before ever*.
Or we go to the declaration of this pfalm, it fhall be convenient to fhew who did write this pfalm.   *Fifher.*

The dead man's knell
Is there fcarce afk'd for whom, and good men's lives
Expire before the flowers in their caps,
Dying *or* ere they ficken.   *Shakefp. Macbeth.*
Learn before thou fpeak, and ufe phyfick *er ever* thou be
fick.   *Ecclus* xviii. 19.

OR. *n. f.* [French.]   Gold.
The fhow'ry arch
With lifted colours gay, *er*, azure, gules,
Delights and puzzles the beholders eyes.   *Philips.*

O'RACH. *n. f.* The flower is without leaves, but confifts of
many ftamina arifing from a five leav'd empalement ; the
pointal becomes a flat orbicular feed, enclofed in the empalement, which becomes a foliaceous capfule, including two
forts of feeds. There are thirteen fpecies ; of which the
firft called garden *erach*, was cultivated as a culinary herb,
and ufed as fpinach, though it is not generally liked by the
Englifh, but ftill efteemed by the French. It was formerly
ufed in medicine.   *Miller.*

O'RACLE. *n. f.* [*oracle*, Fr. *oraculum*, Lat.]

1. Something delivered by fupernatural wifdom.
The main principle whereupon our belief of all things
therein contained dependeth, is, that the fcriptures are the
oracles of God himfelf.   *Hooker, b.* iii. *f. 8.*

2. The place where, or perfon of whom the determinations
of heaven are enquired.
Why, by the verities on thee made good,
May they not be my *oracles* as well,
And fet me up in hope?   *Shakefp. Macbeth.*
God hath now fent his living *oracle*
Into the world to teach his final will,
And fends his fpirit of truth henceforth to dwell
In pious hearts, an inward *oracle*,
To all truth requifite for men to know.   *Par. Reg.*

3. Any perfon *or* place where certain decifions are obtained.
There mighty nations fhall enquire their doom,
The world's great *oracle* in times to come.   *Pope.*

4. One famed for wifdom ; one whofe determinations are not
to be difputed.

To O'RACLE. *v. n.* [from the noun.] To utter oracles. A
word not received.
No more fhalt thou by *oracling* abufe
The gentiles.   *Paradife Regained, b.* i.

ORA'CULAR. ? *adj.* [from *oracle*.] Uttering oracles ; refem-
ORA'CULOUS. } bling oracles.
Thy counfel would be as the oracle of
Urim and thummim, thofe *oraculous* gems
On Aaron's breaft, or tongue of feers old
Infallible.   *Milton's Paradife Reg. b.* iii.
Here Charles contrives the ord'ring of his ftates,
Here he refolves his neigh'ring princes fates ;
What nation fhall have peace, where war be made,
Determin'd is in this *orac'lous* fhade.   *Waller.*
Though their general acknowledgments of the weaknefs
of human underftanding look like cold and fceptical difcourage-
ments ; yet the particular expreffions of their fentiments are
as *oraculous* as if they were omnifcient.   *Glanv Scepf.*
They have fomething venerable and *oracular*, in that un-
adorned gravity and fhortnefs in the expreffion.   *Pop. Pref.*
Th' *orac'lous* feer frequents the Pharian coaft,
Proteus a name tremendous o'er the main.   *Pope.*

ORA'CULOUSLY. *adv.* [from *oraculous*.] In manner of an
oracle.
The teftimony of antiquity, and fuch as pafs *oraculofly*
amongft us, were not always fo exact as to examine the
doctrine they delivered.   *Brown's Vulgar Err. b.* i.
Hence rife the branching beech and vocal oak,
Where Jove of old *oraculofly* fpoke.   *Dryden.*

ORA'CULOUSNESS. *n. f.* [from *oracular*.] The ftate of being
oracular.

O'RAISON. *n. f.* [*oraifon*, Fr. *oratio*, Lat.] Prayer ; verbal
fupplication ; or oral worfhip : more frequently written *orifon*.
Stay, let's hear the *oraifons* he makes.   *Shakefpeare.*
Bufinefs might fhorten, not difturb her pray'r ;
Heav'n had the beft, if not the greater fhare :
An active life, long *oraifons* forbids,
Yet ftill fhe pray'd, for ftill fhe pray'd by deeds.   *Dryden.*

O'RAL. *adj.* [*oral*, Fr. *os*, *oris*, Latin.] Delivered by mouth ;
not written.
Oral difcourfe, whofe tranfient faults dying with the found
that gives them life, and fo not fubject to a ftrict review,
more eafily efcapes obfervation.   *Locke's Effnot.*
St. John was appealed to as the living *oracle* of the church ;
and as his *oral* teftimony lafted the firft century, many have
obferved, that by a particular providence feveral of our Saviour's difciples, and of the early converts, lived to a very
great age, that they might perfonally convey the truth of the
gofpel to thofe times which were very remote.   *Addifon.*

O'RALLY. *adv.* [from *oral*.] By mouth ; without writing.
Oral tradition were incompetent without written monuments to derive to us the original laws of a kingdom, becaufe they are complex, not *orally* traducible to fo great a
diftance of ages.   *Hale's Comm. Laws of Eng.*

O'RANGE. *n. f.* [*orange*, Fr. *aurantia*, Latin.] The leaves
have two lobes or appendages at their bafe like ears, and cut
in form of a heart ; the fruit is round and depreffed, and of
a yellow colour when ripe, in which it differs from the ci-
tron and lemon. The fpecies are eight.   *Miller.*
I will difcharge it in your ftraw-colour'd beard, your *orange*
tawny beard.   *Shakefp. Midf. Night's Dream.*
The notary came aboard, holding in his hand a fruit like
an *orange*, but of colour between *orange* tawny and fcarlet,
which caft a moft excellent odour, and is ufed for a preferva-
tive againft infection.   *Bacon's New Atlantis.*
Fine *oranges*, fauce for your veal,
Are charming when fqueez'd in a pot of brown ale.   *Swift.*
The ideas of *orange* colour and azure, produced in the
mind by the fame infufion of lignum nephriticum, are no
lefs diftinct ideas than thofe of the fame colours taken from
two different bodies.   *Locke.*

O'RANGERY. *n. f.* [*orangerie*, Fr.] Plantation of oranges.
A kitchen garden is a more pleafant fight than the fineft
orangery, or artificial green houfe.   *Spectator*, N°. 477.

O'RANGEMUSK. *n. f.* See PEAR, of which it is a fpecies.

O'RANGEWIFE. *n. f.* [*orange* and *wife*.] A woman who fells
oranges.
You wear out a good wholefome forenoon in hearing a
caufe between an *orangewife* and a foffet feller.   *Shakef.*

ORA'TION. *n. f.* [*oration*, Fr. *oratio*, Lat.] A fpeech made ac-
cording to the laws of rhetorick ; a harangue ; a declamation.
There fhall I try,
In my *oration*, how the people take
The cruel iffue of thefe bloody men.   *Shakefp. Jul. Caf.*
This gives life and fpirit to every thing that is fpoken,
awakens the dulleft fpirits, and adds a fingular grace and
excellency both to the perfon and his *oration*.   *Watts.*

ORATO'RICAL. *adj.* [from *orateur*.] Rhetorical ; befitting an
oratour.
Where he fpeaks in an *oratorical*, affecting, or perfuafive
way, let this be explained by other places where he treats of
the fame theme in a doctrinal way.   *Watts.*

O'RATOUR. *n. f.* [*orateur*, Fr. *orator*, Lat.]

1. A publick fpeaker ; a man of eloquence.
Poor queen and fon ! your labour is but loft ;
For Warwick is a fubtle *orator*.   *Shakefp. Henry VI.*
As when of old fome *orator* renown'd,
In Athens or free Rome, where eloquence
Flourifh'd, fince mute ! to fome great caufe addrefs'd,
Stood in himfelf collected ; while each part,
Motion, each act, won audience.   *Milton's Par. Loft.*
The conftant defign of both thefe *orators* in all their
fpeeches, was to drive fome one particular point.   *Swift.*
I have liftened to an *orator* of this fpecies, without being
able to underftand one fingle fentence.   *Swift.*
Both *orators* to much renown'd,
In their own depths of eloquence were drown'd.   *Dryden.*

2. A petitioner. This fenfe is ufed in addreffes to chancery.

O'RATORY. *n. f.* [*oratorio*, *ars*, Lat.]

1. Eloquence ; rhetorical fkill.
Each pafture ftored with fheep feeding with fober fecurity,
while the pretty lambs with bleating *oratory* craved the dams
comfort.   *Sidney.*
When a world of men
Could not prevail with all their *oratory*,
Yet hath a woman's kindnefs over-rul'd.   *Shakefpeare.*
When my *oratory* grew tow'rd end,
I bid them that did love their country's good,
Cry, God fave Richard.   *Shakefp. Rich. III.*
Sighs now breath'd
Unutterable, which the fpirit of pray'r
Infpir'd, and wing'd for heav'n with fpeedier flight
Than loudeft *oratory*.   *Milton's Paradife Loft, b.* xi.
By this kind of *oratory*, and profeffing to decline their own
inclinations and wifhes, purely for peace and unity, they
prevailed over thofe who were ftill furprifed.   *Clarend.*
The former who had to deal with a people of much more
politenefs, learning, and wit, laid the greateft weight of his
oratory upon the ftrength of his arguments.   *Swift.*
Come

3

divine design (and indeed blessings). Questioning Jenyns's notion of being "born to poverty," he suggested that this privileged member of Parliament "perhaps never saw the miseries which [he] imagine[s] thus easy to be
borne." Depriving poor people of an opportunity to learn to read and write
was "cruel, if not unjust," for it entailed poverty upon "generation after
generation":

> To entail irreversible poverty upon generation after generation only be-
> cause the ancestor happened to be poor is in itself cruel, if not unjust. . . .
> Those who communicate literature to the son of a poor man consider
> him as one not born to poverty, but to the necessity of deriving a better
> fortune from himself.[63]

In the new reading nation, Johnson argued, a basic ability to read and write
was a necessity for all social groups regardless of their occupations. Johnson's
modern belief in the importance of literacy for everyone reflects an ongoing,
gradual shift from older assumptions about literacy as an occupational tool to
a new sense of literacy as a universal good. This shift is reflected in the transformation of the most common understanding of the term "literate" from
the older meaning of literate as "learned" (*litteratus*: a person who knew
Latin, or was learned) to the most common definition today: that is, having
a basic ability to read and write.[64] Johnson refused to reduce poverty to an
abstraction, and he saw poverty and illiteracy as closely linked. "Literature,"
or learning, was no guarantee of opportunity, but the ability to read and write
would at least give "the son of a poor man" a chance to improve his fortunes.
Keeping this in mind will help us to make sense of Johnson's deep distrust
of the efforts of some of his genteel contemporaries to recover and valorize
selected kinds of "oral tradition."[65]

As the son of a bookseller, Johnson was a lifelong armchair traveler. He
read "journals, treatises, diaries, logs, letters, memoirs, chronicles, topographical surveys, atlases, and descriptions of domestic, Continental, and remote
regions."[66] According to Boswell, Johnson first grew interested in seeing the
Highlands when his father put Martin Martin's *Description of the Western
Islands of Scotland* (1703) into his hands.[67] Johnson's first book publication,
A Voyage to Abyssinia (1735), was a translation of a travel narrative, *Relation historique d'Abissinie* (1728), by the French cleric Joachim Le Grand,
whose work was in turn a translation of an account by Portuguese missionary Jerome Lobo recounting his travels to Abyssinia (Ethiopia). In his preface to *Voyage*, Johnson praised the abbé Le Grand for his "dar[ing] . . . disap-
probation" of missionaries who "preach[ed] the Gospel with swords in their

hands, and propagate[d] by desolation and slaughter the true worship of the God of Peace."[68] Twenty-four years later, Johnson published *Rasselas, or the Prince of Abyssinia* (1759), and he wrote an introduction to publisher John Newbery's twenty-volume series of "Travels," *The World Displayed; or, A Curious Collection of Voyages and Travels, Selected from the Writers of All Nations*. Johnson's introduction surveys European exploration and trade up to the time of Columbus, who "made the daring and prosperous voyage, which gave a new world to European curiosity and European cruelty."[69] Refusing to minimize the legacy of *English* "cruelty" by emphasizing Spanish and Portuguese atrocities, he explicitly singled out "the *English* barbarians that cultivate the southern islands of *America*."[70] In a moment of piqued Scottish pride, Boswell claimed in his *Tour* that Johnson "allowed himself to look upon all nations but his own as barbarians" (20). But as one can see from Johnson's explicit condemnation of "*English* barbarians," Boswell's (now often quoted) statement is incorrect.

Johnson also reviewed travel books, and he wrote about "the Narrations of travellers" in his own tellingly titled periodicals *Rambler, Adventurer*, and *Idler*. In one essay, he outlines his philosophy or theory of the duties of "Writer[s] of Travels." Like all authors, travel writers have an obligation to instruct as well as please. Accordingly, a travel writer should "offer *new* images to his reader," for "why should he record excursions by which nothing could be learned"?[71] In Johnson's *Journey to the Western Islands of Scotland*, he focuses (as the title of his work suggests) on the little-known rural regions of the Highlands rather than the better-known commercial towns of the Lowlands. His scant attention to Edinburgh, one of the centers of the European Enlightenment, was (and still is) interpreted by some readers as a snub. But in Johnson's view, Edinburgh was "too well known to admit description" (3). As we can see from his explicitly expressed views of the duties of travel writers, he held that they should always offer something new to their readers.

Finally, for now, to understand the generic innovations and political and moral imperatives of Johnson's *Journey*, it is helpful to situate this work in relation to two kinds of travel writing that were increasingly important in the eighteenth century: the travel guide for tourists and the printed observations of scientific travelers. Well into the eighteenth century, one of the most widely consulted guides was James Howell's *Instructions for Forreine Travel* (1642). Aimed at gentlemen traveling to continental Europe, Howell's book provides relatively little practical information by our standards; instead, it emphasizes the moral and civic ends of touring and the importance of careful intellectual preparation for one's travels. But while

Howell advised extensive prior reading and oral conversation with experienced travelers, he also emphasized that "one's own Ocular view . . . will still find out something new."[72] As this observation suggests, travel writing was greatly influenced by empiricist philosophy and the new emphasis on scientific method. In 1666 the Royal Society of London published Robert Boyle's "General Heads for a Natural History of a Countrey," a checklist for scientific travelers teaching them to record details of a country's terrain, climate, and natural resources. Boyle's "Heads" encouraged a new sense of travel as data collection.[73] In the eighteenth century, mapmakers, botanists, and other recorders accompanied sailors on voyages of exploration. Captain James Cook's voyages to the South and North Pacific between 1768 and 1779 were officially made for scientific purposes (as well as for purposes of colonization), and the information gathered on these expeditions (and later printed) prompted new questions about animal and vegetable species and the development of human societies.

When Johnson undertook his nearly four-month journey to Scotland in the fall of 1773, the Hebrides were not yet a tourist attraction. There were no signposts or inns, and beyond Inverness, he "enter[ed] a country upon which perhaps no wheel has ever rolled" (29). Johnson traveled from London to Edinburgh, then set off with Boswell, traveling by coach, on horseback, on foot, and occasionally by boat. Boswell was thirty-two and Johnson sixty-three: an advanced age to be "climbing crags, and treading bogs" (29).

Johnson was a humanist *and* an empiricist travel writer. He combined older philosophical and social motivations for travel with a new emphasis on scientific method. His commitment to the rules of empirical research can be seen in his advice that travelers should carry ink, paper, and measuring instruments and record their observations as soon as possible. For "he who has not made the experiment, or who is not accustomed to require rigorous accuracy from himself, will scarcely believe how much a few hours take from certainty of knowledge" (146–47). As a literary work, the *Journey* is a complex generic hybrid. Its basic form is that of a travel diary, but it is also an ethnography and a philosophical meditation. Pat Rogers calls it one of Johnson's "most eloquent and challenging works, a great document of cultural studies before the topic was invented."[74]

Johnson regretted that Martin Martin, a native of the Hebrides, did not say more about the traditional way of life in the islands in his *Description of the Western Islands of Scotland*. Although Martin recorded some Highland traditions, he "was hardly sympathetic to them. For him their passing marked a milestone in the islanders' progression to become a useful part of the British state."[75] Martin was a member of the Royal Society of London. He followed Boyle's "General Heads for a Natural History of a Countrey," and his *Description* focuses chiefly on natural resources. In contrast to Martin, Johnson concentrated on "life and manners" (32). But whereas earlier humanists (such as Francis Bacon) advised travel writers to turn their attention to the courts of princes, Johnson focused on "the state of common life":

> The manners of a people are not to be found in the schools of learning, or the palaces of greatness . . . nor is public happiness to be estimated by the assemblies of the gay, or the banquets of the rich. The great mass of nations is neither rich nor gay: they whose aggregate constitutes the people, are found in the streets, and the villages, in the shops and farms; and from them collectively considered, must the measure of general prosperity be taken.[76] (22)

In assessing the landscape, Johnson prioritized its ability to feed and shelter its inhabitants. To him, "mountainous regions" and "naked rock" suggested not sublime aesthetic experience but the likelihood of hardship for peasants forced to till the soil and graze animals on the land (38). Traveling past Anoch—"a village . . . of three huts"—he encounters "regions mountainous and wild, thinly inhabited, and little cultivated" (35, 40). He remarks that "an eye accustomed to flowery pastures and waving harvests is astonished and repelled by this wide extent of hopeless sterility." "Waving harvests" and "flowery pastures" mean well-fed peasants and livestock, but "hopeless sterility" means desperate hunger (39). The "phantoms which haunt" mountainous, infertile regions are not the ghosts of Ossianic heroes but the real-life threats of "want, and misery, and danger" (41).[77] Throughout Britain, hunger and malnutrition were a fact of life for agricultural laborers. But in the especially harsh climate and terrain of the Hebrides, "the dark months are . . . a time of great distress; because the summer can do little more than feed itself, and winter comes with its cold and its scarcity upon families very slenderly provided" (52). To make matters worse, the "petty tenants, and labouring peasants, live in miserable cabins, which afford them little more than shelter from the storms" (101).

As he enters the Highlands, Johnson initially seems to see himself as traveling backward in time. His expectation that he will see representatives of an earlier, primitive form of society suggests the place of the Highlands in conjectural history. Not coincidentally, most leading conjectural historians were Scottish.[78] Typically based in major urban centers such as Edinburgh or Glasgow, these men were becoming increasingly aware of the diversity of societies within Scotland as well as across the globe. After the devastation of 1745–46, the contrast between the thriving commercial centers of the Lowlands and the struggling rural regions of the Highlands was becoming strikingly apparent. R. L. Meek observes that in the Lowlands,

> the whole social life of the communities concerned was being rapidly and visibly transformed, and it was fairly obvious that this was happening as a result of profound changes taking place in economic techniques and basic socio-economic relationships. And the new forms of economic organisation which were emerging could be fairly easily compared and contrasted with the older forms of organisation which still existed, say, in the Scottish Highlands.[79]

Stadial theory allowed conjectural historians to account for these differences by fitting all of Scotland into one line of social development. They posited that the commercial towns of the Lowlands exhibited the most advanced or "refined" stage of progress, while the rural Highlands, with their feudal clans and "hunter-gatherer" and "pastoral" modes of subsistence, represented an earlier, "primitive" stage.

Johnson's diction shows the influence of stadial theory. On the Isle of Skye, he observes that "the state of life, which has hitherto been purely pastoral, begins now to be a little variegated with commerce" (89). But his eyewitness observation soon teaches him that while he "planned to study an exotic, intriguing stage of social development that . . . was still alive, he imagined, . . . in the Western Isles," in reality the Highlands was far from the primitive or feudal society that conjectural history had prepared him to find.[80] Early in the *Journey*, Johnson foregrounds his erroneous assumptions. Although he came "to hear old traditions, and see antiquated manners," the "system of antiquated life" and the manners that he expected no longer exist (128, 57). This change is in no small part due to England's political, legal, and economic incursions. The laws and civil penalties imposed to weaken the clan system have had devastating effects on the Highlanders' way of life. "There was perhaps never any change of national manners so quick, so great, and so general, as that which has operated in the Highlands, by the last conquest, and the subsequent laws" (57). After observing for himself the consequences of "the last conquest," Johnson arguably mocks his own earlier desire to encounter a "barbarous," yet magnificent premodern society. Recalling Shaftesbury's critique of English readers who panted for books of *"Barbarian* Customs . . . [and] *Savage* Manners"—but critiquing such readers for entirely different reasons—Johnson now sardonically reflects that "a longer journey than to the Highlands must be taken by him whose curiosity pants for savage virtues and barbarous grandeur" (58).

Johnson especially lambasts British government efforts to abolish the use of Gaelic. The "late conquest" has stripped the Highlanders of everything but "their language and their poverty," and now, even their language is under "attack":

> Of what they had before the late conquest of their country, there remain only their language and their poverty. Their language is attacked on every side. Schools are erected, in which English only is taught, and there were lately some who thought it reasonable to refuse them a version of the holy scriptures, that they might have no monument of their mother-tongue. (57–58)

Later in the *Journey,* he observes that "there are now parochial schools" where "the children are taught to read; but by the rule of their institution, they teach only English, so that the natives read a language which they may never use or understand" (103). Johnson supported the teaching of English, but he viewed it as tragic when any native language was lost. Languages are themselves accretions of tradition, and in an era of mass emigration, a common linguistic heritage linked a scattered people. If the establishment of public schooling in the Highlands threatened to undermine the native language of Gaelic, it was an "attack" on "the natives" rather than a gift.

Despite the rage for all things "Ossianic," Johnson observed, the true condition of the contemporary Highlanders remained largely unknown. Not only to the English but also "to the southern inhabitants of Scotland, the state of the mountains and the islands is equally unknown with that of Borneo or Sumatra: Of both they have only heard a little, and guess the rest" (88). Later, he reiterates his view that "of the past and present state of the [Highlands] . . . , the Lowlanders are at least as ignorant as ourselves" (119). This ignorance was an especially urgent problem given ongoing attempts to consolidate Great Britain and to ameliorate poverty. For both the English and the Lowland Scots "are strangers to the language and the manners, to the advantages and wants of the people, whose life they would model, and whose evils they would remedy" (88). But whereas Johnson begins his narrative by observing how little the English and the Lowland Scots know about the Highlanders, he ends it by emphasizing his own ignorance:

> Having passed my time almost wholly in cities, I may have been sur-
> prised by modes of life and appearances of nature, that are familiar to
> men of wider survey and more varied conversation. Novelty and igno-
> rance must always be reciprocal, and I cannot but be conscious that my
> thoughts on national manners, are the thoughts of one who has seen but
> little. (164)

One of the most powerful aspects of the *Journey* is the way it shows a stub-
born old man coming to rethink his own assumptions. Johnson's ability to
do this can be seen in his successive comments on the shortage of forests
in Scotland. Early in the *Journey*, he blames the Scots for what he sees as
their moral failure to plant seedlings to provide shelter and timber for future
generations. Later, though, he realizes with sympathy and dismay that the
impoverished Highlanders face more pressing needs: "plantation is naturally the employment of a mind unburdened with care. . . . He that pines
with hunger, is in little care how others shall be fed" (139).

Johnson set out for the Highlands expecting to find exotic otherness.
He also set out fully equipped with typical English biases against the Scots.
But what he ultimately learns is the extent of his own prior ignorance about
the effects of the Act of Union and the plight of the Highlanders after 1745.
"His intent to study life and manners brought him unexpectedly to the
subject of human suffering caused by disturbing historical forces that the
Highland Scots were ill suited to meet."[81] In his aforementioned essay on
"the Narrations of Travellers," Johnson wrote that

> He that would travel for the entertainment of others, should remember
> that the great object of remark is human life. . . . He only is a useful
> Traveller, who brings home something by which his country may be
> benefited; who procures some supply of Want, or some mitigation of
> Evil.[82]

Despite having "seen but little," Johnson's use of print commerce allowed
him to do something "useful." His travel narrative "allowed him to do what
he had not anticipated: he was able not only to record a distant, static history but to enter an ongoing historical process that he could perhaps alter
for the good."[83]

Given his growing awareness of the plight of the Highlanders and the
complex consequences of the Act of Union, why does Johnson spend so
much time addressing the question of oral tradition in the *Journey*? As I
shall suggest now in examining his remarks on oral discourse, oral tradition,

and Macpherson's Ossian poems, Johnson believed that the true history of a nation was at stake. Johnson readily acknowledged that "all history was at first oral." But as we have seen, he also held that when documents were available, they should replace tradition as a historical source. This was especially true when the documents were the scriptures. According to Boswell, when he asked Johnson his view of the Catholic doctrine of transubstantiation, he responded with the standard Protestant view that the scriptures, not tradition, were the rule of faith: "'Tradition, sir, has no place, where the Scriptures are plain; and tradition cannot persuade a man into a belief of transubstantiation'" (*Tour*, 393, 194). Boswell's *Life of Johnson* is now the most canonical source for the study of Johnson's *oral* discourse. As Boswell "venture[d] to predict," his books are no substitute for living witnesses who could "bear testimony" to Johnson's "extemporaneous effusions," but "no other memorial[s]" of greater value remain.[84] But in discussing Johnson's views of the Ossian debate and of oral tradition, it is important to remember that all his originally oral remarks on these issues come to us in the form of *texts*. Boswell's portraits of Johnson in his *Journal of a Tour to the Hebrides* (1785) and *Life of Johnson* (1791) are interpretations and artistic reconstructions, and although Johnson read portions of Boswell's manuscript diaries, both of these works were published after Johnson's death (1784).

Several of the conversations that Boswell records in his *Journal of a Tour* seem far from "extemporaneous." In particular, Boswell appears to have arranged meetings between Johnson and defenders of Macpherson's Ossian so as to provoke good material for his *Journal of a Tour*. Almost as soon as Johnson arrived in Scotland, Boswell hosted an evening's entertainment that brought Johnson together with Sir James Adolphus Oughton, a British military commander who knew some Erse. Boswell appeals to his reader's imagination when he reports that Sir James "expressed his belief in the authenticity of Ossian's Poetry," while Johnson "took the opposite side of that perplexed question" (145). Later in his text, Boswell records a similar confrontation with the Reverend Donald MacQueen. Boswell portrays Johnson as offering MacQueen a compliment even as he holds his ground and attempts to clarify his position: "I am not disputing that you may have poetry of great merit; but that M'Pherson's is not a translation from ancient poetry" (240).

Hugh Blair represented Macpherson as the translator of Ossianic poetry, and Johnson reasoned that "'if the poems were really translated, they were certainly first written down.'"[85] If there *was* a manuscript, Macpherson should settle the authenticity debates by depositing the text "in one of the colleges at Aberdeen, where there are people who can judge" (*Tour*, 95). As for

Macpherson's methods in composing his Ossianic works, Johnson argued a position that has since turned out to be largely the truth: Macpherson "found names, and stories, and phrases, nay, passages in old songs, and with them has blended his own compositions, and so made what he gives to the world as the translation of an ancient poem" (*Life*, 242). Macpherson's texts were contemporary to himself, and accordingly, they were worthless as historical sources. According to Boswell, Johnson observed that if *Fingal* had "been really an ancient work, a true specimen how men thought at that time, it would have been a curiosity of the first rate," but "as a modern production," it was "nothing" (*Tour*, 240–41).

But although Johnson was right in surmising that Macpherson's Ossian poems were literary creations, he was wrong in stating that Erse "never was a written language; that there is not in the world an Earse manuscript a hundred years old." On the one hand, Johnson acknowledged that he did not speak Erse and knew little about the history of the language: "as I understand nothing, I cannot say more than I have been told" (114). On the other hand, he makes several blunt statements about Erse in his text, and "the undeveloped state of Gaelic studies helps to explain, but does not finally excuse" his lack of "restraint in his published remarks."[86] Early in the *Journey*, he asserts that Erse "merely floated in the breath of the people," and in a later passage, he implicitly assigns Erse to what he calls the "childhood" stage of the development of Gaelic. Theorizing the relationship between speech and texts in general, he writes:

> When a language begins to teem with books, it is tending to refinement. . . . [S]peech becomes embodied and permanent; different modes and phrases are compared, and the best obtains an establishment. By degrees one age improves upon another. . . . But diction, merely vocal, is always in its childhood. As no man leaves his eloquence behind him, the new generations have all to learn. (115)

By linking "merely vocal" (or oral) languages to the "childhood" stage of the development of languages, Johnson contributes to a developmental model of modes of communication whereby the childhood of language (orality) is inexorably (and ideally) replaced by adulthood ("letters" and "books").

Still, Johnson not only makes extensive use of oral histories in his *Journey* but also defends his decision to do so.[87] When an "elderly gentleman" narrates a story associated with a bagpipe tune, Johnson asserts that "narrations like this, however uncertain, deserve the notice of a traveller, because they are the only records of a nation that has no historians" (49–50; see also

110). What he cannot learn from books or eyewitness observation, Johnson is eager to learn from oral accounts. When the accounts that he gathers contradict one another, he regrets that the Highlanders' "primitive customs and ancient manner of life" are "faintly and uncertainly remembered by the present race" (112). But his own observation of the suffering of the Highlanders soon teaches him why this "distress[ed]" people must focus on the present rather than on "primitive customs" and manners:

> We soon found what memorials were to be expected from an illiterate people, whose whole time is a series of distress; where every morning is labouring with expedients for the evening; and where all mental pains or pleasure arose from the dread of winter, [and] the expectation of spring. (110–11)

Johnson remains judgmental throughout the *Journey*, but crucially, the object(s) of his judgment shift. As I suggested earlier, he concludes by critiquing his own prior ignorance of the true state of the Highlands, despite his literacy: "I cannot but be conscious that my thoughts on national manners, are the thoughts of one who has seen but little" (164).

While Johnson disputed the authenticity of Macpherson's Ossian poems and complained of the Scots' "easy reception of an improbable fiction," he did not reject the idea of tradition itself (119). Throughout his travels, he expresses interest in how tradition functions. He notes that in areas where books are few, "stated observances" such as "pageants, . . . processions, and commemorations" serve as important "registers" of the past (65). Monuments and features of the landscape also function as forms of historical record. Of the Druid Stones at Banff, Johnson observes that "edifices, either standing or ruined, are the chief records of an illiterate nation" (73). Despite his Protestantism, he expresses regret that he did not have time to visit "the Popish islands" of the Hebrides so as to have observed for himself how Catholic ceremonies did, indeed, preserve tradition: "Popery is favourable to ceremony; and among ignorant nations, ceremony is the only preservative of tradition. . . . We therefore who came to hear old traditions, and see antiquated manners, should probably have found them amongst the Papists" (127–28).

Johnson especially attempts to find out the truth about bards and seanchaí (traditional Celtic historians). He reports what he learns from creditable informants *and* from common report: "it seems to be universally supposed, that much of the local history was preserved by the bards. . . . After these bards were some of my first inquiries. . . . They said that a great family had a bard and a *senachi*, who were the poet and historian of the house" (111). He evaluates what he hears, and he identifies where evidence is lacking: "whether the 'man of talk' was a historian, whose office was to tell truth, or a story-teller . . . it now would be vain to inquire" (112). Like Defoe in his *Essay upon Literature*, he associates the absence of texts with the easy propagation of "fictions." Like classical scholars who increasingly understood that Greek rhapsodes were entertainers, Johnson emphasizes that Celtic bards were dependent on patronage and that this dependence had consequences for the reliability of their histories: "the nation was wholly illiterate. Neither bards nor *senachies* could write or read; but if they were ignorant, there was no danger of detection; they were believed by those whose vanity they flattered." In reciting noble genealogies, the bards "might obtrude fictitious pedigrees, either to please their masters, or to hide the deficiency of their own memories" (112).

But as anthropologists and folklorists now agree, the continuous transformation of tradition should not necessarily be understood as the propagation of "fict[ions]." Change is inherent to the process of tradition, and in societies without any form of writing:

> Myth and history merge into one: the elements in the cultural heritage which cease to have a contemporary relevance tend to be soon forgotten or transformed; and as the individuals of each generation acquire their vocabulary, their genealogies, and their myths, they are unaware that various words, proper names and stories have dropped out, or that others have changed their meanings or been replaced.[88]

Ultimately, to assess tradition on the basis of its truth-value is to misunderstand how tradition functions. Traditions serve psychological, as well as historical, needs, and we learn most if we critically interpret them as such. Johnson never contemplated what might be learned by understanding Ossianic tradition *as tradition*. He refused to see Macpherson's Ossian poems as anything but an instance of fraud. Alluding to myths of Patagonian giants that had circulated since Ferdinand Magellan's circumnavigation of the globe, he urged his readers not to "fill the vacuity" of knowledge with the "delusive opiate of hasty persuasion":

> To be ignorant is painful; but it is dangerous to quiet our uneasiness by the delusive opiate of hasty persuasion. . . . If we know little of the ancient Highlanders, let us not fill the vacuity with Ossian. If we have not

searched the Magellanick regions, let us however forbear to people them
with Patagons. (119)

Uniting empirical observations and humanist motivations and offering
"new images" to his readers, Johnson's political travel narrative helps,
in unexpected ways, to clarify some of the political, social, and moral issues at stake in his genteel contemporaries' relatively sudden craze for oral
tradition.

"STEP[S] IN THE NATURAL HISTORY OF MAN": SITUATING SPEECH, WRITING, AND PRINTING IN STADIAL THEORY

The year that Johnson died, state record keeper Thomas Astle published *The
Origin and Progress of Writing . . . Also Some Account of the Origin and
Progress of Printing* (1784). Like Defoe and Warburton, Astle discussed oral
tradition, the invention of letters, the introduction and spread of printing,
and writing systems across the globe. But whereas earlier authors attempted
to reconcile theological and secular accounts of the origin and development
of writing, Astle's history of mediation is explicitly evolutionary. Whereas
Defoe insisted that writing was a onetime gift from God, Astle explicitly
(and rather boldly) titled a section of his work "Alphabetic Writing not first
communicated to Moses, nor of Divine Original." Significantly, Astle had
no qualms about placing "brute[s]," "savages," and "MAN"—as well as their
forms of communication—along a single evolutionary chain. In the opening sentence of his work, he declared, "The noblest acquisition of mankind is SPEECH, and the most useful art is WRITING. The first, eminently
distinguishes MAN from the brute creation; the second, from uncivilized
savages." In the latter regard, I suggest, Astle's stadial history of modes of
human communication anticipates nineteenth-century *biological* models
of the evolution of humankind.

By the end of the eighteenth century, we detect the idea of communications technologies as themselves part of an unfolding sequence of "stages"
in the development of human societies. From the 1790s, conjectural historians suggested that shifts in communication practices and tools themselves
triggered "stages." In 1792 Dugald Stewart asserted that "the invention of
printing" was the "single event, independently of every other" that was "sufficient to change the whole course of human affairs."[89] He argued that "the
means of communication afforded by the press, have, in the course of two

centuries, accelerated the progress of the human mind, far beyond what the most sanguine hopes of our predecessors could have imagined."[90] Stewart depicted the invention of printing as part of a "natural," inevitable sequence of developments in human societies. The "art of printing" is "a step in the natural history of man":

> if this invention had not been made by the particular person to whom it is ascribed, the same art, or some analogous art, answering a similar purpose, would have been infallibly invented by some other person, at no very distant period. The art of printing, therefore, is entitled to be considered as a step in the natural history of man.

Like Defoe and Johnson, Stewart associated the archiving quality of print with the accumulation of knowledge, and the proliferation of texts with the beneficial comparison of competing accounts. It was "upon these last considerations," Stewart wrote, "much more than on the efforts of original genius, that I would rest my hopes of the progress of the human race."[91]

Meanwhile, across the English Channel, the fugitive philosopher Marie Jean Antoine Nicolas de Caritat, marquis de Condorcet (1743–94), was penning his *Esquisse d'un Tableau Historique des Progrès de l'Esprit Humain.* After he died in prison, this text was published as *Sketch for a Historical Picture of the Progress of the Human Mind* (1795). Like Astle and Stewart, Condorcet divided human history into "ages," then systematically linked stages of social development to stages in the development of communications. In Condorcet's *Sketch*, each new invention or major discovery seems to trigger or enable a new "stage." The "Third Stage" covers "up to the invention of the alphabet," the "Seventh Stage" includes "the progress of science . . . to the invention of printing," and the "Eighth Stage" addresses man's development "from the invention of printing to the time when philosophy and the sciences shook off the yoke of authority." In a move that anticipates (the now much-critiqued) "Great Divide" model of "orality and literacy," Condorcet divided the history of mankind into a "before" and "after" of alphabetic writing, then represented these two stages as the "two great eras of the human race." As a philosophe and an atheist, Condorcet was the product of an Enlightenment tradition different from that of the British writers I have discussed here. But significantly, he too critiqued oral tradition, and he praised letters as the superior means of communicating knowledge across generations. He declared that human progress "would have been impossible if there had not been men who understood the art of writing, the only method of establishing and maintaining a tradition, of communicating and transmitting knowledge as it grows."[92]

Confronted with a wealth of new accounts of the world's peoples, eighteenth-century conjectural historians attempted to make sense of the diversity of human societies by placing these different social formations along a single evolutionary chain. But ironically, in their efforts to *relate* the world's peoples by linking them in a developmental sequence, these philosophers arguably separated them further from one another. As Johannes Fabian suggests in his account of the constitutive function of time in modern anthropology:

> Evolutionary sequences . . . create a universal frame of reference able to accommodate all societies . . . but they are founded on distancing and separation. There would be no raison d'etre for the comparative method if it was not for the classification of entities or traits which first have to be separate and distinct before their similarities can be used to establish taxonomies and developmental sequences.[93]

A similar point might be made about now-naturalized models of media shift. In an attempt to make sense of the profound changes associated with the "electronic age," "digital age," "information age" (and so on), contemporary media theorists now commonly employ a developmental model consisting of a succession of stages, such as "oral culture," "scribal culture," "print culture," and the "electronic era." To a certain extent, of course, we can understand change only in terms of difference. But many studies of media shift (and of "orality and literacy") *begin* by assuming contrasts and even "conflict" between the "forms of social organization and thought" now associated with diverse media forms. In his eight-paragraph introduction to *Orality and Literacy* (1982), for instance, Ong uses the word "differences" four times and "contrast(s)" or "contrasting" five times, and he explicitly states that "the subject of this book is the differences between orality and literacy."[94] Similarly, in *The Domestication of the Savage Mind* (1977), anthropologist Jack Goody cautions against assuming any crude dichotomy between "literate and non-literate societies," but he nonetheless explicitly states that his goal is to "pursue the *contrast* between literate and non-literate societies."[95] Goody warns against binary models and crude developmental sequences, but he also suggests that it is difficult not to employ developmental models when comparing societies: "any resort to comparative work necessarily raises the evolutionary issue."[96] But as I have tried to show in this chapter, these evolutionary or developmental models have lengthy histories, and by understanding these histories, I suggest, we have a greater chance of avoiding ethnocentrism. In demonstrating the integral relationship between the explosion of print commerce and the new literate habit of conjecturing oral societies (or what we now often call "oral cultures"), I hope to have contributed to the project of historicizing these models. There is certainly a sense in which "the modern discovery of primary oral cultures" took place in the twentieth century with the discoveries of Milman Parry, as Ong suggests. But the modern invention of the idea of oral societies, I have argued, took place in the eighteenth century as a consequence of the spread of print.

When Did "Orality" Become a "Culture"?

When did "orality" become a "culture"? As I've suggested in this book, no eighteenth-century author used the term "oral culture," for the anthropological idea of a culture as a "total way of life" did not exist. In the eighteenth century, "culture" typically referred to the care of crops or animals—as when Samuel Johnson defined "culture" as "the act of tilling the ground; tillage" and as the "art of improvement and melioration."[1] It is not impossible to find examples of "culture" used to indicate a process of human improvement, but this usage is rare. In "An Epistle to Mr. Pope. Occasioned by his Characters of Women" (1736), Anne Ingram, Viscountess Irwin, compared untutored female minds to uncultivated crops. Arguing for improved educational opportunities for women, she wrote, "Culture improves all fruits, all sorts we find, / Wit, judgment, sense—fruits of the human mind."[2] In 1748 Lord Chesterfield advised his nephew to cultivate his own mind. He urged, "observe the difference there is between minds cultivated and . . . uncultivated, and you will . . . think that you cannot . . . employ too much . . . time in the culture of your own. A drayman is probably born with as good organs as Milton, Locke, or Newton; but, by culture, they are as much more above him as he is above his horse."[3]

In the nineteenth century, the idea of culture as the outcome of a process of human cultivation developed into what evolutionary anthropologist Edward Burnett Tylor called culture "in its wide ethnographic sense." In the opening sentence of *Primitive Culture* (2 vols., 1871), a work now cited as the earliest "official promulgation of the culture idea"[4] in anthropology, Tylor defined culture as "that complex whole which includes knowledge, belief, art, morals, law, custom, and any other capabilities and habits acquired by man as a member of society."[5] Today, the most common sense of "culture" is "a way of life, or a system of meaning shared among a people."[6] At the heart of this idea of culture, Christopher Herbert suggests, is the assertion (or assumption) that an "array of disparate-seeming elements of social life composes a significant *whole*." In terms that unwittingly evoke what I have argued was eighteenth-century conjectural historians' contribution to our modern idea of oral and print cultures, Herbert observes that "to a certain extent, the entity that Tylor names 'culture' takes on a distinctly hypothetical or conjectural character." The premise of "a culture" allows the ethnographer to "bind . . . into a single scheme . . . all the disparate features of the life of a society."[7] In the nineteenth century, the idea of culture was a conceptual rubric for the emergent disciplines of anthropology, sociology, history, literature, and folklore. It led to "a series of attempts . . . to write something like a totalizing history of social life."[8]

In his "genealogical account of the prehistory of 'the culture concept' in late nineteenth- and early twentieth-century ethnography," Brad Evans cautions that the plural term "'cultures' in its anthropological sense" did not "enter . . . the lexicon with force" until the twentieth century. This was decades after "E. B. Tylor and Franz Boas began . . . to make 'culture' the object of anthropological attention," and more than a century after Johann Gottfried Herder linked the idea of a "culture" to the spirit of a nation's "folk."[9] But by the 1950s, I suggest, culture had become a load-bearing concept: an idea or hypothesis that seemed to generate new thinking by itself.[10] In 1952 sociologists Alfred L. Kroeber and Clyde Kluckhohn cataloged and classified 169 distinct definitions of "culture" on offer in the human sciences, exemplifying at least a dozen different conceptual approaches.[11] Six years later, Raymond Williams published *Culture and Society, 1780–1950* (1958), arguing that the "Arnoldian" idea of culture as a state of mind to strive for through education and self-improvement—an idea that we now associate with school inspector Matthew Arnold—developed in the nineteenth and twentieth centuries as a form of protest against modern market society.[12] In the early 1960s, the compound term "oral culture" was born and baptized, most notably by the prolific interdisciplinary scholar Walter Ong.[13] In 1961–62 Ong referred to "oral-aural cultures" in his review of Albert Lord's study of Serbo-Croatian oral tradition, *The Singer of Tales* (1960).[14] In 1962 Ong's onetime tutor, Marshall McLuhan, used "oral culture" in *The Gutenberg Galaxy*, but in a much looser way than did his former student. McLuhan paradoxically described Alexis de Tocqueville (1805–59) as an author "whose literacy was much modified by his oral culture."[15] In 1965 Ong's widely cited essay "Oral Residue in Tudor Prose Style" was published in *Publications of the Modern Language Association of America*, and by the 1970s the idea of oral culture was generating new arguments and research in such fields as history, sociology, folklore, and literary studies.[16] In 1978 Peter Burke published his influential historical study *Popular Culture in Early Modern Europe* (1978). Burke drew on Kroeber and Kluckhohn in defining culture as "'a system of shared meanings, attitudes, and values, and the symbolic forms (performances, artifacts) in which they are expressed or embodied.' Culture in this sense is part of a total way of life."[17] The following year, two decades after publishing *Culture and Society*, Williams looked back on the extraordinary proliferation of studies of culture over the past twenty years and sighed, "[Culture]: I don't know how many times I've wished that I never heard the damned word."[18]

A study of the late twentieth-century development of the compound terms "oral culture" and "popular oral culture" is beyond the scope of *The Invention of the Oral*. Nonetheless, the widespread eighteenth-century reflection on oral discourse, oral tradition, and oral practices that I have identified and analyzed in this book is, I believe, a key phase in the development (or "prehistory") of these concepts. Today, most of the stories that scholars tell about the development of the culture concept begin at the *end* of the eighteenth century. Raymond Williams's story begins in 1780, and many textbooks and anthologies in anthropology, cultural studies, and other areas of inquiry state briefly that the culture concept originated with the writings of Johann Gottfried Herder (1744–1803), before moving on to more modern terrain. But throughout the eighteenth century, I have shown, one finds protoethnographers, anthropologists, and theorists of what we would now call "oral culture." The term dates to the 1960s, but the idea long preexisted the term. To trace the historical development of an abstract concept of the "oral" has required us to identify and analyze embryonic ideas as well as explicit statements. (Literary texts, in particular, seldom work by explicit statement.) The risk of anachronism is the high price of historical understanding. But at the very least, I hope that we have learned much about the eighteenth-century creative invention of the category of the oral and about "orality" as a back-formation of print.

All italic text in quotations is original unless otherwise noted.

INTRODUCTION

1. The publication history of the *Dunciad* is notorious: writing and printing different versions of the poem preoccupied Pope for nearly half his life. I am quoting here from Alexander Pope, *The Dunciad in Four Books* (1743), ed. Valerie Rumbold (New York: Longman, 1999), bk. 4, ll. 23–26. Unless otherwise specified, further references to the *Dunciad* are to this edition and will be cited parenthetically by book and line number.

2. Nicholas Hudson, "*O Divinum Scripturae Beneficium*! Swift's Satire of Writing and Its Intellectual Context," in *The Age of Johnson: A Scholarly Annual*, vol. 7, ed. Paul J. Korshin (New York: AMS Press, 1996), 343–63, here 358. In *Writing and European Thought, 1600–1830* (Cambridge: Cambridge University Press, 1994) and a series of related articles that I cite throughout this book, Hudson has discussed the disenchantment of the "European literati" with modern, literate culture. See, e.g., Nicholas Hudson, "Constructing Oral Tradition: The Origins of the Concept in Enlightenment Intellectual Culture," in *The Spoken Word: Oral Culture in Britain, 1500–1850*, ed. Adam Fox and Daniel R. Woolf (Manchester: Manchester University Press, 2002), 240–55, esp. 250. As writing and literacy became common, many authors developed a new appreciation for the distinctive characteristics of speech. I am indebted to Hudson's scholarship, but my own central concerns and argument are different. In my account, it was not writing in general that unsettled the "literati"; rather, it was the eighteenth-century *commercialization* of writing and the increasingly pluralist literary marketplace ushered in by new institutional arrangements for printing. In addition, whereas Hudson is an intellectual historian who focuses on major "Enlightenment thinkers," I study social and intellectual history in tandem. The relationship *between* different socioeconomic groups—from philosophers to fishwives—is at the center of my story. Finally, for now, whereas Hudson takes concepts like "print culture" and "orality" largely for granted, an important goal of *The Invention of the Oral* is to help historicize these now-naturalized terms and ideas.

3. *Oxford English Dictionary*, *OED Online*, s.v. "fugitive," *n.*, accessed June 2016.

4. Don Herzog, *Poisoning the Minds of the Lower Orders* (Princeton, NJ: Princeton University Press, 1998), x.

5. In an influential essay "Oral Residue in Tudor Prose Style," *PMLA* 80 (1965): 145–54, Walter J. Ong argued that many early modern texts reveal "habits of thought and expression tracing back to preliterate situations or practice, or deriving from the dominance of the oral as a medium in a given culture, or indicating a reluctance or inability to dissociate the written medium from the spoken" (146). These traces of a prior oral culture include direct addresses to the reader, episodic sentences, formulaic structures, and so on. In Ong's model, "residual orality" is properly speaking a *textual* phenomenon. Although this phenomenon can be traced in eighteenth-century texts, that is not my goal in *The Invention of the Oral*. Nor is my subject the textual reconstruction of oral discourse for literary effect. These types of literary orality (to borrow an oxymoron) have already been well discussed by others. See, e.g., Carey McIntosh, *The Evolution of English Prose, 1700–1800: Style, Politeness, and Print Culture* (Cambridge: Cambridge University Press, 1998); Maureen McLane, *Balladeering, Minstrelsy, and the Making of British Romantic Poetry* (Cambridge: Cambridge University Press, 2008); James Mulholland, *Sounding Imperial: Poetic Voice and the Politics of Empire, 1730–1820* (Baltimore: Johns Hopkins University Press, 2013); and Alexis Tadié, *Sterne's Whimsical Theatres of Language: Orality, Gesture, Literacy* (Burlington, VT: Ashgate, 2003).

6. For representative arguments along these lines, see Roger Chartier, *The Culture of Print*, trans. Lydia Cochrane (Princeton: Princeton University Press, 1989); Michael Warner, *The Letters of the Republic: Publication and the Public Sphere in Eighteenth-Century America* (Cambridge, MA: Harvard University Press, 1990); and Adrian Johns, *The Nature of the Book: Print and Knowledge in the Making* (Chicago: University of Chicago Press, 1998). The charge of technological determinism is most often directed at Elizabeth L. Eisenstein's pioneering work *The Printing Press as an Agent of Change: Communications and Cultural Transformation in Early-Modern Europe* (Cambridge: Cambridge University Press, 1979; in 1 vol., 1980). For Eisenstein's spirited rejoinders, see "An Unacknowledged Revolution Revisited," in "How Revolutionary Was the Print Revolution?" forum, *American Historical Review* 107 (2002): 87–105; and *Divine Art, Infernal Machine: The Reception of Printing in the West from First Impressions to the Sense of an Ending* (Philadelphia: University of Pennsylvania Press, 2011). For further discussion, see the essays in Sabrina Alcorn Baron, Eric N. Lindquist, and Eleanor F. Shevlin, eds., *Agent of Change: Print Culture Studies after Elizabeth L. Eisenstein* (Amherst: University of Massachusetts Press, in association with Center for the Book, Library of Congress, 2007), including my own " 'On the Behalf of the Printers': A Late Stuart Printer-Author and Her Causes," 125–39.

7. Johns, *Nature of the Book*, 2.

8. Hudson, for instance, briefly connects changing attitudes toward "oral and written language" to the invention of the printing press. "It was . . . only after Gutenberg," he says, "that scholars gained a strong awareness of the special characteristics of oral and written language" ("Constructing Oral Tradition," 242). But he doesn't suggest what about Gutenberg's invention generated this new awareness. Nor does he especially distinguish between the fifteenth-century invention of the printing press and the dramatic eighteenth-century proliferation of print.

9. Michael Treadwell, "London Printers and Printing Houses in 1705," *Publishing History* 7 (1980): 5–44, esp. 6.

10. For helpful background, see John Feather, *Publishing, Piracy, and Politics: An Historical Study of Copyright in Britain* (London: Marshall, 1994), 50–53, and the works cited there.

11. Elinor James, *To the Honourable House of Commons. Gentlemen, Since You have been pleased to lay such a heavy Tax upon Paper* (n.d., c. 1696–98), in *The Early Modern Englishwoman: Essential Works; Elinor James*, ed. Paula McDowell (Aldershot, UK: Ashgate, 2005), 96–97.

12. For my understanding of the eighteenth-century British book trade, I am indebted to the work of scholars such as Terry Belanger, Maureen Bell, John Feather, David Foxon, Michael Harris, D. F. McKenzie, James Raven, Richard Sher, William St. Clair, and Michael Treadwell (to name only a few). I cite these scholars' works throughout this book, but I also wish to acknowledge a general debt to D. F. McKenzie, David McKitterick, and I. R. Willison, eds., *The Cambridge History of the Book in Britain* (Cambridge: Cambridge University Press, 1999–2011), esp. vol. 4, *1557–1695*, ed. John Barnard and D. F. McKenzie, with the assistance of Maureen Bell (2002), and vol. 5, *1695–1830*, ed. Michael F. Suarez and Michael L. Turner (2009). For concise overviews of key developments between 1695 and 1800, see Terry Belanger, "Publishers and Writers in Eighteenth-Century England," in *Books and Their Readers in Eighteenth-Century England*, ed. Isabel Rivers (New York: St. Martin's Press, 1982), 5–25; and James Raven, "The Book Trades," in *Books and Their Readers in Eighteenth-Century England: New Essays*, ed. Isabel Rivers (New York: Continuum, 2003), 1–34.

13. James Ralph, *The Case of Authors by Profession or Trade, Stated. With Regard to Booksellers, the Stage, and the Public* (London, 1758), 8, 13. Ralph is chiefly concerned with the book trade and the literary marketplace, but he also briefly discusses writing for the stage.

14. The Engravers' Copyright Act, 1734/35, 8 Geo. 2, c. 13, sometimes called Hogarth's Act, protected the rights of engravers and printsellers. On the implications of the Statute of Anne for authors and ideas of authorship, see Mark Rose, *Authors and Owners: The Invention of Copyright* (Cambridge, MA: Harvard University Press, 1993).

15. Ralph, *Case of Authors*, 67.

16. Thomas Percy, ed., *Reliques of Ancient English Poetry: Consisting of Old Heroic Ballads, Songs, and Other Pieces of Our Earlier Poets, Together With Some Few of Later Date* (1765), ed. Henry B. Wheatley, 3 vols. (London: Swan Sonnenschein, 1886; repr., New York: Dover, 1966), 1:348, 380.

17. Jonathan Swift, "Apology," in *A Tale of a Tub, and Other Works*, vol. 1 of *The Cambridge Edition of the Works of Jonathan Swift*, ed. Marcus Walsh (Cambridge: Cambridge University Press, 2010), 5.

18. *Oxford English Dictionary, OED Online*, s.v. "invent," *n.*, 1, accessed June 2016.

19. Ibid., s.v. "invention," *n.*, 3b, accessed June 2016.

20. John Dryden, preface to *Annus Mirabilus* (London, 1667).

21. Geoffrey C. Bowker and Susan Leigh Star, *Sorting Things Out: Classification and Its Consequences* (Cambridge, MA: MIT Press, 1999), 10, 287, 13, 34.

22. Peter de Bolla, "New Knowledge as the Goal of Research" (lecture, New York University Department of English, September 2014).

23. See Peter de Bolla, "Mediation and the Division of Labor," in *This Is Enlightenment*, ed. Clifford Siskin and William Warner (Chicago: University of Chicago Press, 2010), esp. 87–90.

24. Herzog, *Poisoning the Minds of the Lower Orders*, x.

25. *Oxford English Dictionary*, OED Online, s.v. "oral," 1. a., 2, accessed June 2016.

26. I quote here from Thomas Blount, *Glossographia: or, A dictionary interpreting all such hard words . . . as are now used in our refined English tongue* (London, 1656). Along similar lines, Nathan Bailey, *Universal Etymological Dictionary* (London, 1721), defines "oral" as "delivered by the Mouth or Voice" (s.v. "oral").

27. *Hale's Comm. Laws of Eng.*, quoted in Samuel Johnson, *A Dictionary of the English Language*, 2 vols. (London, 1755), s.v. "orally."

28. *Coriolanus*, act 2, scene 1.

29. These are indeed "modern concepts." Of the long list of compound terms in the *Oxford English Dictionary* under "oral," the only one in use in the eighteenth century was "oral law" (referring to the Jewish notion of the Oral Torah, an idea I discuss later in this book).

30. Adam Fox and Daniel R. Woolf helpfully define "oral culture" as "a collection of communicative habits and practices, premised on primarily face-to-face viva voce communication, and occurring within a variety of contexts," and as "the aggregate of those things which are communicated orally in a specific social, linguistic and geographic setting, together with the vocal means by which they are communicated" (*Spoken Word*, 11–12).

31. Mary Poovey, *A History of the Modern Fact: Problems of Knowledge in the Sciences of Wealth and Society* (Chicago: University of Chicago Press, 1998), 20, 25.

32. Adapting Johannes Fabian, *Time and the Other: How Anthropology Makes Its Object* (1983; repr., New York: Columbia University Press, 2002), 18.

33. The full title of Walter J. Ong's work is *Ramus, Method, and the Decay of Dialogue: From the Art of Discourse to the Art of Reason* (Cambridge, MA: Harvard University Press, 1958; repr., Chicago: University of Chicago Press, 2004).

34. Eric A. Havelock, "The Oral-Literate Equation: A Formula for the Modern Mind," in *Literacy and Orality*, ed. David R. Olson and Nancy Torrance (Cambridge: Cambridge University Press, 1991), 11–27. Havelock suggests that this flurry of works on "orality and literacy" reflected "a common and widespread response . . . to a shared experience of a technological revolution in the means of human communication. . . . Radio, not to mention its immediate predecessor, the telephone, and its successor, television, was transforming the reach of the spoken, that is, of the oral word" (12).

35. McLuhan's reflections on "print culture" were triggered not only by new scholarship on "orality" but also by technologies such as the telephone, radio, and television that were changing the reach of "oral" discourse. But McLuhan was not the first to use "print culture." See, e.g., Gilbert Seldes, *The Public Arts* (New York: Simon and Schuster, 1956; New Brunswick, NJ: Transaction, 1994), 230–31.

36. From today's vantage point, it is difficult to imagine doing work in this area without the invaluable research of pioneering publishing historians such as Terry Belanger, John Feather, David Foxon, D. F. McKenzie, Michael Treadwell, and others I mention in n. 12.

37. Marshall McLuhan, *The Gutenberg Galaxy: The Making of Typographic Man* (Toronto: University of Toronto Press, 1962), 255.

38. Walter J. Ong, *The Presence of the Word: Some Prolegomena for Cultural and Religious History* (New Haven, CT: Yale University Press, 1967; repr., Minneapolis: University of Minnesota Press, 1981), 17.

39. In chapter 8, I trace stadial models of human history to the eighteenth century and suggest that one way eighteenth-century authors conceptualized differences between peoples and societies was according to their "arts of transmission"—a concept similar but not identical to our modern idea of "modes of communication."

40. In "An Interview with Walter J. Ong Conducted by George Reimer," Ong used the phrase "writing-and-print culture." See Thomas J. Farrell and Paul A. Soukup, eds., *An Ong Reader: Challenges for Further Inquiry* (Creskill, NJ: Hampton Press, 2002), 91.

41. For a bibliography of Ong's works, see Farrell and Soukup, *Ong Reader*. I discuss Ong's notion of orality as a mode of consciousness in "Ong and the Concept of Orality," *Religion and Literature* 44 (2012): 169–78.

42. For Ong's definitions of these terms, see Walter J. Ong, *Orality and Literacy: The Technologizing of the Word* (London: Methuen, 1982; repr., London: Routledge, 2002), 1–3.

43. Ong was a Jesuit priest, but ironically, by attending to the etymology of one of his key concepts, "orality," we can see that the concept of oral tradition that he inherited from theorists living in the latter part of the eighteenth century in fact represented a secularization of the earlier theological context of these debates. For this argument see McDowell, "Ong and the Concept of Orality."

44. Swift, *A Tale of a Tub*, 129.

45. Daniel Defoe, *A Journal of the Plague Year* (1722), ed. Paula R. Backscheider (New York: Norton, 1992), 5.

46. Even the decibel, the unit of measurement of sound, is itself a dimensionless unit that expresses a ratio of quantities rather than an absolute.

47. For an overview of recent work in soundscape studies and sensory history, see Mark M. Smith, "Producing Sense, Consuming Sense, Making Sense: Perils and Prospects for Sensory History," *Journal of Social History* 40 (2007): 841–58. I have especially benefited from Bruce R. Smith, *The Acoustic World of Early Modern England: Attending to the O-Factor* (Chicago: University of Chicago Press, 1999); Richard Cullen Rath, *How Early America Sounded* (Ithaca, NY: Cornell University Press, 2003); and Leigh Eric Schmidt, *Hearing Things: Religion, Illusion, and the American Enlightenment* (Cambridge, MA: Harvard University Press, 2000).

48. Thomas Sheridan, *A Course of Lectures on Elocution: Together With Two Dissertations on Language; And Some Other Tracts Relative to Those Subjects* (1762) (New York: Benjamin Blom, 1968), xii.

49. Joseph Addison and Richard Steele, *Spectator* 247 (13 December 1711), in *The Spectator*, ed. Donald F. Bond, 5 vols. (Oxford: Clarendon, 1965), 2:458.

50. Ethnography (from Greek *ethnos*, "people" or "nation" + *graphein*, "writing") is a genre of writing, based on fieldwork, that describes human social phenomena. The term "ethnography" was coined in the nineteenth century with the emergence of the modern discipline of anthropology; the term "fieldwork," in the sense of practical versus theoretical

research, is an even more recent coinage. Yet historians, travel writers, and others have been producing descriptions of other peoples ostensibly based on participant observation since at least Herodotus, and nineteenth- and twentieth-century ethnographies were influenced by prior writings long predating their own defining concepts and terms. The first recorded use of the term "fieldwork" dates to the eighteenth century, where it was used in the context of surveying land, and even today the term retains overtones of research done beyond the confines of urban centers and modern commercial society. But as we shall see, eighteenth-century literary authors often sent their narrators into, rather than out of, the heart of Britain's largest cities (especially London) for their protoethnographic descriptions of "others."

51. Thomas Percy, ed., *Reliques of Ancient English Poetry: Consisting of Old Heroic Ballads, Songs, and Other Pieces of Our Earlier Poets, Together With Some Few of Later Date* (1765), ed. Henry B. Wheatley, 3 vols. (London: Swan Sonnenschein, 1886; repr., New York: Dover, 1966), "An Essay on the Ancient Minstrels in England," 1:345–81, here 348.

52. Sir William Temple, *An Essay Upon the Ancient and Modern Learning* (1690), in *Sir William Temple's Essays on Ancient and Modern Learning and on Poetry*, ed. J. E. Spingarn (Oxford: Clarendon, 1909), 1–42, here 6.

53. Hugh Blair, *A Critical Dissertation on the Poems of Ossian, The Son of Fingal* (1763), in *The Poems of Ossian and Related Works*, ed. Howard Gaskill (Edinburgh: Edinburgh University Press, 1996), 345–408, here 406.

54. Ibid., 353.

55. Fabian, *Time and the Other*, 17. Fabian calls the "denial of coevalness" a "constitutive phenomenon" of the modern discipline of anthropology (Matti Bunzl, foreword to ibid., xi).

56. Dugald Stewart, *Account of the Life and Writings of Adam Smith* (1793), in *Collected Works*, ed. Sir William Hamilton, 11 vols. (Edinburgh: Thomas Constable, 1854–60), 10:1–98, here 54.

57. Kathleen Stewart, "Nostalgia—a Polemic," *Cultural Anthropology* 3 (1988): 227–41, here 227–28. In thinking about nostalgia as a means of coming to terms with perceived discontinuity, I have also especially benefited from Svetlana Boym, *The Future of Nostalgia* (New York: Basic Books, 2001); Nicholas Dames, "Austen's Nostalgics," *Representations* 73 (2001): 117–43; and Susan Stewart, *Crimes of Writing: Problems in the Containment of Representation* (Oxford: Oxford University Press, 1991).

CHAPTER ONE

1. William Blake, *The Complete Poetry and Prose of William Blake*, rev. ed., ed. David V. Erdman (Berkeley: University of California Press, 1981), 39–40.

2. "A Calculation of the Credibility of Human Testimony," *Philosophical Transactions of the Royal Society* 21 (1699): 359–65, here 363–64.

3. "A Calculation" has also been attributed to George Hooper, later bishop of Bath and Wells; for a suggestive but inconclusive case, see A. I. Dale, "On the Authorship of 'A Calculation of the Credibility of Human Testimony,'" *Historia Mathematica* 19 (1992): 414–17. It is not materially important to my argument which member of the Royal

Society wrote this text; in fact, my point is that there was a growing network of scholars, clergymen, poets, and philosophers among whom the question of "oral tradition" was widely addressed.

4. Edward Shils, *Tradition* (Chicago: University of Chicago Press, 1981), 12.

5. *Oxford English Dictionary*, OED Online, s.v. "tradition," accessed June 2016.

6. Mark Salber Phillips, "What Is Tradition When It Is Not 'Invented'? An Historiographical Introduction," in *Questions of Tradition*, ed. Mark Salber Phillips and Gordon Schochet (Toronto: University of Toronto Press, 2004), 3–29, here 11. On tradition in religious thought, see also Yves Congar, *Tradition and Traditions: An Historical and Theological Essay*, trans. Michael Naseby and T. Rainborough (London: Burns and Oates, 1966); Jaroslav Pelikan, *The Christian Tradition: A History of the Development of Doctrine*, 5 vols. (Chicago: University of Chicago Press, 1971–89); and Jacob Neusner, *Oral Tradition in Judaism: The Case of the Mishnah* (New York: Garland, 1987).

7. John Sergeant, *A Letter of Thanks from the author of Sure-Footing to his answerer Mr. J[ohn] T[illotson]* (Paris, 1666), 37.

8. Marcus Walsh, "Text, 'Text,' and Swift's *A Tale of a Tub*," *Modern Language Review* 85 (1990): 290–303, here 295.

9. Alexandra Walsham, "Reformed Folklore? Cautionary Tales and Oral Tradition in Early Modern England," in *The Spoken Word: Oral Culture in Britain, 1500–1850*, ed. Adam Fox and Daniel R. Woolf (Manchester: Manchester University Press, 2002), 175.

10. Early modern authors used the term "mediation" "in reference to divine and human intercession." See Clifford Siskin and William B. Warner, eds., *This Is Enlightenment* (Chicago: University of Chicago Press, 2010), 6. The most important example was that of Jesus Christ as a mediator between God and humanity. For my argument that in the Enlightenment, debates about tradition were the dominant discourse about what we would now call "media," "mediation," and "communication," see Paula McDowell, "Defoe's *Essay upon Literature* and Eighteenth-Century Histories of Mediation," *PMLA* 130, no. 3 (May 2015): 566–83.

11. Phillips, "What Is Tradition?," 14.

12. Francis Bacon, *Francis Bacon*, ed. Brian Vickers (Oxford: Oxford University Press, 1996), 230. I have benefited from John Guillory's discussion of this passage in "The Memo and Modernity," *Critical Inquiry* 31 (2004): 108–32, esp. 108–9; and in "Enlightening Mediation," in Siskin and Warner, *This Is Enlightenment*, 37–63, esp. 40–41.

13. *Oxford English Dictionary*, OED Online, s.v. "organ," accessed June 2016.

14. Samuel Johnson, *A Dictionary of the English Language*, 2 vols. (London, 1755), s.v. "tradition," my emphasis.

15. David Hume published *Philosophical Essays Concerning Human Understanding* in 1748 and retitled it *An Enquiry concerning Human Understanding* in 1756.

16. See D. R. Woolf, *The Social Circulation of the Past: English Historical Culture, 1500–1730* (Oxford: Oxford University Press, 2003), esp. 352–91.

17. John Brand, *Observations on Popular Antiquities* (Newcastle upon Tyne, 1777), preface, iv.

18. John Aubrey, preface to *Remaines of Gentilisme and Judaisme*, in *Three Prose Works*, ed. John Buchanan-Brown (Carbondale: Southern Illinois University Press, 1972), 132.

19. Ibid., 290.

20. John Locke, *Some Thoughts Concerning Education* (1693), ed. John W. Yolton and Jean S. Yolton (Oxford: Clarendon, 1989), 196, 245–46.

21. Joseph Addison, *Spectator* 12 (14 March 1711). All quotations from the *Spectator* are from Donald F. Bond, ed., *The Spectator*, 5 vols. (Oxford: Clarendon, 1965). This paper appears at 1:52–55, and these quotations at 53 and 54 respectively.

22. Walsh, "Text, 'Text,' and Swift's *A Tale of a Tub*," 291.

23. See, e.g., [John Gother], *An Agreement Between the Church of England and the Church of Rome* (London, 1687). Gother's frequently reprinted text *A Papist Misrepresented and represented* (1685), to which Edward Stillingfleet and other eminent Anglican divines responded, was published under the pseudonym J.L[ovell].

24. The full title of Stillingfleet's work is *Origines Sacrae, Or A Rational Account of the Grounds of Christian Faith. As to the Truth and Divine Authority of the Scriptures, And the matters therein contained* (1662). See also Stillingfleet's *A Rational Account of the Grounds of Protestant Religion* (1664/65).

25. Stillingfleet, *Origines Sacrae*, contents page. Stillingfleet's text has rightly been described as "a work with large sections on the history of writing." See Nicholas Hudson, *Writing and European Thought, 1600–1830* (Cambridge: Cambridge University Press, 1994), 36. But the breadth of Stillingfleet's interests in diverse modes of transmission suggests the potential greater usefulness of a broader rubric of "histories of mediation." For this argument, see McDowell, "Defoe's *Essay upon Literature* and Eighteenth-Century Histories of Mediation."

26. J[ohn] Sergeant, *Sure-Footing in Christianity, Or, Rational Discourses On The Rule of Faith*, 2nd ed. (London, 1665), 41, quoted in Sergeant, *Letter of Thanks*, 38.

27. Sergeant, *Letter of Thanks*, 108. See also *Oxford English Dictionary, OED Online*, s.v. "orality," *n.*, accessed June 2016.

28. Sergeant, *Letter of Thanks*, 38.

29. Sergeant, *Sure-Footing*, 202.

30. Ibid., 137.

31. Alison Shell, *Catholicism, Controversy, and the English Literary Imagination, 1558–1660* (Cambridge: Cambridge University Press, 1999), 162. See also Beverly C. Southgate, "Blackloism and Tradition: From Theological Certainty to Historiographical Doubt," *Journal of the History of Ideas* 61 (2000): 97–114.

32. Sergeant, *Letter of Thanks*, 108.

33. Edward Stillingfleet, *Scripture and Tradition compared in a sermon preached at Guild-Hall Chapel, Novemb. 27, 1687* (1688).

34. Jonathan Sheehan, *The Enlightenment Bible: Translation, Scholarship, Culture* (Princeton, NJ: Princeton University Press, 2005), 3–4, my emphasis.

35. Shell, *Catholicism*, 157.

36. Joseph M. Levine, "From Tradition to History: Chillingworth to Gibbon," in *Historians and Ideologues: Essays in Honor of Donald R. Kelley*, ed. Anthony T. Grafton and J. H. M. Salmon (Rochester, NY: University of Rochester Press, 2001), 181–210, here 199, 194, 200–201.

37. John Milton, *Paradise Lost*, bk. 12, ll. 508–14. In its 1667 edition, *Paradise Lost* was divided into ten books; Milton redivided it into twelve books in the second edition of 1674.

38. John Dryden, *Religio Laici* (1682), in *The Works of John Dryden*, ed. H. T. Swedenberg et al., 20 vols. (Berkeley: University of California Press, 1956–2000), vol. 2, *Poems, 1681–1684*, ed. Vinton A. Dearing (Berkeley: University of California Press, 1972), ll. 270–73.

39. Ibid., ll. 228, 350–51, 417, 400–405.

40. John Dryden, *The Hind and the Panther* (1687), in Swedenberg et al., *Works of John Dryden*, vol. 3, *Poems, 1685–1692*, ed. Earl Miner (Berkeley: University of California Press, 1969), pt. 1, l. 1; pt. 2, l. 167.

41. *An Enquiry Whether Oral Tradition Or The Sacred Writings, Be the Safest Conservatory and Conveyance Of Divine Truths* (printed by Robert Clavel, 1685), preface, A6v–A7r, and p. 11.

42. Ibid., A4r–v, 106.

43. Ibid., 215–16.

44. Ibid.

45. Ibid., 11, 161–62, 11, 14, 21–22.

46. Stephen Prickett, *Modernity and the Reinvention of Tradition: Backing into the Future* (Cambridge: Cambridge University Press, 2009), 49. See also Neusner, *Oral Tradition in Judaism*.

47. *An Enquiry*, 58.

48. John Henley, *Oratory Transactions* 1 (1728): 28.

49. David Hume, *An Enquiry concerning Human Understanding*, ed. T. L. Beauchamp (Oxford: Clarendon, 2000), sec. 10, "Of Miracles," 97, 88, 97–98.

50. Ibid., 83–84.

51. Andrew I. Dale, "Craig, John (c.1663–1731)," in *Oxford Dictionary of National Biography*, online ed., ed. David Cannadine (Oxford: Oxford University Press, 2004), accessed 30 June 2016, http://www.oxforddnb.com/view/article/6577; see also Hume, *Enquiry concerning Human Understanding*, 171n85, section 23.

52. David Hume, *The History of England* (1778), rev. ed., 6 vols. (Indianapolis: Liberty Fund, 1983), 1:3.

53. D. R. Woolf, "The 'Common Voice': History, Folklore and Oral Tradition in Early Modern England," *Past and Present* 120 (1988): 26–52, here 39–40; and Walsham, "Reformed Folklore?," 178.

54. Woolf, "'Common Voice,'" 39.

55. Gilbert Burnet, *Some Passages of the Life and Death of . . . John, Earl of Rochester* (1680), 74, quoted in Woolf, "'Common Voice,'" 39–40.

56. Matthew Hale, *The History and Analysis of the Common Law of England* (1713), 1–2.

57. By the first Statute of Westminster, "before time of memory" was declared to be anything before the reign of Richard I, which began on 6 July 1189.

58. Nicholas Hudson, "'Oral Tradition': The Evolution of an Eighteenth-Century Concept," in *Tradition in Transition: Women Writers, Marginal Texts, and the Eighteenth-Century Canon*, ed. Alvaro Ribeiro and James Basker (Oxford: Oxford University Press, 1996), 161–76, here 162.

59. On the ideology of the "Ancient Constitution," see J. G. A. Pocock, *The Ancient Constitution and the Feudal Law: A Study of English Historical Thought in the*

Seventeenth Century (1957; repr., Cambridge: Cambridge University Press, 1987); and J. G. A. Pocock, *The Machiavellian Moment: Florentine Political Thought and the Atlantic Republican Tradition* (Princeton, NJ: Princeton University Press, 1975), 333–60, quotation on 341.

60. Pocock briefly but intriguingly compares this ideology, and appeals to "customary" laws in general, to aspects of late eighteenth- and nineteenth-century European Romanticism. He suggests that the "myths" created by proponents of these ideologies "derived . . . national laws not only from legendary and heroic times, but also from the primitive and inarticulate wisdom of the folk, expressed in age-old custom" (Pocock, *Ancient Constitution*, 19).

61. Walsham, "Reformed Folklore?," 178.

62. Richard M. Dorson, *The British Folklorists: A History* (Chicago: University of Chicago Press, 1968), 3.

63. Woolf, *Social Circulation*, 360, 353, 357.

64. Ibid., 377.

65. John Selden, *Table-talk, being the discourses of John Selden, Esq (1689)*, ed. R. Milward (London: J. M. Dent, 1906), 93, 153, 155.

66. Aubrey, preface to *Remaines of Gentilisme and Judaisme*, 132.

67. Aubrey, *Remaines of Gentilisme and Judaisme*, 290.

68. On Defoe's "filching" from previous printed sources, see Pat Rogers, *The Text of Great Britain: Theme and Design in Defoe's "Tour"* (Newark: University of Delaware Press, 1998), 114.

69. James Howell, *Instructions for Forreine Travell* (1642), 7.

70. Daniel Defoe, *The Great Law of Subordination Consider'd* (1724), 46–47.

71. Rogers, *Text of Great Britain*, 165; and John Glendening, *The High Road: Romantic Tourism, Scotland, and Literature, 1720–1820* (New York: St. Martin's Press, 1997), 32.

72. Daniel Defoe, *A Tour thro' the Whole Island of Great Britain*, vols. 1–3 of *Travel and Historical Writings of Daniel Defoe*, ed. John McVeagh (London: Pickering and Chatto, 2001), 2:11, my emphasis.

73. Laura Gowing, *Domestic Dangers: Women, Words, and Sex in Early Modern London* (Oxford: Clarendon, 1996), 50.

74. *Oxford English Dictionary, OED Online*, s.v. "old wife," 1. b., accessed June 2016.

75. Plato, *Republic* 2.377-78.a–d. This passage can be found in the Loeb Classical Library print edition of *The Republic*, ed. and trans. Chris Emlyn-Jones and William Preddy (Cambridge, MA: Harvard University Press, 2013), vol. 1, pp. 192–95.

76. Men could also be accused of telling "old wives' tales." As we shall see in chapter 3, when Defoe critiques *men* for superstitious oral tale-telling, he accuses them of being "old women too."

77. Defoe, *Tour*, 3:120.

78. Woolf, *Social Circulation*, 361.

79. Daniel Defoe, *The Political History of the Devil* (1726), 332–33.

80. Daniel Defoe, *A System of Magick; or, A History of the Black Art* (London: J. Roberts, 1727), 225.

81. Defoe, *Political History of the Devil*, 333.

82. Defoe, *Tour*, 3:139.

83. See Lorraine Daston and Katherine Park, *Wonders and the Order of Nature, 1150–1750* (New York: Zone Books, 2001), 343–50, here 343.

84. Henry Bourne, *Antiquitates Vulgares* (Newcastle-upon-Tyne: J. White, 1725), passim.

85. Walsham, "Reformed Folklore?," 178–79.

86. Dorson, *British Folklorists*, 13.

87. Brand, *Observations on Popular Antiquities* (1777), preface, iv.

88. Ibid.

89. Ibid.

90. Johann Gottfried Herder's "Auszug aus einem Briefwechsel über Ossian und die Lieder alter Völker," familiarly known as "Essay on Ossian," was written in 1771 and published as a contribution to his *Von deutscher Art und Kunst* [Of German art and kind/nature] (Hamburg, 1773).

91. Dorson, *British Folklorists*, 91.

92. Prickett, *Modernity*, 129, 110.

93. Johann Gottfried Herder, *Sämtliche Werke*, ed. Bernhard Suphan et al., 33 vols. (1877–1913; repr., Hildesheim: Georg Olms, 1967), 25:323. This translation is Robert T. Clark's in *Herder: His Life and Thought* (Berkeley: University of California Press, 1955), 259.

94. See John Brand, *Observations on Popular Antiquities: Chiefly Illustrating the Origin of Our Vulgar Customs, Ceremonies, and Superstitions. Arranged and revised, with additions, by Henry Ellis*, 2 vols. (London, 1813).

95. Dorson, *British Folklorists*, 10.

96. William J. Thoms, "Folklore," *Athenaeum*, 22 August 1846, 862–63.

97. Locke, *Some Thoughts Concerning Education*, 245–46, 196.

98. Persius, *Satires* 5.92, quoted in Addison and Steele, *Spectator* 12 (14 March 1711), in Bond, *Spectator*, 1:52–55; these quotations appear at 54 and 53–54 respectively.

99. Wollstonecraft's *Elements of Morality* is a loose translation of Christian Gotthilf Salzmann, *Moralisches Elementarbuch* (1783; Leipzig: Siegfried Lebrecht Crusius, 1785).

100. Maria Edgeworth and Richard Lovell Edgeworth, *Practical Education*, 2 vols. (London, 1798), 611–13.

101. Hannah More, "Tawney Rachel, Or, The Fortune Teller: With Some Account of Dreams, Omens, and Conjurors," in *The Works of Hannah More*, 18 vols. (London, 1818), 5:448–71, 14.

102. Phillips, "What Is Tradition?," 3–29, here 3 and 14.

103. Raymond Williams, *Keywords: A Vocabulary of Culture and Society*, rev. ed. (New York: Oxford University Press, 1983), "Tradition," pp. 318–20 (originally published 1976).

CHAPTER TWO

1. *A Tale of a Tub* (1704) was bound and paged consecutively in one volume with *Battel of the Books* and *Mechanical Operation of the Spirit*. The list of "Treatises" was originally printed facing the title page but later moved to the title page recto. All quotations (with the single exception of this one, where I am quoting from the list of "Treatises

writ" shown in fig. 2.1) are from *A Tale of a Tub, and Other Works*, vol. 1 of *The Cambridge Edition of the Works of Jonathan Swift*, ed. Marcus Walsh (Cambridge: Cambridge University Press, 2010), where the list of "Treatises" appears on p. 4.

2. Swift's modern editors appear to have reached a consensus that "there is nothing to show that [these statements] are not substantially correct." *"A Tale of a Tub" to Which Is Added "The Battle of the Books" and the "Mechanical Operation of the Spirit,"* ed. A. C. Guthkelch and D. Nichol Smith, 2nd ed. (Oxford: Clarendon, 1958), xliii.

3. I take the "Bookseller" figure to be part of "the theatre of obfuscation with which Swift surrounded the *Tale*" (xxxii).

4. The "Preface" also mentions "the Tax upon Paper" (28), that is, "An Act for granting to His Majesty several Duties upon Paper Vellum and Parchment," May 1697, 8 & 9 Will. 3, c. 2.

5. The "Apology" itself is dated "June 3. 1709" (14).

6. I understand the adjective "Grub Street" to be a rhetorical term of abuse, not a transparent classification. For the purpose of entering into the spirit of Scriblerian satire, however, I usually use "Grub Street" without quotation marks. For a further polemical discussion of these terms, see my *The Women of Grub Street: Press, Politics, and Gender in the London Literary Marketplace, 1678–1730* (Oxford: Clarendon, 1998).

7. Furthermore, England was not at peace in August 1697 (when the "Preface" is dated). Some Swift scholars suggest that this is a proleptic reference to the peace established by the Treaty of Ryswick (signed 20 September 1697), which ended England's involvement in the Nine Years' War.

8. See Michael Treadwell, "Swift's Relations with the London Book Trade to 1714," in *Author/Publisher Relations during the Eighteenth and Nineteenth Centuries*, ed. Robin Myers and Michael Harris (Oxford: Oxford Polytechnic Press, 1983), 1–36.

9. Edward W. Said, *The World, the Text, and the Critic* (Cambridge, MA: Harvard University Press, 1983), 78.

10. Pat Rogers, *Grub Street: Studies in a Subculture* (London: Methuen, 1972), 98–99.

11. Eighteenth-century authors from Joseph Addison to Jane Austen take positions on the issue of "delivery" in the church; see my discussion in chapters 4 and 5.

12. There are three different sets of notes in the 5th ed. (1710) of the *Tale*: (*i*) the marginal notes included from the earliest editions, (*ii*) a set of notes that is unsigned but almost certainly by Swift himself, and (*iii*) a set of notes signed "W. Wotton" but placed there by Swift as "a humorous revenge on the *Tale's* chief critic" (Guthkelch and Smith, *"A Tale of a Tub,"* xxv).

13. See figure 2.4, "The *Pulpit*, the *Ladder*, and the *Stage-Itinerant*," discussed later in this chapter.

14. John Locke, *Two Treatises of Government*, ed. Peter Laslett (Cambridge: Cambridge University Press, 1988), preface, 138.

15. As we shall see in chapter 4, even John "Orator" Henley, who was charged with using his "gilt Tub" to attack the Church of England and "alienate the minds of his Majesty's subjects," defended his own aggressively politicized sermons by declaring that "ye Pulpit has allways been a Warlike place" (BL Add. MSS 10346, fol. 379, n.d.).

16. William Hogarth's *The Idle 'Prentice Executed at Tyburn*, plate 11 of the series "Industry and Idleness," shows a condemned man in a cart on his way to the gallows,

accompanied by a gesticulating Dissenting preacher. A female hawker in the center foreground is crying printed copies of the condemned man's "Last Dying Speech" even before he is dead. For this engraving, which I discuss in detail in chapter 5, see figure 5.1.

17. On Swift and "vagabond entertainments" such as the performances of mountebanks, see Hugh Ormsby-Lennon, *Hey Presto! Swift and the Quacks* (Newark: University of Delaware Press, 2011); and Ormsby-Lennon's earlier articles cited there.

18. Recent revisionary considerations of oral discourse emphasize the materiality of sound and speech. See, e.g., Bruce R. Smith, *The Acoustic World of Early Modern England: Attending to the O-Factor* (Chicago: University of Chicago Press, 1999); and Leigh Eric Schmidt, *Hearing Things: Religion, Illusion, and the American Enlightenment* (Cambridge, MA: Harvard University Press, 2000).

19. In a more accurate translation: "For we must confess that voice and sound also / Have bodies, since they strike upon the senses." T. Lucretius Carus, *On the Nature of the Universe (De rerum natura)*, trans. Ronald Melville (New York: Oxford University Press, 2008), bk. 4, ll. 527–28, pp. 115–16.

20. Ibid., ll. 533–34, 540–41, p. 116.

21. Francis Bacon, *Sylva Sylvarum*, in *The Works of Francis Bacon*, ed. James Spedding, Robert Leslie Ellis, and Douglas Denon Heath (London: Longman, 1857–74), vol. 2, Century III, par. 114, p. 389.

22. Ibid., par. 205, p. 415.

23. Alexander Pope may similarly have found satiric inspiration in Boyle's *General History of Air*. Compare Boyle's "Of Clouds, Mists and Fogs" (chap. 9), for instance, to Pope's representation of the "fog" of Queen Dulness in the *Dunciad*.

24. Robert Boyle, *A Continuation of New Experiments Physico-Mechanical, Touching the Spring and Weight of the Air, and their Effects* (London, 1669), pt. 1, 49. Boyle's works describing his experiments with air are also echoed in Swift's representation of the AEolists (discussed below).

25. William Wotton, *Reflections Upon Ancient and Modern Learning* (1694), 179.

26. Narcissus Marsh, "An introductory Essay to the doctrine of Sounds, containing some proposals for the improvement of Acousticks," *Philosophical Transactions of the Royal Society* 14 (1684): 472–88. On Swift and Marsh, see Edward W. Rosenheim, *Swift and the Satirist's Art* (Chicago: University of Chicago Press, 1963), 74–75.

27. Marsh, "An introductory Essay," 488 and fig. 2 (the "*Phonical* Sphear").

28. Boyle, *Continuation of New Experiments*, pt. 1, 43.

29. The movement of words up or down to reach different sectors of the theater audience in Swift's satire also recalls the movement of water up and down in a suction pump in Boyle's experiments.

30. Pamphlets, newspapers, and broadsides are often grouped together as "ephemera," but in Swift's satire, the ephemerality of a work is not a function of its physical size. Weighty folios can be as ephemeral as pamphlets. In a jab at John Dryden, Swift proposes in "Epistle Dedicatory, To His Royal Highness Prince Posterity" that the poet's lavishly produced folio translation of Virgil, published only a few months earlier, had already (nearly) disappeared: "I do therefore affirm upon the Word of a sincere Man, that there is now actually in being, a certain Poet called *John Dryden*, whose Translation of *Virgil* was lately printed in a large Folio, well bound, and if diligent search were made, for ought I

know, is yet to be seen." Dryden's *Virgil* was published in July 1697. Not coincidentally, Swift explicitly dates his "Epistle" "Decemb. 1697," driving home his joke concerning the ephemerality of Dryden's work.

On Swift's role in constructing the modern category of "ephemera," see Paula Mc-Dowell, "Of Grubs and Other Insects: Constructing the Categories of 'Literature' and 'Ephemera' in Eighteenth-Century British Writing," *Book History* 15 (2012): 48–70.

31. See Jacob Neusner, *Oral Tradition in Judaism: The Case of the Mishnah* (New York: Garland, 1987).

32. Swift's jab at contemporary "*Female* Priests" need not be limited to the Quakers. As I have discussed in "Enlightenment Enthusiasms and the Spectacular Failure of the Philadelphian Society," *Eighteenth-Century Studies* 35 (2002): 515–33, the period of the genesis and publication of the *Tale* was also the heyday of the London-based Philadelphian Society, whose spiritual leader, Jane Lead, published her three-volume spiritual diary in 1696–97 (the same years that Swift was drafting the *Tale*).

33. 1 W. & M., c. 18.

34. In Miguel de Cervantes's *Don Quixote* (Madrid, 1605), two aldermen bray to recover a lost ass (pt. 2, chap. 25); later, Sancho demonstrates his own technique (chap. 27).

35. Re "*Soporiferous* Medicine," readers of Pope's *Dunciad* may recognize a similar pattern of imagery wherein braying authors and Dissenting preachers alike induce drowsiness and sleep. Pope represents bad writing and forms of threatening oral discourse as a kind of "Noise" that dulls, rather than awakens, the consciousness. These textual and oral performances envelop readers and hearers in a fog of "Dulness," so that they can't—or won't—use their brains.

36. Cf. the similar critique in various *Spectator* and *Tatler* papers on different types of plays: Addison and Steele too set up a dichotomy of shallow appeals to "ears" and "eyes" versus thoughtful appeals to the intellect.

37. On the critique of enthusiasm as a "class rhetoric," see Clement Hawes, *Mania and Literary Style: The Rhetoric of Enthusiasm from the Ranters to Christopher Smart* (Cambridge: Cambridge University Press, 1996). In the writings of critics such as Swift, Hawes suggests, "'enthusiasm' . . . is the profoundly ambivalent signifier of two revolutions: the bourgeois revolution that did occur and the far more democratic and egalitarian revolution whose possibility was tantalizingly glimpsed and then suppressed" (2).

38. Irvin Ehrenpreis, *Swift: The Man, His Works, and the Age*, 3 vols. (Cambridge, MA: Harvard University Press, 1962), 1:201. In *Battel of the Books*, the spider and bee each have their own distinctive dialect. When the bee gets tangled in the spider's net, destroying his labor, the spider "stormed and swore like a Mad-man. . . . *A Plague split you . . . for a giddy Son of a Whore; Is it you, with a Vengeance, that have made this Litter here? Could you not look before you, and be d——n'd?*" The bee responds to the spider in his polite, yet similarly proverbial way: "I was never in such a confounded Pickle since I was born" (149–50).

39. John Boyle, 5th Earl of Orrery, *Remarks on the Life and Writings of Dr. Jonathan Swift*, 2nd ed., corrected (London, 1752), 21.

40. In addition to the published plates, we know of eight original designs that were inserted in the display copy of the *Tale* owned by Sir Andrew Fountaine. Photographs of

six of these designs survive in the Forster Collection of the Victoria and Albert Museum, F.47.E, box 12.

41. For a parallel set of images in which one preacher puts his audience to sleep while another exacerbates his listeners' dangerous "enthusiasm," see William Hogarth, *The Sleeping Congregation* (1736) and *Credulity, Superstition, and Fanaticism* (1762) (figs. 5.2 and 5.3). Significantly, while *Sleeping Congregation* depicts an Anglican preacher with only a few congregants visible, *Credulity* depicts a "fanatic" Dissenting preacher inspiring a wide variety of (dangerous) responses in a crowded audience.

CHAPTER THREE

1. Daniel Defoe, *A Journal of the Plague Year* (1722), ed. Paula R. Backscheider (New York: Norton, 1992), 5. All further references to this text will be cited parenthetically.

2. Adrian Johns, *The Nature of the Book: Print and Knowledge in the Making* (Chicago: University of Chicago Press, 1998), 2. See also Michael Warner, *The Letters of the Republic: Publication and the Public Sphere in Eighteenth-Century America* (Cambridge, MA: Harvard University Press, 1990), esp. 1–33.

3. Daniel Defoe, *An Essay upon Literature*, in *"A General History of Discoveries and Improvements" (1725–6) and "An Essay upon Literature" (1726)*, ed. P. N. Furbank (London: Pickering, 2001), 227–308, here 301.

4. Daniel Defoe, *The Storm: Or, A Collection of the Most Remarkable Casualties . . . Which Happen'd in the Late Dreadful Tempest* (1704), A2v. In the *Journal*, Defoe foregrounds the way that print seems to live on after "the Author is forgotten in his Grave" when, in a startling moment, H.F. mentions the Dissenters' burial ground in Bunhill Fields and an unidentified voice intrudes into the text to inform us that "the Author of this Journal [i.e., H.F.], lyes buried in that very Ground" (181). Defoe himself would be buried in Bunhill Fields graveyard in 1731.

5. Defoe, *Storm*, A2r.

6. Watson Nicholson, *The Historical Sources of Defoe's "Journal of the Plague Year"* (1919; Port Washington, NY: Kennikat Press, 1966), 52, 82.

7. Frank Bastian, "Defoe's *Journal of the Plague Year* Reconsidered," *Review of English Studies*, n.s., 16 (1965): 151–73, here 163.

8. Michael Harris, *London Newspapers in the Age of Walpole: A Study of the Origins of the Modern English Press* (London: Associated University Presses, 1987), 19.

9. The most influential twentieth-century proponent of the hermeneutic of "orality and literacy" is Walter J. Ong. See, e.g., Walter J. Ong, *Orality and Literacy: The Technologizing of the Word* (London: Methuen, 1982; repr., London: Routledge, 2002); and Thomas J. Farrell and Paul A. Soukup, eds., *An Ong Reader: Challenges for Further Inquiry* (Creskill, NJ: Hampton Press, 2002). However, as I argue throughout *The Invention of the Oral*, this binary model, if not this terminology, was emergent in the eighteenth century and was related to the spread of printing after the lapse of the Licensing Act in 1695.

For representative arguments for and against the view that major shifts of epistemology, cognition, and narration accompanied the so-called shift *from* orality *to* literacy, see

Ong, *Orality and Literacy*; Farrell and Soukup, *Ong Reader*; Jack Goody, *The Domestication of the Savage Mind* (Cambridge: Cambridge University Press, 1977); Jack Goody, *The Interface between the Written and the Oral* (Cambridge: Cambridge University Press, 1987); and Ruth Finnegan, *Literacy and Orality: Studies in the Technology of Communication* (Oxford: Blackwell, 1988). One of my own goals is to contribute toward the historicizing of these evolutionary models of media shift. For representative attempts to move beyond what Finnegan critiques as "Great Divide" theories, see Harvey J. Graff, *The Legacies of Literacy: Continuities and Contradictions in Western Culture and Society* (Bloomington: Indiana University Press, 1987); and Brian V. Street, *Literacy in Theory and Practice* (Cambridge: Cambridge University Press, 1984).

10. Nicholson, *Historical Sources of Defoe's "Journal of the Plague Year,"* 90.

11. Richelle Munkhoff, "Searchers of the Dead: Authority, Marginality, and the Interpretation of the Plague in England, 1574–1665," *Gender and History* 11 (1999): 1–29, here 2. See also Walter George Bell, *The Great Plague in London in 1665* (London: John Lane, 1924); Thomas R. Forbes, "The Searchers," *Bulletin of the New York Academy of Medicine* 50 (1974): 1031–38; and Paul Slack, *The Impact of Plague in Tudor and Stuart England* (London: Routledge and Kegan Paul, 1985).

12. Johns, *Nature of the Book*, 5.

13. Ian Atherton, "The Itch Grown a Disease: Manuscript Transmission of News in the Seventeenth Century," in *News, Newspapers, and Society in Early Modern Britain*, ed. Joad Raymond (London: Frank Cass, 1999), 39–65, here 47.

14. Manuel Schonhorn, "Defoe's *Journal of the Plague Year*: Topography and Intention," *Review of English Studies* 19 (1968): 387–402. Schonhorn proposes that "a good deal of Defoe's anecdotal detail . . . must have been transmitted to him orally by his uncle [Henry Foe], who was still alive in Defoe's fifteenth year" (392).

Defoe's prose style is known for its distinctly oral quality. H.F.'s narrative is characterized by such "oral residue" as a high degree of repetition and redundancy, cadences reminiscent of the speaking voice, and colloquial phrases and formulaic refrains ("poor dying Creatures"). On oral residue, see Farrell and Soukup, *Ong Reader*, 313–29.

15. Daniel Defoe, *Due Preparations for the Plague* (1722), in *Romances and Narratives by Daniel Defoe*, ed. George A. Aitken (London: J. M. Dent and Sons, 1895; New York: AMS Press, 1974), 15:121.

16. Ibid., 135.

17. John Graunt, *Natural and Political Observations . . . Upon the Bills of Mortality* (London, 1662), 13, 11.

18. See also Munkhoff, "Searchers of the Dead," 13.

19. Bell, *Great Plague*, 19.

20. Quoted in Munkhoff, "Searchers of the Dead," 1.

21. *The Gentleman's Magazine: and Historical Chronicle for the Year 1799*, vol. 69, pt. 2 (London: John Nichols, 1799), 658.

22. Bell, *Great Plague*, 16.

23. Nicholson, *Historical Sources of Defoe's "Journal of the Plague Year,"* 49.

24. There is one possible exception to this statement. H.F. momentarily appears to acknowledge that examiners and searchers performed different duties when he notes,

"Families . . . took all the measures they could . . . if any died in their Houses to get them return'd *to* the Examiners, and *by* the Searchers, as having died of other Distempers" (Defoe, *Journal*, 162, my emphasis).

25. *Applebee's Original Weekly Journal*, 18 November 1721, in *Selected Poetry and Prose of Daniel Defoe*, ed. Michael F. Shugrue (New York: Holt, Rinehart and Winston, 1968), 212–14.

26. Laura Gowing, *Domestic Dangers: Women, Words, and Sex in Early Modern London* (Oxford: Clarendon, 1996), 50.

27. *Oxford English Dictionary*, 2nd ed., s.v. "gossip, *sb*," def. 3.

28. Paul K. Alkon, *Defoe and Fictional Time* (Athens: University of Georgia Press, 1979), 174, 50.

29. Adam Fox, *Oral and Literate Culture in England, 1500–1700* (Oxford: Clarendon, 2000), 335.

30. Samuel Pepys, *Diary*, 14 September 1665, in *The Diary of Samuel Pepys*, ed. Robert Latham and William Matthews (Berkeley: University of California Press, 1972), 4:224.

31. Defoe, *Due Preparations*, 17.

32. On Puritan hermeneutics and Defoe's own habit of reading events such as natural disasters as signs, see J. Paul Hunter, *The Reluctant Pilgrim: Defoe's Emblematic Method and Quest for Form in "Robinson Crusoe"* (Baltimore: Johns Hopkins University Press, 1966). Elsewhere, Hunter proposes more specifically of the *Journal* that H.F.'s "preoccupation . . . with how to read the signs and decide what he should do is an epistemological paradigm for the age." See J. Paul Hunter, *Before Novels: The Cultural Contexts of Eighteenth-Century English Fiction* (New York: Norton, 1990), 46. Cynthia Wall's introduction to the Penguin Classics edition productively links the reading of signs such as tokens with the demands of interpreting written and printed texts (including H.F.'s own narrative). See Cynthia Wall, ed., *A Journal of the Plague Year*, by Daniel Defoe (London: Penguin, 2003), xvii–xxxiii.

33. Daniel Defoe, *A System of Magick; or, A History of the Black Art* (London: J. Roberts, 1727), 225.

34. John Richetti, *Defoe's Narratives: Situations and Structures* (Oxford: Clarendon, 1975), 236.

CHAPTER FOUR

1. Joseph Addison and Richard Steele, *Spectator* 10 (12 March 1711), in *The Spectator*, ed. Donald F. Bond, 5 vols. (Oxford: Clarendon, 1965), 1:44.

2. *Spectator* 1 (1 March 1711), in Bond, *Spectator*, 1:5.

3. See, e.g., Donna T. Andrew, "Popular Culture and Public Debate: London 1780," *Historical Journal* 39 (1996): 405–23; Donna T. Andrew, ed., *London Debating Societies, 1776–1799* (London: London Record Society, 1994); Mary Thale, "The Robin Hood Society: Debating in Eighteenth-Century London," *London Journal* 22 (1997): 32–50; Mary Thale, "Women in London Debating Societies in 1780," *Gender and History* 7 (1995): 5–24; Iain McCalman, *Radical Underworld: Prophets, Revolutionaries and Pornographers in London, 1795–1840* (Cambridge: Cambridge University Press, 1988); and Iain

McCalman, "Ultra Radicalism and Convivial Debating Clubs in London, 1795–1838," *English Historical Review* 102 (1987): 309–33.

4. John Henley, undated lecture notes, cataloged as "'Academical Lectures,' by the Rev. J. Henley: 1726–1740," BL Add. MSS 19925.

5. John Henley, *History and Advantages of divine Revelation* (1725), 14–15. This sermon was later reprinted in black letter type as "The Discourse on Action in the Pulpit," in *Oratory Transactions* 2 (1729): 1–21. The pagination of *Oratory Transactions* is idiosyncratic. Items are sometimes individually paginated; thus, this sermon is paginated 1–21 despite appearing as the last item in this issue. To assist the reader, I have given the titles of individual items in each issue wherever possible.

6. See, e.g., Richard Steele, *Tatler* 66 (10 September 1709) and 70 (20 September 1709), in *The Tatler*, ed. Donald F. Bond, 3 vols. (Oxford: Clarendon, 1987), 1:453–61, 483–89; and Addison and Steele, *Spectator* 147 (18 August 1711) and 407 (17 June 1712), in Bond, *Spectator*, 2:78–81, 3:520–23.

7. Henley, *History and Advantages of divine Revelation*, 18, 16.

8. "An Act for Exempting their Majestyes Protestant Subjects dissenting from the Church of England from the Penalties of certaine Lawes," 24 May 1689, 1 W. & M., c. 18. The word "toleration" is not used in the original statute.

9. John Henley, *Milk for Babes, or a Hornbook for . . . Mr. H——s . . . Being No. V of Oratory Transactions* (1729), 49.

10. John Henley, "The First Sermon Preach'd at the Opening of the Oratory, On Sunday, July 3. 1726. On the Design, and Reasons, of the Institution," *Oratory Transactions* 1 (1728): 40.

11. John Henley, "Plan of the Oratory" (1726), reprinted in *Oratory Transactions* 1 (1728): i.

12. *Grub-Street Journal* 64 (25 March 1731); *A Comparison between Orator H——and Orator P——* (1749), 5; and *Grub-Street Journal* 408 (20 October 1737).

13. Alexander Pope, *The Dunciad in Four Books* (1743), ed. Valerie Rumbold (New York: Longman, 1999), bk. 3, ll. 209–10, p. 247. All further quotations from the *Dunciad* are taken from this edition and will be cited parenthetically by book and line numbers only.

14. Graham Midgley, *The Life of Orator Henley* (Oxford: Clarendon, 1973), viii.

15. Advertisements for 2 and 9 October 1742, in Daniel Lysons, *Collectanea: Or, A Collection of Advertisements and Paragraphs from the Newspapers, Relating to Various Subjects* (Strawberry-Hill, n.d.), 113 (BL shelfmark C.103.k.12).

16. John Henley, undated lecture notes, BL Add. MSS 10346, fol. 379.

17. John Henley, lecture notes dated 1743, BL Add. MSS 10347.

18. Henley, "First Sermon Preach'd," 31.

19. Presentment of the Grand Jury of Middlesex, 9 January 1729, printed in *Weekly Journal or the British Gazetteer* and *Applebee's Original Weekly Journal*, 18 January 1729.

20. As Isabel Rivers suggests, "freethinking is a rational process by which truth is discovered; it does not presuppose what truth is." Isabel Rivers, *Reason, Grace, and Sentiment: A Study of the Language of Religion and Ethics in England, 1660–1780*, vol. 2, *Shaftesbury to Hume* (Cambridge: Cambridge University Press, 2000), 11.

21. For this term, see, e.g., Henley, "Plan of the Oratory," iii; and Henley, "First Sermon Preach'd," 35–36.

22. John Henley, "Narrative," *Oratory Transactions* 1 (1728): 3–4.

23. John Henley, lecture notes dated 1753, BL Add. MSS 11790.

24. Henley, "Narrative," 3–4. The biographical "Narrative" was ostensibly written by Leonard Welsted but was probably penned by Henley himself.

25. Ibid., 10–11.

26. Henley, "First Sermon Preach'd," 35. See also Henley's undated lecture draft, "A Proposition for a New Institute of ye Sciences, School Learning & ye Classicks," BL Add. MSS 19925.

27. Henley, "Narrative," 5.

28. R. C. Alston, ed., *English Linguistics, 1500–1800: A Collection of Facsimile Reprints*, no. 232 (Menston, England: Scolar Press, 1970), n.p.

29. Henley, "Preface," *Oratory Transactions* 1 (1728): iv.

30. Henley, "Narrative," 14.

31. Advertisement for 18 September 1748, in Lysons, *Collectanea*, 154.

32. Henley, "Narrative," 12.

33. William Whiston, *Mr. Henley's Letters and Advertisements, Which concern Mr. Whiston. Published by Mr. Whiston* (1727), 3.

34. Advertisement dated 16 March 1750, in Lysons, *Collectanea*, 162.

35. Henley, "First Sermon Preach'd," 31.

36. For Gibson's letter to Townshend, see Correspondence of the First Lord Hardwicke, BL Add. MSS 36136, no. 63. Gibson's letter to Yorke has not survived, but for a draft of Yorke's response dated 1 August 1726, see BL Add. MSS 36136, no. 53.

37. See Correspondence of the First Lord Hardwicke, BL Add. MSS 36136, no. 64.

38. *Letter to the Reverend Mr. John Henley* (1726), 9.

39. This was one of Christopher Smart's nicknames for Henley in the periodical *Midwife* (1750–53). See my discussion of Smart's satire later in this chapter.

40. John Henley, *Second St. Paul in Equity Hall* (1755), 26.

41. See the British Library's copy of John Henley's *Deism Defeated, And Christianity Defended* (1731), shelfmark 4015.c.21.

42. Advertisement for 24 August 1753, in Lysons, *Collectanea*, 189, quoted in Midgley, *Orator Henley*, 82.

43. Advertisement for 25 October 1729, in Lysons, *Collectanea*, 39, mentioned in Midgley, *Orator Henley*, 77. A satirical print titled *An extempore Epigram made at ye Oratory* (1731) depicts an elite woman departing from the Oratory in a carriage labeled "Folly." See Frederic George Stephens and Edward Hawkins, *Catalogue of Prints and Drawings in the British Museum, Division I: Political and Personal Satires*, vol. 2, *1689–1733* (London: British Museum, 1877), no. 1871, "The Oratory."

44. Midgley, *Orator Henley*, 78.

45. *Grub-Street Journal* 67 (15 April 1731).

46. John Henley, "Butcher's Lecture," *Oratory Transactions* 4 (1729): 30, 25–26.

47. Henley, *Milk for Babes*, 45.

48. John Henley, *Why How now, Gossip POPE? Or, The Sweet Singing-Bird of Parnassus taken out of its pretty Cage to be roasted. . . . Exposing the Malice Wickedness*

and Vanity of his Aspersions on J. H. in that Monument of His Own Misery and Spleen, the Dunciad (1736), 2nd ed. (1743), 12.

49. Anon., *The Art of Speaking in Publick: Or An Essay on the Action of an Orator*, 2nd ed. (London, 1727), "The Editor's Introduction and Apology for this Edition," xiv–xxiv, here xx. See below for further discussion of this edition.

50. Henley, *Why How now, Gossip POPE?*, 13.

51. Advertisements for 7 November 1747 and 28 December 1753, in Lysons, *Collectanea*, 150, 184.

52. Henley, "Plan of the Oratory," "First Sermon Preach'd," and *"An Idea of What is intended to be taught in the Week-Days universal Academy,"* all in *Oratory Transactions* 1 (1728). These quotations are from iii, 28, 35–36, 47–48.

53. Henley's undated lecture notes are bound as "Henley's Academical Orations 1730," BL Add. MSS 19925.

54. See Henry Oldenburg et al., eds., *Philosophical Transactions of the Royal Society* (1665–present); and Thomas Sprat, *The History of the Royal Society of London, For the Improving of Natural Knowledge*, 3 pts. (1667). This quotation is from Sprat, *History of the Royal Society*, pt. 1, sec. 20.

55. "First Sermon Preach'd," *Oratory Transactions* 1 (1728): 37.

56. Sprat, *History of the Royal Society*, pt. 2, sec. 20: "Their manner of Discourse," 113.

57. John Henley, "Laws of the Disputations," *Oratory Transactions* 1 (1728).

58. William T. Costello, *The Scholastic Curriculum at Early Seventeenth-Century Cambridge* (Cambridge, MA: Harvard University Press, 1958), 108.

59. Henley, "Plan of the Oratory," ii–iii; and Henley, "First Sermon Preach'd," 33–34.

60. Henley, *"An Idea of What is intended to be taught," Oratory Transactions* 1 (1728): 49.

61. Henley, *History and Advantages of divine Revelation*, 18.

62. Henley, "Narrative," 3–4.

63. See, e.g., the catalog *Books Written, and Publish'd, By the Reverend Mr. John Henley, M.A. Rector of Chelmondiston, in Suffolk* (1724). Thirty-eight years later, Henley still listed this text as among his works.

64. *Oratory Transactions* 2 (1729): 3 records that this lecture was delivered on 29 March 1727.

65. Henley, "First Sermon Preach'd," 36.

66. Henley, "Butcher's Lecture," 7.

67. For these and other lecture topics, see *Oratory Transactions* 2 (1729).

68. Henley, *Why How now, Gossip POPE?*, 13.

69. Henley, "Laws of the Conferences," *Oratory Transactions* 1 (1728): v, my emphasis.

70. See John Henley, "Laws of the Conferences," "Specimen of a Conference," and "Laws of the Disputations," all in *Oratory Transactions* 1 (1728).

71. Henley, "Laws of the Conferences," vi, viii.

72. *Grub-Street Journal* 88 (9 September 1731).

73. See *Oratory Transactions* 2 (1729): 8. This lecture was delivered on 17 January 1728.

74. Henley, dedication to *The Lord, He is God* (1730), n.p.

75. John Henley, *The Victorious Stroke For Old England* (1748), title page.

76. *Daily Gazette*, 3 July 1736.

77. *Hyp-Doctor*, 28 December 1736, quoted in Midgley, *Orator Henley*, 118.

78. Wilbur Samuel Howell, *Eighteenth-Century British Logic and Rhetoric* (Princeton, NJ: Princeton University Press, 1971), 165.

79. Ephraim Chambers, *Cyclopaedia*, 2 vols. (1728), 2nd ed., 2 vols. (1738), 2:150.

80. Howell, *Eighteenth-Century British Logic*, 193.

81. *Tatler* 66 (10 September 1709), in Bond, *Tatler*, 1:455–56; and *Spectator* 147 (18 August 1711), in Bond, *Spectator*, 2:79–80.

82. *Spectator* 407 (17 June 1712), in Bond, *Spectator*, 3:522; and *Tatler* 66 (10 September 1709), in Bond, *Tatler*, 1:455–56.

83. Henley, *Victorious Stroke*, 29.

84. Henley, lecture notes dated 1743, BL Add. MSS 10347.

85. *Oratory Transactions* 2 (1729): 12.

86. Anon., *Art of Speaking in Publick*, 2nd ed. (1727), "The Editor's Introduction and Apology for this Edition," xiv–xv. The "Mr. Wood" was probably William Wood of Christ Church, Oxford.

87. Ibid., xv–xvi. I discuss this text in more detail in chapter 5 (see pp. 170–73, 175, 180, 186, 206–7, 314n36).

88. *Grub-Street Journal* 166 (1 March 1733) and 117 (30 March 1732).

89. This engraving and commentary appear in *Grub-Street Journal* 147 (26 October 1732) and 148 (30 October 1732).

90. On book prices, see Richard D. Altick, *The English Common Reader: A Social History of the Mass Reading Public, 1800–1900* (Chicago: University of Chicago Press, 1957), 21–23; Margaret Spufford, *Small Books and Pleasant Histories: Popular Fiction and Its Readership in Seventeenth-Century England* (Athens: University of Georgia Press, 1981), 48–51, 91–98; and Robert Mayer, "Nathaniel Crouch, Bookseller and Historian: Popular Historiography and Cultural Power in Late Seventeenth-Century England," *Eighteenth-Century Studies* 27 (1994): 391–419, esp. 398–99, n. 15.

91. There does not appear to be any hard evidence that Henley was a paid informant for Walpole. The "evidence" that Midgley offers, for instance, is either murky, biased, or significantly posthumous; see, e.g., Midgley, *Orator Henley*, 51. The source of the charge appears to be Pope's note in the *Dunciad*, 3.199n, where he claims that Henley was in the pay of Walpole and that he also offered to write for the Tories. But Henley was a lifelong Whig, and the latter charge seems especially unlikely.

92. See, e.g., *Applebee's Original Weekly Journal* and *Weekly Journal or the British Gazetteer* for 18 January 1729.

93. *Oratory Transactions* 2 (1729): 8.

94. *Grub-Street Journal* 286 (19 June 1735).

95. Midgley, *Orator Henley*, 88.

96. *Grub-Street Journal* 63 (18 March 1731).

97. Midgley, *Orator Henley*, 137.

98. *Grub-Street Journal* 117 (30 March 1732), 148 (30 October 1732), 71 (13 May 1731), and 160 (18 January 1733).

99. "Theological, or *Lord's-Day's Subjects* of the Oratory," *Oratory Transactions* 2 (1729): 12.

100. Advertisement for 30 November 1728, in Lysons, *Collectanea*, 27.

101. The Presentment of the Grand Jury appeared in the *Weekly Journal or the British Gazetteer* and in *Applebee's Original Weekly Journal* on 18 January 1729 and is reprinted in Midgley, *Orator Henley*, 134–35, quotation on 135.

102. *London Evening Post*, 23–25 January 1729, quoted in Midgley, *Orator Henley*, 136.

103. Henley, *Milk for Babes*, 45.

104. *Oratory Transactions* 1 (1728): title page.

105. Henley, "Plan of the Oratory," i–ii.

106. Henley, "First Sermon Preach'd," 40–41.

107. Henley, *Hyp-Doctor*, 30 December 1735.

108. Henley, "Plan of the Oratory," iii; and John Henley, "Defence of the Oratory," *Oratory Transactions* 1 (1728): 45–46.

109. *Letter to the Reverend Mr. John Henley* (1726), 9. See also *Letter To The Celebrated Orator* (1727).

110. *A Comparison between Orator H—— and Orator P—— etc.* (1749), 5.

111. *Grub-Street Journal* 71 (13 May 1731).

112. Presentment of the Grand Jury of Middlesex, 9 January 1729, printed in *Weekly Journal or the British Gazetteer* and *Applebee's Original Weekly Journal*, 18 January 1729; and reprinted in Midgley, *Orator Henley*, 134–35, here 135.

113. Advertisement for 1 February 1729, in Lysons, *Collectanea*, 29. In his preface to *Joseph Andrews* (1742), Fielding makes a distinction between "burlesque" and "satire" that has fundamentally shaped modern critical discussions of satire. Henley, however, aligned burlesque and satire rather than opposed them. In fact, I would argue that Henley's contemporary use of "burlesque" may have been one reason why Fielding was determined to distinguish his own ludic practice as "satire" rather than "burlesque."

114. According to a list of "Academical Subjects of the *Oratory*" published in *Oratory Transactions* 2 (1729): 1–20, Henley delivered this lecture on 31 January 1728 (9).

115. For Henley's "Dissertation on Nonsense" and "Oration on . . . Serious Buffoons," see *Oratory Transactions* 2 and 5 (1729), respectively.

116. Henley, "Oration on . . . Serious Buffoons," 10, 14.

117. Henley, *Milk for Babes*, 47. Whereas Pope's comments on Henley are uniformly negative, Swift's one extant comment on Henley is relatively neutral. In his satiric self-obituary *Verses on the Death of Dr. Swift* (wr. 1731; pub. 1739) Swift shows himself to have been well aware of Henley's success in securing an audience. But Swift's satire seems directed at the literary marketplace and at his own aspirations to fame rather than at Henley. Swift depicts a country squire visiting the shop of bookseller Bernard Lintot and "Inquir[ing] for Swift in verse and prose." Lintot vaguely recalls the dean, who "died a year ago," but he tells the squire that he has already remaindered all Swift's works. Instead, he recommends that the squire purchase some more popular items: "Sir Roberts vindication, / And Mr. Henley's last oration. / The hawkers have not got 'em yet: / Your honor please to buy a set?" (ll. 277–80).

118. Henley, *Milk for Babes*, 47.

119. *A Letter To The Celebrated Orator* (1727), "Advertisement," n.p., and 3–4, 6–7.

120. Henley, "Defence of the Oratory," 34.

121. Midgley, *Orator Henley*, 196.

122. Henley, *Hyp-Doctor*, 10 May 1737, quoted in Midgley, *Orator Henley*, 195.

123. Henley, lecture notes dated 1 July 1750, BL Add. MSS 11778.

124. Midgley, *Orator Henley*, 194.

125. Advertisement for 6 April 1745, in Lysons, *Collectanea*, 138.

126. Somerset House (pcc.Glazier.274), quoted in Midgley, *Orator Henley*, 279.

127. This newspaper clipping dated 2 December 1746 is preserved in Lysons, *Collectanea*, 145.

128. See the *Daily Advertiser*, 20 June 1747.

129. See also the anonymous satiric print *The Orator Versus Culloden* (1746), not reproduced here, which depicts Henley at his pulpit, wearing the plaid in support of the Jacobite rebels and brandishing a sword.

130. *An Epistle to O——r H——nl-y; Containing, Some Remarks on the Discourses set forth in the Conventicle the Corner of Lincoln's-Inn-Fields, near Clare-Market* (1746), title page.

131. For another example of his use of mock imprints, see John Henley, *Oratory Magazine* 3 (n.d. [1748?]), "Printed for ENGLISH BIRTHRIGHT, Esq."

132. Henley, *Milk for Babes*.

133. Henley, *Victorious Stroke*, 24, 44, 27, 54, 52.

134. Henley, *Hyp Doctor*, 29 April 1735. Many scholars now agree with Henley's verdict that Savage contributed to the composition of the prose notes.

135. Henley, *Why How now, Gossip POPE?*, 8.

136. Claudia Thomas, "Pope and His *Dunciad* Adversaries: Skirmishes on the Borders of Gentility," in *Cutting Edges: Postmodern Critical Essays on Eighteenth-Century Satire*, ed. James Gill (Knoxville: University of Tennessee Press, 1995), 287.

137. Henley, *Why How now, Gossip POPE?*, 4, 16, 12.

138. Henley more than once suggests that Pope's works were subjects of Oratory debates. In *Why How now, Gossip POPE?*, 13, he responds to Pope: "your Discourse on *Pastoral, your Pastorals, your Notion of Poetic Probability* in the Translation of *Homer*, your *Ethical* Epistles, your Character of *me* in your *Dunciad*, have been disputed upon distinctly."

139. See Ashley Marshall, "Henry Fielding and the Scriblerians," *Modern Language Quarterly* 72 (2011): 20–48, here 29; and Ashley Marshall, "The Myth of Scriblerus," *Journal for Eighteenth-Century Studies* 31 (2008): 77–99.

140. On this period of Fielding's creative life, see Robert D. Hume, *Henry Fielding and the London Theatre, 1728–1737* (Oxford: Clarendon, 1988); J. Paul Hunter, *Occasional Form: Henry Fielding and the Chains of Circumstance* (Baltimore: Johns Hopkins University Press, 1975); and Thomas Lockwood, ed., *The Wesleyan Edition of the Works of Henry Fielding, Plays*, vol. 1, *1728–1731* (Oxford: Clarendon, 2004).

141. Lockwood, *Plays*, vol. 1, act 1, scene 5, p. 235.

142. Charles B. Woods, ed., *The Author's Farce* (1730), by Henry Fielding (Lincoln: University of Nebraska Press, 1966), 104.

143. Lockwood, *Plays*, vol. 1, act. 3, p. 271. Act 3 is not divided into scenes.

144. See ibid., 275.

145. See *Daily Post*, 7 and 29 May 1730.

146. Lockwood, *Plays*, vol. 1, 192.

147. *Daily Post*, 4 August 1730. For other fairground adaptations of Fielding's plays, see Sybil Rosenfeld, *Theatre of the London Fairs in the Eighteenth Century* (Cambridge: Cambridge University Press, 1960); and William Van Lennep et al., eds., *The London Stage, 1660–1800*, pt. 3, *1729–47*, ed. Arthur H. Scouten (Carbondale: Southern Illinois University Press, 1961).

148. L. J. Morrissey, ed., *"Tom Thumb" and "The Tragedy of Tragedies"* (Berkeley: University of California Press, 1970), 1.

149. Henry Fielding, *The History of Joseph Andrews* (1742), ed. Martin C. Battestin (Oxford: Clarendon, 1966), 235.

150. Advertisement dated 3 December 1751, in Lysons, *Collectanea*, 170.

151. Chris Mounsey, *Christopher Smart: Clown of God* (Lewisburg, PA: Bucknell University Press, 2001), 17.

152. *Midwife* 3.2.37–38. Smart's *The Midwife: Or, The Old Woman's Magazine* was published monthly from 16 October 1750 to 31 October 1751, with another three issues on 7 January and 4 August 1752 and 16 June 1753. A collected edition was published in 1753. Quotations are from the collected edition, cited by volume, issue, and page number.

153. See Paula McDowell, *The Women of Grub Street: Press, Politics, and Gender in the London Literary Marketplace, 1678–1730* (Oxford: Clarendon, 1998), 249n56. For an argument that Smart's "Old Woman's Oratory" and *Midwife* were vehicles for political commentary, see Mounsey, *Christopher Smart*.

154. *Midwife* 3.2.40–41.

155. *Midwife* 3.2.49, 98, 49 (again), 37–42.

156. *Midwife* 3.2.99–100.

157. *Grub-Street Journal* 71 (13 May 1731).

158. *Daily Journal* 3893 (21 June 1733).

159. *Grub-Street Journal* 186 (19 July 1733).

160. *Free Mason* [*Hyp-Doctor*], 13 November 1733 to 19 February 1734.

161. Midgley, *Orator Henley*, 262n3.

162. McCalman suggests that meetings were held as early as 1742; see his "Ultra Radicalism," 310. Another address commonly given was "Essex Street in the Strand." See, e.g., Thale, "Robin Hood Society." Surviving records for the Robin Hood Society show a paying attendance of between 50 and 250 persons.

163. Advertisement for 26 January 1751, in Lysons, *Collectanea*, 166.

CHAPTER FIVE

1. I am quoting *Mansfield Park* here (discussed later in this chapter).

2. See Lori Anne Ferrell and Peter McCullough, eds., *The English Sermon Revised: Religion, Literature, and History, 1600–1750* (Manchester: Manchester University Press, 2000), e.g., Tony Claydon, "The Sermon, the 'Public Sphere' and the Political Culture of Late Seventeenth-Century England," 208–34.

3. John Henley, undated lecture notes, BL Add. MSS 10346, fol. 379.

4. See, e.g., Richard Steele, *Tatler* 66 (10 September 1709) and 70 (20 September 1709),

in *The Tatler*, ed. Donald F. Bond, 3 vols. (Oxford: Clarendon, 1987), 1:453–56, 483–89; and Joseph Addison and Richard Steele, *Spectator* 147 (18 August 1711) and 407 (17 June 1712), in *The Spectator*, ed. Donald F. Bond, 5 vols. (Oxford: Clarendon, 1965), 2:78, 3:520–23.

5. *Tatler* 70 (20 September 1709), in Bond, *Tatler*, 1:484; and *Spectator* 407 (17 June 1712), in Bond, *Spectator*, 3:522.

6. Jonathan Swift, "On Sleeping in Church," in *Prose Works*, ed. Herbert Davis, vol. 9, *Irish Tracts, 1720–1723, and Sermons*, ed. Louis Landa (Oxford: Basil Blackwell, 1948), 210–18, here 210.

7. Wilbur Samuel Howell, *Eighteenth-Century British Logic and Rhetoric* (Princeton, NJ: Princeton University Press, 1971), 145, 181.

8. *Tatler* 66 (10 September 1709), in Bond, *Tatler*, 1:453; *Spectator* 407 (17 June 1712), in Bond, *Spectator*, 3:521; and *Tatler* 66 (10 September 1709), in Bond, *Tatler*, 1:457.

9. *Tatler* 70 (20 September 1709) and *Tatler* 66 (10 September 1709), in Bond, *Tatler*, 1:457, 455.

10. *Spectator* 407 (17 June 1712), in Bond, *Spectator*, 3:522; *Tatler* 66 (10 September 1709), in Bond, *Tatler*, 1:455–56; and *Spectator* 147 (18 August 1711), in Bond, *Spectator*, 2:79–80.

11. Vicki Tolar Burton, "John Wesley and the Liberty to Speak: The Rhetorical and Literacy Practices of Early Methodism," *College Composition and Communication* 53 (2001): 65–91, here 71–72.

12. Richard P. Heitzenrater, *Wesley and the People Called Methodists* (Nashville, TN: Abingdon Press, 1995), quoted in Burton, "John Wesley," 75.

13. Benjamin Franklin, *Autobiography*, ed. Joyce E. Chaplin (New York: Norton, 2012), 90. Recent research suggests that Franklin's estimate may not be far from the truth; see Braxton Boren, "The Maximum Intelligible Range of the Human Voice" (PhD diss., New York University, 2014).

14. John Henley, sermon for 2 September 1744, BL Add. MSS 19922.

15. John Henley, sermon [1743?], BL Add. MSS 10347, fols. 87–88.

16. See my discussion of the occasion of this second edition in chapter 4 (pp. 138–39).

17. Anon., *An Essay Upon the Action of an Orator; As to His Pronunciation and Gesture. Useful both for Divines and Lawyers, and necessary for all Young Gentlemen, that study how to Speak well in Publick. Done out of French* (London, 1702), 8.

18. Ibid., 171–72.

19. John Wesley, *Directions Concerning Pronunciation and Gesture* (Bristol, 1749), 9; cf. Le Faucheur, *Essay*, 173.

20. Anon., *Essay Upon the Action of an Orator*, 2.

21. Carolyn Eastman, *A Nation of Speechifiers: Making an American Public after the Revolution* (Chicago: University of Chicago Press, 2009), observes that Demosthenes was also considered "a perfect model for American schoolchildren—and not just because his life epitomized the benefits of hard work and self-improvement. He symbolized the ideal civic orator, the 'good man' whose selfless passion for virtue infused his speech with conviction and moved others to public action" (17).

22. Anon., *Essay Upon the Action of an Orator*, 55–56.

23. Thomas Sheridan, *A Course of Lectures on Elocution: Together With Two Dissertations on Language; And Some Other Tracts Relative to Those Subjects* (1762; New York: Benjamin Blom, 1968), 27.

24. Anon., *Essay Upon the Action of an Orator*, 58. In *Tatler* 66 (10 September 1709), in Bond, *Tatler*, 1:455, Steele suggests that a good orator "add[s] to the Propriety of Speech . . . and Action which would have been approv'd by *Demosthenes*."

25. Wesley, *Directions*, 10; see also 3.

26. Anon., *Essay Upon the Action of an Orator*, 153.

27. David Hume, "Of Eloquence" [1742], in *Essays Moral, Political, and Literary,* ed. Eugene F. Miller (rev. ed. Indianapolis: Liberty Fund, 1985), 97–110, here 105. For a reading of eighteenth-century representations of orators as a form of rhetorical theory in themselves, see Andrew Black, "Neutered Rhetoric: Representations of Orators in the Long Eighteenth Century" (Ph.D. diss., University of Maryland, 2013).

28. Anon., *Essay Upon the Action of an Orator*, 196, 10, 202, 174, 196, 202.

29. John Wesley, *Directions Concerning Pronunciation and Gesture* (Bristol, 1749), 11.

30. Ibid.; cf. Anon., *Essay Upon the Action of an Orator*, 193.

31. Anon., *Essay Upon the Action of an Orator*, 183.

32. Wesley, *Directions Concerning Pronunciation and Gesture*, 10.

33. James Boswell, *"Life of Johnson," Together with Boswell's "Journal of a Tour to the Hebrides" and Johnson's "Diary of a Journey into North Wales,"* ed. George Birkbeck Hill, rev. ed., ed. L. F. Powell, 6 vols. (Oxford: Clarendon, 1934–64), 3:409, 2:211.

34. Thomas Sheridan, *British Education: Or, The Source of the Disorders of Great Britain. . . . With An Attempt to shew, that a Revival of the Art of Speaking, and the Study of Our Own Language, might contribute . . . to the Cure of those Evils* (1756), vi.

35. Sheridan, *Course of Lectures*, 219.

36. Wilbur Samuel Howell, who calls Le Faucheur (or, rather, the 1702 English translation of his *Traitté*) the "first founder" of the elocution movement in Britain, designates Sheridan as the "second founder" (Howell, *Eighteenth-Century British Logic* , 168). Sheridan is also a key figure in studies of the elocution movement in eighteenth- and nineteenth-century America; see, e.g., Jay Fliegelman, *Declaring Independence: Jefferson, Natural Language, and the Culture of Performance* (Palo Alto, CA: Stanford University Press, 1993); Sandra M. Gustafson, *Eloquence Is Power: Oratory and Performance in Early America* (Chapel Hill: University of North Carolina Press, 2000); and Eastman, *Nation of Speechifiers*.

37. Howell, *Eighteenth-Century British Logic*, 214.

38. Paul Goring, *The Rhetoric of Sensibility in Eighteenth-Century Culture* (Cambridge: Cambridge University Press, 2005), 28. In contrast to Howell, Goring is far more willing to admit that "from the *beginning* of the eighteenth century there was a major movement to develop public speaking in Britain" (211, my emphasis). Goring "aim[s] to open up the ramifications of elocutionary writing more widely than Howell, who, as a champion of classical rhetoric . . . is fundamentally dismissive of the movement" (12).

39. Ibid., 98–99.

40. Sheridan, *Course of Lectures*, 1.

41. I.e., William Pitt, 1st Earl of Chatham (Pitt the Elder). As Peter de Bolla suggests, "the elocutionary movement . . . utilize[d] the myth of Pitt's voice . . . for its own

self-promotion. . . . The voice is sacrosanct, an asset of the nation." Peter de Bolla, *The Discourse of the Sublime: Readings in History, Aesthetics, and the Subject* (Oxford: Basil Blackwell, 1989), 143–44.

42. Sheridan, *Course of Lectures*, xii–xiii.

43. Ibid., 1, my emphasis.

44. Patricia Howell Michaelson, *Speaking Volumes: Women, Reading, and Speech in the Age of Austen* (Palo Alto, CA: Stanford University Press, 2002), 143. Michaelson is especially concerned with "performance readings": that is, reading aloud from books. She argues that in the "Age of Austen," the oral performance of literary texts was a means for men and women to practice authoritative speech. But scholars disagree about the prevalence of performance readings. John J. Richetti argues that performance readings were common—so much so that the prospect of performance was an integral aspect of the composition of eighteenth-century verse; John J. Richetti, "Performance in Eighteenth-Century English Verse," in *A Companion to British Literature*, ed. Robert DeMaria, Heesok Chang, and Samantha Zacher (Oxford: John Wiley and Sons, 2014). In contrast, J. Paul Hunter argues that there is little firsthand evidence documenting "performance readings" before the nineteenth century and proposes that scholars' assumptions that performance readings were common may have less to do with *fact* than with own modern nostalgia for a "more oral" past:

> We have been taught to believe that sound in the seventeenth and eighteenth centuries was more crucial than in subsequent ages, and most of us probably imagine frequent public readings and performances. But that assumption seems to have been created merely from retrogressive expectations of harmony and loss; that is, every age believes the previous age to have been more oral than the present one. . . . I have pursued the question at length and find virtually no evidence that performance readings often took place outside the theatre. . . . the firm chiming we associate with the couplet mainly took place in readers' heads.

J. Paul Hunter, "Sleeping Beauties: Are Historical Aesthetics Worth Recovering?," *Eighteenth-Century Studies* 34 (2000): 1–20, here 19.

45. Sheridan, *Course of Lectures*, 139.

46. On the implications of *Donaldson v. Becket* (1774), the House of Lords ruling against perpetual copyright, for the rise of anthologies (including a new print genre tellingly titled "speakers"), see William St. Clair, *The Reading Nation in the Romantic Period* (Cambridge: Cambridge University Press, 2004), esp. 135–38.

47. On the institutionalization of recitation in public schools in nineteenth- and twentieth-century Britain, see Catherine Robson, *Heart Beats: Everyday Life and the Memorized Poem* (Princeton, NJ: Princeton University Press, 2012).

48. Sheridan, *Course of Lectures*, xii–xiii, x, 247, 148, 139.

49. Sheridan, *British Education*, 185, 270, 185–86; Sheridan, *Course of Lectures*, 207; and Sheridan, *British Education*, 187.

50. Sheridan, *Course of Lectures*, 8, 7, 247, 208.

51. Samuel Johnson, *Rambler* 177 (26 November 1751).

52. Sheridan, *Course of Lectures*, 80, 72, 215.

53. Ibid., 174–75.

54. Ibid., 10, 19, 10.

55. Ibid., 113, 11.

56. Anon., *The Art of Speaking in Publick: Or An Essay on the Action of an Orator,* 2nd ed. (London, 1727), xiv.

57. Sheridan, *British Education,* 91; and Sheridan, *Course of Lectures,* xiii.

58. Sheridan, *Course of Lectures,* 120, 128.

59. Ibid., 133–34; and Sheridan, *British Education,* 91.

60. Sheridan, *Course of Lectures,* 30, 207.

61. Letter to John Wilkes, 16 October 1754, in *Letters of David Hume,* vol. 1, *1727– 1765,* ed. J. Y. T. Greig (Oxford: Oxford University Press, 2011), 205.

62. Penny Fielding, *Writing and Orality: Nationality, Culture, and Nineteenth-Century Scottish Fiction* (Oxford: Clarendon, 1996), 21.

63. Sheridan, *Course of Lectures,* 225, 247, 262. On Sheridan's and Johnson's dictionaries and their relationship to questions of linguistic imperialism, see Janet Sorensen, *The Grammar of Empire in Eighteenth-Century British Writing* (Cambridge: Cambridge University Press, 2000).

64. Sheridan, *Course of Lectures,* 262, 246, 256, 262.

65. William Benzie, *The Dublin Orator: Thomas Sheridan's Influence on Eighteenth-Century Rhetoric and Belles Lettres* (Leeds: University of Leeds School of English, 1972), 99.

66. Lynda Mugglestone, *"Talking Proper": The Rise of Accent as Social Symbol* (Oxford: Oxford University Press, 1995), 6, my emphasis.

67. Adam Potkay, *The Fate of Eloquence in the Age of Hume* (Ithaca, NY: Cornell University Press, 1994), 86.

68. Samuel Foote, *The Orators* (1762), 6–7, 30.

69. Linda Ferreira-Buckley and S. Michael Halloran, eds., *Lectures on Rhetoric and Belles Lettres by Hugh Blair* (Carbondale: Southern Illinois University Press, 2005), xxxv.

70. Ibid., 378n1, xxxv, 74, 368.

71. Ibid., 282.

72. Ibid., 69, 268, 345.

73. Hugh Blair, *A Critical Dissertation on the Poems of Ossian, The Son of Fingal,* in *The Poems of Ossian and Related Works,* ed. Howard Gaskill (Edinburgh: Edinburgh University Press, 1996), 345–46. See also Blair's "Lecture 14: Origin and Nature of Figurative Language," in Ferreira-Buckley and Halloran, *Lectures,* 145–56.

74. Ferreira-Buckley and Halloran, *Lectures,* 346; see also 68.

75. On the importance of ancient and modern theories of the passions for seventeenth- and eighteenth-century discussions of acting, see Joseph R. Roach, *The Player's Passion: Studies in the Science of Acting* (Newark: University of Delaware Press, 1985).

76. Anon., *Essay Upon the Action of an Orator,* 99.

77. Charles Le Brun, *A Method to learn to Design the Passions* (1734), 12–13, 39.

78. Sheridan, *Course of Lectures,* x.

79. Ferreira-Buckley and Halloran, *Lectures,* 265, 266.

80. Potkay, *Fate of Eloquence,* 27.

81. Ferreira-Buckley and Halloran, *Lectures,* 292–93, 285, 324, 317–18.

82. John Henley, *Oratory Transactions* 1 (1728): 48.

83. Ferreira-Buckley and Halloran, *Lectures*, 289, 386.

84. Ibid., 387, 265.

85. Ibid., 290.

86. Sheridan, *Course of Lectures*, 225, 17–18, 22.

87. Richard Brinsley Sheridan, *The Rivals* (1775), act 1, scene 2.

88. Benzie, *Dublin Orator*, 54, 52–53.

89. Jane Austen, *Mansfield Park* (1814), ed. James Kinsley (Oxford: Oxford World's Classics, 2008), vol. 3, chap. 3 [chap. 34], 266.

90. Ibid., 266, 267.

CHAPTER SIX

1. Joseph Addison and Richard Steele, *Spectator* 247 (13 December 1711), in *The Spectator*, ed. Donald F. Bond, 5 vols. (Oxford: Clarendon, 1965), 2:458–62.

2. Samuel Johnson, *Lives of the Poets*, 4 vols. (1783), in *Lives of the Poets*, ed. Roger Lonsdale, 4 vols. (Oxford: Oxford University Press, 2006), 2:73.

3. Ashley Montagu, *The Anatomy of Swearing* (New York: Macmillan, 1967), 293.

4. A note on terminology: A "topos" (plural, "topoi") is a rhetorical commonplace—a stock line of argument or invention that authors and orators stored in their memory or in notes, then drew on in discourse as occasions arose. In eighteenth-century rhetoric, the terms "topos" and "topic" were used interchangeably. Rhetoricians such as Smith and Blair advised against the overuse of topoi, but they used them extensively in actual practice. Meanwhile, a "trope" was a figurative or metaphorical use of a word or expression—a use of language to mean something different from the literal meaning of the words ("they fell in love"). In common usage today, however, a "trope" has come to mean almost any recurring theme or motif; it often implies a cliché. Thus, "trope" and "topos" are sometimes conflated today in a way that they were not in the older rhetorical sense. On tropes and figures as rhetorical terms, see Richard A. Lanham, *A Handlist of Rhetorical Terms*, 2nd ed. (Berkeley: University of California Press, 2012).

5. On this tradition, see Pamela Allen Brown, *Better a Shrew than a Sheep: Women, Drama, and the Culture of Jest in Early Modern England* (Ithaca, NY: Cornell University Press, 2003).

6. Rudolf Ackermann, "Bilingsgate [*sic*]," in *The Microcosm of London Or London in Miniature*, 3 vols. (1808–10; London: Methuen, 1904), 1:63.

7. Thomas Sheridan, *A Course of Lectures on Elocution: Together With Two Dissertations on Language; And Some Other Tracts Relative to Those Subjects* (1762) (New York: Benjamin Blom, 1968), 148.

8. Ibid., 174–75.

9. Ibid., 133, 8.

10. *Spectator* 1 (1 March 1711), in Bond, *Spectator*, 1:2.

11. Like Addison, Steele depicted women's voices as "Instruments" that needed tuning (or, sometimes, silencing). In *Tatler* 157 (11 April 1710), in *The Tatler*, ed. Donald F. Bond, 3 vols. (Oxford: Clarendon, 1987), 2:378–83, Isaac Bickerstaff describes an evening that he spent in the company of "an Assembly of very Fine Women." He depicts these

women's discourse as a symphony (or cacophony) of sound. The women communicate not only by their voices but also through body language and gestures. One particularly "alarm[ing]" speaker is highly performative: "The most sonorous Part of our Consort was a She-Drum, or (as the Vulgar call it) a Kettle-Drum, who accompanied her Discourse with Motions of the Body, Tosses of the Head, and Brandishes of the Fan. Her Musick was loud, bold, and masculine. Every Thump she gave alarmed the Company." As this passage suggests, for female speakers the vigorous use of gesture was risky. Steele's "She-Drum" speaker is "loud, bold, and masculine," and her use of gesture "alarmed the Company." But Steele in fact depicts *all* the female speakers in this consort as problematic. For unlike Bickerstaff—paradoxically, the fictional author of a periodical named the *Tatler*—these ladies never stop talking: "there was not any Regard to Time, nor any of those Rests and Pauses which are frequent in the Harmony of the other Sex."

12. W. M. Stern, "Fish Marketing in London in the First Half of the Eighteenth Century," in *Trade, Government, and Economy in Pre-industrial England: Essays Presented to F. J. Fisher*, ed. D. C. Coleman and A. H. John (London: Weidenfeld and Nicolson, 1976), 68–77, here 69.

13. *Tatler* 4 (19 April 1709), in Bond, *Tatler*, 1:36–44.

14. *Spectator* 251 (18 December 1711), 362 (25 April 1712), and 251 (18 December 1711), in Bond, *Spectator*, 2:475, 3:354, and 2:475.

15. Daniel Defoe, *Review* (1709), quoted in Sean Shesgreen, ed., *The Criers and Hawkers of London: Engravings and Drawings by Marcellus Laroon* (Palo Alto, CA: Stanford University Press, 1990), viii (*Four for Six pence Mackrell* is reprinted on 159). For further information on street criers, see also Sean Shesgreen, *Images of the Outcast: The Urban Poor in the Cries of London* (New Brunswick, NJ: Rutgers University Press, 2002).

16. Diana Donald, *The Age of Caricature: Satirical Prints in the Reign of George III* (New Haven, CT: Yale University Press, 1996), 117.

17. Gail Kern Paster, *The Body Embarrassed: Drama and the Disciplines of Shame in Early Modern England* (Ithaca, NY: Cornell University Press, 1993), 39.

18. Phyllis Mack, *Visionary Women: Ecstatic Prophecy in Seventeenth-Century England* (Berkeley: University of California Press, 1992), 25.

19. Even Botticelli, in his painting *The Birth of Venus* (1486), depicts the goddess Venus naked on a half shell, rising from the sea.

20. Eric Partridge, *Shakespeare's Bawdy* (London: Routledge and Kegan Paul, 1947), 106.

21. John Aubrey, *Remaines of Gentilisme and Judaisme*, in *Three Prose Works*, ed. John Buchanan-Brown (Carbondale: Southern Illinois University Press, 1972), 254.

22. William Wycherley, "To a Pretty Young Woman, who opening Oisters said, / She wou'd open for Her, and Me too; since 'twas for her Pleasure. A Song," in *Complete Works*, ed. Montague Summers (London: Nonesuch Press, 1924), 3:169–70.

23. Letter, 9 March 1748, in *The Letters of the Earl of Chesterfield to His Son* (1774), ed. Charles Strachey, 2 vols. (London: Methuen, 1901), 1:213.

24. Daniel Defoe, preface to *A Continuation of Letters Written by a Turkish Spy at Paris* (1718), iv.

25. Eighteenth-century authors from Addison to Rousseau drew on the trope of the "Anatomy of a Woman's Tongue." See Jean-Jacques Rousseau, *Emile* (New York: Basic Books, 1979), 376, for Rousseau's physiological explanation for female loquacity.

26. John Gay, *Trivia: Or, the Art of Walking the Streets of London* (1716), in *Poetry and Prose of John Gay*, ed. Vinton A. Dearing with Charles E. Beckworth, 2 vols. (Oxford: Clarendon, 1974), 2:381–98.

27. Eliza Haywood, *A Spy Upon the Conjurer* (1724), 81.

28. Henry Fielding, *The History of Tom Jones* (1749), ed. Martin C. Battestin and Fredson Bowers, 2 vols. (Oxford: Clarendon, 1974), 1:273, 2:919, 2:602–3.

29. Anon., *An Essay Upon the Action of an Orator; As to His Pronunciation and Gesture. Useful both for Divines and Lawyers, and necessary for all Young Gentlemen, that study how to Speak well in Publick. Done out of French* (London, 1702), 173.

30. Ibid., 28, 32.

31. Sheridan, *Course of Lectures*, 214, 183–84.

32. Brown, *Better a Shrew than a Sheep*, 8.

33. Ibid., 15.

34. Ned Ward, *London Spy*, nos. 2 and 3 (Deccember 1698 and January 1698/99), in *The London Spy*, ed. Paul Hyland (East Lansing, MI: Colleagues Press, 1993), 39–40, 46.

35. Corporation of London Record Office (now London Metropolitan Archives), Journal 22, fol. 378v; Journal 24, fol. 98v.

36. Laura Gowing, *Domestic Dangers: Women, Words, and Sex in Early Modern London* (Oxford: Clarendon, 1996), 15.

37. Ward, *London Spy*, in Hyland, *London Spy*, 46.

38. John Brown, *An Estimate of the Manners and Principles of the Times*, 2 vols. (1757–58), pt. 3, sec. 2, 426–27.

39. Donald, *Age of Caricature*, 116.

40. Ackermann, "Bilingsgate [*sic*]," 1:63–68.

41. For Doll's "shrilling Strain" and Orpheus's "cry," see Gay, *Trivia*, 2:386, 396.

42. The classic study of the literary genre of *poissarde* is A. P. Moore, *The Genre Poissarde and the French Stage of the Eighteenth Century* (New York: Institute for French Studies, Columbia University, 1935). For an interesting update, see Carla Hesse, *The Other Enlightenment: How French Women Became Modern* (Princeton, NJ: Princeton University Press, 2001), 3–30, here 12.

43. Hesse, *Enlightenment*, 26, 12, 26.

44. Pope, *Dunciad*, 2.75n, 3.152n, and 2.291n.

45. John Henley, *Why How now, Gossip POPE? Or, The Sweet Singing-Bird of Parnassus taken out of its pretty Cage to be roasted. . . . Exposing the Malice Wickedness and Vanity of his Aspersions on J. H. in that Monument of His Own Misery and Spleen, the Dunciad*, 2nd ed. (1743), 16.

46. *A Letter to the Celebrated Orator* (1727), "Advertisement," n.p., and 17.

47. Adam Smith, "Of Tropes and Figures of Speech," in *Glasgow Edition of the Works and Correspondence of Adam Smith*, ed. A. S. Skinner, vol. 4, ed. J. C. Bryce (Oxford: Oxford University Press, 1983), 33, my emphasis.

48. Ibid., 25.

49. It must be admitted that Ward's own comic style is relentlessly figurative, and that this is a great source of energy in his writing.

50. See pp. 130–31 re Henley's extension of Royal Society language projects.

51. Thomas Sprat, *History of the Royal Society of London, For the Improving of Natural Knowledge*, 3 pts. (1667), pt. 2, sec. 20, 113.

52. For a helpful taxonomy of the "low," "middle," and "grand" styles, see Kenneth Cmiel, *Democratic Eloquence: The Fight over Popular Speech in Nineteenth-Century America* (Berkeley: University of California Press, 1990).

53. Sprat, *History of the Royal Society*, pt. 2, sec. 20, 113.

54. Hugh Blair, *A Critical Dissertation on the Poems of Ossian, The Son of Fingal*, in *The Poems of Ossian and Related Works*, ed. Howard Gaskill (Edinburgh: Edinburgh University Press, 1996), 345–408, here 345–46.

55. Linda Ferreira-Buckley and S. Michael Halloran, eds., *Lectures on Rhetoric and Belles Lettres by Hugh Blair* (Carbondale: Southern Illinois University Press, 2005), 268, 150.

56. Jean-Jacques Rousseau, *Essay on the Origin of Languages*, in *Two Essays on the Origin of Language*, by Jean-Jacques Rousseau and Johann Gottfried Herder, ed. and trans. John H. Moran and Alexander Gode (Chicago: University of Chicago Press, 1966), 12–13.

57. Tobias Smollett, *The Expedition of Humphry Clinker*, ed. Lewis M. Knapp, rev. Paul-Gabriel Boucé (Oxford: Oxford University Press, 1998), 52. In another form of engagement with contemporary rhetorical discourse, Smollett makes the titular hero of his novel, the penniless but morally admirable Humphry Clinker, turn Methodist preacher—the later eighteenth-century's favorite example of overly "enthusiastic" (and so problematic) public speaking.

58. A collected edition in three volumes was published in 1753.

59. Christopher Smart, *The Midwife: Or, The Old Woman's Magazine* 3.2.37–38. Quotations are from the 1753 collected edition, cited by volume, issue, and page number.

60. J. C. Jeaffreson, ed., *Middlesex County Records*, 4 vols. (London: Middlesex County Records Society, 1886–92), vol. 4, *1667–88*, 285.

61. Ibid., 285–86.

62. For further examples of plebeian women indicted for treasonous statements, see Andy Wood, "The Queen Is 'a Goggyll Eyed Hoore': Gender and Seditious Speech in Early Modern England," in *The English Revolution, c. 1580–1720: Politics, Religion and Communities*, ed. Nicholas Tyacke (Manchester: Manchester University Press, 2007), 81–94.

63. Hesse, *Enlightenment*, 9, 10, 17, 21.

64. See Donald, *Age of Caricature*, 117–18.

65. Hesse, *Enlightenment*, 21.

66. Ibid., 20.

67. Hannah More, "Letter to Horace Walpole, 1789," quoted in William Roberts, *Memoirs of the Life of Mrs. Hannah More*, 2 vols. (London: R. B. Seeley and W. Burnside, 1836), 1:441.

68. Edmund Burke, *Reflections on the Revolution in France*, ed. Connor Cruise O'Brien (London: Penguin, 1982), 165.

69. Mary Wollstonecraft, *A Vindication of the Rights of Men* (1790), 63–64.

CHAPTER SEVEN

1. Walter J. Ong, *The Presence of the Word: Some Prolegomena for Cultural and Religious History* (Minneapolis: University of Minnesota Press, 1981), 17–18.

2. Ibid., 10.

3. Thomas Percy, ed., *Reliques of Ancient English Poetry: Consisting of Old Heroic Ballads, Songs, and Other Pieces of Our Earlier Poets, Together With Some Few of Later Date* (1765), ed. Henry B. Wheatley, 3 vols. (London: Swan Sonnenschein, 1886; repr., New York: Dover, 1966), preface, 1:7–15, here 7; "An Essay on the Ancient Minstrels in England," 1:345–81, here 348, 381.

4. Ibid., 1:380–81.

5. Joseph Ritson, "Observations on the Ancient English Minstrels," in *Ancient Songs, From the Time of King Henry the Third, to the Revolution* (1790 [sic; recte 1792]), i–xxvi, here xvii.

6. William Motherwell, introduction to *Minstrelsy, Ancient and Modern*, 2 vols. (1827; repr., Boston: William D. Ticknor, 1846), 1:1–136, here 58n.

7. Albert B. Friedman, *The Ballad Revival: Studies in the Influence of Popular on Sophisticated Poetry* (Chicago: University of Chicago Press, 1961), 6–7.

8. Ballads were in fact among the largest classes of printed materials since the beginning of printing in England; see Tessa Watt, *Cheap Print and Popular Piety, 1550–1640* (Cambridge: Cambridge University Press, 1991), 11.

9. Dianne M. Dugaw, "Anglo-American Folksong Reconsidered: The Interface of Oral and Written Forms," *Western Folklore* 43 (1984): 83–103, here 83.

10. Adam Fox, *Oral and Literate Culture in England, 1500–1700* (Oxford: Clarendon, 2000), 5.

11. Dugaw, "Anglo-American Folksong," 86.

12. James Macpherson, *Fragments of Ancient Poetry* (Edinburgh, 1760), in *The Poems of Ossian and Related Works*, ed. Howard Gaskill (Edinburgh: Edinburgh University Press, 1996), 1–31.

13. Significantly, Robert Wood's *An Essay on the Original Genius of Homer*, written in 1767 and first published in 1769, was reprinted in 1775 with additions as *An Essay on the Original Genius and Writings of Homer* (note "*and Writings*"). References here are to the 1775 edition.

14. John Pinkerton, *Scottish Tragic Ballads. . . . To Which are Prefixed Two Dissertations, I. On the Oral Tradition of Poetry. II. On the Tragic Ballad* (1781), 9–27; republished with a second volume as *Select Scotish [sic] Ballads* (1783). References here are to the 1781 edition.

15. Francis James Child, "Ballad Poetry," in *Johnson's New Universal Cyclopaedia*, ed. Frederic A. P. Barnard et. al., 4 vols. (New York, 1875–80), 1:365–68; reprinted in *Journal of Folklore Research* 31 (1994): 214–22. This quotation is from 218.

16. Joseph Addison and Richard Steele, *Spectator* 70 (21 May 1711), 74 (25 May 1711), and 85 (7 June 1711), in *The Spectator*, ed. Donald F. Bond, 5 vols. (Oxford: Clarendon, 1965), 1:297–303, 315–22, 360–64.

17. These quotations are from *Spectator* 70, 74, and 85, passim.

18. Jeffrey Sing-Song [Daniel Defoe?], "The Ballad-maker's Plea," *Applebee's Original Weekly Journal* (13 October 1722), reprinted in William Lee, ed., *Daniel Defoe: His Life and Recently Discovered Writings*, 3 vols. (London, 1869), 3:57–60.

19. Ibid., 58–59. I discuss the tradition of political balladry with which "The Ballad-maker's Plea" engages in Paula McDowell, "'The Manufacture and Lingua-facture of

Ballad-Making': Broadside Ballads in Long Eighteenth-Century Ballad Discourse," *The Eighteenth Century* 47 (2006): 151–78; and in Paula McDowell, *The Women of Grub Street: Press, Politics, and Gender in the London Literary Marketplace, 1678–1730* (Oxford: Clarendon, 1998), esp. 82–90.

20. William St. Clair, *The Reading Nation in the Romantic Period* (Cambridge: Cambridge University Press, 2004), 345.

21. *A Collection of Old Ballads. Corrected from the best and most Ancient Copies Extant. With Introductions Historical, Critical, or Humorous, Illustrated with Copper Plates*, 3 vols. (1723–25), 1:3, font reversed.

22. Ibid., 3:3, 3:6–7, 2:5–6, 1:7.

23. Allan Ramsay, advertisement appearing in *The Battel: Or, Morning-Interview. An Heroi-Comical Poem* (Edinburgh, 1716), sig. A2 ("home-manufactory" is in boldface type in the original).

24. On Burns, ballads, and Burns's self-positioning in relation to print commerce, see Robert P. Irvine, ed., *Robert Burns: Selected Poems and Songs* (Oxford: Oxford World's Classics, 2014), and the sources cited there.

25. *Collection of Old Ballads*, 1:3–4.

26. Richard Bentley, *Remarks Upon a Late Discourse of Free Thinking* (1713), 18.

27. Thomas Blackwell, *An Enquiry Into the Life and Writings of Homer* (1735), 101, 103, 118.

28. Wood, *Essay on the Original Genius and Writings of Homer*, 248, 257.

29. Ibid., 279. On the intersection of Homer scholarship and investigations of Ossian, see Kirsti Simonsuuri, *Homer's Original Genius: Eighteenth-Century Notions of the Early Greek Epic (1688–1798)* (Cambridge: Cambridge University Press, 1979); Casey Dué, "The Invention of Ossian," *Classics@* 3 (2006), accessed 19 March 2016, chs.harvard.edu/CHS/article/display/1334; and Maureen N. McLane and Laura M. Slatkin, "British Romantic Homer: Oral Tradition, 'Primitive Poetry' and the Emergence of Comparative Poetics in Britain, 1760–1830," *ELH* 78 (2011): 687–714, esp. 692–95. I regret that I learned of Dué's helpful essay only after this book was completed.

30. [Blair?], preface to Macpherson, *Fragments*, in Gaskill, *Poems of Ossian*, 5.

31. Hugh Blair, *A Critical Dissertation on the Poems of Ossian, The Son of Fingal*, in Gaskill, *Poems of Ossian*, 345–408. These quotations are from "Appendix," 403, and *Critical Dissertation*, 350. On the publication history of Blair's *Critical Dissertation*, see Gaskill, *Poems of Ossian*, 542–43.

32. Blair, "Appendix," 403–6.

33. For a brilliant reading of the editorial work of later eighteenth- and nineteenth-century ballad collectors as itself a kind of *poesis*, or poetic making, see Maureen N. McLane, *Balladeering, Minstrelsy, and the Making of British Romantic Poetry* (Cambridge: Cambridge University Press, 2008), esp. 34–83. On the ballad as a "key index of a romantic attention to intermediality," see Andrew Piper, *Dreaming in Books: The Making of the Bibliographic Imagination in the Romantic Age* (Chicago: University of Chicago Press, 2009), 99; and McLane, *Balladeering*.

34. Percy, preface to *Reliques*, 1:15. On Percy's editorial methods and contributions to textual scholarship, see Nick Groom, *The Making of Percy's "Reliques"* (Oxford: Oxford University Press, 1999). Percy's *Reliques* was by far the most important and influential

scholarly ballad collection of the century, but it should be noted that Percy's interests were shaped by developments that long preceded him. Fifteen years earlier, Samuel Johnson satirized the polite "rediscovery" of popular ballads and the antiquarian collecting of broadside ballads. He depicted "Cantilenus," a member of a "little societ[y] of literature," who "turned all his thoughts upon old ballads"—especially a prized "first edition" of *The Children in the Wood.* See Samuel Johnson, *Rambler* 177 (26 November 1751).

35. Thomas Percy to Robert Jamieson, 4 April 1801, in *Illustrations of the Literary History of the Eighteenth Century*, by John Nichols, 8 vols. (1817–58), 8:341.

36. Thomas Percy to William Shenstone, 19 July 1761, in *The Percy Letters*, ed. David Nichol Smith and Cleanth Brooks, vol. 7, *Correspondence of Thomas Percy and William Shenstone*, ed. Cleanth Brooks (New Haven, CT: Yale University Press, 1977), 108–9. For further information on the Dicey family, see Victor E. Neuberg, "The Diceys and the Chapbook Trade," *Library*, 5th ser., 24 (1969): 219–31; and Dianne M. Dugaw, "The Popular Marketing of 'Old Ballads': The Ballad Revival and Eighteenth-Century Antiquarianism Reconsidered," *Eighteenth-Century Studies* 21 (1987): 7–90.

37. Thomas Percy to George Paton, 11 September 1773, in *Percy Letters*, vol. 6, *Correspondence of Thomas Percy and George Paton*, ed. A. F. Falconer (New Haven, CT: Yale University Press, 1961), 69.

38. I have borrowed this term from Ruth Finnegan, *Literacy and Orality: Studies in the Technology of Communication* (Oxford: Basil Blackwell, 1988), who critiques evolutionary models that postulate a "great divide in human development between 'oral' and 'literate' stages of society" (6 and passim).

39. Percy, *Reliques*, 1:346, 373, 363, 381, 375.

40. Percy, preface to *Reliques*, 1:14.

41. Joseph Ritson, *A Select Collection of English Songs*, 3 vols. (1783), 1:13, 1.

42. For Ritson's "Observations on the Ancient English Minstrels," see n. 5. Ritson's "Dissertation on the Songs, Music, and Vocal and Instrumental Performance of the Ancient English" was prefaced to Ritson, *Ancient Songs*, xxvii–lxxvi, and his "An Historical Essay on the Origin and Progress of National Song" was prefaced to Ritson, *Select Collection*, 1:i–lxxii.

43. Ritson, *Select Collection*, 1:52.

44. Ritson, *Ancient Songs*, xii.

45. Ritson, *Select Collection*, 1:lvi.

46. Ibid., 58–61.

47. Ritson, *Ancient Songs*, 23, 73, 18.

48. Nathan Bailey, *Universal Etymological Dictionary* (1721), s.v., "ballad," my emphasis.

49. Ritson, *Select Collection*, vol. 3, consists entirely of airs to the songs.

50. Ritson, *Ancient Songs*, 75. For Ritson's comments on Macpherson, see Ritson, *Select Collection*, 1:36.

51. John Pinkerton, "A Dissertation on the Oral Tradition of Poetry," in his *Scottish Tragic Ballads*, 16–17, 10, 15, my emphasis.

52. Ibid., 17, 20.

53. See Adam Parry, ed., *The Making of Homeric Verse: The Collected Papers of Milman Parry* (Oxford: Clarendon, 1971), 23–24.

54. Pinkerton, "Dissertation," 27.

55. Walter Scott, *Minstrelsy of the Scottish Border*, 3 vols. (Kelso and Edinburgh, 1802–3), ed. T. F. Henderson, 4 vols. (Edinburgh: William Blackwood and Sons; New York: Charles Scribner's Sons, 1902). Quotations are taken from the one-volume reprint (London, 1931) edited by Henderson. For Scott's "Introductory Remarks," see 501–32; for the quotation, see 512–13.

56. Walter Scott, "Essay on Imitations of the Ancient Ballad" (1830), in *Minstrelsy*, 535–67, here 535, my emphasis.

57. Motherwell, *Minstrelsy*, 1:1, 3.

58. William B. McCarthy, "William Motherwell as Field Collector," *Folk Music Journal* 5 (1987): 295–316, here 300.

59. Motherwell, *Minstrelsy*, 1:23–24.

60. An exception here is McCarthy, "William Motherwell." See also Mary Ellen Brown, *William Motherwell's Cultural Politics, 1797–1835* (Lexington: University Press of Kentucky, 2001), 1, 93.

61. Motherwell, *Minstrelsy*, 1:26.

62. Ibid., 4.

63. William Motherwell to Walter Scott, 28 April 1825, quoted in McCarthy, "William Motherwell," 301–2.

64. Walter Scott to William Motherwell, 3 May 1825, quoted in McCarthy, "William Motherwell," 303.

65. Motherwell, *Minstrelsy*, 1:24–25, 56.

66. Christina Lupton has recently suggested that by the 1760s this self-consciousness about mediation was so normalized that expressions of disgust at the explosion of the literary marketplace had become "a fashionable . . . impulse" or cliché. See Christina Lupton, *Knowing Books: The Consciousness of Mediation in Eighteenth-Century Britain* (Philadelphia: University of Pennsylvania Press, 2012), 1.

67. Motherwell, *Minstrelsy*, 1:58n, 5, 124–26, 132, 6.

68. Francis James Child, *The English and Scottish Ballads*, 2nd ed., 8 vols. (Boston: Little, Brown, 1860), 1:7, 8.

69. Francis James Child to Svend Grundtvig, 25 August 1872, in Sigurd Bernhard Hustvedt, *Ballad Books and Ballad Men: Raids and Rescues in Britain, America, and the Scandinavian North since 1800* (Cambridge, MA: Harvard University Press, 1930), 252–55, here 255.

70. Ibid., 254.

71. Mary Ellen Brown, "Child's Ballads and the Broadside Conundrum," in *Ballads and Broadsides in Britain, 1500–1800*, ed. Patricia Fumerton and Anita Guerrini, with the assistance of Kris McAbee (Burlington, VT: Ashgate, 2010), 57–74, here 67.

72. Child, "Ballad Poetry," 218, 214–15.

73. Dugaw, "Anglo-American Folksong," 103.

74. Brown, "Child's Ballads," 72.

CHAPTER EIGHT

1. Anthony Ashley Cooper, 3rd Earl of Shaftesbury, *Characteristics of Men, Manners, Opinions, Times* (1711), ed. Lawrence E. Klein (Cambridge: Cambridge University Press, 1999), 153.

2. William St. Clair, *The Reading Nation in the Romantic Period* (Cambridge: Cambridge University Press, 2004), 233–34.

3. Hugh Blair, "Appendix" to *The Poems of Ossian and Related Works*, ed. Howard Gaskill (Edinburgh: Edinburgh University Press, 1996), 401–8, here 403.

4. Hugh Blair, *Critical Dissertation on the Poems of Ossian, The Son of Fingal*, in Gaskill, *Poems of Ossian*, 363.

5. Dugald Stewart, *Account of the Life and Writings of Adam Smith* (1793), in *Collected Works*, ed. Sir William Hamilton, 11 vols. (Edinburgh: Thomas Constable, 1854–60), 10:1–98, here 33–34.

6. Dugald Stewart, *Elements of the Philosophy of the Human Mind*, pt. 1 (1792), in Hamilton, *Collected Works*, 2:242.

7. Samuel Johnson, *The Yale Edition of the Works of Samuel Johnson*, vol. 9, *A Journey to the Western Islands of Scotland*, ed. Mary Lascelles (New Haven, CT: Yale University Press, 1971), 58. All further references to this work will be cited parenthetically in the text.

8. Paul Rycaut, trans., *Royal Commentaries of Peru, in two parts* (London, 1688). I am quoting here from the Harold V. Livermore translation, *Royal Commentaries of the Incas, and General History of Peru* by Garcilaso de la Vega (Austin: University of Texas Press, 1966), bk. 6, chap. 9, 332.

9. Sir William Temple, *An Essay Upon the Ancient and Modern Learning* (1690), in *Sir William Temple's Essays on Ancient and Modern Learning and on Poetry*, ed. J. E. Spingarn (Oxford: Clarendon, 1909), 1–42, here 6.

10. Jonathan Swift, *Battel of the Books* (1704) depicts the Moderns as angry with the Ancients on Mount Parnassus for spoiling their "Prospects . . . especially towards the *East*." See Jonathan Swift, *A Tale of a Tub, and Other Works*, vol. 1 of *The Cambridge Edition of the Works of Jonathan Swift*, ed. Marcus Walsh (Cambridge: Cambridge University Press, 2010), 144. For Temple's phrase "*Eastern* Regions," see Temple, *Essay*, 5–6.

11. Temple, *Essay*, 15, 6, 6.

12. The phrase "total way of life" is from Edward B. Tylor, *Primitive Culture* (London: John Murray, 1871). I discuss the origins of the modern anthropological idea of "cultures" in my coda, below.

13. Temple, *Essay*, 5–6, 3–4.

14. A fuller title is Baron de Lahontan, *New Voyages to North-America. Containing An Account of the Several Nations of that Vast Continent; their Customs, Commerce, and Way of Navigation [and so on]*, 2 vols. (London, 1703).

15. Nicholas Hudson, "'Oral Tradition': The Evolution of an Eighteenth-Century Concept," in *Tradition in Transition: Women Writers, Marginal Texts, and the Eighteenth-Century Canon*, ed. Alvaro Ribeiro and James G. Basker (Oxford: Clarendon, 1996), 161–76, here 165.

16. Ronald L. Meek, *Social Science and the Ignoble Savage* (Cambridge: Cambridge University Press, 1976), 64.

17. Joseph Francis Lafitau, *Customs of the American Indians Compared With the Customs of Primitive Times* (1724), ed. and trans. William N. Fenton and Elizabeth L. Moore, 2 vols. (Toronto: Champlain Society, 1974–77), 1:lxxxvi, 1:xxxiii.

18. Ibid., 298–99.

19. Ibid., 297–99, 308, 81. Three years later, Cadwallader Colden, the lieutenant governor for the Province of New York, represented native American leaders as eloquent orators who preferred to use persuasion rather than brute force to achieve their ends. In his *History of the Five Indian Nations* (New York: William Bradford, 1727), Colden compared contemporary "Indian Nations" to ancient Greek and Roman republics. He suggested that "the Greeks and Romans . . . [were] once as much Barbarians as our Indians now are." Contributing to the emergent trope of the noble savage, he argued that contact with European explorers and colonists was making the Iroquois barbarous rather than vice versa: "instead of Vertues we have only taught them Vices, that they were entire free of before" (iv–v). On the trope of Indian eloquence, see Sandra M. Gustafson, *Eloquence Is Power: Oratory and Performance in Early America* (Chapel Hill: University of North Carolina Press, 2000); and Carolyn Eastman, *A Nation of Speechifiers: Making an American Public after the Revolution* (Chicago: University of Chicago Press, 2009).

20. Thomas Percy, ed., *Reliques of Ancient English Poetry: Consisting of Old Heroic Ballads, Songs, and Other Pieces of Our Earlier Poets, Together With Some Few of Later Date* (1765), ed. Henry B. Wheatley, 3 vols. (London: Swan Sonnenschein, 1886; repr., New York: Dover, 1966), 3:340.

21. This is an example of what critical anthropologist Johannes Fabian calls "allochronism," or the denial of coevalness to a people. See Johannes Fabian, *Time and the Other: How Anthropology Makes Its Object* (1983; repr., New York: Columbia University Press, 2002).

22. Joseph Ritson, "An Historical Essay on the Origin and Progress of National Song," preface to *A Select Collection of English Songs*, 3 vols. (1783), 1:iv, note on iii, ii.

23. Jonathan Swift, *Gulliver's Travels* (1726), bk. 4, chaps. 9 and 3 (in this order). Swift's depiction of the poetry-loving Houyhnhnms seems indebted to Rycaut, *Royal Commentaries* (trans. Livermore, chap. 27), where Garcilaso de la Vega describes the Incas' love of poetry and their passing down of arts, laws, and customs by tradition.

24. See, e.g., Terry Castle, "Why the Houyhnhnms Don't Write: Swift, Satire, and the Fear of the Text," *Essays in Literature* 7 (1980): 31–44.

25. See Nicholas Hudson, "*O Divinum Scripturae Beneficium!* Swift's Satire of Writing and Its Intellectual Context," in *The Age of Johnson: A Scholarly Annual*, vol. 7, ed. Paul J. Korshin (New York: AMS Press, 1996), 343–63.

26. Daniel Defoe, *An Essay upon Literature: or, An Enquiry into the Antiquity and Original of Letters* (London, 1726), in *"A General History of Discoveries and Improvements" (1725–26) and "An Essay upon Literature" (1726), by Daniel Defoe*, ed. P. N. Furbank (London: Pickering, 2001), 302. I coin the term "histories of mediation" and discuss Defoe's views on the consequences of printing for oral tradition in Paula McDowell, "Defoe's *Essay upon Literature* and Eighteenth-Century Histories of Mediation," *PMLA* 130, no. 3 (May 2015): 566–83.

27. William Warburton, *The Divine Legation of Moses Demonstrated*, 2 vols. (1738–41); rev. ed., 4 vols. (1741–42).

28. The (145-page) section of Warburton's *Divine Legation* devoted to hieroglyphics was translated by Marc-Antoine Léonard des Malpeines as *Essai sur les hiéroglyphes* (Paris, 1744). Two years later, Etienne Bonnot de Condillac acknowledged his debt to Warburton in his own *Essay on the Origin of Human Knowledge* (1746). He wrote, "from

[Warburton's] work I have borrowed practically all I say about this subject." See Etienne Bonnot de Condillac, *Essay*, ed. Hans Aarsleff (Cambridge: Cambridge University Press, 2001), pt. 2, sec. 13, 178n48. Today, *Divine Legation* is perhaps better known as the springboard for Derrida's essay "Scribble (Writing Power)." Derrida's essay served as a preface to a reissue of the 1744 translation of Warburton's writing on hieroglyphics, published as *Essai sur les hieroglyphs des Egyptiens* (Paris: Auberge-Montaigne, 1977), and it was reprinted with minor changes in *Yale French Studies* 58 (1979): 117–47.

29. See Kirsti Simonsuuri, *Homer's Original Genius: Eighteenth-Century Notions of the Early Greek Epic (1688–1798)* (Cambridge: Cambridge University Press, 1979), esp. chap. 6.

30. In Giambattista Vico, *La Scienza Nuova* (Naples, 1725), the Italian philosopher suggested that the Homeric poems were the myths of an entire people rather than the work of an individual, but Vico's work was not widely known before the nineteenth century.

31. Richard Bentley, *Remarks Upon a Late Discourse of Free Thinking* (1713).

32. Thomas Blackwell, *An Enquiry Into the Life and Writings of Homer* (1735), 104, 5, 103.

33. Ibid., 4, 112, 118.

34. Simonsuuri, *Homer's Original Genius*, 107.

35. Henry Fielding, *The History of Joseph Andrews* (1742), ed. Martin C. Battestin (Oxford: Clarendon, 1967), 90–91.

36. [Hugh Blair?], preface to *Fragments of Ancient Poetry* (1760), by James Macpherson, in Gaskill, *Poems of Ossian*, iii–vii.

37. Blair, *Critical Dissertation*, 401, 358.

38. Ibid., 353. Shortly after Macpherson published *Fragments* (1760), Smith taught his students at the University of Glasgow that "there are four distinct states which mankind pass thro: 1st, the Age of Hunters; 2dly, the Age of Shepherds; 3dly, the Age of Agriculture; and 4thly, the Age of Commerce." See Adam Smith, "Of Jurisprudence" (1762), in *Glasgow Edition of the Works and Correspondence of Adam Smith*, ed. A. S. Skinner, vol. 5, *Lectures on Jurisprudence*, ed. R. L. Meek, D. D. Raphael, and P. G. Stein (Oxford: Oxford University Press, 1978), i.27.

39. Blair, "Appendix," 401–8.

40. For a concise overview of this debate and the vast scholarship that it has generated, see Thomas M. Curley, *Samuel Johnson, the Ossian Fraud, and the Celtic Revival in Great Britain and Ireland* (Cambridge: Cambridge University Press, 2009), 1–21.

41. On Macpherson's methods, see ibid., 22–44.

42. In 1765 Blair predicted the imminent demise of oral tradition in Scotland. In his "Appendix," he tied oral tradition to the earliest stages in the development of human societies. He then suggested that in the quickly changing Highlands, these stages had (nearly) passed:

> if enquiries had been made fifty or threescore years ago, many more particulars concerning these poems might have been learned . . . but . . . the manners of the inhabitants of the Highland counties have of late undergone a great change. Agriculture, trades, and manufactures, begin to take place of hunting, and the shepherd's life. The introduction of the busy and laborious arts has considerably abated that poetical enthusiasm which is better suited to a vacant and indolent state. (404)

43. Ibid., 405.

44. Macpherson depicted bards passing down history via tradition, and he used print to evoke what he took to be the style of bardic performance. For discussions of the literary and textual effects that Macpherson created in his works—effects that I call literary or textual orality (to coin an oxymoron)—see Nick Groom, "Celts, Goths, and the Nature of the Literary Source," in Ribeiro and Basker, *Tradition in Transition*, 275–96; and James Mulholland, *Sounding Imperial: Poetic Voice and the Politics of Empire, 1730–1820* (Baltimore: Johns Hopkins University Press, 2013), esp. 93–119.

45. Fiona J. Stafford, *The Sublime Savage: A Study of James Macpherson and the Poems of Ossian* (Edinburgh: Edinburgh University Press, 1988), 171.

46. Fiona Stafford, introduction to Gaskill, *Poems of Ossian*, v–xxi. This quotation is from p. x. Curley describes Macpherson as "an ambitious and unsettled opportunist who would indeed transform himself from a patriotic Highland poet posing as Ossian to a conservative British propagandist for George III's ministry in a highly successful quest to get ahead" (*Samuel Johnson, Ossian Fraud, and Celtic Revival*, 82).

47. Linda Ferreira-Buckley and S. Michael Halloran, eds., *Lectures on Rhetoric and Belles Lettres by Hugh Blair* (Carbondale: Southern Illinois University Press, 2005), xvi. Blair's lectures were published in two volumes in 1783 and in three volumes in the expanded edition of 1785.

48. St. Clair, *Reading Nation in the Romantic Period*, 272.

49. Thomas Percy, "On the Ancient Metrical Romances," in *Reliques*, 3:339–40.

50. Blair, *Critical Dissertation*, 350.

51. Katie Trumpener, *Bardic Nationalism: The Romantic Novel and the British Empire* (Princeton, NJ: Princeton University Press, 1997), 125.

52. Vicesimus Knox, "On the Prevailing Taste for the Old English Poets," in *Essays Moral and Literary*, 3 vols. (1782), 9th ed. (1787), 1:414–15.

Ironically, in describing the origins of the *Reliques*, Percy portrayed himself as having literally "rescue[d] oral tradition from the *hands* of the vulgar." In a letter to a friend, he described how, when staying with another friend in the country, he discovered "a very curious Old Manuscript lying dirty on the floor under a bureau in ye Parlour: being used by the Maids to light the fire." Quoted in Nick Groom, *The Making of Percy's "Reliques"* (Oxford: Oxford University Press, 1999), 20. This "Old Manuscript" turned out to be a commonplace book filled with ballads, metrical romances, and popular songs, many of them apparently surviving only in this transcription. In collecting his ballads from manuscript and printed texts rather than from recitation, Percy literally collected them from "hands" rather than "mouths."

53. Robert Wood, *An Essay on the Original Genius of Homer* (1769); repr., with additions, as *An Essay on the Original Genius and Writings of Homer* (1775), 270, 248.

54. Ibid., 259, 257, 249, 260.

55. Jean-Jacques Rousseau, *Essay on the Origin of Languages*, in *Two Essays on the Origin of Language*, by Jean-Jacques Rousseau and Johann Gottfried Herder, ed. and trans. John H. Moran and Alexander Gode (Chicago: University of Chicago Press, 1966), 300–301.

56. Friedrich August Wolf, *Prolegomena ad Homerum* (Halle, 1795), ed. and trans. Anthony Grafton et al. (Princeton, NJ: Princeton University Press, 1985), pt. 1, chap. 20, 100–101.

57. See Walter J. Ong, *Orality and Literacy: The Technologizing of the Word* (London: Methuen, 1982; repr., New York: Routledge, 2002), where this phrase is the title of chapter 2. For Milman Parry's contributions, see Adam Parry, ed., *The Making of Homeric Verse: The Collected Papers of Milman Parry* (Oxford: Clarendon, 1971), ix–lxii. See also Albert B. Lord, *The Singer of Tales*, 2nd ed., ed. Stephen Mitchell and Gregory Nagy. (Cambridge, MA: Harvard University Press, 2000).

58. Ong, *Orality and Literacy*, 16–17, 24, 20.

59. As I suggested in chapter 4, John Henley was taken up for treason for using his Oratory forum to condemn the English forces. He was also satirized in several prints that depict him wearing the Scottish plaid; see, e.g. *Oratory Chappel* (fig. 4.1) (probably 1746) and *The Orator Versus Culloden* (1746).

60. For an elegant early reading of Macpherson's Ossian poems as a "reshaping of the past . . . designed to restore the Highlanders' self-esteem in post-Culloden Britain," see Leith Davis, "Origins of the Specious: James Macpherson, Samuel Johnson, and the Forging of the Nation," in *Acts of Union: Scotland and the Literary Negotiation of the British Nation, 1707–1830* (Palo Alto, CA: Stanford University Press, 1998), 74–106, quotation on 15. See also Howard D. Weinbrot, *Britannia's Issue: The Rise of British Literature from Dryden to Ossian* (Cambridge: Cambridge University Press, 1993). Weinbrot additionally discusses the role of "Celtomania" in the consolidation of "British Literature" after 1745.

61. Matthew Hale, *The History and Analysis of the Common Law of England* (1713), chap. 4, 60. Johnson cites this work as Hale, *Comm. on the Laws of England*; see Samuel Johnson, *A Dictionary of the English Language*, 2 vols. (London, 1755), s.v. "orally."

The editors of the *Oxford English Dictionary* (first pub. 1928) appear to have worked to undo Johnson's binary opposition of "oral" and "written." They define "oral" as "done or performed with or by the mouth" and as "of or relating to communication by speech." The *OED* entry for "oral" also lists numerous compound terms that emerged only in the twentieth century (such as "oral culture"). Of these "special uses," only one dates to the eighteenth century. Significantly—and in keeping with my argument in *The Invention of the Oral* about the religious origins of the idea of oral tradition—this term expresses a *religious* concept. Dating to 1731, "Oral Law" is defined as "the part of Jewish religious law believed to have been passed down by oral tradition before being collected in the Mishnah; the Oral Torah" (*Oxford English Dictionary, OED Online*, s.v. "oral," 1. a., 2, and "special uses," accessed June 2016).

62. Soame Jenyns, *A Free Inquiry Into The Nature and Origin of Evil* (1757), 34.

63. Samuel Johnson, review of *A Free Inquiry Into The Nature and Origin of Evil*, by [Soame Jenyns], *Literary Magazine*, nos. 13–15 (April–July 1757); reprinted in *The Oxford Authors: Samuel Johnson*, ed. Donald Greene (Oxford: Oxford University Press, 1984), 522–43, here 527, 529.

64. Johnson, *Dictionary*, defines "literacy" as "learning," but his use of "literature" in this review of Jenyns arguably reflects the ongoing transformation of the idea of literacy.

65. To what extent was Johnson himself "the son of a poor man"? Johnson was the son of a failed bookseller of modest means, and he struggled to make ends meet for most of his life. Although he managed to attend Oxford for a year, he left partly for financial reasons, and in retrospect, we might read the tagline to his first major publication, *London* (1738), as a motto for his own life: "Slow Rises Worth, by Poverty Depressed." Johnson

was by no means destitute; he was not one of those whom Defoe categorized as "the miserable, who really pinch and want." But he experienced periods of what Boswell called "extreme indigence," and throughout his writings, he thematized the physical and psychological suffering of the poor. In *Rambler* 53 (18 September 1750), he observed:

> There is scarcely, among the evils of human life, any so generally dreaded as poverty. . . . It is impossible to pass a day or an hour in the confluxes of men, without seeing how much indigence is exposed to contumely, neglect, and insult; and, in its lowest state, to hunger and nakedness.

As Nicholas Hudson suggests, "Johnson was no mere foot-soldier for the privilege and power of the literate ruling classes." See Nicholas Hudson, *Writing and European Thought, 1600–1830* (Cambridge: Cambridge University Press, 1994), 111.

66. Thomas M. Curley, *Samuel Johnson and the Age of Travel* (Athens: University of Georgia Press, 1976), 52.

67. James Boswell, *Life of Johnson, Together with Boswell's "Journal of a Tour to the Hebrides" and Johnson's "Diary of a Journey into North Wales,"* ed. George Birkbeck Hill, rev. ed., ed. L. F. Powell, 6 vols. (Oxford: Clarendon, 1934–64), vol. 5, *The Tour to the Hebrides and the Journey into North Wales* (1950), 13. All further references to Boswell's *Tour to the Hebrides* and *Life of Johnson* are to this Oxford edition and will be given parenthetically in the text.

68. Samuel Johnson, *A Voyage to Abyssinia* (1735), in *Works*, vol. 15, *A Voyage to Abyssinia*, ed. Joel Gold (New Haven, CT: Yale University Press, 1985), 4.

69. Allen T. Hazen, ed., *Samuel Johnson's Prefaces and Dedications* (New Haven, CT: Yale University Press, 1937), 236.

70. Ibid., 227, my emphasis.

71. Samuel Johnson, *Idler* 97 (23 February 1760), my emphasis.

72. James Howell, *Instructions for Forreine Travel* (1642), 49.

73. Boyle's emphasis on the importance of noting a country's trees suggests that Johnson's (and Defoe's) much-discussed comments on the shortage of forests in Scotland might be seen less as xenophobic than as exemplifying their efforts to be good systematic observers of nature. See Robert Boyle, "General Heads for a Natural History of a Countrey," *Philosophical Transactions* 1 (1665–66): 186–89, here 188.

74. Pat Rogers, "Johnson, Samuel (1709–1784)," in *Oxford Dictionary of National Biography*, online ed., ed. David Cannadine (Oxford: Oxford University Press, 2004), accessed 1 September 2015, http://www.oxforddnb.com/view/article/14918.

75. Domhnall Uilleam Stiùbhart, "Martin, Martin (d. 1718)," in *Oxford Dictionary of National Biography*, accessed 1 September 2015, http://www.oxforddnb.com/view/article/18201.

76. Johnson's expression of surprise at the number of Scots who "go barefoot" (*Journey*, 28) brings to mind Boswell's account of Johnson's worn-out shoes while a student at Oxford. Boswell relates that when Johnson was at Pembroke College, he regularly picked up lecture notes from a friend at Christ Church College, "till his poverty being so extreme that his shoes were worn out, and his feet appeared through them, he saw that this humiliating circumstance was perceived by the Christ Church men, and he came no more" (Boswell, *Life*, 1:76–77).

77. This is not to say that Johnson never views the landscape through a Romantic lens. On "the verge of the Highlands," for instance, he describes Fores as "the town to which Macbeth was travelling, when he met the weird sisters in his way." But he also seems to satirize himself for retreating from reality to literary "amusements": "Our imaginations were heated, and our thoughts recalled to their old amusements" (*Journey*, 25).

78. Among these luminaries were Adam Smith, James Millar, Adam Ferguson, William Robertson, Dugald Stewart, and Henry Home, Lord Kames.

79. Meek, *Social Science*, 127–28.

80. John Glendening, *The High Road: Romantic Tourism, Scotland, and Literature, 1720–1820* (New York: St. Martin's Press, 1997), 78.

81. Ibid.

82. Samuel Johnson, *Idler* 97 (23 February 1760).

83. Glendening, *High Road* 119.

84. In an "Advertisement" prefixed to the third edition of the *Tour* (1786), Boswell compared the evanescence of Johnson's conversation with the relative permanence of texts: "I will venture to predict, that this specimen of [Johnson's] . . . colloquial talents and extemporaneous effusions . . . will become still more valuable, when, by the lapse of time, . . . all those who can now bear testimony to the transcendent powers of his mind, shall have passed away; and no other memorial of this great and good man shall remain but the following Journal [and other texts]" (Boswell, "Advertisement to the Third Edition," in *Tour*, 3–4). As other critics have noted, Boswell took great pains to capture in print the distinctive characteristics of Johnson's oral conversations, employing careful transcription methods, scene painting, and "move[ment] . . . in and out of written and oral registers." See, e.g., Michael Gavin, *The Invention of Criticism, 1650–1750* (Cambridge: Cambridge University Press, 2015), 134–56.

85. In *Samuel Johnson, Ossian Fraud, and Celtic Revival*, Curley provides a careful reading of Johnson's remarks on the Ossian question. Surprisingly, though, he pays little attention to the ways that Johnson's Protestantism shaped his attitudes toward oral tradition. In contrast, I have foregrounded what I take to be the crucial (and revealing) intersection of sacred and secular notions of tradition in his works.

86. Curley, *Samuel Johnson, Ossian Fraud, and Celtic Revival*, 100.

87. Oral history is the study of the relatively recent past by means of orally narrated recollections. The term "oral history" originated in the twentieth century, but as Johnson was aware, the practice dates to Herodotus in the fifth century BCE.

88. Jack Goody and Ian Watt, "The Consequences of Literacy," in *Literacy in Traditional Societies*, ed. Jack Goody (Cambridge: Cambridge University Press, 1968), 27–68, here 34.

89. Stewart, *Elements*, 2:242.

90. Stewart, *Account of the Life*, 10:54.

91. Stewart, *Elements*, 2:243, 246. As Maureen McLane and Laura Slatkin have observed in another context, stadial theory "involved a new consideration of media across the board, as oral tradition, the invention of alphabetic writing and printing, the status of writing and reading were all newly and conjointly theorized along stadial lines." See Maureen N. McLane and Laura M. Slatkin, "British Romantic Homer: Oral Tradition, 'Primitive Poetry' and the Emergence of Comparative Poetics in Britain, 1760–1830," *ELH* 78

(2011): 687–714, here 702. See also McLane's reading of James Beattie's "The Minstrel; or, the Progress of Genius" and other statements about poetry as exhibiting an "aspiration to periodize cultural development as a succession of medial, as well as socio-economic, phases." See Maureen N. McLane, "Dating Orality, Thinking Balladry: Of Milkmaids and Minstrels in 1771," *The Eighteenth Century* 47, no. 2/3 (2006): 129–47, here 132.

92. Antoine-Nicolas de Condorcet, *Sketch for a Historical Picture of the Progress of the Human Mind* (1795), trans. June Barraclough (London: Weidenfeld and Nicolson, 1955), 36.

93. Fabian, *Time and the Other*, 27.

94. Ong, *Orality and Literacy*, 1.

95. Jack Goody, The *Domestication of the Savage Mind* (Cambridge: Cambridge University Press, 1977), 3, my emphasis. Goody's book title was intended as a play on—and, importantly, a critique of—*La pensée sauvage* by Claude Lévi-Strauss (Paris: Librarie Plon, 1962), translated as *The Savage Mind* (Chicago: University of Chicago Press, 1966).

96. Goody, *Domestication*, ix. Goody notes that most anthropologists now tend to "set aside evolutionary or even historical perspectives," but he argues that many have simply substituted an empty relativism "that looks upon discussions of development as necessarily entailing a value judgment on the one hand and as over-emphasizing or misunderstanding the differences on the other" (2). Ultimately, he suggests, orality and literacy studies need to reject evolutionary narratives, crude dichotomies, *and* the "diffuse relativism" (26) that fails to engage seriously with and attempt to understand social difference.

CODA

1. Samuel Johnson, *A Dictionary of the English Language*, 2 vols. (London, 1755), s.v. "culture." See also Raymond Williams, *Keywords: A Vocabulary of Culture and Society*, rev. ed. (New York: Oxford University Press, 1985), 87 (originally published 1976).

2. Anne Ingram, "An Epistle to Mr. Pope" (1736), ll. 7–8, in *Eighteenth-Century Women Poets*, ed. Robert Lonsdale (New York: Oxford University Press, 1989), 150.

3. Letter, 1 April 1748, in *The Letters of the Earl of Chesterfield to His Son* (1774), ed. Charles Strachey, 2 vols. (London: Methuen, 1901), 1:220. A drayman delivers beer.

4. Christopher Herbert, *Culture and Anomie: Ethnographic Imagination in the Nineteenth Century* (Chicago: University of Chicago Press, 1991), 4.

5. Edward B. Tylor, *Primitive Culture* (London: John Murray, 1871), 1.

6. Brad Evans, *Before Cultures: The Ethnographic Imagination in American Literature, 1865–1920* (Chicago: University of Chicago Press, 2005), 3.

7. Herbert, *Culture and Anomie*, 5.

8. Fredric Jameson, foreword to *Noise: The Political Economy of Music*, by Jacques Attali, trans. Brian Massumi (Minneapolis: University of Minnesota Press, 1985), vii. In *The Work of Writing: Literature and Social Change in Britain, 1700–1830* (Baltimore: Johns Hopkins University Press, 1998), Clifford Siskin describes "culture" as a constitutive category of modern knowledge. See esp. chap. 2, "Engendering Disciplinarity."

9. Evans, *Before Cultures*, 3.

10. The term "load-bearing concept" is Peter de Bolla's; see my discussion in the introduction, above.

11. Alfred L. Kroeber and Clyde Kluckhohn, with the assistance of Wayne Untereiner, *Culture: A Critical Review of Concepts and Definitions* (Cambridge, MA: Peabody Museum of American Archaeology and Ethnology, Harvard University Press; New York: Vintage, 1952).

12. Raymond Williams, *Culture and Society, 1780–1950* (New York: Columbia University Press, 1958; repr., New York: Harper and Row, 1966). By the Arnoldian idea of culture I am referring to Matthew Arnold's influential arguments as developed, for instance, in Matthew Arnold, *Culture and Anarchy* (London: Smith, Elder, 1869).

13. For a bibliography of Ong's more than 450 individual books, essays, reviews, and interviews, see Thomas J. Farrell and Paul A. Soukup, eds., *An Ong Reader: Challenges for Further Inquiry* (Creskill, NJ: Hampton Press, 2002).

14. Walter J. Ong, review of *The Singer of Tales*, by Albert B. Lord, *Criticism: A Quarterly for Literature and the Arts* 4 (Winter 1962): 74–78, reprinted in Farrell and Soukup, *Ong Reader*, 301–6, here 304.

15. Marshall McLuhan, *The Gutenberg Galaxy: The Making of Typographic Man* (Toronto: University of Toronto Press, 1962), 7.

16. Walter J. Ong, "Oral Residue in Tudor Prose Style," *PMLA* 80 (1965): 145–54. Although he did not specifically focus on "oral culture," I would be remiss here if I did not also mention (and note the timing of) Clifford Geertz, *The Interpretation of Cultures: Selected Essays* (New York: Basic Books, 1973), a book that was listed in the *Times Literary Supplement*, 6 October 1995, as one of the "one hundred most influential publications since the Second World War."

17. Peter Burke, *Popular Culture in Early Modern Europe* (New York: Harper and Row, 1978), xi, citing Kroeber and Kluckhohn, *Culture*.

18. Raymond Williams, *Politics and Letters: Interviews with "New Left Review"* (London: NLB, 1979), 87, regarding Williams, *Culture and Society*.

INDEX

Page numbers in italics indicate figures, and page ranges in boldface indicate a chapter discussion of the topic.